Discursive Constructions of Consent in the Legal Process

OXFORD STUDIES IN LANGUAGE AND LAW

Oxford Studies in Language and Law includes scholarly analyses and descriptions of language evidence in civil and criminal law cases as well as language issues arising in the area of statutes, statutory interpretation, courtroom discourse, jury instructions, and historical changes in legal language.

The Legal Language of Scottish Burghs: Standardization and Lexical Bundles (1380-1560)
Joanna Kopaczyk

"I'm Sorry for What I've Done": The Language of Courtroom Apologies
M. Catherine Gruber

Dueling Discourses: The Construction of Reality in Closing Arguments
Laura Felton Rosulek

Entextualizing Domestic Violence: Language Ideology and Violence Against Women in the Anglo-American Hearsay Principle
Jennifer Andrus

Speak English or What?: Codeswitching and Interpreter Use in New York City Small Claims Court
Philipp Sebastian Angermeyer

Law at Work: Studies in Legal Ethnomethods
Edited by Baudouin Dupret, Michael Lynch, and Tim Berard

Speaking of Language and Law: Conversations on the Work of Peter Tiersma
Edited by Lawrence M. Solan, Janet Ainsworth, and Roger W. Shuy

Confronting the Death Penalty: How Language Influences Jurors in Capital Cases
Robin Conley

Discursive Constructions of Consent in the Legal Process
Edited by Susan Ehrlich, Diana Eades, and Janet Ainsworth

Discursive Constructions of Consent in the Legal Process

Edited by Susan Ehrlich,
Diana Eades, and Janet Ainsworth

OXFORD
UNIVERSITY PRESS

OXFORD
UNIVERSITY PRESS

Oxford University Press is a department of the University of Oxford. It furthers the University's objective of excellence in research, scholarship, and education by publishing worldwide.

Oxford New York
Auckland Cape Town Dar es Salaam Hong Kong Karachi
Kuala Lumpur Madrid Melbourne Mexico City Nairobi
New Delhi Shanghai Taipei Toronto

With offices in
Argentina Austria Brazil Chile Czech Republic France Greece
Guatemala Hungary Italy Japan Poland Portugal Singapore
South Korea Switzerland Thailand Turkey Ukraine Vietnam

Oxford is a registered trademark of Oxford University Press in the UK and certain other countries.

Published in the United States of America by
Oxford University Press
198 Madison Avenue, New York, NY 10016

Cataloging-in-Publication data is on file at the Library of Congress
ISBN 978–0–19–994535–1

CONTENTS

SECTION 4 The Coercive Force of Cautions

ACKNOWLEDGMENTS

Many people have made the production of this book possible. We thank Roger Shuy and the members of the editorial board for the Oxford Studies in Language and Law series for encouraging us with this project in the first place. Roger, in particular, has been extremely supportive of the book throughout its various stages of production and has provided us with sage advice when needed. We thank Hallie Stebbins, our Oxford editor, and Suvesh Subramanian, our production manager, for skillfully guiding us through the production process. Mary Anne Shahidi, our copy editor, was not only very careful and meticulous in her work, but also tactful and respectful. Special thanks go to our amazing editorial assistant, Rick Grimm, whose careful eye and sense of rigor meant that our final submission to Oxford was in much better shape than it might otherwise have been. And, of course, we thank our contributors, who engaged with the book's concerns to produce original and insightful chapters, and who exhibited much patience during the book's somewhat lengthy route to completion.

CONTRIBUTORS

Janet Ainsworth is the John D. Eshelman Professor of Law at Seattle University, and was appointed Research Professor in the Research Center for Legal Translation, China University of Political Science and Law in Beijing. Prior to accepting a teaching position, she practiced law as a public defender, trying felony cases and pursuing criminal appeals. Her current research interests lie at the intersection of law, language, and culture.

Philipp Sebastian Angermeyer is Associate Professor of Linguistics at York University in Toronto. His research investigates language contact and bi- and multilingual language use from a sociolinguistic perspective, in different spoken and written contexts, focusing on codeswitching and pragmatic aspects of interpreting. He is the author of *Speak English or What? Codeswitching and Interpreter Use in New York City Courts* (2015, Oxford University Press).

Susan Berk-Seligson is Research Professor in the Department of Spanish and Portuguese, and Faculty Fellow, Latin American Public Opinion Project at Vanderbilt University. She is author of the award-winning book *The Bilingual Courtroom: Court Interpreters in the Judicial Process* (1990, 2002, University of Chicago Press) and *Coerced Confessions: The Discourse of Bilingual Police Interrogations* (2009, Mouton de Gruyter). Berk-Seligson is currently completing a book-length manuscript on justice systems in contact, focusing on the Quichua indigenous peoples of Ecuador.

R. Jean Cadigan is Assistant Professor in the Department of Social Medicine at the University of North Carolina at Chapel Hill. She received her PhD in anthropology from the University of California at Los Angeles. Much of her work involves empirical studies on the ethical, legal, social, and policy implications of large-scale genomic research.

John Conley is William Rand Kenan, Jr. Professor of Law at the University of North Carolina–Chapel Hill. He holds an AB from Harvard and a JD and PhD (Anthropology) from Duke. He has conducted ethnographic and linguistic studies of the informal justice system, institutional investing (both with William O'Barr), corporate social responsibility (with Cynthia Williams), corporate boards of directors (with Lissa Broome and Kimberly Krawiec), and, most recently, the emerging field of genetic medicine.

Arlene Davis is an attorney and Associate Professor of Social Medicine, as well as core faculty in the Center for Bioethics at the University of North Carolina–Chapel Hill. Her work focuses on clinical and research ethics and draws upon her prior experience in private practice and in pediatric and public health nursing. Over the past 20 years, Arlene has been a member of a research ethics committee and a co-investigator on a series of research projects funded by the National Institutes for Health for the examination of the ethical, legal, and social implications of the human genome project.

Paul Dwyer is a Senior Lecturer in the Department of Performance Studies in the Faculty of Arts and Social Sciences at the University of Sydney. In addition to his research collaboration with Michele Zappavigna and Jim Martin on multimodal discourse analysis of restorative justice conferencing, Paul publishes on applied theater practices in the fields of health, education, welfare, and political activism. He is also a performance maker with extensive experience in documentary theater, including several works based on transcripts from parliamentary inquiries, royal commissions, coronial inquests, and other legal proceedings.

Diana Eades, an Adjunct Professor at the University of New England in Australia, is a critical sociolinguist whose main research examines communication with Australian Aboriginal speakers of English in the legal process. Her books include *Courtroom Talk and Neocolonial Control* (2008, Mouton de Gruyter) and *Sociolinguistics and the Legal Process* (2010, Multilingual Matters). She also applies sociolinguistic research in training lawyers and judicial officers, as expert witness, and as advisor to inquiries.

Derek Edwards is Emeritus Professor of Psychology in the Department of Social Sciences, Loughborough University, England. His interests are in the analysis of language and social interaction in everyday and institutional settings. He specializes in discursive psychology, in which relations between psychological states and the external world are studied as discourse categories and practices, including accounts of actions, events, and intentionality in legal settings. His books include *Discursive Psychology* (with Jonathan Potter, 1992, Sage) and *Discourse and Cognition* (1997, Sage).

Helen Edwards is a Senior Lecturer at Nottingham Law School, Nottingham Trent University. She specializes in criminal law, evidence, and advocacy. She is a barrister and maintains an associate tenancy at KCH Garden Square Chambers in Nottingham and Leicester. Helen is also a qualified mediator.

Susan Ehrlich is Professor of Linguistics at York University in Toronto. She has published in the areas of language, gender, and sexuality, discourse analysis, and language and the law. Her books include *Representing Rape* (2001, Routledge), *"Why Do You Ask?": The Function of Questions in Institutional*

Discourse (2010, Oxford, co-edited with Alice Freed), and *The Handbook of Language, Gender, and Sexuality* (2014, Wiley Blackwell, co-edited with Miriam Meyerhoff and Janet Holmes).

Philip Gaines is Associate Professor of English Language Studies at Montana State University, United States. His research interests focus on the discourse of trial lawyers and police interrogators. A monograph on the discursive history of trial advocacy manuals will be published by Oxford in 2016. New research deals with the discourse structure of police interrogations leading to false confessions.

Fleur van der Houwen is affiliated with the Department of Language, Literature, and Communication, VU University, Amsterdam. Her research interests include institutional interaction (especially legal and medical settings), lay-professional communication, new media technologies for communication, and authorship analysis. She also serves as linguistic consultant and expert for the police as well as private parties and teaches courses in forensic linguistics and presents workshops for (legal) professionals.

Guusje Jol is a PhD Candidate at the Center for Language Studies at Radboud Universiteit, Nijmegen (the Netherlands). She has degrees in both law and Dutch language and culture, and she studies police interviews with child witnesses. Other research interests include institutional interaction and language in legal context.

J. R. Martin is Professor of Linguistics at the University of Sydney and at the Martin Centre for Appliable Linguistics, Shanghai Jiao Tong University. His research interests include systemic theory, functional grammar, discourse semantics, register, genre, multimodality, and critical discourse analysis, focusing on English and Tagálog. Recent publications include *Learning to Write, Reading to Learn* (2012, Equinox, with Clare Painter and Len Unsworth), *Reading Visual Narratives* (2013, Equinox), and *Systemic Functional Grammar: A Next Step into the Theory* (2013, Higher Education Press, Beijing).

Frances Rock is Reader in the Centre for Language and Communication Research at Cardiff University. Her work investigates the mediation of experiences in social worlds. Her research examines language and policing, workplaces, and ecolinguistic topics. Her publications include the monograph *Communicating Rights: The Language of Arrest and Detention* (2007, Palgrave Macmillan) and *Legal-Lay Communication: Textual Travels in the Law* (2013, Oxford University Press, co-edited with Chris Heffer and John Conley). She is an Editor of the *International Journal of Speech, Language and the Law.*

Lawrence M. Solan is the Don Forchelli Professor of Law and Director of the Center for the Study of Law, Language and Cognition at Brooklyn Law School. His books include *The Language of Judges* (1993, University of Chicago Press), *Speaking of Crime* (with Peter Tiersma, 2005, University of Chicago Press), *The Language of Statutes: Laws and their Interpretation*, (2010, University of Chicago Press) and *The Oxford Handbook of Language and Law* (co-edited with Peter Tiersma, 2012, Oxford University Press). Solan has been a Visiting Professor at the Yale Law School and in the Psychology Department and Humanities Council at Princeton University.

Elizabeth Stokoe is Professor of Social Interaction in the Department of Social Sciences at Loughborough University, United Kingdom. She has published extensively her analyses of interaction in settings including police interrogations, commercial sales calls, and inquiries to mediation and other services. She has also studied the implications of role-played or simulated interaction for communication training, and developed a pioneering alternative based in conversation analysis. She is the author of *Discourse and Identity* (2006, with Bethan Benwell) and editor of *Conversation and Gender* (2011, with Susan Speer).

Michele Zappavigna is a Lecturer in the School of Arts and Media at the University of New South Wales. Her major research interest is the discourse of social media, and she has published two books in this area: *Discourse of Twitter and Social Media* (2012, Continuum) and *Researching the Language of Social Media* (2014, Routledge, with Ruth Page, Johann Unger, and David Barton). Forthcoming is *Discourse and Diversionary Justice: An Analysis of Ceremonial Redress in Youth Justice Conferencing* (with J. R. Martin and Paul Dwyer).

Discursive Constructions of Consent in the Legal Process

1

Introduction

LINGUISTIC AND DISCURSIVE DIMENSIONS OF CONSENT

Susan Ehrlich and Diana Eades

Introduction

Consent is one of the foundational principles of Western liberal legalism, although legal doctrine is surprisingly inattentive to how it is constructed and contested. In a very general way, consent by citizens to the exercise of governmental power can act to legalize state conduct that otherwise would violate their civil and human rights; that is, the legitimacy of the state itself rests on the notion of the "consent of the governed." Consent is also relevant to both criminal and civil law: for example, in the criminal law, consent polices the boundaries between rape and sex, between theft and gift; and, in the civil law, consent to the terms of agreements is the basis of contract law enforcement. Additionally, many aspects of police-citizen encounters involve the notion of free and voluntary consent: for example, suspects in police interviews have the right to answer questions without being unduly pressured by police officers as well as the right to not answer questions; valid confessions must be voluntary and not the result of coercion; individuals in police custody must voluntarily consent to waive their rights; and searches conducted without the "free and voluntary consent" of property owners can be deemed illegal. Nonetheless, while consent figures prominently within the legal system and language often plays a central role in its negotiation, there are few, if any, publications in the language and law literature that have systematically investigated it by bringing together research from the disparate legal settings in which it is relevant. This book aims to fill this gap by exploring the linguistic and discursive dimensions of consent—and the processes involved in

We gratefully acknowledge our co-editor, Janet Ainsworth, for her insightful comments on a previous version of this chapter.

eliciting what the law considers to be consent—in a wide variety of sociolegal contexts. Tiersma (2007: 91) has argued that consent is "a mental state that may or may not be expressed verbally"; the chapters in this book reveal the central role of "verbal expression" in the complex ways that consent is sought, steered, scaffolded, given, resisted, or withheld.

Legal Settings and Scholarly Approaches

The book's examination of the linguistic and discursive dimensions of consent presents an array of legal settings and scholarly approaches. Four of the chapters consider consent in individual case studies (Ehrlich; Eades; Gaines; Berk-Seligson), while six draw on larger corpora (Rock; Conley, Cadigan and Davis; Angermeyer; Zappavigna, Dwyer and Martin; van der Houwen and Jol; Stokoe, Edwards and Edwards), with the remaining two chapters taking a wider sociolegal approach (Ainsworth; Solan). Although most of the chapters focus on the construction of consent within the legal process (such as consent to answering police questions or being searched by police), four chapters consider actions in other contexts over which there can be legal issues concerning consent (engaging in sexual activity, going for a car ride, signing a contract, or participating in medical research).

In linguistic research to date, the most extensively studied legal context in which the law requires a determination of whether someone has consented to the exercise or non-exercise of rights has been the police-suspect interview—the setting for chapters by Rock and Stokoe et al. in England and Wales, and Berk-Seligson and Gaines in the United States. For both Rock and Stokoe et al., the focus is on one aspect of suspects' rights in this context, namely, waiving their right to have a lawyer present, and exercising their right to remain silent, respectively. Rock also examines another kind of police-citizen interaction, that is, between police call center operators and individuals making nonemergency telephone calls. Each of these two chapters draws on a large corpus of recorded interactions between officers and laypeople: 30 nonemergency telephone calls and 60 suspect interviews (Rock), and 125 suspect interviews (Stokoe et al). Berk-Seligson's case study of issues involved in the comprehension of US Miranda rights—including the right to remain silent and the right to confer with a lawyer during interrogation—examines a recorded interview with a Spanish-speaking Mexican immigrant suspected of being an accessory to murder. Gaines's chapter, also a case study, analyzes a post-sting interview between a police officer and a suspect. This police questioning followed a police undercover operation in which the suspect was covertly and deceptively observed by the police, but where the suspect had no knowledge that he was under police surveillance and thus could not have consented to this surveillance. One further chapter deals with police-citizen interactions, but not in formal interviews.

This is Ainsworth's consideration of the impact of abusive swearing by street police on the capacity of individuals to voluntarily consent to a search of their person or property.

Several of the chapters scrutinize courtroom proceedings. Angermeyer draws from a corpus of 60 recorded US small claims court proceedings, as well as on ethnographic fieldwork in three courthouses. Looking mainly at litigants who speak languages other than English and who have the assistance of interpreters, his chapter investigates the purported consent by such litigants to have their case heard by an arbitrator rather than a judge. In a criminal case study, Eades examines some of the linguistic mechanisms used to secure the consent of a young teenage Aboriginal witness in an Australian court to a lawyer's recontextualized account of an incident. This chapter involves "layers of consent," as this recontextualization contests the witness's claim that he and his two friends did not give their consent to being taken for a ride by police. Ehrlich follows the trajectory of a US rape case from trial to two consecutive appeals, focusing on several levels of recontextualization of crucial parts of the complainant's evidence, first by lawyers in trial, and then by appellate judges in their decisions.

The single chapter that deals with the continental legal system (van der Houwen and Jol) examines an important part of Dutch trials, which has no counterpart in the common law. Judges in the Dutch system are required to warn suspects that they are not obliged to answer questions in court, and van der Houwen and Jol's chapter reveals some of the legal and interactional factors that can compromise this right.

The chapter by Zappavigna et al. takes us to a legal context barely considered by linguists to date, namely, that of alternative criminal justice practices (see Eades 2010: 220–228). The authors examine a small Australian corpus of recorded youth justice conferences, one of the diversionary procedures within the restorative justice tradition. The main focus in this chapter is on the discursive mechanisms used to secure the compliance of young offenders to a particular subject position, that of a person who articulately acknowledges their transgression and apologizes for it.

But, issues of consent in the law are not restricted to the criminal law, despite the fact that current linguistic research on the topic has been skewed in this direction. Consent is at the heart of contract law, and Solan's chapter identifies a linguistic problem with how judges determine the nature and scope of consent to the terms of a contractual agreement in contract disputes. Conley et al.'s chapter investigates another context in which laypeople sign legal documents that constitute their consent to a transaction, namely, informed consent documents that allow participants' genetic material to be used for medical research.

The research approaches used by the contributors to this volume represent a range of current methods for investigating language in the law. Fine-grained analysis of interaction is achieved with Conversation Analysis (van der Houwen and Jol, Stokoe et al.), and related discourse analytic tools

(Gaines, Berk-Seligson). The chapters by Ehrlich, Eades, Rock, Conley et al., and Angermeyer combine discourse analytic approaches, such as interactional sociolinguistics and/or critical discourse analysis, with ethnographic methods. Zappavigna et al.'s main analytical tool is systemic functional linguistics, a kind of discourse analysis that has only recently been introduced into studies of language and the law. Ainsworth takes a primarily sociolegal approach, while Solan's chapter uses concepts from semantics and philosophy of language in order to shed light on a legal problem. Most of the chapters also draw on research from a range of social sciences—including anthropology, sociology, feminist studies, and criminology—in order to explore the significance of the linguistic and discursive practices examined to important legal and social questions.

Key Themes

Although each of the chapters addresses the issue of consent in a specific legal setting, and in many cases using very specific kinds of data to make its argument, there are many overlapping and crosscutting themes in the chapters, making linear organization of the book a somewhat challenging exercise. Our solution has been to group chapters into sections according to what we feel are their primary thematic contributions:

- free and voluntary consent,
- informed consent or ritualized consent?
- the influence of discursive practices, and
- the coercive force of cautions.

This structure, however, is not intended to suggest that any one chapter deals with only one theme or that our organizing principles are the only means by which the chapters could have been grouped and categorized.

SECTION 1: FREE AND VOLUNTARY CONSENT

In many areas of the law, it is specified that in order for consent to be legally effective, it must be freely and voluntarily given. For example, Ainsworth in this volume refers to case law interpreting the Fourth Amendment of the US Bill of Rights, which stipulates that police searches based on consent "are legally permissible . . . only if that consent is freely and voluntarily given," and Ehrlich in her chapter notes that an important aspect of rape law reform in the Anglo-American legal system has been the (re)defining of consent in some jurisdictions as "agreement to sex that is freely or willingly given." In spite of this statutory emphasis on the issuing of free and voluntary consent, a number of scholars have argued that courts frequently take a decontextualized approach to the question of what constitutes consent, ignoring the ways in which social and situational context can imbue expressions of consent—and nonconsent—with meaning. According to Ainsworth (2008: 1), courts in the Anglo-American legal system have generally failed to "use ordinary norms of conversational implicature" in their judicial decision making; rather, they have imposed normative judgments about how language *should* be used and interpreted by speakers and hearers in ways that are at odds with insights from pragmatics and sociolinguistics. With respect to consent specifically, Solan and Tiersma (2005) have argued that courts are reluctant to view police-citizen encounters as inherently coercive—a view that has significant implications for how language produced within these encounters comes to be understood. Specifically, while police officers may produce utterances that look like polite requests in the context of police-citizen encounters, given the power asymmetry that exists between police officers and citizens such utterances will undoubtedly have the illocutionary force of commands for the ordinary citizens to whom they are directed. Yet, Solan and Tiersma (2005) discuss a number of US Supreme Court decisions regarding the legality of searches, in which courts interpreted these polite requests *literally*, that is, as requests that citizens could freely decline. Such decisions, according to Nadler and Trout (2012), typically downplay important dimensions of the police-citizen encounter, namely, that police officers are armed. Indeed, Nadler and Trout (2012: 333) cite a 2002 Supreme Court decision which asserted that, when an armed officer seeks to secure consent for a search, "[t]he presence of a holstered firearm . . . is unlikely to contribute to the coerciveness of the encounter absent active brandishing of the weapon."

Eades, in her chapter for this volume, makes an argument about police-citizen interactions similar to that of Solan and Tiersma (2005). Specifically, she argues that contextual factors were erased when judicial officers ruled in the Pinkenba case that three young Aboriginal boys were not forced by six armed police officers to enter three police cars, but rather did so voluntarily. This decision ignored not only the power asymmetries of police-citizen encounters discussed above, but also the specificities of the relationship between police and Aboriginal people in Australia. Eades points out that "the two centuries of police harassment and violence towards Aboriginal people . . . would have certainly led the three boys to fear armed police approaching them in the middle of the night" and, crucially, would have undermined their capacity to exercise free will when told to enter a police car by six armed police officers.

Ainsworth's chapter also reflects upon the narrow interpretations that courts have taken in determining whether citizens voluntarily consent to police. However, according to Ainsworth, in order to understand the "hidden architecture of coercion" in police-citizen encounters, it is necessary to broaden one's inquiry beyond the institutional roles of police and citizen to the institution of policing itself. In particular, Ainsworth argues that the use of abusive language by police officers is an integral part of police culture and its "perlocutionary impact creates a form of coercion" that undermines the ability of ordinary citizens to voluntarily consent to police searches. Ainsworth's chapter, then, builds upon previous work (e.g., Solan and Tiersma 2005; Nadler and Trout 2012): it considers not only the effect of asymmetrical social/institutional roles on the interpretation of speech acts in police searches, but also the way that linguistic practices (i.e., swearing by police) can intensify these pre-existing asymmetries in particular interactions, encouraging acquiescence on the part of citizens as opposed to the free expression of consent/nonconsent. That lawyers and judges disregard this wider interactional context means, according to Ainsworth, that they "blind themselves to the discursively created coercion" that often occurs when police attempt to secure consent to searches.

In attempting to account for the legal system's decontextualized approach to language documented in the research discussed above, recent work in language and the law has drawn attention to the importance of meta-level understandings of language—what linguistic anthropologists have called linguistic ideologies (Schieffelin, Woolard and Kroskrity 1998)—in the interpretation of both spoken and written "texts" in the legal system (e.g., Haviland 2003; Mertz 2007; Ainsworth 2008; Eades 2012). Consistent with this trend, the chapters by Eades and Ehrlich identify a specific linguistic (or language) ideology—what has been variously labeled "the correspondence theory of language" (Ainsworth 2008), the "referentialist" ideology (Collins 1996; Mertz 2007), or the "referential transparency" theory of language (Haviland 2003)—that they argue is "at work" in courts' assessments of what constitutes free and voluntary consent. Under the "referentialist" ideology, meaning is located exclusively in linguistic forms irrespective of the social and interactional context in which those forms occur. For Eades, then, when adjudicators ruled that three young Aboriginal boys voluntarily entered a police car, they were operating according to this view of language, imputing a meaning to the police officers' utterance, "Jump in the car," that ignored the social, historical, and interactional context in which it occurred. In a similar way, Ehrlich argues that the rape case analyzed in her chapter was transformed into one focused on the legal status of postpenetration rape because it relied on an understanding of language that decoupled the propositional content of linguistic forms from their surrounding context. In particular, the alleged expression of consent produced by the complainant in this case, "You can take your turn as long as you stop when I say so," seemed to have been divorced from the context in which it occurred—a series of nonconsensual acts of sexual aggression perpetrated by both the accused and his friend—by at least some of the jurors. And, according to Ehrlich, "without the series of non-consensual sexual acts that comprised the context for, and gave meaning to, [the complainant's] one instance of qualified agreement," this utterance was ascribed its propositional, context-free meaning, losing its significance as an act of submission or compliance motivated by a fear of more intense or prolonged violence. Thus, for both Eades and Ehrlich, it was the courts' privileging of literal meaning over more context-dependent meaning that led to a very narrow interpretation of consent. The courts disregarded the overall coerciveness of the interactions in question, coerciveness that, according to Eades and Ehrlich, would call into question a finding of free and voluntary consent.

SECTION 2: INFORMED CONSENT OR RITUALIZED CONSENT?

The extent to which consent can be said to be free and voluntary is also related to how well informed the consenter is about what they are consenting to, a question taken up by the chapters in Section 2. Indeed, all of the chapters in this section demonstrate that the issuing of consent in the absence of sufficient information or knowledge can run the risk of becoming mechanistic or ritualistic. Of relevance to this issue is Philips's (1998) pioneering study of guilty plea hearings in Arizona courts. Philips found that some judges took a routinized approach to the process of determining that defendants were pleading knowingly and voluntarily, in the sense that these judges asked identical questions of each defendant. By contrast, other judges tailored their questions to the individual in order to establish the knowing and voluntary nature of the plea, taking pains to carefully inform defendants about what the plea would mean in their particular situation. This study, demonstrating the impact of judges' ideologies on the seeming neutrality of their work, is significant to chapters in this section in its focus on how the law can ritualize the enactment of consent (for Philips, in the waiving of the right to a trial).

The ritualization of consent is a theme of Rock's chapter, the first chapter of Section 2. Rock's chapter focuses on seemingly innocuous requests for consent in interactions between police personnel and the public—consent requests that are framed as mere formalities mandated by the institution and, correspondingly, as banal and unimportant. Rock refers to the "consent" that is secured by these kinds of requests as "tick-box consent," a term that is reminiscent of "the boxes we complete on forms and websites" without paying full attention to what we are consenting to and without being sufficiently informed about the specifics of what we are consenting to. Here, then, it is not only the unequal status of interlocutors that interferes with a layperson's ability to consent to something in a free and voluntary way, but also the ritualistic and formalistic nature of the consent requests. Rock points out that "voluntariness can be undermined if the consent exchange is cast as a mere formality to dash through." Accordingly, her term for the speech act that results from these kinds of consent exchanges is "*disengaged* acquiescence" (emphasis added), a term that highlights the lack of engagement and knowledge that typically accompanies such expressions of "consent." For Rock, then, what is potentially dangerous about "tick-box" consent requests is that individuals (both the consenter and the elicitor of that consent) orient to them as if they concern unimportant matters, when, in fact, the consequences of acquiescing to such matters can be very serious. Indeed, Rock argues that the increasing use of consent routines by police personnel is part of a wider "ethical turn" in social life whereby morally and socially questionable activities are legitimized through the codification of consent. In the case of policing specifically, the securing of consent to "apparently minor impositions" is one means of camouflaging the coercive nature of police work.

With the notion of "tick-box" consent, Rock calls attention to the issue of what it means to be informed in the context of consent, and the extent to which individuals can be knowledgeable about what they are consenting to when consent requests are presented as if they are merely institutional "hoops" to "jump through." As Rock points out, tick-box consent routines tend to "close down opportunities for information exchange ... instead of opening up a space to explore facts and implications" of consent decisions.

The extent to which individuals are informed about consent is also a theme investigated in Solan's chapter. However, rather than focusing on what individuals know or do not know about the matters they appear to consent to (like the other two chapters in this section: Rock and Conley et al.), Solan is interested in how the law understands the scope of what people consent to when they enter into certain kinds of contractual agreements, and how these understandings may be at odds with consumers' own understandings of the terms of their contracts. American consumer contracts, according to Solan, typically display a semantic ambiguity: consenting to the terms of a contract can mean either consenting to each of a set of identifiable terms (i.e., the transparent reading) or consenting to a set of general terms, none of which may be specifically read and/or understood by the consenting party (i.e., the opaque reading). In other words, these two possible interpretations make a difference in the legal scope of the contract terms agreed to, depending on whether the consumer is deemed to have consented to the particular terms of the contract or to the contract as a whole (which may happen to contain a variety of terms). In contemporary commercial life, opaque consent to the terms of consumer contracts has become the norm. That is, as Solan says, "actual consent to individual terms occurs much less frequently than does blanket consent to a group of unread terms." Indeed, we live in a world where the vast majority of commercial transactions are "accomplished through ... forms that people cannot be expected to read." Nonetheless, Solan argues that the law surrounding contracts has been inadequate in its response to this move from transparent to opaque consent as it continues to assume "that consent to terms means consent to specific terms." Following law in the European

Union, Solan advocates a different kind of approach—a hybrid approach combining transparent and opaque consent in the interpretation of consumer contracts—whereby transparent consent should be required for important or variable terms of a contract (for example, in a mobile phone service agreement, the cost of the service and what is covered by it); otherwise, where the consumer would not expect a choice in the terms of the contract and would not be surprised at their content, opaque consent would be sufficient.

Solan's chapter, like Rock's, draws our attention to the formulaic or ritualistic nature of certain kinds of consent procedures. If the terms in a contract are not understood as specified, there is a sense in which opaque consent to form contracts is like the tick-box consent discussed by Rock, and often, interestingly, actually involves the ticking of a box. As with the people being interviewed by police in Rock's study, a consumer's consent to this kind of contract is constructed as a bureaucratic nicety that has to be done in order for the main business of an interaction to occur (such as proceeding with an interview, as discussed in Rock's chapter, or being able to download a computer program, as discussed in Solan's chapter). And, in these situations, the strong imperative to move quickly through the consent procedure imbues the entire process with a ritualistic quality and can seriously undermine the consenter's ability to be "informed" about what is being consented to.

The question of whether consent is truly informed is also a theme developed by Conley et al. in their analysis of interviews conducted with people who contributed, or in some cases declined to contribute, their genetic material to genomic biobanks. The authors in this study are interested in the extent to which their participants understood what they were agreeing to when they signed so-called informed consent documents, allowing their DNA to be part of repositories of genetic material. Rather than analyzing the discursive dynamics of actual consent interactions, however, as Rock's chapter does, or the law's interpretation of whether or not consent should be seen as valid, as Solan's chapter does, Conley et al. use ethnographic methods that focus on participants' later reflections on whether they gave truly informed consent. Thus, this study makes a unique contribution to our examination of consent, by shedding light on what consenters themselves say about the process. Despite this different methodological approach, however, Conley et al. characterize their participants' experience of expressing consent in ways not so dissimilar to Rock's description of "tick-box" consent: as ceremonial or ritualistic in nature, a description we also suggest well describes the consumer who agrees to opaque contractual terms when signing a form contract. That is, although the individuals who joined biobanks remembered signing the informed consent form, they could recall little about the form's content or substance. Conley et al. report that participants who joined the biobanks said "almost uniformly that they gave their consent at a time when they were not well-informed." Thus, although medical researchers generally treat the securing of informed consent as a singular event that coincides with the signing of a consent form, for Conley et al., the "locating" of informed consent at the moment of signing a form does not adequately capture the way their participants' understandings of what they were consenting to evolved and developed over time. Rather, Conley et al. argue that the giving of informed consent is better understood "as a discursive process, unfolding over time and contexts, and likely to have many twists and turns." The signing of an informed consent form may be one point in this discursive process, but ironically, for the vast majority of Conley et al.'s interviewees, it was not a significant one, given that they had virtually no understanding of what they were agreeing to when they signed the form. For both Conley et al. and Rock, then, the securing and giving of informed consent turns out to have an important temporal dimension: in order for consent to be voluntary and genuinely informed, it cannot be, as Rock says, "a mere formality to be dashed through," or, as one of Conley et al.'s interviewees said in commenting on the negative aspects of the form signing event, "really quick" and "rushed." As Conley et al. point out, individuals become "informed" about what they are consenting to over time and in response to their engagement with a variety of interlocutors and texts (see also Conley, Cadigan, Davis, Dobson, Edwards, Fortson, and Mitchell 2013). And, although many consenters to opaque contractual terms may also have had little understanding of what they were agreeing to at the contract signing time (when the law will say that they gave their consent), many will never discover that they did not understand the terms they agreed to unless they pursue the terms of the contract through the courts.

SECTION 3: THE INFLUENCE OF DISCURSIVE PRACTICES

In arguing that informed consent is a "discursive production" (Conley et al. 2013: 251), Conley et al.'s chapter resonates with other chapters in this volume that have as their focus the influence of discursive practices on laypersons' abilities to freely choose among options in various kinds of legal and sociolegal settings. For example, Eades's chapter from Section 1, in investigating "layers of consent" in the Pinkenba case, considers not only the coercive nature of the police-citizen interaction that was the subject of the criminal proceedings, but also the coercive force of questions in the hearing. Eades examines some of the linguistic mechanisms used in cross-examination of the Aboriginal boys to gain their "apparent consent" to confusing leading questions that supported the defense's main argument (i.e., that the boys consented to go for a ride with the police officers).[1] Such mechanisms are particularly problematic in the examination of Australian Aboriginal witnesses because of "the Aboriginal tendency to answer yes to a question ... regardless of whether the speaker agrees with the proposition being questioned." Indeed, this phenomenon of "gratuitous concurrence" meant that the Aboriginal boys in the Pinkenba hearing were probably even more susceptible than other witnesses would have been to the discursive control of cross-examining lawyers in their attempts to elicit the boys' agreement to a particular version of events.

The chapters in Section 3 also attend to how individuals' ability to accept or consent to certain kinds of representations, identities, or legal options may be discursively influenced, to varying degrees, by institutions or particular institutional representatives. Angermeyer's chapter, for example, explores the decisions that lay litigants make in small claims court about whether to have their cases heard by judges or by volunteer arbitrators. Consistent with the studies in Section 2, this procedure is frequently routinized. Although in theory this choice is a free and voluntary one that each litigant makes individually, Angermeyer argues that the courts, arbitrators, and even interpreters do not assume an impartial stance vis-à-vis the litigants' decisions. The lower costs and shorter processing times associated with arbitration hearings make them the preferred option of the institution, despite the fact that for many claimants a trial before a judge would better serve their interests. Angermeyer shows how, at different points in their court appearances, litigants are channeled in ways that encourage them to choose arbitration over trials. One way this is achieved is by the court presenting arbitration as the default option that will be the choice unless it is affirmatively rejected: "litigants are put in a position where they have to actively 'opt out' of arbitration and assert their preference for trial by judge." And, often this choice must be asserted in front of the arbitrator who will potentially hear the litigant's case, a context in which a litigant's "choice" to opt for a trial amounts to a face-threatening act against the arbitrator—an act that a litigant may be reluctant to commit. Of particular relevance to the question of whether these choices are truly informed is Angermeyer's description of the means by which the litigants become "informed" about their decision to choose arbitration as opposed to a trial by judge. Consistent with the ideas of Conley et al., this is not a one-time event, but rather a discursive process that unfolds over time. However, as a process that is controlled by the institution, the information essential to litigants in making an "informed" choice is either withheld or presented selectively. As a result, litigants generally "choose" the option that is preferred by the institution.

Angermeyer's study focuses on litigants who speak languages other than English, and, as noted above, it is not only the arbitrators who may fail to adopt an impartial stance in relation to litigants' decision but also the interpreters. According to Angermeyer, interpreters "interfere in the consent procedure in ways that demonstrate their alignment with the goals of the court system, while at the same time contravening professional norms for court interpreting." Thus, Angermeyer's study makes a valuable contribution to the discussion of two of the central ethical principles of interpreting, namely, neutrality and impartiality: while the ethic of impartiality "forbids the interpreter from taking sides for or against the other-language speaker," it does not "automatically prohibit actions on behalf of the legal institution." Because courts see themselves as "neutral and impartial by definition," interpreter alignment with the court is not seen to "compromise the perception that they are neutral in the legal dispute." But, this study of consent procedures in small claims court shows how aligning with the court's preference for arbitration rather than trial actually prevents interpreters from remaining neutral in an interaction between a layperson and a representative of the institution.

The extent to which laypeople can be discursively influenced by institutions or institutional representatives is also an issue within informal legal contexts—contexts that, in theory, are meant to eschew the hierarchical relationships inherent in more formal legal procedures. Zappavigna et al.'s chapter provides an analysis of one such legal process, youth justice conferencing in the state of New South Wales (NSW) in Australia. This type of conferencing represents "an attempt to divert young offenders away from formal court proceedings" and is part of a more general "restorative justice" reform movement that conceptualizes justice as less about punishment and retribution and more about reparation and reconciliation. As such, youth justice conferencing in NSW brings a young person who has admitted to an offense together with the victim of that offense; the ultimate goal of the conference is to broker an "outcome plan" whereby the offender engages in reparative actions that, according to the Young Offenders Act, are meant to help the young person take responsibility for his or her behavior and ultimately "become a fully autonomous individual." Conferences are made up of various stages, which Zappavigna et al. call elemental genres of the macrogenre (i.e., the conference as a whole), and consent by the young offender figures in the conferencing process both at the beginning, when the offender consents to participate in the proceedings, and at the end, when the offender agrees to the "outcome plan" that has been developed over the course of the conference. While the securing of consent at each of these two points is a discrete event that typically involves a yes/no response to a formulaic question, there is a further kind of consent that "unfolds across the whole macrogenre." That is, as several of these chapters have detailed in other contexts, this kind of consent is a discursive production, one that, in this context, involves the offender implicitly agreeing to 'take on' a particular kind of identity that is in keeping with the macrogenre's expectation: "a forthcoming, remorseful young person." Like the small claims litigants in Angermeyer's chapter, these young people, according to Zappavigna et al., do not freely choose to enact these institutionally preferred identities; rather, they comply with identities actually produced to a large extent by the conveners and other powerful participants in the conferences. More specifically, the offenders' discourse is heavily structured, or "scaffolded," by the discursive contributions of powerful actors within the conferencing process, in particular, by the conveners' discursive contributions, despite the fact that the conveners are supposed to be "transparent, neutral cypher[s]." The authors conclude that the "relative informality of the conferencing talk" can mask "relations of power" that make it difficult for the young offenders to construct identities of their own choosing; indeed, they say that "it would be naïve to think that the relative informality of the conferencing talk could be, in and of itself, sufficient to persuade 'at risk' YPs [young people] from 'targeted' communities, that they can . . . have a voice in [the conference]."

Although compliance with the subject positions provided by the conferencing discourse was the usual stance adopted by the offenders, Zappavigna et al. discuss one conference in their sample in which two young participants did resist the remorseful offender identities made available to them by the conveners. For Zappavigna et al., this kind of resistance put into stark relief the acquiescence exhibited more typically by the young people in all of the other conferences they observed. It is also an example of how it is possible for an individual to withstand, as opposed to comply with, the attempts by an institution or particular institutional representatives to gain consent to a damaging account—a theme that is explored in Gaines's contribution to this volume.

Gaines's chapter takes as its focus of analysis the police interview that followed a "sting" operation in which Larry Craig, a US senator, was accused of sexual solicitation in a public restroom in the Minneapolis–St. Paul airport. On June 1, 2007, unbeknownst to Craig, an undercover police officer, Dave Karsnia, was seated in one of the stalls in this public restroom. According to Karsnia, Craig entered the adjacent stall and engaged in supposed signaling practices (e.g., foot tapping, foot touching, hand movements) intended to solicit sex from Karsnia. Craig was ultimately arrested and pled guilty to solicitation charges. A post-arrest police interview of Craig by Karsnia was intended to solidify the case by getting Craig to adopt Karsnia's version of the events in the restroom. However, as Gaines points out, Craig did not "consent to" the version of events put forward by Karsnia; on the contrary, Craig went to great lengths to resist this version of events and to substitute in its place a narrative in which he was merely an innocent commuter using a public restroom for its intended purpose.

One of the discursive strategies that Craig used in producing his counter-narrative is referred to by Gaines as "reformulation by question." That is, Gaines shows how Craig reformulates many of the damaging propositions put forward by Karsnia in the form of questions that represent the events under scrutiny as completely proper and innocent. Moreover, after posing his own, benign, questions, Craig proceeds to answer them "unequivocally, as though he is being cooperative, forthcoming and honest." In an interesting twist, then, on the literature that shows questioners in legal contexts (typically, legal representatives such as police and lawyers) to exert interactional control over answerers (typically, laypeople), Gaines's analysis illustrates Craig usurping the police officer's role as questioner and, in turn, discursively controlling the way the events under investigation are characterized. Here Gaines notes parallels with the strategies adopted by the physician, Harold Shipman, in the police interviews analyzed by Haworth (2006) and Newbury and Johnson (2006). As was also true of the then-Ontario premier whose participation in a public inquiry was analyzed by Ehrlich and Sidnell (2006), Senator Craig and Dr. Shipman undoubtedly had the social capital and the discursive resources to enable them to resist damaging representations of their actions and intentions (see Eades 2008: 154).

This resistance to the adoption of damaging representations is more likely to be interactionally (although not necessarily legally) successful when the agent of resistance has the social capital and discursive resources typified by a politician like Craig than when the target of these tactics is a young person in trouble with police. For example, the two noncompliant young offenders in Zappavigna et al.'s chapter who eschewed the remorseful subject position that other young offenders typically adopted—and that was preferred by the institution—were negatively evaluated by the conference conveners, and their successful outcome plan was achieved, Zappavigna et al. argue, only because of the "hyper-compliant" identity performed by the sister of one of these offenders. (See Eades 2008: 223 and Harris 1984 for similar examples of witnesses whose resistance is expressed as defiance or as "answering back.") Indeed, compliance seems to be the norm for laypeople in the legal system who lack social power or are socially marginalized, as various chapters in this book demonstrate. That is, the majority of the young people in youth justice conferences (Zappigna et al., this volume), the Aboriginal boys in the Pinkenba case (Eades, this volume), and the lay litigants in NYC small claims courts for whom English was a second language (Angermeyer, this volume) were all subject to the discursive influence of institutional representatives, making little or no attempt at resistance. As a result, the identities, versions of events, or hearing options that they inevitably ended up adopting were not ones that they freely and voluntarily chose.

SECTION 4: THE COERCIVE FORCE OF CAUTIONS

Within the context of police interviews, the issue of consent arises not only in relation to suspects' adherence or resistance to the institution's preferred version of events (as is illustrated by Gaines's chapter; see also Heydon 2005), but also in relation to suspects' ability to waive or invoke their rights in an uncoerced way. Suspects who are detained and interviewed by police must be advised of their rights (e.g., the right to remain silent, the right to a lawyer) as part of an opening "caution," and the way in which these rights are communicated, interpreted, and understood has received considerable attention within the language and law literature. Rock (2007) represents the most detailed and comprehensive of these works: she examined, among other things, how rights were delivered and responded to in over 150 police cautions given by four police forces in England and Wales. One of the issues she was interested in was the discrepancy between suspects' seemingly positive assertions of comprehension within the police interview itself and the lack of understanding they exhibited of the cautions after the interviews. Why would detainees indicate to police officers that they understood their rights (and often, on that basis, waive them) when in fact they did not? Rock's chapter in this current volume provides one kind of answer to this question: the "tick-box" quality of consent routines within police interviews encourages "disengaged acquiescence" on the part of suspects in spite of the fact that suspects may not understand their rights. In fact, Rock shows that even when suspects' supposed waivers of their rights are equivocal at best, the institutional imperative for police officers to move through such "formalities" is so strong that, according to Rock, it is "as if they have no idea how to orient to the exchanges except as tick-boxes." It is in such examples, then, that we see the coercive potential of tick-box consent routines for the waiving of suspects' rights.

The coerciveness of rights talk is also a theme investigated in Berk-Seligson's chapter in this volume. Berk-Seligson's work concerns the delivery of Miranda rights to Spanish speakers in police custody in the United States. As the largest linguistic minority in the United States, Hispanics are frequently provided their Miranda rights in Spanish. However, there is no standardized version of these rights in English or in Spanish. English versions of the Miranda rights tend to be reasonably consistent, since they can draw from the exact language used in the Supreme Court opinion itself, and most Miranda warnings in English do so. Berk-Seligson notes, in contrast, that the lack of "quality control" over the numerous Spanish translations means they can vary dramatically in "their fidelity to the English language source." Beyond the problems connected with inaccurate translations of the constitutionally required rights warnings, Berk-Seligson argues that there are a variety of other factors that can negatively impact Spanish speakers' comprehension of the Miranda warnings even when such warnings are delivered in Spanish by native speakers of Spanish. According to US law, the "totality of circumstances surrounding an interrogation" (a principle put forward in the 1986 US Supreme Court decision *Moran v. Burbine*) must be considered when determining whether a suspect in the United States has adequately understood their Miranda rights and, thus, waived these rights voluntarily, in other words, without coercion. Applying this notion of "totality of circumstances" to her own case study, Berk-Seligson demonstrates how "factors beyond the wordings of the warnings" can interfere with suspects' comprehension of their Miranda rights (including the suspects' educational background, cognitive ability, cultural familiarity with police cautions, and fear of the police) and, by extension, with their ability to waive their rights in a voluntary way. In this respect, the Mexican suspect who is the focus of Berk-Seligson's case study resembles the non-English-speaking litigants in Angermeyer's chapter: in spite of the presence of interpreters, in each case, their ability to voluntarily consent to choices with important legal consequences is compromised by the legal system's failure to provide comprehensible information about these rights. More generally, while linguists call for the use of professional interpreters and translations in police interviews and courtrooms to assist second language speakers (e.g., Pavlenko 2008; Berk-Seligson 2009), and this is certainly essential, Berk-Seligson's chapter is significant in highlighting the possible limitations of such solutions for the delivery of suspects' Miranda rights. Even when Spanish translations by native speakers of Spanish are involved in the transmission of these rights, suspects' comprehension is not guaranteed.

The next two chapters in this section also examine the potential for coercion in the language of cautions; however, while Rock and Berk-Seligson call attention to the importance of suspects' understanding of the cautions in order that rights waivers are truly voluntary, the chapters by van der Houwen and Jol and Stokoe et al. probe a different dimension of coercion in the giving of cautions—namely, the coercive potential inherent in the caution itself. Van der Houwen and Jol investigate cautions in a setting that has received little attention in the Anglophone literature—courtroom hearings in an inquisitorial legal system, specifically, the Dutch legal system. While cautions are not typically delivered in courtrooms in common law jurisdictions, inquisitorial systems feature judges as active participants in the examination of suspects and witnesses and, in the Dutch system, before judges can begin to question suspects, they must issue a caution, advising suspects that they are not obligated to answer questions. As van der Houwen and Jol point out, a suspect's right not to answer questions creates "an interactionally difficult task" for both suspects and judges. Suspects do not want to incriminate themselves but, at the same time, they want to avoid the negative inferences that can be drawn from their failure to answer questions. (Within the Dutch system, suspects' attitudes within trials, translated from the Dutch as "procedural attitudes"—for example, their perceived cooperativeness, remorse, openness, and silence—can be taken into consideration by judges in the sentencing phase of a trial.) Judges need to hear the evidence in order to arrive at a verdict but, at the same time, they do not want to appear to be pressuring suspects into answering questions, given that suspects do have the legal right not to do so. Despite the legal protection of the right not to answer questions, van der Houwen and Jol show that judges, in subtle and not so subtle ways, apply pressure on suspects to answer questions. During the examination phase of the trials, for example, judges, on the one hand, refer to the caution while simultaneously, on the other hand, inviting suspects to tell their side of the story. According to van der Houwen and Jol, this double message (discussed in Komter 1998) "enables the judge to ask a question that may be considered coercive . . . while also making clear that the suspects' rights have been observed." Perhaps even more coercive than the "double messages" are points in the questioning of suspects when judges make explicit reference to a suspect's uncooperative "procedural attitude." Given that suspects' procedural attitudes can have consequences for sentencing, these kinds of examples are illustrative of the suspects' interactional dilemmas. Either they answer questions and risk incriminating themselves or they remain silent and appear uncooperative. Ultimately, van der Houwen and Jol question the extent to which it is possible for suspects to answer questions voluntarily when there are negative consequences associated with their exercising of the right to not answer questions.

Stokoe et al.'s chapter also explores the exercising of suspects' rights in cautions; however, in an interesting departure from most work in this area, which has focused on the apparent waiving of such rights, Stokoe et al. investigate the way that suspects invoke rights in UK police interviews. More specifically, Stokoe et al. analyze how suspects exercise their right to silence through the use of "no comment" responses to questions. Changes to the law in England and Wales in 1994 mean that the police caution there not only stipulates a detainee's right to silence under questioning, but also includes "a caveat on the possibility of negative inferences being drawn from the exercise of that right."[2] (This is analogous in effect to the Dutch cautions analyzed by van der Houwen and Jol, where negative assessments of suspects' "procedural attitudes" are a possible result of suspects' exercising their right to not answer questions.) Indeed, one of the issues addressed by Stokoe et al. is the extent to which "no comment" responses may function to avoid or "block" the negative inferences potentially generated by a suspect's remaining silent.

Stokoe et al. show how "no comment" responses have different interactional consequences relative to possible paraphrases such as "I have nothing to say" or "I don't wish to comment": this precise formulation, "no comment," "regularly forestalls" police officers' pursuits of answers in ways that paraphrases do not. It is this formulaic quality of "no comment" that, according to Stokoe et al., makes it recognizable as an "action in its own right, a *device for doing* not-answering" (emphasis in original). That is, suspects who use this device are not simply saying nothing: they are affirming their right to say nothing. And, because suspects are doing so in this legally recognizable way, Stokoe et al. suggest that suspects' "no comment" responses may "obviate as much as possible" the negative inferences that can arise when suspects invoke their right to silence. Interestingly, while formulaic elicitations of consent have been found to cause problems for consent (Rock, this volume), the availability of a formulaic answer ("no comment") appears to provide suspects with some protection from coercion. However, as Stokoe et al. point out, there are limits to the protection afforded by the "no comment" answer, because the law itself (since 1994) "risks being considered coercive on this point."

Conclusion

The publication of a book on consent in the legal system is a timely undertaking given the attention the topic has received of late in both news media and public discourse. As we write this, there are countless examples throughout the world. For instance, since the fall of 2014 the American comedian Bill Cosby has been accused by numerous women of sexual assault over several decades; during this same period, a popular Canadian radio broadcaster, Jian Ghomeshi, who has claimed that he engages in consensual sadomasochistic sex, was criminally charged with sexual assault following complaints by a number of women. At the level of the institution, universities and government agencies have responded to what has been characterized as a rape crisis on university campuses. For example, in 2014 the state of California instituted a "positive consent" standard for colleges and universities in an attempt to change the culture in that state surrounding sexual violence; and, in England, Oxford and Cambridge Universities introduced compulsory workshops on sexual consent for new students. While these very public conversations primarily concern consent within the context of sex and sexual violence, the chapters in this book bear testimony to the more *general* and much more widespread importance of consent in the legal system. By investigating consent across multiple and diverse legal domains, the book highlights what is common about the interpretation and representation of consent in these settings, while exemplifying the need to focus on socially situated linguistic interactions in order to understand the variety of ways in which it can be sought, negotiated, and controlled. Moreover, these studies showcase the ways in which a wide spectrum of linguistic perspectives and methodologies can illuminate problematic issues in legal practices and procedures that may otherwise be uncritically accepted.

Notes

1. This dimension of Eades's chapter builds in some ways on earlier work in language and the law, which examined the syntactic structure of questions in court in order to establish hierarchies of coerciveness (e.g., Danet, Hoffman, Kermish, Rafn and Stayman 1980), control (e.g., Woodbury 1984), and manipulation (Walker 1987) (see Eades 2000 for discussion of these approaches).

2. Rock (2010: 315) points out that the Home Office specifically states that suspects "may choose not to answer questions but police do not require the suspect's consent or agreement to interview them."

References

Ainsworth, Janet. 2008. "You have the right to remain silent …" but only if you ask for it just so: The role of linguistic ideology in American police interrogation law. *International Journal of Speech, Language and the Law* 15(1): 1–22.

Berk-Seligson, Susan. 2009. *Coerced Confessions: The Discourse of Bilingual Police Interrogations.* Berlin: Mouton de Gruyter.

Collins, James. 1996. Socialization to text: Structure and contradiction in schooled literacy. In Michael Silverstein and Greg Urban (eds.) *Natural Histories of Discourse.* Chicago: University of Chicago Press. 203–228.

Conley, John, Jean Cadigan, Arlene Davis, Allison Dobson, Erin Edwards, Wendell Fortson and Robert Mitchell. 2013. The discourse of DNA: Giving informed consent to genetic research. In Chris Heffer, Frances Rock, and John Conley (eds.) *Legal-Lay Communication: Textual Travels in the Law.* New York: Oxford University Press. 247–265.

Danet, Brenda, Kenneth Hoffman, Nicole Kermish, H. Jeffrey Rafn and Deborah Stayman. 1980. An ethnography of questioning. In Roger Shuy and Anna Shnukal (eds.) *Language Use and Uses of Language.* Washington, D.C.: Georgetown University Press. 222–234.

Eades, Diana. 2000. "I don't think it's an answer to the question": Silencing Aboriginal witnesses in court. *Language in Society* 29(2): 161–196.

Eades, Diana. 2008. *Courtroom Talk and Neocolonial Control.* Berlin: Mouton de Gruyter.

Eades, Diana. 2010. *Sociolinguistics and the Legal Process.* Bristol, U.K.: Multilingual Matters.

Eades, Diana. 2012. The social consequences of language ideologies in courtroom cross examination. *Language in Society* 41(4): 471–497.

Ehrlich, Susan and Jack Sidnell. 2006. "I think that's not an assumption you ought to make": Challenging presuppositions in inquiry testimony. *Language in Society* 35(5): 655–676.

Harris, Sandra. 1984. Questions as a mode of control in the magistrates' courts. *International Journal of the Sociology of Language* 49: 5–28.

Haviland, John. 2003. Ideologies of language: Some reflections of language and U.S. law. *American Anthropologist* 105: 764–774.

Haworth, Kate. 2006. The dynamics of power and resistance in police interview discourse. *Discourse & Society* 17: 739–759.

Heydon, Georgina. 2005. *The Language of Police Interviewing: A Critical Analysis.* Basingstoke, U.K.: Palgrave Macmillan.

Komter, Martha. 1998. *Dilemmas in the Courtroom: A Study of Trials of Violent Crime in the Netherlands.* Mahwah, New Jersey: Lawrence Erlbaum.

Mertz, Elizabeth. 2007. *The Language of Law School: Learning to Think Like a Lawyer.* New York: Oxford University Press.

Nadler, Janice and J. D. Trout. 2012. The language of consent in police encounters. In Peter Tiersma and Larry Solan (eds.) *The Oxford Handbook of Language and Law.* New York: Oxford University Press. 326–339.

Newbury, Phillip and Alison Johnson. 2006. Suspects' resistance to constraining and coercive questioning strategies in the police interview. *The International Journal of Speech, Language and the Law* 13: 213–240.

Pavlenko, Aneta. 2008. Non-native speakers of English and the Miranda warnings. *TESOL Quarterly* 42: 1–30.

Philips, Susan. 1998. *Ideology in the Language of Judges: How Judges Practice Law, Politics and Courtroom Control.* New York: Oxford University Press.

Rock, Frances. 2007. *Communicating Rights: The Language of Arrest and Detention.* Basingstoke, U.K.: Palgrave Macmillan.

Rock, Frances. 2010. Collecting oral evidence: The police, the public and the written word. In Malcolm Coulthard and Alison Johnson (eds.) *The Routledge Handbook of Forensic Linguistics.* London: Routledge. 126–138.

Schieffelin, Bambi, Kathryn Woolard and Paul Kroskrity (eds.). 1998. *Language Ideologies: Practice and Theory.* Oxford: Oxford University Press.

Solan, Lawrence and Peter Tiersma. 2005. *Speaking of Crime: The Language of Criminal Justice.* Chicago: University of Chicago Press.

Tiersma, Peter. 2007. The language of consent in rape law. In Janet Cotterill (ed.) *The Language of Sexual Crime.* Basingstoke, U.K.: Palgrave Macmillan. 83–103.

Walker, Anne Graffam. 1987. Linguistic manipulation, power, and the legal setting. In Leah Kadar (ed.) *Power through Discourse.* Norwood, New Jersey: Ablex Publishing Company. 57–80.

Woodbury, Hanni. 1984. The strategic use of questions in court. *Semiotica* 48: 197–228.

SECTION 1

Free and Voluntary Consent

2

Culture, Cursing, and Coercion

THE IMPACT OF POLICE OFFICER SWEARING ON THE VOLUNTARINESS OF CONSENT TO SEARCH IN POLICE-CITIZEN INTERACTIONS

Janet Ainsworth

Why do people allow police to search their persons or property when they know that incriminating items will be found? Consider the following scenario: a police officer asks someone to permit a search of his or her person or property, the targeted person assents to the search, and the search turns up evidence of a crime that the police would not otherwise have had. In fact, when the evidence in question is illegal drugs—as it often is—the search can result in a criminal prosecution that would not have occurred at all but for the search. Given this reality, it is hard for legal practitioners to believe that any rational person would consent to a search likely to result in such serious negative consequences. As one US federal judge (*Higgins v. United States* 1954: 820) succinctly put it more than half a century ago, "No sane man would actually be willing that policemen search his room for contraband which is certain to be discovered." And yet, as every American criminal lawyer knows, this behavior apparently occurs with surprising frequency. So, the question remains: why would anyone who knows that he or she is in possession of something that could result in their going to jail voluntarily permit the police to search for it?

To answer this question, it is first necessary to appreciate the legal constraints under which American police investigation occurs. Police officers are not constitutionally empowered to search people or places simply because they have a hunch they might find evidence of a crime in doing so. The framers of the US Bill of Rights were acutely aware that unconstrained governmental power to search people and property was subject to abuse. This concern provided the impetus for the inclusion of the Fourth Amendment in the Bill of Rights limiting the search and seizure powers of the government.

Under case law interpreting the strictures of the Fourth Amendment (see, e.g., Whitebread and Slobogin 2008: 299–307), police ordinarily cannot conduct a search unless they have a strong factual basis to believe that evidence will be found in the place searched. In addition, they must have either a warrant or a delineated justification for a warrantless search. Without those required circumstances, a police search cannot be lawfully conducted on a mere hunch or hope that evidence will be found—unless, that is, the target of the investigation were to consent to the search. It is this simple fact—that consent to search permits police searches that would otherwise not be lawful—that impels officers to seek consent on a regular basis (LaFave 2004).

Police searches based on consent are legally permissible, however, only if that consent is freely and voluntarily given (*Schneckloth v. Bustamonte* 1973: 227). Mere submission to asserted police authority is not enough to establish a voluntary consent to search (*United States v. Johnson* 1948: 13; *Bumper v. North Carolina* 1968: 548–549). If someone were to be coerced into allowing the police to conduct a search, any purported "consent" procured under those circumstances would be invalid, and the fruits of that search would thus be inadmissible in a prosecution. Overt police coercion such as use of physical violence, or even direct threat of violence, may well be uncommon. When criminal defendants tell their lawyers that their decision to permit the police search did not feel voluntary to them, they seldom allege that kind of bald coercion.[1] Yet, despite the lack of physical violence—actual or threatened—many people in these situations nevertheless experience the interaction in question as so coercive that they feel they had no choice but to acquiesce to a police search (Cole 1999: 19–20; Lichtenberg 2001).

Legal commentators (see, e.g., Stuntz 1995: 1064; Sklansky 1997: 318–323; Nadler 2002: 172–197; Tiersma and Solan 2004: 230–231) have expressed skepticism that most purported consents to search by suspects are truly voluntary and uncoerced. While such skepticism may be warranted, a generalized sense of skepticism is not terribly useful to lawyers and judges who must determine on a case-by-case basis (*Schneckloth v. Bustamonte* 1973; *Ohio v. Robinette* 1996) whether a particular defendant's supposed consent was voluntary or the product of coercion. If we are to progress from generalized intuitive skepticism to a demonstration in individual cases of how some purported consents are in fact the product of coercion, it is necessary to have a more complete understanding of the nature of the interactions that culminate in these supposed consents. To that end, a discursive analysis of police-citizen street encounters can reveal factors and circumstances that promote coercion in some instances.

In this chapter, I consider the way in which verbal interactions between police and citizens in street encounters in the United States can create the kind of coercion that undermines the voluntariness of resulting consents to search. Consideration of the discursive attributes of these street encounters, coupled with an understanding of the dynamics of police culture derived from the work of anthropologists and sociologists, can help uncover the discursive means through which coercion is deployed—the beneath-the-surface architecture of coercion that results in otherwise inexplicable "consents" to search.[2] This chapter will examine one particular kind of linguistic practice by law enforcement officers that has a coercive impact on the subjects of the discourse: abusive swearing by officers at the persons with whom they interact in street encounters. Although I will focus only on swearing, much of the linguistic and social interactionist analysis that applies to swearing would be equally pertinent to other forms of transgressive language used by police, such as the use of racial or ethnic slurs.

Social scientists studying police behavior have begun to recognize the importance of studying police verbal behavior and have urged more scholarly attention to language used by police in their interactions with the public. For example, Stephen Mastrofski and Roger Parks (1990: 476) have argued that research on police behavior pays too little attention to "what the police say and how they say it and why they say it." Phillip C. H. Shon (2000, 2002) echoes this concern, criticizing the adequacy of most ethnographies of police-citizen encounters because of lack of attention to the language used in the encounters, and asserting that language used by police plays a major role in the overall dynamics of these interactions.

A number of scholars have fruitfully used a social interactionist framework in studying police interactions with the public (Mastrofski, Snipes and Supina 1996; McCluskey, Mastrofski and Parks 2000; Mastrofski, Reisig and McCluskey 2002; McCluskey 2003), an approach that has been particularly useful in uncovering and articulating the dynamics that create coercion by situating linguistic practices in police-citizen street interactions in the context of what sociologists and anthropologists have called "police culture." This chapter will show how features of police occupational culture help explain why police officers may be inclined to use abusive language in their street interactions with citizens, and the consequences that such language use has on the dynamics those interactions. Swearing is a form of linguistic behavior with special characteristics; sociolinguistic features of swearing as a practice highlight the characteristics of such language that are particularly revealing in the context of patrol officers engaged in street interactions. Specifically, abusive swearing by a police officer is a linguistic resource that can systematically undermine the ability of a person to resist acquiescing to police domination. What may be phrased by the officer as a request to search comes instead to be understood as a demand to search that cannot be refused (see Solan and Tiersma 2005: 35–51).

Police Culture: What Does It Mean to Be a "Street Cop"?

> It's a Cop Thing, You Wouldn't Understand.
>
> —Slogan seen on on an off-duty police officer's T-shirt (Crank 1998: 13)

In order to appreciate the specifics of police linguistic behavior, one must first understand the overall dynamics of what social scientists call "police culture." Many occupations are characterized by a distinctive culture—that is, a pattern of shared identities, roles, beliefs, norms, and behaviors that infuse meaning into the experiences of those in that occupation. Occupational culture, like culture more generally, operates both as a lens through which the world is seen and as a template that structures and gives meaning to actions by those who participate in that culture. In other words, an occupational culture is both interpretive—shaping how one sees oneself and the rest of the world—and prescriptive—shaping how one should behave as a member of that culture.

Police culture, as a specific type of occupational culture, has been extensively studied by social scientists (see, e.g., Bennett 1984; Reiner 1992: 111–129; Kappeler, Sluder and Alpert 1994; Skolnick 1994: 40–68; Crank 1998; Paoline 2001; Chan 2003; Henry 2004: 85–107; Skolnick 2008; Loftus 2010). In doing so, social scientists have accompanied officers in their day-to-day street interactions and have interviewed and surveyed officers to get officers' own articulations of their beliefs and experiences. In the process of investigating this occupational niche, social scientists have painted a picture of police culture among patrol officers that is remarkably consistent across jurisdictions and communities in the United States (Loftus 2010; Skolnick 2008).

It must be borne in mind that police culture is not univocal—there are subcultures within the overall framework of police culture, such as "street cop culture" and "police management culture" (Reuss-Ianni 1983: 2–7; Chan 2003: 19–29). Nevertheless, the concept of "police culture" as an overarching description of a consistent set of norms, values, and behaviors has been shown by social scientists to be remarkably robust and persistent in a wide variety of law enforcement contexts. Aspects of police culture are inculcated through a reinforcing network of social mechanisms in which the role of "street cop" is rehearsed, practiced, and perfected. It begins even before the would-be officer dons a uniform for the first time. Images of policing transmitted through popular culture supply a ready-made model of policing even before formal training begins (Bennett 1984: 48). The sense of what it is like to be a police officer that prospective recruits bring to the job is reinforced (Bennett 1984; Chan 2003: 246–269) through the introductory immersive training that refines and amplifies the new officer's ideas of how to act out the role of police officer. Further acculturation into police culture occurs through the rookie officer's on-the-job experiences on the street. Here, rookies learn from their initial street policing experiences and from their partners which aspects of police academy training should be considered pertinent and useful and which should be minimized or ignored (Bennett 1984: 52; Brown 1988: 238–254; Crank 1998: 29–31; Paoline 2001: 10). By expressing approval or disapproval of the rookie officer's conduct on the job, partners and other peer officers supply positive and negative feedback that lets new officers know whether they are successfully adapting to their new identity.

Police culture is developed and sustained narratively as well as experientially, through the telling and sharing of "war stories"—stories of situations faced on the street and the consequences of what the officer in question did or failed to do (McNulty 1994; Crank 1998: 166–175). War stories can be humorous, ironic, tragic, or heroic in their gloss on the officer's situation, but, regardless of tone, these stories consistently serve as a powerful vehicle for the transmission of the underlying values and norms of behavior of police culture—a reaffirmation of police identity and a reminder of the unique nature of their experiences. As a practical guide for police day-to-day behavior, shared "war stories" easily trump the advice given at the training academy—advice that comes to seem out-of-touch and irrelevant to the actual demands of street policing (Paoline 2001: 10; Chan 2003: 155–162).

Police culture, and more specifically "street cop" culture, is understood by police officers themselves to be an especially powerful framework for understanding the world (Kappeler, Sluder and Alpert 1995: 243). Patrol officers insist that people who aren't police officers have no ability to understand or empathize with their experiences, their norms, and the reasons for their actions. Believing that their perspective is unique and unavailable to the outside world tends to engender in police a sense of social isolation from the rest of society. It also provides a ready defense against external criticisms of police practices and norms. If outsiders cannot know what it is like to be a "street cop," then any outside disapproval of police behavior can hardly be respected or validated (Kappeler et al. 1995: 127–142). The organizational structure of American police departments as paramilitary organizations (Auten 1981; Bittner 1995; Erickson and Haggerty 1997: 134–137; Kraska and Kappeler 1997; Crank 1998: 65–75; Chan 2003: 34–36) helps shape police culture as analogous to military culture. Officers wear uniforms similar to those worn by military personnel. They are organized by military rank, calling their supervisors sergeants, lieutenants, and captains instead of supervisors or foremen. Police training, like military training, is marked by a heavy emphasis on weaponry and its uses (Kappeler et al. 1994: 98–100), and even when officers are performing administrative jobs, they carry firearms (Betz 1988). Metaphors dominating contemporary street-level policing are explicitly derived from a military context—police are seen as *fighting a war* on crime or drugs. Not surprisingly, some officers come to see themselves as soldiers occupying enemy territory as they patrol the streets.

Another defining attribute of police culture is the belief that the world is divided into two salient categories: fellow officers and everybody else—and the corollary belief that members of the category "everybody else" should be assumed to be at least potentially hostile to police interests (see, e.g., Bouza 1990: 74). This belief leads officers to conclude that they can't depend on or trust anyone except their fellow officers (Skolnick and Bayley 1987: 49–50; Kappeler at al. 1994: 97; Crank 1998: 187–190). Good officers are said to have a suspicious turn of mind, always alert to the possibility that a citizen is involved in hitherto unknown crime or capable of displaying hitherto unsuspected violence (Crank 1998: 95–109).

Patrol officers in the United States thus see themselves as a discrete force operating in an environment of hostility and danger. The idea that policing is a highly dangerous enterprise is an important foundational belief in police culture (Cullen, Link, Travis and Lemming 1982). While it is undeniably true that police work can at times be dangerous, policing has always been objectively much less risky than officers believe it to be (for statistics, see Violanti 1996). This hyper-awareness of danger is reinforced among officers through retelling "war stories" about dangerous policing episodes. Such stories serve to confirm the "truth" that policing is a uniquely dangerous occupation in which violent suspects are a constant, omnipresent danger (Kappeler et al. 1994: 100–102). The consequence of this belief in the danger of police work is the resulting article of faith that it is essential for an officer to maintain physical and psychological control over any street encounter to minimize the risk to officer safety (Strecher 1995: 217).

The emphasis on being in control of any situation is reinforced by what is probably the central cultural feature of "street cop" culture—its essential masculinity. Police culture has been described as thoroughly masculine in terms of the attributes valued and the behavioral norms espoused (Martin 1982; Hunt 1990; Martin 1990; Young 1991: 192; Heidensohn 1992: 244; Kappeler et al. 1994: 106–107; Martin 1997; Martin and Jurik 1997: 59–72; Crank 1998: 179–182; Chan 2003: 30–32, 279–300).

This is true not merely because policing has traditionally been—and continues to be—overwhelmingly the work of men (Sklansky 2006: 1235–1239), but also because the cultural constructs concerning authority and control inherent in police culture map onto the cultural constructs of hegemonic masculinity nearly seamlessly. Hegemonic masculinity has been defined (Connell 1995; Connell and Messerschmidt 2005) as the ideology and associated practices that equate masculinity with such characteristics as dominance, aggression, risk-taking, courageousness, emotional self-control, independence, and superiority to women. Many of the contemporary scholars studying police culture (e.g., Prokos and Padavic 2002; Franklin 2005; Brown 2007; Cheng 2008; Shelley, Morabito and Tobin-Gurley 2011) have seen the concept of hegemonic masculinity as key to understanding the dynamics of police culture, since street-level policing occurs in an environment in which the characteristics associated with hegemonic masculine identity—strength, aggressiveness, dominance, and bravery—are valorized. Prokos and Padavic (2002: 446) describe what they call the "hidden curriculum" in police training that teaches rookie officers that only those who fully subscribe to the ideology of hegemonic masculinity can be considered "real cops," a process that alienates and discourages women recruits as well as men whose masculinities fail to conform to that norm (Cheng 2008). Even those scholars who more favorably assess police culture have noted the tight connection between police culture and a valorization of a certain kind of masculinity. For example, Waddington (1999: 298) wrote what he termed an "appreciation" of police culture, in which he described police culture's "cult of masculinity" and observed that "the exercise of coercive authority is . . . the preserve of 'real men' who are willing and able to fight."

As a result of this emphasis on hegemonic masculinity in police culture, those aspects of the police role that conform to hegemonic masculine norms—especially the active, physical confrontation of criminals—are considered "real" policing (Crank 1998: 180–182; Chan 2003: 30–32). Ironically, most modern police work consists of activities other than confronting and apprehending criminals (Livingston 1998), such as mediating neighborhood disputes, establishing a visible presence in the community, negotiating bureaucracies for citizens who are unsure how to get their needs met, transporting ill or injured persons to get medical assistance, responding to noise complaints, assisting motorists who have been in traffic accidents, dealing with medical and mental health emergencies, overseeing crowds at public events, giving directions, and so forth. Although administrative and peacekeeping functions dwarf crime-fighting functions in the actual work that patrol officers do—actual criminal law enforcement occupies only 15–30% of a patrol officer's time (Skogan and Frydl 2004: 71)—the imagined core of the police role in police culture is still the tough, macho crime-fighter. Even female patrol officers, if they are to succeed in the world of "street cops," feel pressured to take on masculine characteristics and behaviors—including linguistic behavior—or risk being seen to be not "real cops"[3] (Martin 1982; McElhinny 1995; Martin 1997; Shelley et al. 2011).

A key expression of masculinity in the context of police patrol work is the need to establish dominance on the street: being the "top dog" in any interaction. Officers must go to great lengths not only to assert control but also to be objectively perceived as being in control. To be perceived as not in control of any street interaction is seen by officers as hugely risky. At the very least, such officers have lost their position of unquestioned dominance and suffered a successful challenge to their authority. Worse yet, once having lost the assumed position of dominance, officers may then be vulnerable to further overt challenges to their authority, including potential physical assault

(Kappeler et al. 1994: 114–115). Thus, it is not enough merely to *be* masculine and fully in control, the patrol officer must be *seen and acknowledged* by others to be demonstrably masculine and in complete control. As one observer put it (Reuss-Ianni 1983: 14), the masculine ethos of street policing can be summed up as a behavioral norm in two words: "Show balls."

Linguistically speaking, how is "top dog" positionality and control made manifest in police-citizen street interactions? Here, the discursive repertoire available for the performance of masculinity—especially the use of abusive swearing—serves as a linguistic resource available for the instantiation of the behavioral norms and values of police culture, and, in the context of street interactions, this linguistic repertoire serves to enhance police dominance and discourage citizens from contesting that dominance.

A Linguistic Analysis of Swearing: Its Communicative and Meta-communicative Functions

LANGUAGE AND SOCIAL MEANING

The language that we choose in our interactions with others is not an idiosyncratic, purely individual matter. Language use is a culturally freighted activity in which each participant is communicating both surface propositional information and a variety of contextually situated meta-messages. As Gumperz and Cook-Gumperz put it, "in conversation ... we simultaneously signal both content and about content" (1982: 13). Goffman (1959: 1–2) calls this the difference between information given—the literal meaning of an utterance—and information given off—or what the hearer understands because of culturally shared frames of reference entailed by the utterance. In any communicative interaction, these two forms of meaning—the surface meaning of the utterances and the meta-communicative information about what kind of communication this utterance should be taken as—helps define the relationship between the parties and the overall meaning of the interaction (Watzlawick, Bavelas and Jackson 1967: 51–52). In our social interactions, we are both expressing ourselves and interpreting responses on a number of levels at once, engaging in both communicative and meta-communicative exchanges of information as the interaction unfolds, and reevaluating our interpretations of the communication as it proceeds. Communication always entails a kind of meta-comment to the effect of "This is how I see myself . . . , this is how I see you . . . , this is how I see you seeing me . . . ," and so forth in theoretically infinite regress.

It may seem obvious—even circular—to say that competent speakers ordinarily select the language they use in order to communicate what it is that they want to say. What makes this observation less than circular, however, is that speakers have a wide range of linguistic strategies from which to choose for their communicative purposes. For example, a speaker may adopt a particular speech register—a "linguistic repertoire that is associated, culture internally, with particular social practices and with persons who engage in those practices" (Agha 2001: 212) from among multiple available speech registers that could be deployed. The choice of a particular register may be associated with certain settings or situations or may be correlated with a social role or relationship. In fact, the deployment of a register, what Goffman (1974: 44) calls the "linguistic requirements of a particular kind of social situation," serves itself in part to define the social context of speech. Selection of one register rather than another available register serves as a linguistic cue carrying vast amounts of socially contextualized information about the speaker, the speaker's attitude toward the addressee, the speaker's perspective about the interaction in question, and so on.

The choice of language used in an interaction conveys information to hearers regardless of whether the speaker consciously intends to transmit such information. Tannen (1994: 47) suggests that a nondeliberate adoption by a speaker of a particular linguistic strategy should not be thought of as unconscious in the Freudian sense but rather as "automatic." In other words, the register of language used in an interaction may not be self-consciously and deliberately selected at the time of speaking, but speakers, if asked afterward, would be aware that they had made certain choices in expressing themselves and would be able to specify the reasons behind their choices.

Understanding the social meaning of a communication, then, occurs within a process of dynamic interpretation in which both speaker intent and hearer interpretation contribute to meaning. Austin (1975: 98–132), in his germinal work on speech act theory, conceptualized this process by disaggregating communication into locutions bearing illocutionary force and perlocutionary impact. Locution refers to the surface propositional meaning of what is said. By illocutionary force, Austin meant the conventionalized intent of the utterance by the speaker—for example, to threaten, or promise, or reassure, or persuade, or insult. By perlocutionary impact, he meant the effect of the utterance on the hearer—an effect that can be, but need not necessarily be, the reciprocal version of its intended illocutionary force. For instance, the locution "I am going to kill you" has as a propositional meaning that the speaker will cause the death of the hearer in the future; it might have the illocutionary function of threatening, seen from the perspective of the speaker and the reciprocal perlocutionary impact of induced fear in the addressee. On the other hand, the illocutionary force might instead be to express mild annoyance or to make a joke, and the perlocutionary impact of such a locution could likewise be amusement, contempt, or annoyance if the hearer believes that the speaker is unable to or unlikely to mount a legitimate threat of lethal violence.

Austin's analytic framework provides a useful tool for describing how certain utterances can directly or indirectly have a coercive impact on hearers by articulating the dynamic relationship between a speaker's illocutionary intent and the hearer's perlocutionary reaction. Later sociolinguistic analyses of the language of threats (e.g., Storey 1995; Fraser 1998) have used Austin's framework, coupled with an emphasis on the importance of context to meaning, as the basis for further refinements in understanding the speech act aspects of threatening language. This Austinian vocabulary and framework are useful in examining the coercive power of police swearing on those sworn at, but before applying that framework, let's look more closely at the special sociolinguistic attributes of swearing as a linguistic practice.

SWEARING AS SOCIALLY CODED LINGUISTIC PRACTICE

What are the social, cultural, and linguistic uses of swearing generally? Although, as already noted, the meaning of any utterance can be fully understood only in its social context, understanding the meaning of swearing depends even more crucially on context than most other kinds of language. Swearing as a coded social practice derives its significance from shared social frames of meaning and identity. Jay (2000: 18), in his psycholinguistic analysis of swearing, observed, "Curse words ... contain and are produced by social practices. The articulation of a curse word thus has incorporated into it social rules about gender identity, race, power, formality, prohibition, etc." In contrast to most other language used, swearing often has little or no literal or surface meaning. That is not to say that swear words have no intrinsic meaning, but only that the communicative meaning of swearing is almost entirely social and contextual and very seldom literally referential (Hughes 1991: 207; Jay 1992: 12–13; Winters and Duck 2001: 68). In fact, swearing has been called the most thoroughly contextual of any kind of language (Jay 1992: 13). Ironically, despite the fact that swearing comprises a very limited vocabulary, swear words have remarkably varied syntactic properties (Zwicky, Salus, Binnick and Vanek 1992) and an enormous semantic range (Wajnryb 2005: 72), providing swearers with a capacious set of communicative functions (see, e.g., Montagu 1967: 105–106; Pinker 2007: 327–372; Hobbs 2013: 149–176).

Swearing is a linguistic resource that serves a number of different expressive functions for its users. As interjections, swearing serves to denote a strong emotional state of the swearer, expressing pain, fear, surprise, or anger without any other semantic content. Swearing can also serve as an intensifier bearing either a positive or negative valence; this semantic ambiguity of swearing as an intensifier makes it particularly problematic to use in writing, where lack of prosodic and body language cues make it difficult to determine which of those valences is intended.

The usage most pertinent for our analysis, however, is swearing that is abusive or insulting—which can be achieved by using nouns, verbs, modifiers, or complex syntactic forms. In some instances, the swearing acts directly as an abusive descriptor or label of the person being addressed. In other instances, the swearing does not directly label the addressee but still indirectly communicates anger and contempt for the addressee. For example, "Get the hell out of the car" does not label the addressee, but is nevertheless insulting and abusive. To understand the many meanings that swearing can communicate indirectly, consider the meta-communicative functions of swearing.

Meta-communicative Functions of Swearing

Swearing can entail a variety of social meanings, but all of them turn on the fact that swearing is a socially transgressive act. Inherently, swearing explicitly violates norms in its rejection of the accepted conventions of "proper" speech. It also blatantly exercises social power, which we recognize when we euphemistically call swearing "strong" language. What makes swearing "strong" language is that its use overtly breaks a fundamental social language taboo (de Klerk 1991: 157). Swearing is a way of establishing one's identity as someone who is willing to situate oneself outside the established rules of social order, able and willing to use one's power to break those rules. Jay (1992: 160) asserts that differences in the frequency and types of swearing by individuals result from "our attempts to present ourselves as congruent with the expected behavior for our position in society." For example, in certain contexts swearing can be a means of marking in-group solidarity (Winters and Duck 2001; Daly, Holmes, Newton and Stubbs 2004; Wajnryb 2005: 34–38), often by those in a self-perceived marginal social group (McEnery 2006: 43). Whenever a person swears, the primary meta-communicative message is this: "I am a person who is willing and able to break established social rules of linguistic conduct."

Abusive swearing signals more than merely social transgression, however; it additionally expresses anger, hostility, and contempt (Jay 1992: 73–85; Jay 2000: 81–84). Depending on the situation, it can be either a linguistic substitute for physical violence or it can be a prelude to violence (Wajnryb 2005: 32), serving to "cue ... the swearer's state to other participants/onlookers in the vicinity so they can select appropriate responses" (Wajnryb 2005: 143). Unfortunately, the addressee has no failsafe way of knowing whether swearing in any particular instance makes violence on the part of the speaker more or less likely—that is, whether this particular act of swearing is a substitute for or a precursor to more overt violent behavior.

Because this kind of swearing communicates both transgression and aggression, it operates both to signal and to establish dominance by the speaker over the addressee (de Klerk 1991: 156; Jay 2000: 157–163). It is an exercise of power, marking the speaker as "tough, fearsome, or dominant," "claiming power and asserting self" (Winters and Duck 2001: 62, 72). The combination of dominance and aggression inhering in swearing constitute a linguistically created declaration that the swearing speaker is the "top dog" in the interaction.

Given the linkage between swearing and expressions of aggression, power, and dominance, it is unsurprising that swearing is strongly associated with the linguistic performance of hegemonic masculinity. Linguistic practices, after all, serve as one of the many resources through which masculinity can be constructed, signaled, and performed (Cameron 1997; Johnson 1997; Mullany 2010). The relationship between swearing, masculinity, and assertion of power was first noted in the literature of psychology more than a hundred years ago by Patrick (1901: 17), who wrote that "among boys and some classes of men" it is considered "manly to swear." Empirical research on gendered patterns in swearing (Ginsburg, Ogletree and Silakowski 2003; Stapleton 2003; McEnery 2006: 34–43; Jay and Janschewitz 2008; Jay 2009) suggests that, in general, males swear more frequently and with harsher swear words than do females. Recent work analyzing the extensive corpora of spoken Englishes available found that both in the British corpus (McEnery and Xiao 2004) and the Irish corpus (Murphy 2009), men swore somewhat more frequently, but markedly more harshly than did females. A study of verbal interactions in a nursing home (Stone, McMillan, Hazelton and Clayton 2011) found that male patients were more verbally abusive of staff than were female patients, and that their verbal aggression was frequently accomplished with swearing. When male and female respondents are surveyed on their own language use (Selnow 1985; de Klerk 1997), males self-report greater frequency and strength of swearing than do females, lending further support to the idea that swearing is thought of as a gendered linguistic resource. More to the point, whether or not males and females *actually* diverge in their swearing practices, there is a shared social *belief* that swearing is both more prevalent and more socially acceptable for male speakers than for female speakers, and it is this shared social belief that marks swearing as a gender-liminal linguistic activity. For example, both male and female survey respondents (de Klerk 1997: 153–154) reported that they considered swearing to be less appropriate for female speakers than they do for males. This attitude apparently is instilled in children from an early age. By the time children reach school age, they already have a robust understanding of the nature of nature of taboo language, including both a considerable vocabulary of swear words and a sense that their use is more taboo for girls than for boys (Jay and Jay 2013). Although swearing is understood generally to be socially transgressive behavior, swearing by males is nevertheless seen as exemplifying a kind of true masculinity. De Klerk noted, "We may overtly disapprove but we covertly value strong language as coding strength, hardness, and masculinity" (1991: 157). Thus, in contexts in which masculinity and power are contested, swearing can be an important linguistic resource in that contest. As Wajnryb put it, "Swearing has to do with power; gender, power, and swearing are intertwined" (2005: 149).

Impact of Swearing on Addressees

Understanding swearing from a sociolinguistic perspective requires consideration of the sworn-at as well as the swearer. Just as swearing has linguistic and meta-communicative functions for the swearer—its illocutionary force—it also has distinctive linguistic and meta-linguistic effects on those at whom such language is directed—its perlocutionary impact. Because the illocutionary force of swearing derives from socially shared conventions—its association with transgression, aggression, and hegemonic masculinity—its perlocutionary impact in any particular swearing episode will turn on the addressee's understanding of the meta-linguistic functioning of the swearing within its specific context.

The perlocutionary impact of swearing on the person who is sworn at can be disaggregated into separate but interrelated aspects. First, the reaction of someone who is sworn at will turn on the addressee's perception of why the swearer chose to swear. If the hearer believes that the swearing is chosen as a marker of social solidarity, the hearer will react quite differently than if it is perceived as insulting or aggressive in intent (Young 2004: 338–344). In interpreting the meaning of swearing in the specific context in which it occurs, the hearer will take into account contextual factors such as the nature of the episode in question, the relationship between the parties to the interaction and their social identities, the tone of voice and facial expressions that accompany the swearing, and so forth. Given the multiplicity of social meanings that swearing can have, the hearer must pick from among the culturally available meanings the one that best seems to fit the context in question.

The meta-linguistic communicative aspects of swearing create perlocutionary impacts that go far beyond just affecting the hearer's interpretation of the immediate language in question, however (Mulac 1976). Swearing causes the hearer to re-evaluate the entire context of the interchange in which it occurs—both before and after the swearing. It simultaneously is a kind of linguistic practice that must be interpreted in context by its recipient and is a kind of meta-linguistic practice that serves to define the context of the interchange itself. As Winters and Duck observed, "Swearing is most often part of a much larger social episode and so is both a cause and a result of individuals' feelings about one another, of the tone of the interaction, and of the broader flow of experience" (2001: 66).

Abusive Swearing by Police in Street Encounters

In light of the importance in police culture of matters of dominance and masculinity, it would seem predictable that swearing would be a prominent linguistic resource deployed by patrol officers in street encounters. Unfortunately, by the very nature of the police-citizen street encounters, social scientists (see discussion of this issue in Linfoot-Ham 2007: 23–25) have little concrete linguistic data for empirical analysis. Neither party records these interactions, and thus no corpus of police-citizen encounter language is available. There are good reasons, however, to conclude that swearing by US patrol officers in their street interchanges is a common occurrence. Social scientists who have studied the police by embedding themselves in patrol rounds (e.g., White, Cox and Basehart 1991: 276–277; Reisig, McCluskey, Mastrofski and Terrill 2004: 251) have observed that this kind of language is frequently used by the police in their street interactions. In fact, the incidence of police swearing observed by social scientists in fieldwork likely understates the frequency of such language use by officers in contexts in which they are not being observed due to the so-called observer's paradox (Labov 1972: 209–210)—namely, that speakers aware of being observed tend to self-consciously change the way in which they express themselves in order to be seen in a better light by the observer. Specifically, police officers who know their behavior is being observed by researchers might well be inclined to minimize socially offensive language like swearing, and this tendency to avoid displays of transgressive language would be further compounded by the fact that most police departments explicitly forbid their officers from swearing in their dealings with the public (Seron, Pereira and Kovath 2004: 665). Indeed, the very fact that most law enforcement administrators maintain formal policies prohibiting the use of profanity by officers, but must nonetheless issue frequent reminders to patrol officers about adhering to these policies (Reisig et al. 2004: 244) is itself an indication that abusive swearing by officers on the job cannot be an uncommon occurrence and that police administrators consider this to be a significant problem worthy of disciplinary attention.

Police misconduct complaints are another source of data about the use of abusive language in police-citizen interactions. Every US police department of any appreciable size has some kind of institutional mechanism to assess and act on citizen complaints of police misconduct. Goldstein (1994) has argued that citizen complaints about police use of abusive language are almost certainly drastically underreported. Even citizens who feel deeply aggrieved by police swearing may not file a formal complaint, recognizing that such claims are hard to prove due to lack of physical evidence and may not be taken seriously given the lack of objectively measurable harm. Perhaps surprisingly, then, reports of police swearing are nevertheless among the most frequent complaints lodged by citizens about police. For example, in the District of

Columbia (Government of the District of Columbia 2005: 25–26), complaints about obscene and humiliating language by police actually constitute the single most frequently alleged type of police misconduct reported to the Office of Police Complaints, constituting more than 40% of all complaints.

In short, there is good reason to conclude that swearing as a linguistic resource is in fact frequently deployed in patrol officers in street policing.[4] What, then, is the impact of police swearing in street interactions on the citizens at whom they swear? In the context of police-citizen interactions on the street, the overall perlocutionary impact of police officer swearing is arguably to undermine exercises of agency on the part of the citizens. Because, as earlier observed, swearing is a linguistic signal of dominance by the swearer, the person sworn at must choose how to react to this linguistic assertion of dominance. One possibility is that the citizen might choose to contest dominance and react with a linguistic or physical expression of dominance in return. Such a response is fraught with peril, however. Most people in this situation recognize that the police have an uncontestable edge in power and authority, including the legal right to use physical force to compel compliance and the ability to summon additional officers for backup to reinforce police dominance if it is seriously threatened. Thus, in any contest over dominance on the street, the odds are stacked in favor of the police—if not necessarily in the short run, then certainly in the long run—and everyone in the situation understands this. As a result, the only rational choice in the face of police exercise of power and dominance is to concede dominance and become acquiescent.

Acquiescence to police authority creates a kind of passivity on the part of the citizen in such an interaction—a passivity inconsistent with the exercise of agency inhering in the claiming of a right such as the right not to permit a search by the officer. This is particularly so given the fact that the officer asking for consent to search is not indifferent to the citizen's decision—the officer instead has a strong preference that the citizen not exercise his or her right to refuse permission to search. Citizen submission to officer dominance is inconsistent with behavior that asserts one's rights against the wishes of that officer.

Police swearing can have a second perlocutionary impact in these interchanges that further undermines the possibility of a person successfully refusing consent to search. A police officer who swears at someone in a street encounter is linguistically enacting a performance of social role transgression, communicating a willingness to break the rules of appropriate language use in an interaction. In effect, swearing officers are letting the person sworn at understand that they are not by-the-book, follow-the-rules officers, but instead are, at least in their language, transgressive officers. Once the citizen comes to appreciate that a particular officer has been marked linguistically within the interaction to be a transgressive officer, then the citizen's decision about whether to consent to a search are severely constrained by that fact. Before taking the confrontational step of asserting a right that the citizen knows that the police don't want asserted, the citizen must believe that any exercise of that right would be respected and effectuated by the police. A citizen faced with a linguistically transgressive officer, however, might well conclude that there is little point in trying to refuse to consent to a search, since a transgressive officer is unlikely to respect the claim of a right by the citizen that would inhibit the officer's unfettered exercise of investigatory power. Asserting the right to refuse to permit a search would be pointless if the citizen felt that the officer would simply override the assertion.

Worse yet, the citizen in this situation would have antagonized the transgressive officer for no gain, since a search would seem the inevitable outcome, no matter what the citizen said. Further, the attempt to claim one's rights from a transgressive officer might not be merely a pointless act but potentially even a dangerous one. After all, an officer who is willing to break rules about appropriate language use may also be willing to violate other norms of police conduct, including perhaps the norm against gratuitous physical abuse of citizens. Under these circumstances, the citizen must consider the real possibility that a transgressive swearing officer might be willing or even eager to use force in the course of this interaction. It is a hardy, perhaps even foolhardy, soul who would interpose an objection to a police search under these circumstances.

Thus, police officer swearing at someone during a street encounter creates two mutually reinforcing perlocutionary impacts on the person sworn at, both of which act to coercively undermine the possibility that the subject will attempt to exercise the right to forbid the police to search. Instead, "consent" to search in such a situation is the nearly inevitable consequence.

Legal Regulation of Searches Based on Consent: The Need for Context

Swearing by police in street encounters with citizens is highly coercive, as indeed it is arguably intended to be, and its perlocutionary impact creates a form of coercion that undermines voluntariness to subsequent officer "requests" that the citizen consent to a search by the officer of person or property. In this way, the constitutional protections designed to insulate the citizenry from arbitrary police intrusions into their lives have been rendered ineffective. This sidestepping of the constitutional constraints on government intrusion into the lives of the citizenry is especially troublesome given the racially disproportionate impact of these intrusions in the United States (see, e.g., Maclin 1991; Sklansky 1997; Cole 1999: 27–34).

The tests originally outlined by the US Supreme Court for determining whether a purported consent is voluntary validate the necessity for lawyers and trial judges to go beyond considering the immediate question-and-answer exchange constituting the supposed consent to search, and instead to undertake an examination of the wider context of the entire interaction between the police and the target of the search in the light of the linguistic practices situated within police occupational culture. In its earliest consideration of the problem of when consent to search would be considered sufficiently voluntary to be given legal effect, the Supreme Court rejected taking a narrow and cramped interpretive approach to assessing whether a purported consent to search had been procured through means that rendered it involuntary. Instead, the Supreme Court held that the totality of the circumstances of the episode needed to be considered (*Schneckloth v. Bustamonte* 1973: 227). Three years later, in *United States v. Watson*, the Supreme Court held that coercion in this context can be shown not only by demonstrating overt threats or violence but also by a showing of "more subtle forms of [police] coercion that might flaw [the target's] judgment" (1976: 424).

Regrettably, however, in more recent cases, the Supreme Court appears to have backpedaled from requiring this contextual analysis (*United States v. Drayton* 2002: 207) and proposed instead that a bare examination of the language used by the police in asking to search and of the citizen in acquiescing is sufficient to show a valid consent, without any consideration of the fuller context of the interaction in question. Such a narrow examination is unlikely to reveal the existence of the kind of coercion that operates to undermine meaningful choice by citizens in these encounters because an acontextual analysis ignores the way in which police culture engenders discursively created mechanisms of coercion throughout the interaction.

Taking into account the values and norms of police culture in assessing the degree of coercion present in specific instances of police-citizen interaction is crucial to their appropriate interpretation. The more a particular police officer adheres to the norms of police culture, the greater chances that such an officer will be involved in coercive interactions with the public that culminate in searches. For example, attitudinal survey research (Paoline and Terrill 2005) has shown that the police officers who identify most strongly with the norms of police culture are the officers who proportionately do the greatest number of citizen searches. Even more telling, empirical research indicates that those officers with the greatest degree of adherence to the norms and values of police culture express a greater willingness to use overt coercion in their dealings with members of the public (Terrill, Paoline and Manning 2003). Unless the entire police-citizen encounter is considered in assessing the voluntariness of an eventually obtained "consent" to search, police coercion—grounded in police cultural norms and values—that systematically undermines citizen voluntariness will be invisible to judicial scrutiny.

Given the potential for police abuse in procuring consents to search, it might well be better that the law refrain from validating searches on that basis, and instead insist on the same factual basis to justify a search purportedly based on consent that is required of other searches. However, it is unlikely that courts will agree to constrain law enforcement in that way, despite the risks of their inadvertently ratifying police coercion in seeking consent. As long as the judiciary continues to permit police searches based solely on the alleged consent of the target of the search, it will be necessary for courts to closely examine the circumstances of the purported consents in order to determine their voluntariness. This chapter is intended to give a concrete example of the kind of linguistic practices that a "thick description" of police-citizen interactions would see as relevant in uncovering the hidden architecture of coercion in those situations. Instead of focusing narrowly on only what the officer said when asking for authority to search and the citizen's reply, a wider analysis of the entire context of the interaction in question demonstrates the importance of broadening the inquiry to look carefully at the linguistic dynamics of the entire encounter. When lawyers and judges frame their factual inquiry on the question of consent too narrowly, they cannot help but misunderstand the dynamics of the interaction considered as a whole and thereby blind themselves to the discursively created coercion in that interaction.

Notes

1. There have been no empirical studies on this point, since access by researchers to the pool of criminal defendants in this situation for interviewing is understandably not possible. However, as a former criminal defense lawyer who has maintained ties with the local and national criminal defense bar for more than thirty years, I am aware of very few instances in which suspects claimed actual or threatened violence if they did not comply with a police-desired search. Yet they nevertheless describe the experience as one in which they felt coerced, even absent overt threats of violence.

2. It is with reluctance that I use the term "police-citizen" interaction here. The term "citizen" to refer to non-police community members is used extensively in the sociological literature, notwithstanding its misleading implication that it is limited to those with national citizenship status. It is difficult to substitute other terms, however. "Police-civilian" bears an unwanted military connotation, "police-community member" (besides being awkward) implies a limitation to persons who happen to reside in a particular physical site of policing, and "police-suspect" is far too narrow, since many of these interactions involve people who are not suspected of anything particular.

3. During an interview with a social science researcher, a female police officer recounted her process of adaptation to workplace behavioral norms: she and other female officers "start[ed] to act in masculine ways" (McElhinny 1995: 225). When asked for specific examples of how she had adopted "masculine ways," the officer gave as an example her use of what she called "tough" language, describing her own language on the job "atrocious," though the officer noted that she was attempting to "tone[] down her [use of] profanity" (McElhinny 1995: 225–226).

4. One recent example from Seattle, Washington, sheds light on why police use of such language may be so unfortunately prevalent in street encounters. In the course of investigating a robbery, Seattle police officers kicked and swore at an unarmed, handcuffed man, saying they would "beat the fucking Mexican piss out of him." Later, that individual, who was never charged with any crime, sued the police department for his mistreatment. In deposition testimony, the officers involved testified that the use of racially inflammatory and obscene language was used as a control technique, and that the Seattle Police Department was aware of this practice and tolerated it. This case, among others, was cited in a complaint filed by the US Justice Department alleging that Seattle Police Department practices were unconstitutional. U.S. Department of Justice, Civil Rights Division, Investigation of the Seattle Police Department, December 16, 2011, p. 27.Subsequently, the City of Seattle and the Justice Department entered into a consent decree to overhaul police training and street policing practices.

Cases Cited

Bumper v. North Carolina, 391 U.S. 543 (1968).
Higgins v. United States, 209 F.2d 819 (D.C. Cir. 1954).
Ohio v. Robinette, 519 U.S. 33 (1996).
Schneckloth v. Bustamonte, 412 U.S. 218 (1973).
United States v. Drayton, 539 U.S. 194 (2002).
United States v. Johnson, 333 U.S. 10 (1948).
United States v. Watson, 423 U.S. 411 (1976).

References

Agha, Asif. 2001. Register. In Alessandro Duranti (ed.) *Key Terms in Language and Culture.* Oxford: Blackwell. 212–215.
Austin, John. 1975. *How to Do Things with Words* (2nd ed.). Oxford: Oxford University Press.
Auten, James. 1981. The paramilitary model of police and police professionalism. *Police Studies: The International Review of Police Development* 4: 67–78.
Bennett, Richard. 1984. Becoming blue: A longitudinal study of police recruit occupational socialization. *Journal of Police Science and Administration* 12: 47–58.
Betz, Joseph. 1988. Police violence. In Frederick Ellison and Michael Feldberg (eds.) *Moral Issues in Police Work.* Lanham, Maryland: Rowman and Littlefield. 177–196.
Bittner, Egon. 1995. The quasi-military organization of the police. In Victor Kappeler (ed.) *The Police and Society: Touchstone Readings.* Long Grove, Illinois: Waveland Press. 173–183.
Bouza, Anthony. 1990. *The Police Mystique: An Insider's Look at Cops, Crime, and the Criminal Justice System.* New York: Perseus Publishing.
Brown, Jennifer. 2007. From cult of masculinity to smart macho: Gender perspectives in police occupational culture. In Megan O'Neill, Monique Marks and Anne-Marie

Singh (eds.) *The Police Occupational Culture, New Debates and Directions*. Oxford, U.K.: Elsevier Press. 205–226.

Brown, Michael. 1988. *Working the Street: Discretion and the Dilemmas of Reform*. New York: Russell Sage Foundation.

Cameron, Deborah. 1997. Performing gender identity: Young men's talk and the construction of heterosexual masculinity. In Sally Johnson and Ulrike Hanna Meinhof (eds.) *Language and Masculinity*. Oxford, U.K.: Blackwell. 47–64.

Chan, Janet. 2003. *Fair Cop: Learning the Art of Policing*. Toronto: University of Toronto Press.

Cheng, Cliff. 2008. Marginalized masculinities and hegemonic masculinity: An introduction. *Journal of Men's Studies* 7: 295–315.

Cole, David. 1999. *No Equal Justice: Race and Class in the American Criminal Justice System*. New York: New Press.

Connell, R. W. 1995. *Masculinities*. Berkeley: University of California Press.

Connell, R. W. and James Messerschmidt. 2005. Hegemonic masculinity: Rethinking the concept. *Gender and Society* 19: 829–859.

Crank, John. 1998. *Understanding Police Culture*. Cincinnati: Anderson Publishing.

Cullen, Francis, Bruce Link, Lawrence Travis and Terrence Lemming. 1982. Paradox in policing: A note on the perception of danger. *Journal of Police Science and Administration* 11: 457–462.

Daly, Nicola, Janet Holmes, Jonathan Newton and Maria Stubbs. 2004. Expletives as solidarity signals in FTAs on the factory floor. *Journal of Pragmatics* 36: 945–964.

de Klerk, Vivian. 1991. Expletives: Men only? *Communication Monographs* 58: 156–169.

de Klerk, Vivian. 1997. The role of expletives in the construction of masculinity. In Sally Johnson and Ulrike Hanna Meinhof (eds.) *Language and Masculinity*. Oxford, U.K.: Blackwell. 144–158.

Erickson, Richard and Kevin Haggerty. 1997. *Policing the Risk Society*. Toronto: University of Toronto Press.

Franklin, Cortney. 2005. Male peer support and the police culture: Understanding the resistance and opposition to women in policing. *Women and Criminal Justice* 16: 1–25.

Fraser, Bruce. 1998. Threatening revisited. *Forensic Linguistics* 5: 159–173.

Ginsburg, Harvey, Shirley Ogletree and Tammy Silakowski. 2003. Vulgar language: Review of sex differences in usage, attributions, and pathologies. *North American Journal of Psychology* 5: 105–116.

Goffman, Erving. 1959. *The Presentation of the Self in Everyday Life*. New York: Anchor Books.

Goffman, Erving. 1974. *Frame Analysis*. New York: Harper Colophon.

Goldstein, Herman. 1994. Controlling and reviewing police-citizen contacts. In Thomas Barker and David Carter (eds.) *Police Deviance*. Cincinnati: Anderson Publishing. 323–354.

Government of the District of Columbia. 2005. Office of Police Complaints, Annual Report for Fiscal Year 2005.

Gumperz, John and Jenny Cook-Gumperz. 1982. Introduction: Language and the communication of social identity. In John Gumperz (ed.) *Language and Social Identity*. Cambridge: Cambridge University Press. 1–21.

Heidensohn, Frances. 1992. *Women in Control? The Role of Women in Law Enforcement*. Oxford, U.K.: Clarendon Press.

Henry, Vincent. 2004. *Death Work: Police, Trauma, and the Psychology of Survival.* Oxford: Oxford University Press.

Hobbs, Pamela. 2013. "Fuck" as a metaphor for male sexual aggression. *Gender and Language* 7: 149–176.

Hughes, Geoffrey. 1991. *Swearing: A Social History of Foul Language, Oaths, and Profanity.* Oxford, U.K.: Blackwell.

Hunt, Jennifer. 1990. The logic of sexism among police. *Women and Criminal Justice* 1: 3–30.

Jay, Kristin and Timothy Jay. 2013. A child's garden of curses: A gender, historical, and age-related evaluation of the taboo lexicon. *American Journal of Psychology* 126: 459–475.

Jay, Timothy. 1992. *Cursing in America: A Psycholinguistic Study of Dirty Language in the Courts, in the Movies, in the Schoolyards and on the Streets.* Amsterdam: John Benjamins.

Jay, Timothy. 2000. *Why We Curse: A Neuro-Psycho-Social Theory of Speech.* Amsterdam: John Benjamins.

Jay, Timothy. 2009. The utility and ubiquity of taboo words. *Perspectives in Psychological Science* 4: 153–161.

Jay, Timothy and Kristin Janschewitz. 2008. The pragmatics of swearing. *Journal of Politeness Research* 4: 267–288.

Johnson, Sally. 1997. Theorizing language and masculinity: A feminist perspective. In Sally Johnson and Ulrike Hanna Meinhof (eds.) *Language and Masculinity.* Oxford, U.K.: Blackwell. 8–26.

Kappeler, Victor, Richard Sluder and Geoffrey Alpert. 1994. *Forces of Deviance: Understanding the Dark Side of Policing.* Long Grove, Illinois: Waveland.

Kappeler, Victor, Richard Sluder and Geoffrey Alpert. 1995. Breeding deviant conformity: Police ideology and culture. In Victor Kappeler (ed.) *The Police and Society: Touchstone Readings.* Long Grove, Illinois: Waveland. 243–262.

Kraska, Peter and Victor Kappeler. 1997. Militarizing American police: The rise and normalization of paramilitary units. *Social Problems* 44: 1–18.

Labov, William. 1972. *Sociolinguistic Patterns.* Philadelphia: University of Pennsylvania Press.

LaFave, Wayne. 2004. The "routine traffic stop" from start to finish: Too much "routine," not enough Fourth Amendment. *Michigan Law Review* 102: 1843–1905.

Lichtenberg, Illya. 2001. Miranda in Ohio: The effects of Robinette on the "voluntary" waiver of Fourth Amendment rights. *Howard Law Journal* 44: 349–427.

Linfoot-Ham, Kerry. 2007. Conversational maxims in encounters with law enforcement officers. *International Journal of Speech, Language and the Law* 13: 23–54.

Livingston, Debra. 1998. Police, community caretaking, and the Fourth Amendment. *University of Chicago Legal Forum* 1998: 261–481.

Loftus, Bethan. 2010. Police occupational culture: Classic themes, altered times. *Policing and Society* 20: 1–20.

Maclin, Tracey. 1991. "Black and blue encounters"—Some preliminary thoughts about Fourth Amendment seizures: Should race matter? *Valparaiso University Law Review* 26: 243–279.

Martin, Susan Ehrlich. 1982. *Breaking and Entering: Policewomen on Patrol.* Berkeley: University of California Press.

Martin, Susan Ehrlich. 1990. *On the Move: The Status of Women in Policing*. Washington, D.C.: Police Foundation.

Martin, Susan Ehrlich. 1997. Women officers on the move: An update on women in policing. In Roger Durham and Geoffrey Alpert (eds.) *Critical Issues in Policing*. Long Grove, Illinois: Waveland Press. 363–384.

Martin, Susan Ehrlich and Nancy Jurik. 1997. *Doing Justice, Doing Gender*. Thousand Oaks, California: Sage Publications.

Mastrofski, Stephen and Roger Parks. 1990. Improving observational studies of police. *Criminology* 28: 475–496.

Mastrofski, Stephen, Michael Reisig and John McCluskey. 2002. Police disrespect toward the public: An encounter-based analysis. *Criminology* 40: 519–552.

Mastrofski, Stephen, Jeffrey Snipes and Anne Supina. 1996. Compliance on demand: The public's response to specific police requests. *Journal of Research in Crime and Delinquency* 33: 269–305.

McCluskey, John. 2003. *Police Requests for Compliance: Coercive and Procedurally Just Tactics*. El Paso, Texas: LFB Scholarly Publishing.

McCluskey, John, Stephen Mastrofski and Roger Parks. 2000. To acquiesce or rebel: Predicting citizen compliance with police requests. *Police Quarterly* 2: 389–416.

McElhinny, Bonnie. 1995. Challenging hegemonic masculinities: Female and male police officers handling domestic violence. In Kira Hall and Mary Bucholtz (eds.) *Gender Articulated: Language and the Socially Constructed Self*. New York: Routledge. 217–244.

McEnery, Anthony. 2006. *Swearing in English: Bad Language, Purity and Power from 1586 to the Present*. New York: Routledge.

McEnery, Anthony and Zhonghua Xiao. 2004. Swearing in modern British English: The case of fuck in the BNC. *Language and Literature* 13: 235–268.

McNulty, Elizabeth. 1994. Generating common-sense knowledge among police officers. *Symbolic Interaction* 17: 281–294.

Montagu, Ashley. 1967. *The Anatomy of Swearing*. New York: Macmillan.

Mulac, Anthony. 1976. Effects of obscene language upon three dimensions of listener attitude. *Communication Monographs* 43: 300–307.

Mullany, Louise. 2010. Gender and interpersonal pragmatics. In Miriam Locher and Sage Graham (eds.) *Interpersonal Pragmatics*. Berlin: DeGruyter Mouton. 225–244.

Murphy, Bróna. 2009. "She's a *fucking* ticket": The pragmatics of FUCK in Irish English—an age and gender perspective. *Corpora* 4: 85–106.

Nadler, Janice. 2002. No need to shout: Bus sweeps and the psychology of coercion. *Supreme Court Review*: 153–222.

Paoline, Eugene. 2001. *Rethinking Police Culture: Officers' Occupational Attitudes*. El Paso, Texas: LFB Scholarly Publishing.

Paoline, Eugene and William Terrill. 2005. The impact of police culture on traffic stop searches. *Policing: An International Journal of Police Strategies and Management* 28: 455–472.

Patrick, G. T. W. 1901. The psychology of profanity. *The Psychology Review* 8: 113–127.

Pinker, Steven. 2007. *The Stuff of Thought: Language as a Window on Human Nature*. New York: Viking Press.

Prokos, Anastasia and Irene Padavic. 2002. "There ought to be a law against bitches": Masculinity lessons in police academy training. *Gender, Work, and Organization* 9: 439–459.

Reiner, Robert. 1992. *The Politics of the Police*. Oxford: Oxford University Press.

Reisig, Michael, John McCluskey, Stephen Mastrofski and William Terrill. 2004. Suspect disrespect toward the police. *Justice Quarterly* 21: 241–268.

Reuss-Ianni, Elizabeth. 1983. *Two Cultures of Policing: Street Cops and Management Cops*. Somerset, New Jersey: Transaction Publishers.

Selnow, Gary. 1985. Sex differences in uses and perceptions of profanity. *Sex Roles* 12: 303–312.

Seron, Carroll, Joseph Pereira and Jean Kovath. 2004. Judging police misconduct: "Street-level" versus professional policing. *Law and Society Review* 38: 665–701.

Shelley, Tara O'Connor, Melissa Schaefer Morabito and Jennifer Tobin-Gurley. 2011. Gendered institutions and gender roles: Understanding the experiences of women in policing. *Criminal Justice Studies* 24: 351–367.

Shon, Philip Chong Ho. 2000. "Hey, you c'me here!": Subjectivization, resistance, and the interpellative violence of self-generated police-citizen encounters. *International Journal for the Semiotics of Law* 13: 159–179.

Shon, Philip Chong Ho. 2002. Bringing the spoken words back in: Conversationalizing (postmodernizing) police-citizen encounter research. *Critical Criminology* 11: 151–172.

Sklansky, David. 1997. Traffic stops, minority motorists, and the future of the Fourth Amendment. *Supreme Court Review* 1997: 271–329.

Sklansky, David. 2006. Not your father's police department: Making sense of the new demographics of law enforcement. *Journal of Criminal Law and Criminology* 96: 1209–1243.

Skogan, Wesley and Kathleen Frydl (eds.) 2004. *Fairness and Effectiveness in Policing: The Evidence*. Washington, D.C.: National Research Council.

Skolnick, Jerome. 1994. *Justice Without Trial: Law Enforcement in a Democratic Society*. New York: Macmillan.

Skolnick, Jerome. 2008. Enduring issues of police culture and demographics. *Policing and Society* 18: 35–45.

Skolnick, Jerome and David Bayley. 1987. Potential obstacles to community policing. In National Institute of Justice, *Community Policing: Issues and Practices Around the World*. Washington, D.C.: National Institute of Justice. 49–62.

Solan, Lawrence and Peter Tiersma. 2005. *Speaking of Crime: The Language of Criminal Justice*. Chicago: University of Chicago Press.

Stapleton, Karen. 2003. Gender and swearing: A community practice. *Woman and Language* 26: 22–33.

Stone, Teresa, Margaret McMillan, Michael Hazelton and Edward Clayton. 2011. Wounding words: Swearing and verbal aggression in an inpatient setting. *Perspectives in Psychiatric Care* 47: 194–203.

Storey, Kate. 1995. The language of threats. *Forensic Linguistics* 2: 74–80.

Strecher, Victor. 1995. People who don't even know you. In Victor Kappeler (ed.) *The Police and Society: Touchstone Readings*. Long Grove, Illinois: Waveland. 201–233.

Stuntz, William. 1995. Privacy's problem and the law of criminal procedure. *Michigan Law Review* 93: 1016–1078.

Tannen, Deborah. 1994. *Gender and Discourse*. Oxford: Oxford University Press.

Terrill, William, Eugene Paoline and Peter Manning. 2003. Police culture and coercion. *Criminology* 41: 1003–1034.

Tiersma, Peter and Lawrence Solan. 2004. Cops and robbers: Selective literalism in American criminal law. *Law and Society Review* 38: 229–265.

Violanti, John. 1996. *Police Suicide: Epidemic in Blue*. Springfield, Illinois: Charles C Thomas Publishing.

Waddington, P. A. J. 1999. Police (canteen) sub-culture: An appreciation. *British Journal of Criminology* 39: 287–309.

Wajnryb, Ruth. 2005. *Expletive Deleted: A Good Look at Bad Language*. New York: Free Press.

Watzlawick, Paul, Janet Beavin Bavelas and Don Jackson. 1967. *Pragmatics of Human Communication*. New York: W. W. Norton.

White, Mervin, Terry Cox and Jack Basehart. 1991. Theoretical considerations of officer profanity and obscenity in formal contacts with citizens. In Thomas Barker and David Carter (eds.) *Police Deviance*. Cincinnati: Anderson Publishing. 275–291.

Whitebread, Charles and Christopher Slobogin. 2008. *Criminal Procedure: An Analysis of Cases and Concepts* (5th ed.). New York: Foundation Press.

Winters, Alaina and Steve Duck. 2001. "You ****!": Swearing as an aversive and a relational activity. In Robin Kowalski (ed.) *Behaving Badly: Aversive Behaviors in Interpersonal Relationships*. Washington, D.C.: American Psychological Association. 59–77.

Young, Malcolm. 1991. *An Inside Job: Policing and Police Culture in Britain*. Oxford: Oxford University Press.

Young, Stacy. 2004. "What the—is your problem?": Attribution theory and perceived reasons for profanity usage during conflict. *Communication Research Reports* 21: 338–347.

Zwicky, Arnold, Peter Salus, Robert Binnick and Anthony Vanek (eds.). (1970) 1992. *Studies Out in Left Field: Defamatory Essays Presented to James D. McCawley*. Amsterdam: John Benjamins.

3

Post-penetration Rape

COERCION OR FREELY GIVEN CONSENT?

Susan Ehrlich

Introduction

An important aspect of rape law reform in the United States and Canada over the last number of decades has been the requirement that consent be "voluntary" and "freely given" (Schulhofer 1998; Caringella 2009). That is, many rape statutes in the United States and Canada set the boundary between legal sex on the one hand, and rape or sexual assault on the other hand, by defining consent either as agreement to sex that is freely or willingly given (what Schulhofer 1998 and Caringella 2009 call "affirmative consent" statutes) or by specifying a series of conditions, including submitting to sex by reason of force, fear, or threats, under which the law will deem an absence of consent. These types of statutes, then, go some way in recognizing that women can submit or acquiesce to sex because of fear, physical intimidation and/or the threat of violence and that "agreement" which occurs under these circumstances does not constitute consent. In other words, sex that is coerced or forced in these ways is not considered to be consensual sex, according to these statutes, and can be subject to charges of sexual assault or rape. The case that forms the focus of this chapter took place in Maryland, a state whose rape statute has undergone reform in the ways described above: it requires a finding that consent be uncoerced in order to count as consent under the law.

Portions of this chapter are based on some of my previous work (Ehrlich 2012, 2013). Portions are also based on a paper given at the 2011 American Anthropological Association Meeting on a panel titled "Bodies of Law: Regrounding Reason and Mind in the Interactionally-Situated Legal Subject" organized by Robin Conley and Hadi Nicholas Deeb. I thank Diana Eades and Janet Ainsworth for very useful comments on a previous version of this chapter. All remaining errors are, of course, my own.

As part of a widespread, legislatively ambitious, rape law reform movement from the 1970s through the 1990s, the statutory requirement that consent be voluntarily and freely given, like other reform measures of this period, has been difficult to implement in practice. Caringella (2009: 97–98) comments that "discretionary decision making is what determines implementation of any reform provision" and that "the research on [rape law] reform has shown that old-fashioned attitudes about females lying about rape, asking for rape, and so on influence discretionary decision making to undermine reform goals." Tiersma (2007: 93) makes a similar point in relation to the notion of consent specifically, arguing that juries and judges must often draw inferences in determining whether a woman has consented to sex or not and these inferences may be based "on questionable or offensive (some would say: patriarchal) assumptions." In this chapter, like Caringella and Tiersma, I am interested in the ideological forces that inform discretionary decision making in legal cases involving sexual assault and rape and that often undermine the goals of rape law reform. However, here I focus less on gendered ideologies (i.e., Caringella's "old-fashioned attitudes about females lying about rape, asking for rape, and so on" and Tiersma's "offensive [some would say: patriarchal] assumptions") and more on linguistic ideologies that have been shown to influence interpretation in the legal system. I do this by examining a particular type of rape case that has appeared relatively recently in courts in the United States—what has been termed a post-penetration rape case. More specifically, I argue, on the basis of one particular case, *Maouloud Baby v. the State of Maryland*, that its framing as a post-penetration rape case was predicated on an interpretation of an instance of *coerced sex* as consensual sex. That is, even though the judge in this case defined consent as "actually agreeing to the sexual act rather than merely submitting as a result of force or threat of force" (*Maouloud Baby v. State of Maryland*, Court of Special Appeals of Maryland 2005), I attempt to show how a specific linguistic ideology, in combination with constraints imposed by textual hierarchies in the legal system (Mertz 2007), were responsible for transforming the meaning of this case: submission to coerced sex was reinterpreted by at least some of the jurors as consent and the legal question then became whether continued sexual activity following withdrawal of this consent after penetration could legally constitute rape. In this case, then, what began as an investigation of whether consent ever existed in the first place evolved into one in which initial consent was assumed by at least some of the jurors, and the question at issue for the courts was the legal status of post-penetration rape.

Post-penetration Rape

So, what is post-penetration rape? The first post-penetration rape case was heard in a United States court in the late 1970s, and since that time post-penetration rape cases have increasingly been heard in US courts. Post-penetration rape is defined as a situation in which both parties initially consent to sexual intercourse, but at some time during the act of intercourse, one party, typically the woman, withdraws her consent; after this withdrawal of consent, the other party, typically the man, forces the woman to continue intercourse against her will (Davis 2005: 732–733). The question that has arisen in these cases is whether a rape can legally occur if a victim initially consents to intercourse but then withdraws her consent "post-penetration." The answer to this question has been different in different jurisdictions and different courts. Some courts have found post-penetration rape to be a legal impossibility—that is, if a woman consents to sexual intercourse, that initial consent prevents the sexual act from ever legally becoming a rape (e.g., *State v. Way*, North Carolina, 1979). Other courts have held that a withdrawal of consent post-penetration negates any earlier consent and thereby subjects the defendant to rape charges if he continues what has become nonconsensual sexual intercourse (e.g., *In re John Z*, California, 2003).

The case that I analyze in this chapter, *Maouloud Baby v. the State of Maryland*, has a complex procedural history revolving around the issue I have just described. The accused, Maouloud Baby, was convicted of first degree rape and some other sexual offenses in December 2004 and was sentenced to 15 years in jail.[1]

Baby appealed this decision and, upon appeal, the Maryland Court of Special Appeals (the second highest court in Maryland) reversed Baby's convictions in September 2006, arguing that the trial judge erred in failing to give instructions to the jury consistent with a 1980 higher court case, *Battle v. Maryland*, which determined that if a woman "consents [to sexual intercourse] prior to penetration and withdraws the consent following penetration, there is no rape" (*Maouloud Baby v. State of Maryland*, Court of Special Appeals of Maryland 2005). In other words, the Court of Special Appeals believed that, as a lower appellate court, it was bound by the Maryland Court of Appeals' *Battle* decision—that post-penetration rape was a legal *impossibility*—and ordered a new trial to be conducted in light of this decision. In April 2008, after Baby and the state cross-appealed to the Maryland Court of Appeals (the highest court in Maryland), the Court of Appeals also determined that the trial judge erred in not responding to the jury's questions about the legal possibility of post-penetration rape. For this reason, like the Court of Special Appeals, it reversed Baby's convictions and ordered a new trial.[2] In contrast to the Court of Special Appeals, however, the Court of Appeals concluded that the crime of first degree rape in Maryland *does* include post-penetration rape: "the crime of first degree rape includes post-penetration vaginal intercourse ... without the consent of the victim, even if the victim consented to the initial penetration" (*State of Maryland v. Maouloud Baby*, Court of Appeals of Maryland 2007). That is, while the Court of Appeals also reversed Baby's convictions and ordered a new trial, it determined that the Court of Special Appeals, in ruling post-penetration rape a legal impossibility, had invoked a part of the *Battle* decision that was not binding (i.e., was not the "holding" of the case). In doing so, it clarified the Maryland rape statute, holding that a woman may say "no" at any time during intercourse and a man can be subject to a conviction for rape if he does not stop.

Although the *Baby* case, as I have just described, came to be understood in its appellate decisions as a case about the legal status of post-penetration rape, the issue at trial was not framed in this way by either the prosecution or by the defense. Rather, the prosecution in the case argued that the complainant never consented to the sexual acts initiated by Baby (or to the sexual acts initiated by Baby's friend, Michael Wilson), while the defense argued that she did consent to these acts. Crucially, as the next section demonstrates, neither the prosecution nor the defense invoked the categories of pre- versus post-penetration consent or withdrawal of consent.

The Trial "Facts" as Represented by the Prosecution and the Defense

Unlike many trials for serious crimes in the (adversarial) common law system, there were a number of "facts" in the *Baby* trial that the prosecution and the defense agreed upon. The complainant, J.L., and the accused, Baby, met through mutual friends the night of the events in question—December 13, 2003.[3] After participating in a number of activities that involved a group of people, including the complainant, the accused, and their mutual friends, J.L. said she would drive Baby and his friend, Michael Wilson, to a residential neighborhood where J.L. parked her car and agreed to sit in the back seat of the car with the two young men. It was at this point in the testimonies of J.L. and Baby that their stories began to diverge, although it should be noted that the Court of Special Appeals remarked in its opinion that the accused's testimony "was surprisingly consistent" with the complainant's (*Maouloud Baby v. State of Maryland*, Court of Special Appeals of Maryland 2005). The following are excerpts from both the prosecution's and the defense's opening statements regarding the events that transpired once J.L. agreed to sit in the back seat of the car with Baby and Wilson.[4]

Excerpt 1 (see appendix for transcription conventions)

She climbed in thuh back seat, (.) She took with her a: an accessory
magazine a car accessory magazine, she was gonna show thuh two guys
.hh she got into thuh back seat between them (.) and as soo:n as she

got in thuh back seat (.) they both started grabbing her. (.)
Maouloud Baby grabbed her shirt and said "why don't you flash me."
(.) Michael Wilson grabbed her ha:nd and tried to put it down his
pants. (.) She told them to stop. (   ) They didn't stop. (   ) She said
"I have to go." (.) They didn't let her go. (.) Maouloud Baby and
Michael Wilson refused to stop, (.) They flipped her over onto her
stomach, (0.2) J.L.'s face was in Michael Wilson's lap, (.) he
asked her and forgive me for thuh language these are his words not
mine. He asked her to "lick it" so he could get ha:rd. (.) A:nd
meanwhile Maouloud Baby (.) was trying to pull her pants down, (.)
She tried to pull her pants up but her arms were pinned to her
si:de, (.) This is uh-thuh back seat of a two-door car:, there's
three people in thuh back seat, .h and J.L. was unable to move her
arms. .hh J.L. kept saying no. (.) J.L. kept saying stop. (.) but
Maouloud Baby and Michael Wilson persisted.(.) Michael Wilson and
Maouloud Baby both put their fingers in J.L.'s vagina, (.)
She told them to hurt-th-that it hurt she told them to stop, (.)
They did not stop, (.) At one point Michael Wilson (.) was trying to
put his penis in her vagina and he put it in his-her rectum and she
yelled (.) and said it hurt (.) and they laughed. (.) At one point,
(.) Maouloud Baby r:olled up thuh window. (.) Thuh window was down a
little bit.=He rolled up thuh window to keep anyone from hearing
J.L. scream. (.) J.L. kept telling them to stop. (0.4) They didn't
stop. (.).h Now as you can imagine it was crowded in that back seat
with Maouloud Baby, (.) he's six feet tall and Michael Wilson, and
J.L. Michael Wilson a:sked Maouloud Baby to get outta
thuh car. He didn't do that right away (.) but ultimately he did get
outta thuh car:, (.) stood by:, and while he was outta thuh car
while M-Maouloud Baby was outta thuh car Michael Wilson (.) finished
raping J.L., vaginally,=he climaxed, (.) J.L. saw that Michael
Wilson was wearing a condom and she remembered that it was white in
color. (.) .h And after Michael Wilson was finished he told (.)
Maouloud Baby, that it was his turn ( ) and they traded places. (.)
Maouloud Baby got into thuh car Michael Wilson got outta thuh car
(.) and Michael Wilson wa:tched (.) while Maouloud Baby (.) himself
(.) raped () J.L. (.) A:nd you'll hear that when Maouloud Baby got

back in thuh car J.L. (.) was very tired and was in shock, .hh and
he said "are you gonna let me have my turn". (.) and she said "Will
you stop when I say stop" (.) and he started to put his penis in
her: and she said "stop it hurts" (.) and you'll hear that Maouloud
Baby did not stop (.) and that he proceeded to put his penis in
J.L.'s vagina. (.) Maouloud Baby was also wearing a condom
(.) but J.L. did not think that he: had had a climax. (.) A:nd (.)
when Maouloud was finished,=Maouloud Baby was finished=Michael
Wilson (.) with Maouloud Baby, a:nd J.L. in thuh back
seat=Michael Wilson got into thuh driver's seat (.) a:nd started
thuh car. (.) And when J.L. protested ( ) Maouloud Baby said-he
reassured her he said "Don't worry Michael Wilson he knows how to
drive he's cool."

Excerpt 1 is from the prosecution's opening statement. What we see in this excerpt is that after enduring much nonconsensual sex from the two young men (i.e., Baby grabbing J.L.'s shirt and trying to get her to show her breasts (line 5); Wilson grabbing J.L.'s hand and trying to put it down his pants (lines 6 and 7); Wilson trying to get J.L. to lick his penis (lines 10 to 12); Baby trying to pull J.L.'s pants down (lines 13); Wilson and Baby putting their fingers in J.L.'s vagina (lines 18 and 19); Wilson putting his penis in J.L.'s rectum (lines 21 and 22); Mike raping J.L. (lines 32 and 33)), J.L. agrees to allow Baby "to take his turn" (when he re-enters the car) as long as he stops when she tells him to stop (lines 42 to 44). And it was this "agreement" that came to be understood as J.L. consenting to sexual intercourse with Baby, once the case became framed as a post-penetration rape case. As noted above, the issue for the appellate courts *then* became whether this initial "consent" protected the sexual intercourse from legally becoming a rape or not.

Excerpt 2 describes the same set of events, but from the perspective of the defense.

Excerpt 2

She voluntarily goes in thuh ba:ck seat, (.) of thuh sma:ll two door
car, (.) and she says to: Miss Winfrey[5] that she went in thuh back
seat >in thuh middle a thuh night with two guys that were smoking
pot< to show them (.) a: magazine. (.) Common sense. (.) An' I-I
don't wanna be in this courtroom (.) ta:lking about an eighteen year
old girl: badly, (.) but I-he-I- (.) sixteen year old boy:. ( ) Gotta

7 defend 'im.=I gotta DO this. (.) So don't ha:te me for saying ba:d
8 things about pe:ople, (.) I don't know why people do things, (.) but
9 I gotta represent him (.) with a thousand percent of my energy. (.)
10 'cause he's <N:OT GUILTY> of a GANG RAPE. () <N:OT GUILTY> of
11 A:NY of those six charges. (.) She consented with Him. ( ) She consented
12 with HIm. (.) Six times she consented with HIm. (.) Wilson,=I don't
13 know he's not he:re. (.) Okay:? (.) conSENT, conSENT, conSENT,
14 conSENT, conSENT, conSENT. Six counts. (.) All consent. (.) Wilson I
15 dunno. (.) E's got his o:wn penis. (.) And during thuh ti:me that
16 Wilson was with her he was outside uh THUH CAr::. (.) HE's OUTSIde
17 uh thuh car then he gets ba:ck in. (.) An' she didn't say no: tuh
18 him, (.) When he gets back in thuh car >she doesn't say no=eh's a
19 sixteen year old kid.< (.) lookin' tuh pa:rty. (.) What do sixteen
20 year old boys wanna do,=They wanna have SE:X. (.) That's what he
21 wanted to ha:ve. (.) He didn't r:ape anybody, (.) An' when he gets
22 ba:ck in thuh car after Wilson. does what he doe:s with his o:wn
23 penis, (.) He gets in thuh car with his penis. (.) An' she doesn't
24 tell him no: (.) She consents to: him. (.) doing whatever he did.
25 His semen's not- (.) You're not gonna find his semen in the:
26 evidence, (.) He: unfortunately:=I hate to use this language-I-I
27 hate using this language. (.) He couldn't penetrate her. (.) He had
28 difficulty-he couldn't penetrate her. (.) He tri:ed >but he
29 couldn't,< (.) Wanted to: yeah(s)=Sixteen year old- ( ) red blooded
30 boy:, (.) That's what sixteen year old boys wanna do:, (.) He
32 couldn't penetrate her.=his semen is no:t in the: evidence, (.)
33 Wilson's se:men's in the: evidence, (.) His se:men's not in the:
34 evidence, (.) Did you hear:=no weapon:? (.) Nobody had a gun: or a
35 knife,>=I didn't hear that.< NO weapon. (.) No weapon. (.) No gun no
36 knife. (.) No weapon. (.) No threats=>he didn't threaten her-<he
37 a:sked her could do certain things and they did it consensually. (.)
38 ConSENT times six. (.) Times six.

In this excerpt, the series of events that preceded Baby getting back in the car are not itemized, as they were in Excerpt 1; rather, the defense lawyer asserts generally that there was consent with respect to all six counts of Baby's sexually related charges in lines 10 to 14 and again in lines 37 and 38. The only events that are described in some detail in Excerpt 2 are those that occurred once Baby re-entered the car and "tried to penetrate" J.L. but was unsuccessful (lines 27 to 29). And these events, according to the defense lawyer, were also consensual: for example, the lawyer says in lines 23 and 24 "an she doesn't tell him no" and "she consents to him doing whatever he did." Thus, as noted above, the primary difference between the prosecution's and the defense's versions of events is the issue of consent: the prosecution argued that J.L. did not consent to any of the sexual activities initiated by Baby, while the defense argued that she did. The other difference is that the defense argued that Baby was ultimately unable to penetrate J.L., while the prosecution said that he penetrated her and, furthermore, did not stop when J.L. told him to stop. Important for the purposes of my argument here, as indicated above, is the fact that neither the prosecution nor the defense invoked the categories of post-penetration rape or post-penetration withdrawal of consent. Indeed, for the prosecution, there was never consent, and for the defense, there was never penetration. So, how did the case become framed as a post-penetration rape case in the appellate decisions—a framing that is predicated on the assumption that the complainant at some point consented to sexual intercourse with Baby and then withdrew her consent after penetration? The following sections reveal that the post-penetration framing of this case had its genesis in two questions that the jury asked of the judge once it had begun its deliberations.

The Jury's Communication with the Judge

Ordinarily, appellate courts are not privy to the decision-making processes of a jury. The only evidence of how the jurors decide disputed "facts" is that provided by their verdict—guilty or not guilty. But in this case, the jury submitted two notes to the judge that reveal how at least one or more jurors were deciding the disputed "fact" in this case—namely, whether or not the sexual acts were consented to or not. After the jury began its deliberations, it submitted two questions to the judge. The first question read, "If a female consents to sex initially and, during the course of the sex act to which she consented, for whatever reason, she changes her mind and the man continues until climax, does the result constitute rape?" (*State of Maryland v. Maouloud Baby*, Court of Appeals of Maryland 2007). The second question, submitted a day after the first note, read, "If at any time, the woman says stop, is that rape?" (*State of Maryland v. Maouloud Baby*, Court of Appeals of Maryland 2007). While the judge did not answer these questions and instead directed the jurors to answer them for themselves based on the legal definitions of rape and of consent provided during jury instructions, what these questions suggest is that at least some of the jurors considered the idea that J.L.'s qualified agreement to have sex with Baby (represented in lines 41 to 45 of Excerpt 1) *was* consent. In other words, these questions seem to indicate that the jurors (or at least some of the jurors) assumed that J.L. consented to sex with Baby once he re-entered the car and that she subsequently told him to stop. And, in asking the judge whether a man's failure to stop under such conditions constituted rape, it was the jurors who were in a sense responsible for introducing the notion of post-penetration rape into the case. Recall that the foundation of the defense's appeal to the Maryland Court of Special Appeals was that the trial judge had erred in not answering the jurors' questions and, in particular, in not giving the jury an instruction consistent with a 1980 Court of Appeals case *Battle v. Maryland*, which determined that if a woman "consents [to sexual intercourse] prior to penetration and withdraws the consent following penetration, there is no rape" (cited in *Maouloud Baby v. State of Maryland*, Court of Special Appeals of Maryland 2005). That is, it was the defense's position that the judge should have answered the jurors' questions by instructing them according to a governing Maryland appellate case, which said that initial consent protects a sexual act from ever becoming rape.

The jurors found the accused guilty of rape and of some other sexually related charges—an indication that they found the testimony of the complainant credible. As I have noted above, what ultimately led the jury to find the accused guilty is not known. However, it appeared from the jurors' questions that at least some of them may have concluded that there was initial consent on the part of the complainant. In other words, it was the jury's questions that introduced the notion of post-penetration rape into the case and once these questions became the basis for the defense's appeal, the meaning of the case was transformed into one focused on the legal status of post-penetration rape.

So, given that the jury seemed to accept the prosecution's version of events, an obvious question arises: how did the kind of qualified agreement that we see represented in lines 41 to 45 of Excerpt 1 come to be understood as consistent with the judge's definition of consent provided during jury instructions? Consent was defined by the judge as "actually agreeing to the sexual act rather than merely submitting as a result of force or threat of force" (*Maouloud Baby v. State of Maryland*, Court of Special Appeals of Maryland 2005). But, given that J.L.'s agreement to allow Baby to take his turn occurred after she had endured much nonconsensual sex from both Baby and Wilson according to the prosecution's version of events, it seems difficult to view this "agreement" as an instance of "actually agreeing to the sexual act rather than merely submitting."

Research on violence against women has demonstrated that women's submission to sex can, in many circumstances, be a better strategy for surviving violence than physical resistance, given that physical resistance has the potential to escalate and intensify men's violence (Dobash and Dobash 1992). For example, the literature on battered women has demonstrated that seemingly passive behavior on the part of women can be the result of carefully thought-out, creative strategies for dealing with the threat of domestic violence: Campbell, Rose, Kub and Nedd (1998), based on interviews with approximately 100 battered women over a three-year period, found clear support for agency on the part of their subjects even when the women adopted compliant and submissive behaviors. For Campbell et al. (1998: 755), "subordinating the self" was one of these behaviors; it was characterized as a woman's "conscious decision to be as non-responsive as possible [in order] to stop the escalation of [her partner's] anger." In a similar way, research conducted on rape victim impact statements in the United Kingdom (Woodhams 2008) has demonstrated that there are a wide variety of ways that women "resist" the threat of rape, some of which involve acquiescence and submission. One set of strategies, what Woodhams (2008) refers to as "offender management strategies," involve women negotiating with their perpetrators in order to minimize the harm inflicted upon them. For example, women may agree to submit to "lesser" forms of sexual assault in exchange for being let go.

In the following excerpt from J.L.'s redirect examination, we can see evidence that J.L. adopted just such a strategy.

Excerpt 3

L: Okay, and by the time Mike got out of the car and Maouloud got in the car, you had been, correct me if I'm wrong, uhm Mike had put his fingers in your- in your vagina.
J.L.: Yes. Uh- and Maouloud.
L: And Maouloud. And Mike had tried to put his penis in your mouth.
J.L.: Yes.
L: And Maouloud had uhm, grabbed your- your shirt and touched you on the breast.
J.L.: Yes.
L: And Mike had put his penis in your rectum.
J.L.: Yes.
L: And Mike had put his penis in your vagina.
J.L.: Yes.

L: And that was all before Maouloud got out of the car.
J.L.: Yes.
L: And so by the time Maouloud got back in the car, and you
said- and- and he said to you, "Are you gonna let me have my
turn." (2.0) Did you think that if you allowed that to happen,
then you would be able to leave and go home?
CEL: Objection, your honor. Leading.
Judge: Sustained as leading.
L: What did you think, J.L., would happen if you let him do it
at that point.
J.L.: I just wanted to go home.
L: (1.0) You just wanted to go home. (2.0) And you said, did
you- you said that you told him, "Okay, if I tell you to stop,
will you stop?" Did he say anything when you said that to him?=
J.L.: =He
said "Okay."
L: And then he tried to put his penis in you. And what did you
say J.L. .
J.L.: I said, "Ow, it hurts." And I was pushing his knees.
((sniffles)) But he kept pushing. ((sniffles))
L: Did you tell him to stop?
J.L.: Yes.
L: Did he stop?
J.L.: No, after uh- he stopped after like, ten seconds or so.
((sniffles))
L: After he continued to push his penis inside you?
J.L.: Yes.
L: (3.0) J.L., at any point that night did you ever give either
of them permission to touch you?
J.L.: No. (4.0) ((sniffles))
L: Did you ever consent to any of this?
J.L.: No.
L: (4.0) Did you ever willingly engage in any sexual acts with
Maouloud or Mike?
J.L.: No.
L: That's all, your honor. Thank you.

In lines 1 to 15 of this excerpt, we see the state lawyer itemizing the acts of nonconsensual sex inflicted upon J.L. by Wilson and Baby before Baby gets back in the car and asks to take his turn. And, while J.L. acknowledges in lines 17 to 30 that she allowed Baby "to take his turn," it is significant to note that this ostensible "agreement" occurs after much nonconsensual sexual activity at a point in time when J.L. "just wanted to go home" (line 25). Thus, one way of understanding J.L.'s submission to Baby's request/demand that he be able "to take his turn" is as an "offender management strategy." That is, J.L. can be viewed as attempting to resist a prolonging and/or intensification of the sexual aggression she has already experienced from Baby and Wilson in order that she can go home sooner rather than later. But, if J.L.'s agreement to have sex with Baby was, arguably, more understandable as an act of submission or compliance than as one of freely given consent, then what sorts of ideological and/or institutional factors were responsible for the jurors' questions and the subsequent reframing of this case as a post-penetration rape case in the appellate decisions?

THE "REFERENTIALIST" LINGUISTIC IDEOLOGY

Recent research on language and the law has highlighted the importance of meta-level understandings of language—what linguistic anthropologists have called linguistic ideologies (Schieffelin, Woolard and Kroskrity 1998)—in the interpretation of both spoken and written "texts" in the legal system (e.g., Haviland 2003; Mertz 2007; Ainsworth 2008; Eades 2010). Eades (2010) argues that the most fundamental of these ideologies to legal interpretation is what has been variously labeled "the correspondence theory of language" (Ainsworth 2008), the "referentialist" ideology (Collins 1996; Mertz 2007) or the "referential transparency" theory of language (Haviland 2003)—essentially, the idea that meaning resides exclusively in linguistic forms, irrespective of the interactional or social context in which these forms occur. As Mertz says, the referentialist ideology focuses attention on the "decontextualized aspects of meaning, to the exclusion of the more contextually dependent aspects of meaning" (2007: 48). Put somewhat differently, under this view of language, the propositional content of words, phrases or sentences can be "detached" or "decoupled" from their "actual saying" with no alteration to the "truth-functional core" of that propositional meaning (Haviland 2003: 768).

As indicated above, this decontextualized view of meaning has been shown to have an impact on legal interpretation. Solan and Tiersma (2005), for example, argue that US courts do not generally acknowledge the contextual features of police-citizen encounters (i.e., their power asymmetries) and, as a result, interpret utterances produced by police officers in a literal way: as having the illocutionary force of polite requests, when undoubtedly they are interpreted as commands by ordinary citizens. In a similar way, Eades (2008) argues, in her book-length study of the Pinkenba case, that the power asymmetries of police-citizen encounters were ignored when adjudicators ruled that three young Aboriginal boys voluntarily entered a police car, as opposed to being forced to do so by the police. Such an interpretation also disregarded the long history of police harassment of Aboriginal people within the context of Australia and the kind of fear that this harassment would instill in young Aboriginal boys in their encounters with the police. Like these decontextualized interpretations, I am suggesting that the interpretation of J.L.'s coerced agreement as freely given consent—an interpretation that was presupposed by the jurors' questions—has its basis in a view of meaning that "decouples" the propositional content of utterances from their contexts of use. If J.L.'s agreement to allow Baby "to take his turn" is extracted from the broader context in which it occurred and is assigned its propositional meaning, then the questions asked by the jury make a certain kind of sense. That is, without the series of nonconsensual sexual acts that comprised the context for, and gave meaning to, J.L.'s one instance of qualified agreement (i.e., J.L. saying that Baby could take his turn as long as he stopped when she said so), the significance ascribed to this utterance would be its propositional, context-independent meaning—agreement or consent—and not submission or compliance motivated by a fear of more prolonged or more extreme instances of violence.

The Appellate Opinions

As the previous sections have shown, it was the jurors who first introduced the notion of post-penetration rape into the *Baby* case by way of the questions they posed to the trial judge. Once they did so, the defense appealed Baby's convictions, arguing that the trial judge had erred in not answering the jurors' questions in the negative, given the precedential *Battle* decision (1980), which, appeared to the Court of Special Appeals to hold that post-penetration rape was a legal impossibility in Maryland. In other words, the legal status of post-penetration rape in Maryland was the basis of Baby's appeal, and, in turn, became the primary issue addressed by the appellate courts. In a discussion of how legal professionals understand the textual authority of legal cases, Mertz (2007) highlights the extent to which the procedural history of a case is instrumental in determining what a case comes to "mean." In particular, appellate courts can only address issues in their opinions that have been invoked during appeals; "issues not raised at trial or on appeal may generally not be addressed by an appellate court: (Mertz 2007: 62). In Mertz's words, "the semiotic frame imposed by ... litigants as they [choose] particular issues to appeal" constrains "the issues to which an appellate court may speak" (2007: 62). In addition, the law divides the decision-making realms in a legal case between judges and juries—judges are the final arbiters of what the law is, and juries what the facts are. In the *Baby* case, then, once the jurors raised the issue of withdrawal of consent post-penetration, then the defense's appeal inevitably revolved around this issue.[6] In effect, the case *became* a post-penetration rape case: while the two appellate courts (the Court of Special Appeals and the Court of Appeals) disagreed about whether post-penetration rape was a legal possibility in Maryland, they both treated post-penetration rape as the central issue in the case.

In spite of the fact that appellate courts are ostensibly concerned with legal issues, and not factual ones, Mertz (2007) has argued that the version of "facts" represented in appellate courts' opinions will be influenced by the legal issues under consideration in appeals. Consistent with Mertz's claims, the appellate courts in the *Baby* case seemed to retrospectively frame the "facts" of the case in a way that was consistent with post-penetration rape, undoubtedly because that was the basis of the appeals in the case. In particular, when the appellate courts represented the sexual events under investigation, they decontextualized J.L.'s one instance of agreement, textually foregrounding J.L.'s recounting of the series of events that occurred once Baby re-entered the car (Baby saying he wanted to take his turn; J.L. agreeing as long as he stopped when she said stop, etc.) while textually backgrounding her representation of the series of nonconsensual sexual acts that preceded Baby's re-entry into the car. Consider Excerpt 4 below from the Court of Special Appeals opinion at a point in the opinion when the "facts" of the case are represented from the perspective of the prosecution or J.L.

Excerpt 4

Upon their arrival at McDonald's, Lacey left the group to join a friend, after which the complainant agreed to drive appellant and Mike to a residential neighborhood where she parked her car.[7] The complainant complied with the request of appellant and Mike to sit between them on the back seat of her car. Mike put her hand down in his pants and asked her "to lick it." Appellant then asked her to expose her breasts; when she did not comply, he fondled her breast with his hand.

After J.L. acquiesced to the boys' insistence that they stay ten more minutes, she found herself on her back with appellant removing her jeans and Mike sitting on her chest, attempting to place his penis in her mouth. After she told them to stop, the pair moved her around so that her body was up in appellant's lap as he held her arms and Mike tried to insert his penis in her, but briefly inserted it into her rectum by mistake. After Mike again tried to insert his penis in the complainant's vagina, appellant inserted his fingers in her vagina. After appellant exited the car, Mike inserted his finger, then his penis into her vagina.

Mike then got out of the car and appellant got in. Appellant told J.L. that it was his turn and, according to the complainant, the following transpired:

> Q. [ASSISTANT STATE'S ATTORNEY]: And what else did he say?
>
> A. He, after that we sat there for a couple seconds and he was like so are you going to let me hit it and I didn't really say anything and he was like I don't want to rape you.
>
> * * *
>
> Q. So when Maouloud said I don't want to rape you, did you respond?
>
> A. Yes. I said that as long as he stops when I tell him to, then -
>
> Q. Now, that he could?
>
> A. Yes.
>
> * * *
>
> Q. Did you feel like you had a choice?
>
> A. Not really. I don't know. Something just clicked off and I just did whatever they said.
>
> * * *
>
> Q. Now when you told [appellant] if I say stop, something like that, you have to stop. What did he do after you spoke those words?
>
> A. Well he got on top of me and he tried to put it in and it hurt. So I said stop and that's when he kept pushing it in and I was pushing his knees to get off me.
>
> Q. You were on your back and he was on top of you?
>
> A. Yes.
>
> Q. Did he stop pushing his penis into your vagina?
>
> A. Not right away.
>
> Q. About how long did he continue to put his penis into your vagina?
>
> A. About five or so seconds.
>
> Q. And then what happened?
>
> A. And that's when he just got off me and that's when Mike got in the car . . .

(*Maouloud Baby v. State of Maryland*, Court of Special Appeals of Maryland 2005)

What we see in this excerpt from the appellate court's opinion is a difference in the way that various parts of J.L.'s testimony are represented: when the opinion represents the events following Baby's re-entry into the car (i.e., J.L.'s so-called consent), it directly quotes J.L.'s trial testimony; when the opinion represents the events preceding Baby's re-entry (i.e., the series of nonconsensual activities that J.L. reports preceded her "agreement" to have sex with Baby), it represents her trial testimony indirectly. Previous research on the use of reported speech in legal contexts (e.g., Philips 1986; Rumsey 1990; Trinch 2010) has pointed to the greater authority and reliability that direct speech (i.e., direct quotes) is understood to convey (relative to indirect speech), given its (supposed) exactitude in the reporting of speech. Philips (1986: 169), for example, argues that the different ways of representing reported speech indicate to listeners or readers that the reported speech has different functions or meanings in the discourse. In particular, she shows, on the basis of transcripts from a criminal trial, that direct speech was used to represent evidence that was crucial to the case, while indirect speech was used to represent evidence that was less crucial to the case and/or information that provided the background to crucial evidence. In Philips's words, "quoting is reserved for information being presented as evidence directly related to proof of the elements of a criminal charge, to foreground this information, and to give it more fixedness and credibility as 'exact words' than other forms of reported speech are given" (1986: 154). The differential use of reported speech in the excerpt above, then, functions to highlight the importance of the events related to J.L.'s so-called agreement, while downgrading the significance of the events leading up to this so-called agreement. These backgrounded events, of course, are the ones that, I argue, provide contextualizing information that is *crucial* to understanding what J.L. is actually doing when she agrees to have sex with Baby—submitting or complying to coerced sex, as opposed to freely consenting to sex. Rather than creating a sense of this contextualizing relationship, however, the textual foregrounding and backgrounding that we see in Excerpt 4 has the effect of detaching J.L.'s "agreement" from the broader context in which it occurs by creating a distinction or separation between the two sets of events. So, even though appellate courts are meant to address legal issues and not factual ones, I am arguing that the appellate courts' representation of the "facts" of the *Baby* case supports an interpretation of J.L.'s agreement as consent, rather than as submission or acquiescence, which, in turn, supports an understanding of this case as a post-penetration rape case.[8]

The textual foregrounding/backgrounding seen in Excerpt 4 is even more striking when compared to Excerpt 5—a representation of the "facts" of the *Baby* case as presented by the prosecution in one of their appeal documents.

This version of the facts, like Excerpt 4, is also depicted from the point of view of the prosecution or J.L.

Excerpt 5

J.L. climbed over the center console into the back seat and sat between Baby and Wilson. She took off her jacket because it was getting warm in the car, "and that's when [Baby] started putting his hands between my legs and then [Wilson] was trying to put my hand down his pants." Baby was on one side telling her to "flash" him, and Wilson was on the other side telling her "to just lick it." The situation escalated when Baby pulled J.L.'s bra off to the side and grazed her breast while she was trying to extricate her hand from Wilson's pants. The victim insisted that she had to leave, that "[t]he 10 minutes are up." Baby and Wilson replied, "[N]o, just 10 more minutes." J.L. ended up on her back. Baby was trying to take off her pants and Wilson was sitting on her chest trying to force his exposed penis into her mouth. J.L. said, "[N]o, I'm not like that. I don't do things like that." She told them to stop. Wilson was unable to get his penis into her mouth because J.L. clenched her mouth shut. Baby and Wilson then switched places. Baby sat on the passenger's side of the car. He held J.L.'s arms while her upper body lay on his lap. J.L.'s knees were on the floor of the car. Wilson positioned himself behind J.L., and, attempting vaginal intercourse, he put his penis in her rectum. When J.L. cried out in pain, Baby and Wilson laughed. After that, Baby rolled up the passenger window, which had been cracked open. With J.L. now on her back, Wilson tried to "put it in," but could not. He told Baby, "[W]ell, if I can't put it in, then you're not going to be able to fit in. And that's when [Baby] stuck his fingers in [the victim's] vagina." J.L. again cried out in pain and pulled back while Baby continued to push his fingers inside her vagina. Baby got out of the car. Wilson continued trying to put his penis in her vagina, and he also pushed his fingers into her vagina. J.L. refused to help him "put it in," as Wilson asked. Wilson eventually got his penis into the victim's vagina and the victim believed he ejaculated. Wilson exited the car "and that's when [Baby] came in and was like well it's my turn now. And he came in and sat down." After sitting in silence for a couple of seconds Baby said, "[S]o are you going to let me hit it[?]" J.L. did not respond. Baby "was like I don't want to rape you." Wilson and Baby had earlier told J.L. that she could not leave until she had finished "whatever they told me to do" and so she did not "really" feel she had a choice. After enduring the multiple sexual assaults up to this point, J.L. testified that "[s]omething just clicked off"; she was tired, and she just wanted to go home. J.L. told Baby "that as long as he stops when I tell him to" he could, as Baby put it, "hit it." J.L. testified that Baby "got on top of me and he tried to put it in and it hurt." The victim "yelled stop, that it hurt," and tried to push Baby off of her by pushing against his legs and knees. J.L. testified that Baby nevertheless continued to push his penis into her vagina for about five or ten seconds before he finally got off of her.

(from Brief of Petitioner [Attorney General of Maryland] For Writ of Certiorari to the Court of Special Appeals of Maryland)

In contrast to Excerpt 4, Excerpt 5 does not create a textual separation between the two sets of events (i.e., the events before and after Baby's re-entry into the car) via a differential use of reported speech. In fact, Excerpt 5 directly quotes the testimony of Baby, Wilson, and J.L. at various points in the representation of events that occurred both before and after Baby's re-entry into the car. Important for my argument here is the fact that many of the acts of nonconsensual sex that preceded J.L. allowing Baby "to take his turn" are represented, in part, by direct quotes, thereby establishing them, in Philips's words, "as evidence directly related to proof of the elements of a criminal charge." Consider lines 2 to 5 as examples: direct quotes are used to represent Baby putting his hands between J.L.'s legs, Wilson trying to put J.L.'s hand down his pants, and Baby and Wilson telling J.L. to "flash him" and "just lick it," respectively. And, in lines 11 and 12, J.L.'s expressions of nonconsent to Baby's and Wilson's acts of sexual aggression are directly quoted. Excerpt 5 thus assigns as much importance to the events preceding Baby's re-entry into the car as those following his re-entry and, as a result, the context for J.L.'s allowing Baby to take his turn is textually more apparent than in Excerpt 4. Moreover, Excerpt 5 explicitly makes the connection between J.L.'s "agreement" and the "multiple sexual assaults" that J.L. had endured up to that point (line 33). That is, it is only "after enduring *multiple* sexual assaults" (my emphasis) that "J.L. told Baby 'that as long as he stops when I tell him to' he could, as Baby put it, 'hit it'" (lines 32 to 35).

Equally as significant about the version of events relayed in Excerpt 5 is the representation of J.L.'s emotional states and affective stances during the "multiple sexual assaults" that preceded Baby's re-entering the car—representations that are absent in Excerpt 4 even though Excerpt 4 also conveys the events from J.L.'s point of view. So, for example, after Wilson puts his penis in J.L.'s rectum (lines 16 and 17) and after Baby puts his fingers in her vagina (lines 21 to 23), Excerpt 5 reports that J.L. "cried out in pain" (lines 17 and 22). And, when representing J.L.'s acts of resistance to these "multiple sexual assaults," Excerpt 5 portrays their forcefulness: Excerpt 5 reports that "J.L. clenched her mouth shut" (line 13) and "refused" to help Wilson put his penis in her vagina (line 24). Thus, by comparison with Extract 5, not only does Excerpt 4 function to textually detach J.L.'s so-called agreement from the "multiple sexual assaults" that preceded this "agreement," it also omits representations of J.L.'s pain and trauma during these multiple sexual assaults when it indirectly reports on J.L.'s testimony (in the first two paragraphs of Excerpt 4). In other words, the first two paragraphs of Excerpt 4 provide an "affectless" retelling of the events preceding Baby's re-entry into the car. In work on the narratives of asylum seekers in Belgium, Maryns (2013: 678) has identified a similar kind of discursive transformation that occurs when asylum seekers' narratives of traumatic events are recontextualized in asylum officers' reports: "The asylum officer's report is clearly confined to a chronology of the facts and leaves out most of the threat, grief and uncomfortable resonance of the original." And, just as such "objectified" reports may pose difficulty for the categorization of asylum seekers' experiences as "systematic persecution" (as is required by the Geneva Convention), so a chronology of facts that omits J.L.'s expressions of fear and trauma, like those represented in Excerpt 4, makes difficult an interpretation of J.L.'s "agreement" as coerced sex. In this way, Excerpt 4 (by contrast with Excerpt 5) is consistent with a post-penetration "reading" of the *Baby* case, and, more generally, supports the claims of Gewirtz (1996) and Bogoch (2007), who argue that legal opinions tend to recount facts in ways that explain and justify "the inevitability of a particular decision" (Bogoch 2007: 160).

Conclusion

I began this chapter by considering the discrepancies that often exist between "law enacted" and "law in action" (Cargingella 2009: 5). In particular, despite the fact that widespread reforms to rape and sexual assault statutes in Canada and the United States over the last four decades have been hailed as a triumph for feminists, many theorists have pointed to the "androcentric cultural stereotypes" (Sanday 1996: 285) or the "traditional cultural mythologies about rape" (Comack 1999: 234) that can shape "discretionary decision making" (Caringella 2009: 97–98), often undermining the goals of rape law reform. In the same way that cultural mythologies about gender and sexuality have been shown to be powerful ideological forces in the trial and adjudication phases of rape trials (see, for example, Ehrlich 2001 and Matoesian 2001), in this chapter I have attempted to show how a specific linguistic ideology can be equally as influential. Although the opinion from Maryland's highest court used the occasion of the *Baby* case to clarify Maryland's rape statute, giving women the right to retract consent after penetration, this chapter has shown that the framing of the *Baby* case as a post-penetration rape case did not resonate with the version of events put forward by either the prosecution or the defense in the trial. In particular, the notion of post-penetration rape was predicated on the assumption that the complainant, J.L., at some point consented to sex with Baby; yet, such an understanding of consent relied on a view of meaning—the referentialist ideology—that detaches the propositional content of linguistic forms from their "sayings." Specifically, the propositional content of J.L.'s utterance, "you can 'take your turn' as long as you stop when I tell you to," was detached from both the social and interactional context in which it was produced. Once decontextualized in this way, this apparent agreement seemed to lose its meaning as an act of compliance or submission—as a way of attempting to end the ongoing violence sooner rather than later—and instead became interpreted as consent, despite the judge's definition of consent as "actually agreeing to the sexual act."

In sum, while the decision from the highest court in Maryland in the *Baby* case deemed post-penetration rape a legal possibility (presumably a positive result), I am suggesting that the overall framing of this case as one focused on post-penetration rape relied upon an understanding of consent that ignored the kinds of circumstances (e.g., threats, physical intimidation, the abuse of power and authority) under which women often submit to unwanted sex in order to avoid more prolonged or more severe instances of violence.[9] Put somewhat more generally, although the propositional content of acts of compliance or submission may seem identical to acts of freely given consent according to a textualist view of meaning, it is in fact the social and situational context that endows this propositional content with meaning. Thus, ignoring the contexts of use in which these speech acts of "agreement" are embedded is to ignore what is at the essence of voluntary consent.

Appendix: Transcription Conventions

The following transcription conventions are based on and slightly adapted from Jefferson's (2004) glossary of transcript symbols.

Temporal and Sequential Relationships

[	A left bracket indicates the onset of overlapping speech
]	A right bracket indicates the point at which overlapping utterances end

=	An equals sign indicates latched speech (no break or gap between talk)
(0.5)	Silences are indicated as pauses in tenths of a second
(.)	A period in parentheses indicates a hearable micropause (less than two tenths of a second)

Aspects of Speech Delivery

.	A period indicates a falling intonation contour
,	A comma indicates continuing intonation
?	A question mark indicates rising intonation contour
_	An underscore indicates a level intonation contour
:	Colons indicate lengthening of preceding sound (the more colons, the longer the lengthening)
ye-	A hyphen indicates an abrupt cutoff sound (phonetically, a glottal stop)
yes	Underlining indicates stress or emphasis, by increased amplitude or pitch
YES	Uppercase letters indicates noticeably louder speech
°yes°	The degree sign indicates noticeably quiet or soft speech
^	A caret indicates a sharp rise in pitch
>yes<	Indicates talk that is noticeably faster than surrounding talk
<yes>	Indicates talk that is noticeably slower than surrounding talk
hh	The letter "h" indicates audible aspirations (the more hs, the longer the breath)
.hh	A period preceding the letter "h" indicates audible inhalations (the more hs, the longer the breath)
y(h)es	h within parentheses within a word indicates "laugh-like" sound
£yes£	A pound sign indicates smile voice

OTHER NOTATIONAL DEVICES

(guess)	Words within single parentheses indicate likely hearing of that word
((coughs))	Information in double parentheses indicate the transcriber's descriptions of events rather than representations of them
( )	Empty parentheses indicate hearable yet indecipherable talk

Notes

1. The first trial, also in 2004, was declared a mistrial because of a hung jury.

2. According to the state attorney (personal communication), there will not be another trial because the complainant is unwilling to testify once again.

3. The state requested that the Court of Special Appeals refer to the complainant as J.L., and this is how she is referred to in both appellate decisions.

4. Michael Wilson was also charged with rape and some other sexually related charges, but did not have a trial because he pled guilty to all charges.

5. Miss Winfrey was a lawyer for the prosecution.

6. Once the jurors introduced the possibility of the withdrawal of consent, no competent lawyer could have ignored it in the appellate framing of the case (personal communication, Janet Ainsworth).

7. Lacey was J.L.'s best friend and the person who introduced J.L. to Baby and Wilson.

8. It should be noted that the Maryland Court of Appeals, the highest court in the state of Maryland, represented these events in the same way as the Maryland Special Court of Appeals. That is, when the opinion represented the events following Baby's re-entry into the car (i.e., J.L.'s so-called consent), it directly quoted J.L.'s trial testimony; when the opinion represented the events preceding Baby's re-entry (i.e., the series of nonconsensual activities that J.L. reports preceded her "agreement" to have sex with Baby), it represented her trial testimony indirectly.

9. The extent to which my analysis of this post-penetration rape case applies to post-penetration rape cases more generally is an open question, one difficult to determine without data from the trials themselves. Nonetheless, there are some indications from the descriptions of other cases (descriptions that are based on the cases' appellate decisions) that the initial "consent" upon which the post-penetration framing is based on may be more accurately characterized as coerced sex, as in the *Baby* case. See Davis (2005).

Cases Cited

Battle v. Maryland, 414 A.2d 1266 (Md. 1980).

In re John Z., 60 P.3d, 183, 189–90 (Cal. 2003).

Maouloud Baby v. State of Maryland, Court of Special Appeals of Maryland, 2005. 172 Md. App. 588, 916 A.2d 410; 2007 Md. App. LEXIS 60.

State of Maryland v. Maouloud Baby, Court of Appeals of Maryland, 2007. 404 Md.220, 946 A.2d 463; 2008 Md. LEXIS 190.

State v. Way, 254 S.E.2d 760, 762 (N.C. 1979).

References

Ainsworth, Janet. 2008. "You have the right to remain silent . . . But only if you ask for it just so": The role of linguistic ideology in American police interrogation law. *International Journal of Speech, Language and the Law* 15: 259–322.

Bogoch, Byrna. 2007. The victim as 'other': Analysis of the language of acquittal decisions in sexual offences in the Israeli Supreme Court. In Janet Cotterill (ed.) *The Language of Sexual Crime*. Basingstoke, U.K.: Palgrave Macmillan. 159–179.

Campbell, Jacquelyn, Linda Rose, Joan Kub and Daphne Nedd. 1998. Voices of strength and resistance: A contextual and longitudinal analysis of women's responses to battering. *Journal of Interpersonal Violence* 13: 743–762.

Caringella, Susan. 2009. *Addressing Rape Reform in Law and Practice*. New York: Columbia University Press.

Collins, James. 1996. Socialization to text: Structure and contradiction in schooled literacy. In Michael Silverstein and Greg Urban (eds.) *Natural Histories of Discourse*. Chicago: University of Chicago Press. 203–228.

Comack, Elizabeth. 1999. Theoretical excursions. In Elizabeth Comack (ed.) *Locating Law: Race/Class/Gender Connections*. Halifax: Fernwood Publishing. 19–68.

Davis, Amanda. 2005. Clarifying the issue of consent: The evolution of post-penetration rape law. *Stetson Law Review* 34: 729–766.

Dobash, R. Emerson and Russell Dobash. 1992. *Women, Violence and Social Change*. London: Routledge.

Eades, Diana. 2008. *Courtroom Talk and Neocolonial Control*. Berlin: Mouton de Gruyter.

Eades, Diana. 2010. *Sociolinguistics and the Legal Process*. Bristol, U.K.: Multilingual Matters.

Ehrlich, Susan. 2001. *Representing Rape: Language and Sexual Consent*. London: Routledge.

Ehrlich, Susan. 2012. Text trajectories, legal discourse and gendered inequalities. *Applied Linguistics Review* 3: 47–73.

Ehrlich, Susan. 2013. Post-penetration rape and the decontextualization of witness testimony. In Chris Heffer, Frances Rock and John Conley (eds.) *Legal-Lay Communication: Textual Travels in the Legal System*. Oxford: Oxford University Press. 189–205.

Gewirtz, Paul. 1996. Narrative and rhetoric in the law. In Peter Brooks and Paul Gewirtz (eds.) *Law's Stories*. New Haven, Connecticut: Yale University Press. 2–22.

Haviland, John. 2003. Ideologies of language: Some reflections of language and U.S. law. *American Anthropologist* 105: 764–774.

Jefferson, Gail. 2004. Glossary of transcript symbols with an introduction. In Gene Lerner (ed.) *Conversation Analysis: Studies from the First Generation*. Amsterdam: John Benjamins. 13–31.

Maryns, Katrijn. 2013. Disclosure and (re)performance of gender-based evidence in an interpreter-mediated asylum interview. *Journal of Sociolinguistics* 17: 661–686.

Matoesian, Greg. 2001. *Law and the Language of Identity: Discourse in the William Kennedy Smith Rape Trial*. New York: Oxford University Press.

Mertz, Elizabeth. 2007. *The Language of Law School: Learning to Think Like a Lawyer*. Oxford: Oxford University Press.

Philips, Susan. 1986. Reported speech as evidence in an American trial. In Deborah Tannen and James Alatis (eds.) *Georgetown University Roundtable in Languages and Linguistics 1985: The Interdependence of Theory, Data and Application*. Washington, D.C.: Georgetown University Press. 154–170.

Rumsey, Alan. 1990. Wording, meaning and linguistic ideology. *American Anthropologist* 92: 346–361.

Sanday, Peggy. 1996. *A Woman Scorned: Acquaintance Rape on Trial.* New York: Doubleday.

Schieffelin, Bambi, Kathryn Woolard and Paul Kroskrity (eds.). 1998. *Language Ideologies: Practice and Theory.* Oxford: Oxford University Press.

Schulhofer, Stephen. 1998. *Unwanted Sex: The Culture of Intimidation and the Failure of Law.* Cambridge, Massachusetts: Harvard University Press.

Solan, Lawrence and Peter Tiersma. 2005. *Speaking of Crime: The Language of Criminal Justice.* Chicago: University of Chicago Press.

Tiersma, Peter. 2007. The language of consent in rape law. In Janet Cotterill (ed.) *The Language of Sexual Crime.* Basingstoke, U.K.: Palgrave Macmillan. 83–103.

Trinch, Shonna. 2010. Disappearing discourse: Performative texts and identity in legal contexts. *Critical Inquiry in Language Studies* 7: 207–229.

Woodhams, Jessica. 2008. *How victims behave during stranger sexual assaults.* Unpublished manuscript.

4

Erasing Context in the Courtroom Construal of Consent

Diana Eades

Introduction

Late one night in downtown Brisbane (in the Australian state of Queensland), six armed police officers approached three young teenage Aboriginal boys, said something to them, and then escorted each of them into a different police vehicle. The three vehicles then drove the boys 14 kilometers out of town to a dark industrial wasteland at Pinkenba (hence this case is usually referred to as the Pinkenba case). Here the police officers and the boys got out of the cars, and the police said various things to the boys and then drove off without them. Many hours later the boys found their way back to town, mostly by walking, and also by taking a $5 taxi ride for a small part of the way, with money given to them along the way by a security guard.

A complaint from the boys' families led to an investigation by the Criminal Justice Commission, which resulted in criminal charges being laid against the six police officers. They were charged with unlawful deprivation of liberty: that they had "unlawfully deprived" the three boys of their liberty by "carrying them away in a motor vehicle against their will."[1] The boys were never charged with any offense on that night or related to that night, and thus they were not under arrest. The police officers never denied the facts outlined here. In fact, the head of the police union told the media that the boys were taken to Pinkenba by the police *to reflect on their misdemeanors* (ABC 1996). The defense case was that *the deprivation of liberty was not unlawful* because the boys had willingly got into the police cars despite knowing that *they had the right to refuse*—that is that the boys had consented to going for a ride.

This chapter draws in part on my work in Eades (2002, 2006, 2008).

The first stage in the trial process against the six charged police officers was the committal hearing in the magistrate's court, in which the boys' evidence was tested in cross-examination.[2] As child-victim witnesses in the prosecution of adult defendants, the boys had to give evidence in the regular adult court, with none of the protections afforded accused children (who typically appear in a closed Children's Court, with a magistrate trained and experienced in dealing with children, and with specialized support services). The police officers exercised their right not to answer questions, which is part of the protection of the right to be presumed innocent until proven guilty.

In the Queensland criminal code, the offense that I'm referring to here as "abduction" is termed "deprivation of liberty," and it is defined in terms of "unlawfully confin[ing] or detain[ing] another [person] in any place against the other person's will." Like rape cases, abduction cases revolve around the issue of consent, what it is that the complainant agreed to, or consented to. The activity involved is legal if the participants give their consent (that is, to going for a ride or engaging in sex). But if one of the participants in the activity has not consented, then it is illegal, and the other participant can be found guilty of abduction (that is, unlawful deprivation of liberty) or rape. Thus, the central issue in the case was the dispute between prosecution and defense over whether or not the boys had consented to being taken for a ride by the police. Addressing this consent to go with police should have been sufficient for the cross-examination of these prosecution witnesses. However, more than half of their cross-examination was not about the night in question, but about their characters, their earlier experiences with police, and their criminal records. In Eades (2008) I argue that this was because of the work being done by the defense to address an underlying sociopolitical question that was at the heart of this case: namely, whether police officers should have the right to remove Aboriginal young people from public places, when they are not even under investigation for having committed an offense. In addressing this underlying question, the defense worked hard to construct these three young teenage Aboriginal boys as lying criminals who were a threat to public safety, and who had so much experience with police that they knew their legal rights.[3] This chapter will not deal directly with this aspect of the cross-examination, as the aim is to focus on the discursive constructions of consent in this case. The analysis here involves three main interconnecting strands, or layers of consent, summarized as follows:

Consent 1 (C1): The boys' "consent" to the central proposition in cross-examination

The defense counsel used several linguistic mechanisms in their cross-examination of the boys to elicit their apparent consent to the central proposition that at the time that they got in the police cars, they knew they had the right to refuse to do so. I will argue that this apparent consent was actually coerced, and thus cannot count as free and voluntary consent to the cross-examination questions.

Consent 2 (C2): The boys' "consent" to go for a ride with the police
But the boys' answers to these coercive cross-examination questions were taken as consent, and this apparent (but questionable and problematic) consent in cross-examination was the basis of the defense argument that the boys had gone for a ride with the police *of [their] own free will*—that is that they had consented to go for the ride—and that therefore the *deprivation of liberty* was *not unlawful*.

Consent 3 (C3): The justice system's consent to the police removal of young people
This case resulted in the charges against the police officers being dropped, without going to a jury trial. Thus, the defense counsel had gained the consent of the justice system to this style of policing of Aboriginal young people. In Gramscian terms, the coercive power of the police to remove Aboriginal young people from the streets (even when they were not charged with any offense), was legitimized by the hegemonic power—power by consent—exercised in the courtroom.

The linguistic mechanisms used to secure apparent consent to the defense propositions in cross-examination (C1) are introduced in the next section, "Linguistic Mechanisms Involved in the Layering of Consent." This discursive construction of C1 is examined with the analysis of a key extract from the cross-examination of the youngest witness, under "Example of Apparent Construction of Consent 1 about Consent 2." The section "Erasing Context in Construal of Consent 2" then turns to the interpretation of this apparent consent (C1), and problematizes the erasure of context in the courtroom investigation of the alleged consent of the boys to go with police (C2). The concluding section, "Consent, Context, and Equality," takes up the layering of Consent 1 and Consent 2 to construct Consent 3, which relied on problematic ideologies about interpreting speech acts, and about what it means to be equal before the law.

Linguistic Mechanisms Involved in the Layering of Consent

According to a leading trial textbook (Mauet 2000: 250), cross-examination has two major aims: "eliciting favorable testimony" and "discredit[ing] the witness." Lawyers are taught to achieve these aims by developing a "theory of the case," which they can present "in storytelling form" (Mauet 2000: 507) in court. The theory of the case is defined as "simply a logical, persuasive story of 'what really happened.'" Thus, the central strategy for defense counsels' questions in this specific case was to recontextualize what happened on the night in question, in order to provide a different (and persuasive) version of the boys' story. This defense story was that the boys had consented to going for a ride with the police officers.

Several linguistic mechanisms were central to this recontextualization, and this chapter will focus on the three most important ones: namely, defense counsels' use of pseudo-declarative questions, their exploitation of the Aboriginal tendency to gratuitous concurrence, and their skillful and successful strategies in the lexical struggle that was central to the transformation of the boys' story. Following a brief explanation of these three mechanisms in this section, "Example of Apparent Construction of Consent 1 about Consent 2" exemplifies their operation with an extract from the cross-examination of the first of the three witnesses, in which he was directly questioned about his claim of being *forced* into the police car.

This chapter concentrates on the mechanisms relevant to the boy's alleged consent to go with police (Consent 2). In Eades (2008) I examine further linguistic mechanisms used by the lawyers in this case, many of which figured prominently in the construction of the boys as lying criminals who deserved to be removed from the streets. These mechanisms include presuppositions in questions, cultural presuppositions, metapragmatic directives, and strategies used to recontextualize the boys' accounts of numerous events and situations. None of the linguistic mechanisms considered in this chapter or in Eades (2008) are distinctive to abduction hearings or rape hearings—they are the everyday linguistic tools of cross-examination, expected to be used by competent lawyers (see Conley and O'Barr 2005: 37–38). However, there is variation in the extent to which these tools are used, or even exploited, by lawyers, or conversely, controlled by the presiding judge or magistrate (see Eades 2012).

PSEUDO-DECLARATIVE QUESTIONS

Linguists for more than two decades have been interested in the structure of courtroom questions and their power to control witnesses' stories (in examination-in-chief) and to coerce them into agreeing with the questioning lawyers' versions (in cross-examination) (see, for example, Woodbury 1984; Cotterill 2003; Gibbons 2003). It has been widely agreed that the most controlling questions are yes/no questions that present the questioner's version of an event or situation as an assertion to be confirmed. These assertions take the form of declarative statements with question intonation or questioning tag, and following Ehrlich (2001: 72–75) I refer to them as "pseudo-declarative" questions. (These question types are also described as prosodic and tag questions, respectively, e.g., Woodbury 1984.) As Eades (2000, 2008) and others (e.g., Ehrlich and Sidnell 2006) have shown, question types do not necessarily restrict the types of answer that can be given. However, in aggressive cross-examination with intimidated witnesses who have little opportunity to argue, pseudo-declarative questions can be highly effective in gaining a witness's apparent consent to lawyers' recontextualization of the story, as we will see. Thus, it is not surprising that a large proportion of the questions in this cross-examination are pseudo-declaratives.

GRATUITOUS CONCURRENCE

Pseudo-declarative questions aim to elicit an answer of agreement to the cross-examining lawyer's proposition, and they can be particularly effective with Aboriginal witnesses. This is because of the Aboriginal tendency to answer *yes* to a question (or *no* to a negative question) regardless of whether the speaker agrees with the proposition being questioned (and in some instances regardless of whether they even understand it).[4] This pragmatic feature, labeled "gratuitous concurrence" by Liberman (e.g., 1981), has been frequently observed in intercultural communication with Aboriginal Australians for more than a century.

Aboriginal use of gratuitous concurrence cannot be explained only in terms of responses to colonization and subjugation. Liberman found that Aboriginal discourse patterns favor decision making by consensus, involving considerable time and indirectness, as people often work to keep immediate surface harmony, and then work "behind the scenes" over time to deal with disagreements. While Liberman worked in remote Central Australia, the same decision-making patterns are also relevant to many Aboriginal English speakers in rural and urban Australia, who tend not to use direct questioning on important personal issues, and who often express strong opinions with some distance or indirectness (see Eades 2008: 92–96).

My observations over a number of years indicate that certain factors appear to increase the likelihood of gratuitous concurrence: namely, repeated and pressured questioning, particularly if over a lengthy period of time; complex question structures, such as one question that includes two or more propositions; lack of opportunity for the person being questioned to take control of the discourse; and pressure from the questioner—for example, by shouting. These are all factors that can be found in courtroom cross-examination and that characterized the cross-examination in this highly contested case.

More than 60% of the answers from the three boys in this case were either *yes* (or equivalents such as *yeh*), *no* (or equivalents such as *nuh*), or *I don't know/I dunno*. Given the strong tendency of Aboriginal people to use gratuitous concurrence, it is highly likely that some of the *yes* answers (or *no* answers to negative questions) should not be literally interpreted as agreement with the proposition in the question. It is impossible to know exactly what is in any witness's mind, and thus to say with certainty about any answer to a specific question: *the witness answered yes, but he/she did not agree with the proposition*. But for many Aboriginal witnesses, *yes* may signal something like *It's easiest if I agree with your questioning, and I hope that this answer will help bring the questioning to an end*. On the other hand, it may signal agreement to a proposition. Thus, it can clearly be dangerous to rely for important decisions on literal interpretations of *yes, yeh*, or *mm* answers from Aboriginal witnesses to cross-examination questions that can easily elicit gratuitous concurrence. But this is exactly what happened in this case.

LEXICAL STRUGGLE

Pseudo-declarative questions and gratuitous concurrence were central to the defense elicitation from the boys of apparent Consent 1 (to cross-examination questions) to the defense argument about Consent 2—namely, their consenting to go with police. The third mechanism, which I label "lexical struggle," was central to the construction of Consent 2 and was greatly supported by the first two mechanisms, as we will see in the example in the section that follows. Since Danet's (1980) discussion of the 40 lexical items used to refer to the object of abortion in a high-profile US abortion case, sociolinguists have been interested in how lawyers and witnesses define "opposing realities" through lexical contest. I use the general term "lexical struggle" for the process that has been given various names: relexicalization (Cotterill 2001), lexicalization (Cotterill 2003), lexical negotiation (Cotterill 2004), alternative description (Drew 1992), (re)formulation (Ehrlich 2001, 2002), recontextualization (Ehrlich 2002). The central strategies used in this lexical struggle are the overt correction and covert substitution of expressions used by witnesses. And the term "lexical perversion" describes a particular strategy in which the substitution of words and phrases by a lawyer distorts (or perverts) the way in which a witness reports their own experiences (Eades 2006, 2008). We will see an example of this in the extract below.

Example of Apparent Construction of Consent 1 about Consent 2

Extract 1, which illustrates the operation of these three main linguistic mechanisms, is taken from the cross-examination of the first and youngest witness, referred to with the pseudonym David. Aged 12 at the time of the ride with police, and 13 at the committal hearing some 10 months later, David had been cross-examined for close to two and a half hours on the previous day, mostly by the aggressive first defense counsel. He had been visibly upset for much of this time, even crying on occasions. Now on his second day on the witness stand, David was answering questions from the (superficially, at least) more reasonable of the two defense counsel.[5]

In his examination-in-chief David had said that the police *told us to jump in the car.* He was then asked *Did they tell you, or ask you?*, to which he replied, *Told us.* (The other two boys also used *told* in their examination-in-chief to report the same speech act.) In Extract 1, taken from the final 10 minutes of David's cross-examination, the second defense counsel (DC) used the three linguistic mechanisms introduced in the preceding section to cleverly undo the impact of David's account, by constructing Consent 1 to the argument about Consent 2 and thus demolishing the complaint on which the criminal charge relied. Compared to the first DC, the second DC mainly questioned David in a relatively low-key style (but see the raised volume in turn 35). However, his seemingly common-sense recontextualization of David's report of being forced resulted in a *coup de grâce* for the defense, and provides a textbook exemplification of successful cross-examination.

It is relevant to point out that the witness silences in this extract cannot necessarily be interpreted as prefacing dispreferred responses. The widespread Anglo convention of interpreting silences as indicating that something is not working is not shared with Aboriginal people, who often use lengthy silences in either formal or informal interaction, and who find them neither uncomfortable nor remarkable (e.g., Eades 2007; Mushin and Gardner 2009). This contrasts with the dominant assumption in the legal system that silence in answer to a question is generally "interpreted to the detriment of the silent person," such as implying that the person asked the question has something to hide (Kurzon 1995: 56).

Extract 1 (see appendix for transcription conventions)

1. DC: David- let me just try to summarise if I can- what you- what you've told us (3.1) you told us yesterday that the <u>real</u> problem wasn't anything that happened getting into the car or in the car- but the fact that you were left at Pinkenba- that right?
2. David: (1.5) Mm.
3. DC: Mm- that's the truth isn't it?
4. David: Mm.
5. DC: (4.3) You see- you weren't de<u>prived</u> of your liberty at all- uh in going out there- it was the fact that you were <u>left</u> there that you thought was wrong.
6. David: (1.2) °Yeh°.
7. DC: Eh?
8. David: Yeh.
9. DC: (3.5) You got <u>in</u> the car (2.1) without being forced- you went <u>out</u> there without being forced- the <u>prob</u>lem began when you were <u>left</u> there.

10. David: (1.5) [Mm.
11. Pros: [With respect Your Worship- there are <u>three</u> elements to that question and I ask my friend to break them down.
12. Mag: Yes- just break it up one by one Mr Humphrey.
13. DC: You got in the car without being forced David- didn't you?
14. David: (1.5) No.
15. DC: You told us- you've told us a ((laughs)) number of times today you did.
16. David: (1.3) They forced me.
17. DC: Eh?
18. David: They forced us.
19. DC: Tell us- tell us how David come on.
20. David: They told us to jump in the car.
21: DC: They told you to jump in the car?=
22. David: =Yeh.
23. DC: That's <u>all</u> that was said?
24. David: (1.0) Yeh.
25. DC: Nothing else was said to you apart from- jump in the car (2.2) that right?
26. David: (1.2) Yeh.
27. DC: And you did get in the car?
28. David: Yeh.
29. DC: (1.2) You weren't <u>push</u>ed in the car- or held in the car?
30. David: No.
31. DC: You never asked to get <u>out</u> of the car?
32. David: (1.4) No.
33. DC: (4.6) And- all that happened because- <u>you</u> didn't <u>think</u> you were in any trouble- did you?
34. David: (1.8) No.
35. DC: CORRECT?
36. David: (1.9) °Yeh°.
37. DC: And that's why you had no trouble going <u>out</u> there getting in the car and travelling with the police- you <u>didn't</u> think you were in any <u>trouble</u>- did you?
38. David: We weren't.

[five turns involving DC's difficulty in hearing the answer omitted here]

39. DC: You weren't- that's right- that's right- what you're saying is I think- that if you'd just been walking along the street- you wouldn't have jumped in the car yourselves- you got in the car because the police said to.
40. David: Yeh.
41. DC: OK- that's what you mean isn't it?
42. David: Yeh.
43. DC: When you say <u>forced</u>- all <u>you</u> mean is- the police <u>said</u> so.
44. David: Yeh.
45. DC: Mm?
46. David: Yeh.

(Eades 2008: 101–102, 140–141; names are pseudonyms)

PSEUDO-DECLARATIVE QUESTIONS AND ASSERTED PROPOSITIONS

Turn 35 illustrates a common strategy in this hearing: when a witness gave an unacceptable answer, a follow-up question, with raised volume that repeated the previous question in some way, often succeeded in eliciting the opposite answer. Thus, the shouted tag *CORRECT?* resulted in David changing his answer to the question *And- all that happened because-* <u>you</u> *didn't* <u>think</u> *you were in any trouble- did you?* from *No* (in turn 34) to a barely audible *Yeh* (in turn 36). This exchange in turns 33 to 38 illustrates a recurring pattern in the cross-examination of the boys: lawyers' use of confusing questions to elicit contradictory answers from the witnesses. Turn 33 appears from its opening to be a question about why *all that happened*, with the vague *that* presumably referring to the circumstances of the car ride and David not asking to *get out of the car*. However, the closing tag question *did you?* suggests that the proposition being questioned was *you didn't think you were in any trouble*. But, David's answer *we weren't* (in turn 38) to this question when it was repeated (in turn 37), suggests that he may have been answering a question such as *were you in any trouble?* Regardless of the propositional outcome of the answers to these questions, such cross-examining strategy would have added to the pressure, confusion, and exhaustion being experienced by these child witnesses, while increasing the likelihood of gratuitous concurrence, and casting doubt on the credibility of the witness.

In this extract, three of the lawyer turns have the minimal form *Eh?* or *Mm?*, apparently eliciting the repetition of the previous answer, whether because it had been hard to hear or because the lawyer wanted to emphasize the answer (turns 7, 17, 45). But most of the remaining lawyer turns addressed to David by DC in this extract are pseudo-declarative questions: statements with rising intonation in turns 21, 23, 27, 29, 31, or statements with questioning tag in turns 1, 3, 13, 25, 33, 37, 41; and in turn 35 a contraction of a statement with rising intonation. However, six of the lawyer turns do not even have question form. Five of these turns—5, 9, 15, 39, 43—have the form of asserted propositions. And turn 19 has the form of a directive *Tell us- tell us how David come on*. However, all lawyer turns addressed to witnesses are counted as questions in the court, as illustrated by the prosecutor in turn 11 referring to the three elements to *that question*, which is the asserted proposition in turn 9. The official transcript also gives all lawyer turns as questions, with a question mark, and it is commonplace for lawyers, magistrates, and judges to refer to whatever a lawyer has said to a witness as a question. It is also obvious that, typical of many witnesses under cross-examination, David counted the asserted propositions as questions to which he had to provide an answer. (If there had been any chance of David not understanding this expectation, the earlier highly pressured cross-examination of more than two hours by the first defense counsel would have ensured that he learned it quickly.)

GRATUITOUS CONCURRENCE

Pseudo-declaratives and asserted propositions are syntactic structures central to cross-examination that are highly coercive and can easily lead to gratuitous concurrence. It is impossible to know what was in David's mind, but there are reasons to suggest that some or all of his *yeh* and *mm* answers in turns 2, 4, 6, 8, and 10 were gratuitous concurrence. These reasons can be found in the interaction in this extract, combined with the general evidence about situations that favor the elicitation of gratuitous concurrence, referred to under "Linguistic Mechanisms Involved in the Layering of Consent." First, DC questioned about two propositions in the same question in turns 1 and 5, and three propositions in turn 9. Turn 5 also used a legalese term, in the assertion *you weren't deprived of your liberty*, which may not have been familiar to the 13-year-old witness. The combination of this misleading way of asking a yes/no question, with the tendency of Aboriginal people to answer *yes* to repeated questions of this form, even when they don't agree with the proposition, results in an ideal situation for the elicitation of gratuitous concurrence. Further, any or all of these first three answers of *mm* and *yeah*, may have been given without the witness understanding the question. But a stronger indication that these early *mm* and *yeah* answers may have been gratuitous concurrence is found after the prosecutor's objection (in turn 11) to the triple question in turn 9. This objection resulted in the magistrate directing DC to question just one proposition at a time. In answer to the much shorter question (in turn 13) that addressed the first of the three propositions from turn 9, David gave a different answer, one of contradiction rather than agreement (in turn 14). This was followed in turn 16 with his clear statement

They forced me. Complete sentences were relatively rare with this witness, with 65% of his answers to a total of 1,333 questions in cross-examination being *Yes*, or *No*, or *I don't know*. It is impossible to know whether any or all of the remaining monosyllabic answers of apparent agreement were gratuitous concurrence. However, the final four *Yeh* answers may well have been gratuitous concurrence, especially given the difficulty for someone of David's obvious exhaustion, intimidated state, youth, and poor education record to deal with hypothetical questions and semantic argument.

LEXICAL STRUGGLE

This extract highlights the lexical struggle between lawyer and child witness over the meaning of the word *force*. Having provided the clear accusation that the police *forced* him and his friends to get in the car (in turns 16 and 18), David was challenged in turn 19 to explain how the police forced them. His explanation was *They told us to jump in the car.* DC's subsequent turns developed an argument that *nothing else was said*, there was no physical violence by the police and no active resistance from the boys. We see a number of contextual presuppositions here, for example in turn 31, that if he had been forced, he would have *asked to get out of the car.*

This lexical struggle culminated at the end of this extract with DC's lexical perversion, taking David's report that the police *forced* them to get in the cars and transforming that to *all you mean is- the police said so.* It is not surprising that a 13-year-old Aboriginal part-time street kid with a poor record of school attendance did not enter into a semantic argument with the lawyer about the word *force*. Another witness may perhaps have pointed out that although *force* is often used to convey some physical contact, even violence, it does not have to involve this. For example, one could say, *The police officer forced me to pull over to the side of the road*, referring to an incident which involved no physical contact.

As explained above, David's apparent consent to this assertion is likely to be gratuitous concurrence. But it was a strategic coup for the defense, who had now effectively destroyed David's characterization of the crucial speech act that resulted in him getting in the car as a command. But what was the speech act involved if it is referred to as *the police said so*? On the grounds of linguistic form alone, it seems quite difficult to interpret the syntactic form *jump in the car* (accepted by DC in turns 21 to 26) as advice or an offer or a suggestion. Indeed, this imperative form is typically associated with the speech act of commanding. Elsewhere (Eades 2006, 2008) I have reported that throughout the cross-examination, as well as the concluding addresses by both DCs, they almost never labeled the event in question in terms of its speech act, referring to it by such expressions as *this business, that night, this night*, and *when you got in the police car.* The only times in which either of the

DCs labeled the speech act was when it is referred to in an adverbial clause with the agentless passive as *when it was said to jump in the car*, and in vague terms (also as adverbial clauses, introduced with *when*) as *when these police spoke to you that night*, and *when you spoke with these six police in the Valley*. The only instance of the speech act referred to with a noun phrase occurred in DC2's concluding address, when he twice referred to what the police said to the boys as a *statement*.

Erasing Context in Construal of Consent 2

Extract 1 provides an excellent example of how lawyers can control a witness's story and coercively construct a competing version, although it would arguably have not been so easy with an adult witness, or a witness who had not been socialized in using gratuitous concurrence. In controlling and transforming David's story about the speech act that resulted in him getting in the car and being driven out of town, DC has relied on linguistic trickery, especially the three mechanisms highlighted. Pseudo-declaratives and lexical struggle arguably comprise the essence of good cross-examination, while the easy elicitation of gratuitous concurrence from Aboriginal witnesses is a bonus for cross-examining counsel. But, even allowing for DC taking David's account of being *forced* to get into the police car and transforming it to the police *saying so*, there is something problematic—even unbelievable—about construing a 12-year-old boy's action of getting into the police car as an act of his free will amounting to consent. And it is arguably more problematic that both the magistrate and later the review judge accepted this defense version of David's consent (as well as parallel versions of the stories of his two friends). Central to this problematic interpretation is the view that meaning can be understood without taking into account contextual factors, starting with the relationships between interlocutors. Thus, the fictitious example utterance above—*The police officer forced me to pull over to the side of the road*—makes perfect sense as a report of an interaction in which no physical contact occurred, precisely because of the relationship understood between a driver and a police officer. The police officer has the institutional and situational power to enforce the action required for the driver to pull over to the side of the road, simply by activating sirens, or by *saying* to do so. The power imbalance recognizable in this fictitious example is even more recognizable in the situation in which three young teenage Aboriginal children were approached by six armed police officers late at night.

But there is more to the interpretation of speech acts than a literal understanding of linguistic forms. DC's recontextualization of David's story, complete with the construction of Consent 2 to the ride with police, could have been accepted by the judicial decision makers only if they ignored important elements of the immediate social and historical context from the consideration of events on the night in question. This erasure of context enabled the lawyers and the magistrate to conclude that *they all knew that they had the right to refuse to get in the police motor vehicle, but despite of [sic] this knowledge they proceeded and got in* (magistrate's decision).

In Eades (2008: Chapter 3), I provide an account of the social and historical context, which is briefly summarized here (see also Eades 2012). Since the beginning of the colonization of Queensland in the early 1800s, police fought a "bloody frontier war" against Aboriginal people. From the end of the 19th century, legislation gave police the powers to remove Aboriginal people from their land, and to relocate them in missions and government settlements, or to incarcerate them for a wide range of offenses not applied to non-Aboriginal people, including traditional dancing and "immoral behavior." And from 1897 to 1984 police were at the forefront of the widespread removal of Aboriginal children from their families, now referred to as the Stolen Generations. According to criminologist Cunneen (1994: 154), the current policing of Aboriginal young people "may be similarly genocidal in ... impact [to the Stolen Generations], if not in ... conscious intent." Cunneen's convincing argument is that contemporary police intervention in the lives of Aboriginal young people has the effect of making many of them illegal because of their Aboriginality. The extent to which police intervention is overly focused on Aboriginal people is seen in a 2011 report which found that throughout Australia Indigenous young people are in juvenile detention at about 22 times the rate of their non-Indigenous counterparts (SCRGSP 2011: 4.130). Further, the two centuries of police harassment and violence toward Aboriginal people, which climaxed in Brisbane in the decades preceding the Pinkenba incident, would have certainly led the three boys to fear armed police approaching them in the middle of the night. While Queensland legal and judicial practitioners would not necessarily know the details of this context, it would have been impossible to be ignorant of the ongoing role of the police in controlling Aboriginal people, in proportions greatly exceeding their interventions in the lives of other citizens and residents. Moreover, regardless of this context specific to Aboriginal people, the ability of any person—particularly a child—to exercise his or her free will when being told by police to get into a police vehicle was never raised.

These contextual elements are essential to DC's lexical struggle with David over what he meant when he said that the police *forced* them to *get in the police car.* Thus, the erasure of this context was essential to the construal of David's Consent 2. Given this immediate social and historical context, the police did not need to say any more than *jump in the car* (turns 20 to 26), and the boys did not need to be *pushed* or *held* in the car (turns 29 to 30), and it was arguably impossible for them to have *asked to get out of the car* (turns 31 to 32). Yet, as we have seen, DC's questioning assumes that it was common sense that these elements would have been required for the activity to count as the police *forc*ing them to *get in the police car*. But, whether or not the boys knew that it was their legal right to refuse, the social and historical context of this encounter arguably made it impossible for the boys to exercise this right. Yet, a fundamental assumption about questioning that pervades the legal system is that the social context of a speech act (such as the police interaction with the boys) can be ignored in the analysis of what had happened. This assumption about how language works—or language ideology—is completely at odds with the everyday experience of language users, who can never interpret what interlocutors say without taking into account a range of contextual factors.

In legal terms this action of the boys getting in the police cars when they allegedly knew they had the right to refuse is "implied consent": not consent that is verbalized, but which can be inferred from a person's actions, or inactions. As expressed by a Canadian judge, implied consent is "consent by conduct" (see Ehrlich 2005: 154), and it is commonly invoked in rape cases. As is common in rape cases, in this abduction case apparent absence of resistance is taken to imply consent, although the context makes it unbelievable that the boys would have been able to exercise "free will."

The problematic interpretation of speech acts involving police encounters with citizens in the United States has been highlighted in the work of Ainsworth (1993, 2008) and Solan and Tiersma (2005), as discussed in Eades (2010). Ainsworth shows how suspects in police interviews are not considered to have invoked their Miranda rights unless what they say has the linguistic form of a bald and completely unmodified imperative, such as *Give me a lawyer*, or an unmodified statement, such as *I want a lawyer*. So, for example, a court held that *I think I would like to talk to a lawyer* was not an invocation of the suspect's right to a lawyer (Ainsworth 2008). In her discussion of the judicial emphasis on linguistic form in suspects' invocation of their rights, Ainsworth points to this as an example of the "correspondence theory of language," also referred to as a "referentialist" or "textualist" ideology (Collins 1996, cited in Ehrlich 2012: 58). Ehrlich explains that this ideology holds that "meaning resides exclusively in linguistic forms and, as a result, words, phrases, or sentences can be extracted from their original interactional and social context and moved to other contexts without any change in meaning." In its removal of any contextual considerations, there is a parallel in this Australian example in the construal, by both defense and the judicial decision makers, of the bald, unmodified imperative *jump in the car* as a *statement* that the boys were free to ignore. This construal, in addition to erasing the context in which the utterance was produced, also denies the frequent use of imperative forms as commands.

The rights of citizens to exercise their free will and ignore the commands of police officers has been discussed by Solan and Tiersma (e.g., 2005), who have highlighted the selective literalism of US courts. For example, in a US Supreme Court case, an officer's question *Does the trunk open?* was interpreted by the motorist being questioned as a request or command to open the trunk, but it was interpreted literally by the court as merely a question. On the other hand, an "impetuous youth" who sent a letter to President Reagan that contained the sentence "Resign or You'll Get Your Brains Blown Out" was convicted of threatening the life of the president. What is literally a prediction was given its indirect speech act interpretation as a threat. In contrasting these two judicial decisions, Solan and Tiersma show how US courts are selective in their use of literal interpretations. They conclude (2005: 47–48) that "it is hard to avoid the impression that courts have somewhat of a double standard when it comes to considering pragmatic information, such as specifics of context. They are significantly more likely to take it into account when it benefits the government, and less so when it helps the accused." This highly contested Australian case, which was testing the rights of police officers to remove Aboriginal people from public places, suggests the relevance of this double standard finding beyond the United States to Australia.

Consent, Context, and Equality

The defense construction of the boys' consent (C2) in going with the police, through problematic linguistic mechanisms used to gain their apparent consent to propositions in cross-examination questions (C1), resulted in the charges against the police officers being dropped. Thus, in accepting these constructions of consent, the magistrate and the review judge effectively gave the consent (C3) of the legal system to the contested form of policing that allows police to remove Aboriginal people from the streets even when there is no suggestion that they have committed an offense. In this way, the layered discursive constructions of consent in this case played an important role in the perpetuation of the neocolonial control of the state over Aboriginal people.

This case shows the social consequences of a language ideology that promotes the decontextualized interpretation of speech acts, as exemplified in the assumption that anyone (including young teenage Aboriginal part-time street kids) can exercise free will in responding to being *told* by police to *jump in the [police] car*. The larger ideology at work in this case is that courtroom questioning treats all people equally, that it can equally protect the rights of all concerned and enable "the facts" to emerge. These related assumptions rely on the arguably indefensible fiction about equality: that because all people should be treated equally by the law, this must mean that all people are equal in any situation dealt with by the law. In Philips's (1998) study of the ideological diversity of US judges, this was the view of the judges with a conservative political ideological stance. On the other hand, those with a liberal political ideological stance held that to "render some people equal to others, the state must give them special protection and help" (1998: 79), such as taking more time to ensure that they have understood what it means to enter a guilty plea, and what the possible legal consequences can be.

The conservative ideology about equality can promote an interpretation of actions that is demonstrably unfair, as we have seen in this case. When three young teenage Aboriginal boys are told by six armed police officers to get into three police vehicles, they do have the right to decline (and it is possible that they realized at the time that they had that right, as the defense insisted). But what is involved in the exercise of this right? And when each of these boys is asked repeated, often haranguing questions in court, he can give his answer in order to present his side of the story—but only to the extent that he speak only in direct answer to the questions asked, while navigating linguistic trickery, such as we have seen. Considering what is involved in the exercise of the right to present your story in court, we see that the essential factors that mediate between the right and the exercise of the right are again ignored by the legal system—namely, the contextual dimensions, particularly of power relations between lawyers and witnesses. Thus the fiction about equality is sustained both by the assumption that all people have the same opportunity to exercise their rights and by the resulting erasure of any recognition of power asymmetries or other contextual details.

This case provides a startling illustration of the ways in which discursive constructions of consent in the legal process can be involved in the perpetuation of social inequality, and of the central role of the language ideology that promotes the decontextualized interpretation of speech acts. But the legal system is not monolithic or static. Guidance for Australian judicial officers in their day-to-day practice in court is clear about equal treatment not being the same as the same treatment, as seen in the opening section of the NSW *Equality before the Law Bench Book* (Judicial Commission of NSW 2011: 1103):

> Equality before the law is sometimes misunderstood. It does not necessarily mean "same treatment." As McHugh J succinctly explained: "discrimination can arise just as readily from an act which treats as equals those who are different as it can from an act which treats differently persons whose circumstances are not materially different [*Waters v Public Transport Corporation* (1991) 173 CLR 349 at 402.]"[6]

This point is arguably relevant to the consideration of the conditions in which judicial decision makers interpreted the extent to which young teenage Aboriginal children have any opportunity to exercise their free will when told by armed police officers late at night to *jump in the car*. It is also relevant to the courtroom hearing, which pitted six (silent) individual defendants—who were adult police officers represented by the two most highly paid barristers in the state—against three individual plaintiffs—who were young teenage Aboriginal part-time street kids, as if both sides were on a *tabula rasa* or level playing field.

It is something of a paradox that the adversarial cross-examination process, which is structured so centrally around *interaction* within the courtroom, at the same time relies so heavily on an analysis of what has happened outside the courtroom, which effectively excludes interaction. Thus the boys' story had to be filtered in court through cross-examination interaction, about which there is considerable legal attention. Yet legal consideration of what happened in the interaction between them and the police officers on the night in question was restricted to a decontextualized interpretation of a single utterance—namely, *jump in the car.* And in other cases analyzed by Ainsworth (2008) and Solan and Tiersma (2005), such decontextualization results in legal consideration of solely one utterance—such as *I think I would like to talk to a lawyer* or *Does the trunk open?*

In examining the discursive construction of consent in this abduction case study, we have seen the powerful operation of a language ideology that enables the court to ignore the social context of a conversation when they interpret it, something that is impossible for people who participated in the conversation. The encounter between the police officers and the boys was presented in cross-examination questions in terms of an utterance and an action, completely removing what is arguably the most important dimension of any encounter: its contextual details, especially those related to the power relations. And the questioning of the boys in court by defense counsel was the opportunity for the legal system to test the boys' story, as well as to assess their reliability and honesty. Again, it did this by removing contextual details, especially those related to the power relations in court. It is through language ideologies such as the one discussed here, about decontextualized interpretation of speech acts, that the linguistic mechanisms such as we have seen here are able to do their work. The result is the erasure of the contexts of interaction, both in the consideration of the events that lead to the courtroom hearing and in the consideration of what happened in the conduct of the hearing, particularly the interpretation of witness answers to lawyer questions. In this way, consent, both in relation to this abduction episode and in the conduct of courtroom cross-examination, is conceived of as an individualized mental construct (as Ehrlich 2001: 92 has found in rape cases). Sociolinguistic analysis shows us how problematic it can be to ignore the interactional and contextual dimensions involved in the construction of consent, and the far-reaching hegemonic consequences that can result.

Appendix: Transcription Conventions

°	Utterance spoken in a very low volume
[	Indicates talk overlapping with that of another speaker, marked at the point in each utterance where overlap begins
-	Indicates a pause within a turn of less than 0.5 of a second
(3.2)	A number in parentheses indicates the length of a pause in seconds
YES	Small capitals indicates raised volume
yes	Underlining indicates emphasis
=	Latched utterances: no pause between end of one utterance and start of next
((laughs))	Information in double parentheses indicate the transcriber's descriptions of events rather than representations of them

Notes

1. Quotations from this hearing are based on my transcription of official tape recordings. Italics are used in this chapter for any quotation from a spoken source, which includes tape recordings, and radio and television interviews.

2. The Australian committal hearing fulfills some of the functions of the US grand jury trial. But it differs in being heard in an open court in front of a magistrate (analogous to a lower court judge), with no jury. As with trials, committal hearings must follow the rules of evidence, and there is no obligation on the defense to provide any evidence.

3. While the character and previous criminal record of an accused person is not usually allowed to be brought up during a criminal hearing, there is no such restriction for the questioning of witnesses (as it can be argued that such issues are relevant to a witness's credibility).

4. Morrow (1996) reports a communicative pattern similar to gratuitous concurrence among English-speaking Yup'ik Eskimos, as does Berk-Seligson (2009) for US Hispanics.

5. The boys were each cross-examined by two defense counsel, who each represented three of the charged police officers. In an apparent courtroom version of the good-cop-bad-cop routine, the first defense counsel was aggressive, and used much shouting and verbal abuse (see Eades 2008), while the second defense counsel rarely shouted and spoke with less aggression.

6. See also Queensland Supreme Court (2005: 14).

References

ABC (Australian Broadcasting Commission). 1996. *Black and Blue*. Four Corners TV documentary, March 8.

Ainsworth, Janet. 1993. In a different register: The pragmatics of powerlessness in a police interview. *Yale Law Journal* 103: 259–322.

Ainsworth, Janet. 2008. "You have the right to remain silent . . ." but only if you ask for it just so: The role of linguistic ideology in American police interrogation law. *International Journal of Speech, Language and the Law* 15(1): 1–22.

Berk-Seligson, Susan. 2009. *Coerced Confessions: The Discourse of Bilingual Police Interrogations.* Berlin: Mouton de Gruyter.

Collins, James. 1996. Socialization to text: Structure and contradiction in schooled literacy. In Michael Silverstein and Greg Urban (eds.) *Natural Histories of Discourse.* Chicago: University of Chicago Press. 203–228.

Conley, John and William O'Barr 2005. *Just Words: Law, Language and Power* (2nd ed.). Chicago: University of Chicago Press.

Cotterill, Janet. 2001. Domestic discord, rocky relationships: Semantic prosodies in representations of marital violence in the O. J. Simpson trial. *Discourse and Society* 12(3): 291–312.

Cotterill, Janet. 2003. *Language and Power in Court: A Linguistic Analysis of the O. J. Simpson Trial.* Houndmills, Baskinstoke, U.K.: Palgrave Macmillan.

Cotterill, Janet. 2004. Collocation, connotation, and courtroom semantics: Lawyers' control of witness testimony through lexical negotiation. *Applied Linguistics* 25(4): 513–537.

Cunneen, Chris. 1994. Enforcing genocide? Aboriginal young people and the police. In Rob White and Christine Adler (eds.) *The Police and Young People in Australia.* Cambridge: Cambridge University Press. 128–158.

Danet, Brenda. 1980. "Baby" or "fetus"? Language and the construction of reality in a manslaughter trial. *Semiotica* 32(3/4): 187–219.

Drew, Paul. 1992. Contested evidence in courtroom cross-examination: The case of a trial for rape. In Paul Drew and John Heritage (eds.) *Talk at Work: Interaction in Institutional Settings.* Cambridge: Cambridge University Press. 470–520.

Eades, Diana. 2000. "I don't think it's an answer to the question": Silencing Aboriginal witnesses in court. *Language in Society* 29(2): 161–196.

Eades, Diana. 2002. "Evidence given in unequivocal terms": Gaining consent of Aboriginal kids in court. In Janet Cotterill (ed.) *Language in the Legal Process.* Houndmills, Basingstoke, U.K.: Palgrave Macmillan. 162–179.

Eades, Diana. 2006. Lexical struggle in court: Aboriginal Australians vs the state. *Journal of Sociolinguistics* 10(2): 153–181.

Eades, Diana. 2007. Understanding Aboriginal silence in legal contexts. In Helga Kotthoff and Helen Spencer-Oatey (eds.) *Handbook of Intercultural Communication.* Berlin: Mouton de Gruyter. 285–301.

Eades, Diana. 2008. *Courtroom Talk and Neocolonial Control.* Berlin: Mouton de Gruyter.

Eades, Diana. 2010. *Sociolinguistics and the Legal Process.* Bristol, U.K.: Multilingual Matters.

Eades, Diana. 2012. The social consequences of language ideologies in courtroom cross-examination. *Language in Society* 41(4): 471–497.

Ehrlich, Susan. 2001. *Representing Rape: Language and Sexual Consent.* London: Routledge.

Ehrlich, Susan. 2002. (Re)contextualizing complainants' accounts of sexual assault. *Forensic Linguistics* 9(2): 193–212.

Ehrlich, Susan. 2005. Trial discourse and judicial decision-making: Constraining the boundaries of gendered identities. In Judith Baxter (ed.) *Speaking Out: The Female Voice in Public Contexts*. Houndmills, Basingstoke, U.K.: Palgrave Macmillan. 139–158.

Ehrlich, Susan. 2012. Text trajectories, legal discourse and gendered inequalities. *Applied Linguistics Review* 3(1): 47–73.

Ehrlich, Susan and Jack Sidnell. 2006. "I think that's not an assumption you ought to make": Challenging presuppositions in inquiry testimony. *Language in Society* 35(5): 655–676.

Gibbons, John. 2003. *Forensic Linguistics*. Oxford: Basil Blackwell.

Judicial Commission of NSW. 2011. *Equality before the Law Bench Book*. Sydney: Judicial Commission of NSW.

Kurzon, Dennis. 1995. The right of silence: A socio-pragmatic model of interpretation. *Journal of Pragmatics* 23: 55–69.

Liberman, Kenneth. 1981. Understanding Aborigines in Australian courts of law. *Human Organization* 40: 247–255.

Mauet, Thomas. 2000. *Trial Techniques* (5th ed.). Gaithersburg, Maryland: Aspen Publishers, Inc.

Morrow, Phyllis. 1996 Yup'ik Eskimo agents and American legal agencies: Perspectives on compliance and resistance. *Journal of the Royal Anthropological Institute* 2: 405–423.

Mushin, Ilana and Rod Gardner. 2009. Silence is talk: Conversational silence in Australian Aboriginal talk-in-interaction. *Journal of Pragmatics* 41: 2033–2052.

Philips, Susan. 1998. *Ideology in the Language of Judges: How Judges Practice Law, Politics and Courtroom Control*. New York: Oxford University Press.

Queensland Supreme Court. 2005. *Equal Treatment Benchbook*. Brisbane: Supreme Court of Queensland Library.

SCRGSP (Steering Committee for the Review of Government Service Provision). 2011. *Overcoming Indigenous Disadvantage: Key Indicators 2011*. Melbourne: Productivity Commission.

Solan, Lawrence and Peter Tiersma. 2005. *Speaking of Crime: The Language of Criminal Justice*. Chicago: University of Chicago Press.

Woodbury, Hanni. 1984. The strategic use of questions in court. *Semiotica* 48(3/4): 197–228.

SECTION 2

Informed Consent or Ritualized Consent?

5

Talking the Ethical Turn

DRAWING ON TICK-BOX CONSENT IN POLICING

Frances Rock

Introduction

In contemporary "Western" social life, we are frequently asked to make minor, relatively inconsequential decisions about consent. Websites instruct, "Check this box if we may share your details with our trusted partners," implicitly seeking consent to what might become undesirable contact. Automated telephone greetings declare, "This call will be recorded for training and monitoring," implicitly gaining consent to recording as soon as we speak. Requests for consent come with such frequency and in so many forms and modalities that disengaged acquiescence can seem appealing to avoid constant negotiation. Sometimes, then, people consent without really knowing what they are consenting to or why. This is not only a feature of consent; almost any decision necessitates a leap of faith. We opt in or out of things on the basis of best guesses of likely consequences but we can rarely if ever be sure how our choices will pan out nor hope to grasp all of the variables in play. Usually, this does not matter. However, despite the apparent triviality, irrelevance, or remoteness of many consent requests, the resulting change of state can have serious consequences. Sometimes these consequences cannot be envisaged at the time of consent by either party.

The exchanges examined here are between police personnel and the public. In policing settings, laypeople might be particularly ill-equipped to evaluate the implications of their consent decisions given that the institutional world is, for many, closed and mysterious, and laypeople encounter it infrequently (although see Sarangi 2001). This might make it difficult to distinguish those consent exchanges likely to result in a little metaphorical junk mail from the truly consequential. Consent requests that seem innocuous are potent because their very banality can camouflage the real issues that they concern. The banality can be elevated by foregrounding consent procedurality. This chapter examines ostensibly innocuous consent exchanges in policing using the notion of "tick-box consent talk." This is talk, about consent, which, for one reason or another, gives the impression that consent is a mere formality, whether or not it actually concerns important matters. The chapter illustrates that when one or more participant orients to a consent exchange as if it is merely a box to be ticked, negative consequences may follow. After introducing my stance on consent and the notion of tick-box consent, the chapter presents interactions in which individual police forces, or officers, recruit tick-box consent as a resource to accomplish ends or resolve difficulties. I consider how laypeople might go along with the tick-box consent routine but also how, if they do not or cannot do this, the institutional representative takes steps to get the interaction back on course. I close by considering the implications of this for policing and consent.

Consent

The *Oxford English Dictionary* (*OED*) defines the noun *consent* as "voluntary agreement to or acquiescence in what another proposes or desires; compliance, concurrence, permission" (2014). This definition cues up four important aspects of consent that are recognized in academic literature across disciplines (cf. Homan 1991; Shrader-Frechette 1994). First, it indicates that consent is about *voluntariness*, consenting willingly, which entails *informedness* in that to consent willingly, one must understand what one consents to. Second, consent's *expression* can take different forms. The definition suggests that these forms occupy a continuum: from explicit, positive "agreement" to mere "acquiescence." Third, the *OED* notes that consent requires the *involvement* and influence of "another," a point reinforced by its definition of consent as a verb: "agree together." Finally, "compliance, concurrence, permission" indicate that consent initiates *outcomes* with different degrees of enthusiasm from, or involvement by, the consenter. These four themes provide a useful organizing principle for a brief review of literature on consent, raising concepts that underpin the chapter and organize its conclusion.

Aside from deliberate attempts to trick people into consenting, *voluntariness* can be undermined by coercion, even unintentional coercion that results from police authority (Reich 2003: 1061–1064). Laypeople may assume that police who make requests and seek consent have "the power and the right" to force compliance (Solan and Tiersma 2005: 41; see also Eades 2008: 312). As a result, any response might be "coerced" through social rather than interactional pressure. Furthermore, voluntariness can be undermined if the consent exchange is cast as a mere formality to dash through. If consent is to be voluntary it must be genuinely informed. The connection between *voluntariness* and *informedness* leads scholars to recommend "plain," "appropriate" language for consent requests (Green, Duncan, Barnes and Oberklaid 2003), yet such language is difficult to specify (Rock 2007; Berk-Seligson 2009: 138). Even without these challenges, it can be difficult for laypeople to evaluate whether a particular consent exchange is significant or trivial. Furthermore, complete comprehension requires full understanding of all implications of a consent decision, something that is rarely possible at the moment of consent when those full implications are impossible to foresee and thus to detail.

Opportunities for the *expression* of consent potentially save individuals from simply going along with consent-seekers' expectations (Zoller 2003: 128–32; Kärreman and Alvesson 2009). Yet those accused of rape often claim that they "knew" their victims consented because they did not explicitly refuse sex (e.g., say "no") or apparently participated (Ehrlich 2001: 123). Similarly, in a police encounter, Eades shows how withholding consent would be recognized only if "realised in a verbalised objection" (2008: 142). Through the absence of resistance (Ehrlich 2001; 1998) or "apparent agreement" (Eades 2008: 144), consent is assumed even when expressing refusal might be inconceivable due to fear of violence (Ehrlich 2001: 25) or punishment (Eades 2008: 312). Even simple affirmative answers to consent questions can poorly indicate genuine, knowing consent (Rock 2007). For example, the expression of consent becomes potentially meaningless if the consenter assumes that saying "yes" is simply a formality.

We can see *involvement* as the "co" or "con" in consent. Involvement is inherent because consenting involves at least two people. It is a dialogic process. Consenting ideally empowers would-be consenters to make decisions through discursive processes, as they work out their responses to definitions of key concepts, for example (Young, Kim, Li, Baker, Schmidt, Camp and Barfield 2010). Yet this presents an idealized picture of consent not only from a practical standpoint but also from a sociolinguistic one. For example, linguistic style, just one aspect of dialogue, can influence consent exchanges with informal talk minimizing social distance, and potentially being manipulative (Shuy 1998: 179–183). Conversely, although positively evaluated by courts (Nadler and Trout 2012: 329, 333) excessive formality can create distance and potentially result in incomprehension (Berk-Seligson 2009: 122–123). Consent is interpersonal. Soliciting written consent can disrupt trust (Nash 2012: 328) and reduce "the quality of the relationship" among participants (Granero-Molina, Fernández-Sola and Aguilera-Manrique 2009: 803) by shifting the footing of encounters. It can accordingly be resented by participants who, despite objectively valuing consent, see it as serving institutional interests and not their own (Nash 2012: 329).

Consent is a state of mind (Tiersma 2007: 86) and therefore not available for linguists to directly observe. However, it has what we might call communicative *outcomes* in the form of the conversational and paralinguistic traces it creates, such as saying "yes" or "no," nodding or shaking the head—the *expressions* of consent discussed earlier. It also has a set of resulting or instrumental *outcomes* in the form of actions in the social world, such as participating in activities from interviews to sex, depending on the context. It is these communicative and instrumental outcomes that are accessible to the linguist.

The data that I will discuss in this chapter suggest that, in addition to the factors above, we also need to recognize the situatedness of consent in its contexts of negotiation, a point reinforced in relation to both language research (e.g., Wiles, Charles, Crow and Heath 2006) and legal decision making (Solan and Tiersma 2005: 37). Interactions are "located in" times, places, institutions, and power relations (Barton, Hamilton and Ivanič, 2000: 1). This situatedness comes through contextual factors such as who is speaking, where, and when (Gee 2005: 57), and individuals' sociocultural understanding (Nadler and Trout 2012: 329). Thus context can change the meaning of consent requests (Nadler and Trout 2012: 332). Contemporary discourse analysis confirms that language and context are reflexive or mutually determining (Gee 2005: 57): instances of language influence context, which in turn influences instances of language. For example, we consent to a minor imposition, such as a computer cookie, which influences our view of consent (context) such that when we next encounter a consent request, we orient to it with the prior request in mind and so on, through successive more or less important requests. Relationships between consent and context may be changing currently as consent requests proliferate in response to an influential phenomenon discussed below, the "ethicization" of social institutions.

Tick-Box Consent Talk

In this chapter, "tick-box consent talk" refers to consent interactions that might appear to require only cursory attention, inviting an acquiescent response. The term recalls the boxes we complete on forms and websites without perhaps paying full attention. Encounters that feature "tick-box consent talk" do not necessarily concern unimportant matters, however. Therefore, the power of tick-box consent talk is primarily in its potential to allow the consent-seeker to downplay the importance of questions about consent, potentially to the extent that those questions do not seem to be about consent at all. Tick-box consent talk has further potency in that even if consent-givers realize that they are being asked to consent, it allows them to ignore that this is what is going on because tick-box consent talk can be dismissed as "just another question in a context where I have no real choice anyway." The international campaign organization "Terms of Service; Didn't Read" (ToS;DR) raises public awareness about what we consent to when blithely ticking terms of service agreements during sign-up to online services such as Facebook and YouTube. ToS;DR observes, "Terms of service are often too long to read, but it's important to understand what's in them" (2014). Such campaigners remind us that we acquiesce to more than might be prudent when we allow ourselves not to engage with information about our decisions. Even in medical settings, where the stakes are high, patients overlook the importance of consent documents to such an extent that many sign without even reading them (Granero-Molina et al. 2009: 803–804). Thus "tick-box consent" indicates "going along with it," a socially and, as I will show, empirically recognizable phenomenon.

Tick-box consent talk recalls the term "tick-box" as it is used in a pejorative sense in some academic literature, invoking bureaucratization, managerialism, or overly simplistic quantification of complex issues (e.g., Bhui 2009: 94; Thurlow and Bell 2009: 1043; Baxter and Clarke 2013). This usage, implying gradually growing, insidious institutional change, is developed in this chapter by connecting tick-box consent to wider social phenomena. Tick-box consent can be seen as part of professionalization's (Fairclough 2001) tendency to create fixity, and in so doing to overlook social complexity. One recent manifestation of professionalization, noted by Brecher (2010), is a neoliberal shift of attention toward professional and political ethics and resulting codes of practice with a corresponding shift away from attending to moral agency. For Brecher (2010) this shift, which he calls "ethicization," is evidenced in the appeals to ethics frameworks that legitimate a vast range of morally dubious activities, from wars to clinical trials, offering their agents protection from radical critique. Bogner and Menz note that this "ethical turn" (2010: 888) is influential and wide-ranging, "the decisive semantic form" for governance discourses (2010: 890). I suggest that tick-box consent is a productive strand of ethicization, part of what Brecher (2010) calls the *codification* of ethics that leads to gross oversimplification of human action. As Brecher (2010: 354) explains, "Codification ... opens the door to measurement and quantification: whether or not a nurse is working 'ethically' all too easily becomes a matter of checking and, *checking off*, against a list of rules ... [that] remain morally and politically unexamined" (cf. Petersen 2005). His italics marks the notion of "checking off" as particularly noteworthy. This notion connects to consent-seeking activities that are recruited in policing settings in order to legitimate actions. Through this checking off, or tick-boxing, it becomes totally acceptable for a police officer to interview a suspect without the suspect having the benefit of legal advice, provided that the suspect has been given the opportunity to consent to that arrangement. Ethicization and its codification require that ever more minor matters are formally consented to. For this reason, we have become numb to the tick-boxes, click-boxes and website radio-buttons that require us to conform to institutional requirements by confirming our acquiescence. The ubiquity of such consent practices has led consent-seekers and consent-givers to orient to consent in institutions in ways that respectively obscure and ignore the potential importance of consent.

In examining individual, naturally occurring consent exchanges, this chapter considers "the unique, one-time and micro-situatedness" (Blommaert 2005: 76) of consent exchanges. Yet by considering these individual exchanges as manifestations of the ethicized framing of social life, the chapter also considers "higher-level situatedness" above the level of single texts, context that is "large, general, supra-individual, typical, structural and higher than the single society" (Blommaert 2005: 76). This connection between individual experiences of consent and the super-societal phenomenon of ethicization makes it possible to move beyond simply noting tick-box consent in interaction, to interrogating its social significance, too.

Ethicization appears in policing most obviously in institutionally mandated consent procedures. However, my data show that police personnel and individual police forces also use consent routines, sometimes without an institutional imperative. I suggest, through my analysis, that there are two reasons for both institutions and individuals to use tick-box consent talk. First, such talk allows police personnel to get things done, that is, these consent exchanges are a recognizable tool with delineated outcomes. Tick-box consent is usefully viewed as a hoop through which both police worker and layperson must jump. If things go smoothly they both recognize the tick-box as something to just get through. If they do not both recognize this, the institutional actor must work out how to draw the layperson toward them so that both can move through the hoop together and on into the next phase of their interaction. The consent exchange can thus be seen as a microscopic gatekeeping encounter in that one person has "authority to make decisions that affect the other's future" (Erickson and Schultz 1982: xi). The second reason that police personnel recruit consent routines is that being seen to ensure consent is part of a wider tendency in policing to, as Ashford and Kreiner (1999: 414) put it, "reframe, refocus and recalibrate" the image of the "dirty work" of policing through talk. Police personnel recognize that their work may be seen as routinely overly coercive (Dick 2005: 1371) and individual instances of policing, such as extraction of confessions, influence this view (Dick 2005: 1374). Individual instances of a performance of caring, attentive, clinically clean policing through overt attention to consent might be seen to performatively redress this view (Butler 1990; Kulick 2003). Thus tick-box consent is a resource through which both institutions and individuals can enable interactions to progress while at the same time ethicizing the "dirty" work of policing.

Previous usages of "tick-box consent" place the term in opposition to "substantial" consent, suggesting that tick-box consent is, by definition, deficient as consent (McFee 2014: 100). Likewise, the label has described something superficial, "no more than a nod in the direction of informed consent," denying the consenter "the capacity to be sufficiently informed to make an autonomous choice" (McNamee, Olivier and Wainwright 2007: 72). These senses of "tick-box consent," like the sense discussed here, may feature a lackadaisical, overly bureaucratic or loaded delivery of information (McNamee et al. 2007: 72). For these authors, "tick-box consent" necessarily fails to establish genuinely informed consent. On the other hand, "tick-box consent talk," the term used here, is not concerned with whether or not consent was genuine as this is not amenable to linguistic analysis, as noted in my discussion of the *outcomes* of consent, earlier. The next section specifies exactly what is meant by the term in this chapter.

Theorizing Tick-Box Consent Talk

My framework recognizes that all consent talk has the potential to take on a tick-box quality. The notions of "potential" and "quality" are important as "tick-box talk" is not a rigid category or designation. Rather, it a point of contact between the emic social recognizability of particular kinds of consent exchanges and the etic idea that the language analyst can identify features that distinguish different forms of talk. In other words, many people might recognize a consent exchange where there is an element of "going through the motions" (the emic dimension) yet linguistic analysis might offer a way to examine where this feeling originates in talk (the etic dimension) (cf. Stokoe and Edwards 2008, 2009). The potential for consent exchanges to become "tick-box" is ever-present. This potential or quality is activated by the situated occurrence of each consent exchange rather than being a function of only participant or analytic attention. Nonetheless, the particular features that the linguist can identify will not be capable of uniquely and unequivocally identifying an instance as "tick-box" or "not tick-box" so the concept of tick-box is merely a means to interrogate data, not to classify it (recognizing a "potential" and "quality" only, not seeking to categorize talk). Tick-box consent focuses on a recognizable phenomenon, its realization in naturally occurring talk and speakers' orientations to it. It is not intended as a diagnostic tool, but a way of interrogating interactions.

"Tick-box" is first a quality of the consent request. This quality is entailed in its macro- and messo-level contextualized meaning, for example, in that the request is apparently an institutionally mandated formality and made at a time that the hearer might feel compelled to acquiesce. Tick-box consent might be inadequately supported by institutional measures such as training so that those seeking consent, such as police officers, might "muddle through" seeking consent as best they can. Conversely, it might be institutionally over-specified so that those seeking consent take an institutional line that involves going through the motions of consent seeking, rather than a professional one in which they seek to achieve full information exchange (after Sarangi and Roberts 2002: 203–204). This tick-box quality is also entailed in the consent request's local contextualization, for example, its lack of fit, and lack of congruity, with co-text; its location in openings and closings of interactions and its precipitation by an institutionally salient event such as a crime report. Tick-box consent is next a matter of interaction. Particular linguistic forms and paralinguistic behaviors frequently co-occur with tick-box questions, including laughter or smile voice, minimization or downplaying through words such as *just*, problematizing the formulation of the consent request (e.g., characterizing it as "difficult"), and marked delivery. These forms and behaviors do not universally identify tick-box consent talk, but they do frequently characterize it and can be used to identify its *potential* occurrence. The notion of tick-box consent talk becomes particularly useful when one interactant orients to the talk as "tick-box" and one does not.

Stevens and Harper (2007: 1481) note that doctors seeking to "manage patients" concerns' about electroconvulsive therapy will "draw on" informed consent. These doctors use, strategically, the notion that the treatment, though controversial, has been presented fairly. In this way they rationalize their practice by analogy with established medical procedures like major surgery. This raises the possibility that consent-seeking could become a tool to legitimize actions and facilitate activities. This can be further explored through the notion of tick-box consent. If consent can be "drawn on," used, to manage interactions, how much more power is vested in a form of consent that participants will just go along with. This phenomenon is connected to that of invoking procedure, through which institutional actors, by recounting how something "can, will, should or usually does proceed" (Nielsen, Nielsen, Gravengaard and Due 2012: 1457), are able to achieve a range of interactional ends. Here, we will see how, similarly, using consent exchanges imbued with the freedoms of the tick-box light-touch has similar potency.

Data

Much classic literature on consent, language, and law deals, unavoidably, with something hidden: exchanges that occurred before the linguistic study began and have therefore not been audio-recorded and are not available for study (e.g., those that took place during searches [Reich 2003: 1061, 1087] or rape [Meyer 2010]). This chapter, in contrast, presents consent exchanges that have been audio-recorded. This permits consideration of consent as a situated social practice: "ethics-in-interaction" (Barton and Eggly 2009: 312). I have drawn data from two areas of policing (in England and Wales). This is not to imply that these settings are homogenous (cf. Olufowote 2008: 292). Rather, in combination, they begin to illustrate ethicized policing.

I turn first to nonemergency telephone calls to the police, presenting two examples from a data set of 30 calls. As part of the closing routine, call handlers ask callers whether they consent to have their details passed to a counseling and support service, Victim Support. These data therefore concern consent to an administrative activity. A case study introduces and exemplifies tick-box consent talk and shows its power to draw participants through the "hoop" of consent, mentioned earlier, and to get consent done, even when the consenter is reluctant.

The other set of data occur in police interviews, this time in openings, and with suspects, rather than those reporting crimes. I present three examples from a data set of 60 in which suspects who opted not to have legal advice during interviews are asked to consent to, and account for, that choice. These data illustrate how a police force ethicizes through consent but also how tick-box consent can misfire.

Using Consent in Mundane Talk

We begin with the nonemergency police call center, and the seemingly trivial consent topic of whether the caller is willing to allow personal details to be passed on to the charity Victim Support. Call handlers in this particular call center are guided on what to say by a document titled "Occurrence Log—Questions to Ask for Crimes." Some of the "questions" on this log feature specialist terminology such as the acronym CSI (crime scene Investigation), which might be unfamiliar to callers, suggesting that it is not a term which is to be addressed directly to them. Indeed, the document uses this term within a question: "Is CSI applicable?," which is directed toward call handlers, asking them to make a decision based on their assessment of the affordances of crime-scene investigation, rather than offering a form of words that they should recite to the caller. Therefore, the "Questions to Ask" document does not appear to be a script that provides "a full specification of every word uttered by the operator" (Cameron 2000: 330). Rather, it can be seen as a mixture of "prompt sheet" (specifying "interactional moves" but not "a standard form of words" [Cameron 2000: 330]) and "general guidelines" on "staging" (Cameron 2000: 330). Given this, when the document asks, "ANY OBJECTIONS TO VICTIM SUPPORT?" [capitalization as in original], it is likely that this addresses the call handler, and does not require a verbatim reading to the caller. The "Questions to Ask" document offers further detail through what seems to be a more scripted turn:

> *CITY POLICE OPERATE A VICTIM SUPPORT SCHEME, WE RECOMMEND THEIR SERVICES, IT IS AN INDEPENDANT* [sic] *CHARITY AND WE OPERATE A DIRECT REFERAL* [sic] *OF YOUR DETAILS TO THEM UNLESS YOU ASK US NOT TO DO SO.*

The "Questions to Ask" document thus does not prescribe an exchange about consent and indeed seems to recommend merely informing rather than asking about this. Furthermore, the wording above suggests that consent, if sought, would be redundant as victims' details are passed to Victim Support automatically, with the onus evidently being on the caller to object, not consent. A consent request is therefore by no means obligatory, so, why and how does it happen?

Excerpt 1, below, exemplifies. In this excerpt, Jack has called to report that his mobile telephone was stolen from his pocket covertly in a crowded street. Although this crime might be extremely traumatic for some people in some circumstances, Jack did not orient to it as distressing during the call. Indeed, he indicated that he was reporting the theft only so that his telephone provider could finalize cancellation of his contract. Claire, the call handler, likewise confined herself to questions about the incident, the stolen telephone, and contact information, rather than ascribing any negative emotional response to Jack in contrast to other calls. We join the call after Jack's crime report and Claire's allocation of service:

Excerpt 1: Would you mind? (see appendix for transcription conventions)

1	Claire	would you mind if I passed your details to
2		Victim Support they're a charity organisation
3		based within our force just to help victims of
4		crime they ((will)) send you a leaflet is that
5		okay
6	Jack	hh (.) um:: (.) yeah that's fine
7	Claire	right

Victim Support's publicity materials state that they help victims of crime to "find the strength to deal with what [they've] been through" (Victim Support 2014). Given this, in Jack and Claire's unemotional conversation, the mention of Victim Support, particularly in the form of a consent request, seems incongruous. Claire downplays (Camiciottoli 2012) the consent request by using the deferential "would you mind" (line 1), minimizing it, using "just" (line 3) (Grant 2011), and exemplifying the likely outcomes of Jack's consent as merely receiving a posted "leaflet" (line 4). At the end of her turn she revisits the consent request with the minimizing "is that okay" (line 4). Additionally she characterizes Victim Support as a "charity organization based within our force" (turn 4) rather than using the idea from the "Questions to ask" document that "South Wales Police operate" Victim Support. This distancing of Victim Support from the police further downplays (Reyes-Rodriguez 2008) institutional intervention in Jack's life. The consent request seems at odds with Jack's experiences, and Claire's strategies can be seen to recognize this. She has to tick the box of consent, despite it being unlikely that Jack will require the services offered.

Jack's acquiescence to the consent request (line 6) is cautious, prefaced by an outbreath, pauses, and long hesitation "um::." His eventual emphatic consent, through "yeah" and "that's fine" in combination, make the consent appear marked. His repetitive agreement perhaps thinly veils discomfort, yet he does consent despite no overt pressure to do so. Like individuals described by Lichtenberg (2004) and Nadler and Trout (2012: 338), he may or may not believe that refusing consent will genuinely alter his treatment. Acquiescence is perhaps the path of least resistance to what might appear an inconsequential and unnecessary consent query. Jack's specific formulation "yeah that's fine" was common in my data when callers agreed to contact from Victim Support. Berk-Seligson (2009) points out that particular forms of agreement in consent exchanges can raise questions about the validity of the consent. She cites a case in which a suspect consents using simply "yeah" tokens that are delivered "in isolation without further explanation," with a telltale "mechanical quality," with little variation in form and in contexts that render the token frequently "linguistically inappropriate or even meaningless" (2009: 137). Although her example is from a bilingual interaction, the risks of such gratuitous concurrence have been widely reported (Eades 1995: 164). In this instance, Jack consents to something that is extremely unlikely to harm him, or any other caller in his position, and may even positively affect callers who become worried about the crime they have encountered after the fact. Thus, we can see this as ticking a fairly inconsequential box, akin to agreeing to receive direct mail from a company that might turn out to sell a product that we want. Both Jack and Claire move swiftly through the consent exchange, ticking the box of consent and moving on.

Call handlers made individual decisions about how to broach the topic of Victim Support. Many, like Claire, did not simply recite the script provided, but framed the information as requiring consent. Why do these call handlers opt to mention Victim Support using a consent routine, given that they could simply gloss over this matter, as their colleagues did? I suggest that this is an example of ethicization: Claire neutralizes the dirty work of circulating people's personal details and generating what they might construe as "junk mail" (rightly or wrongly) by framing the process as concerned with consent but with a kind of consent that is an inconsequential formality. Both she and Jack orient to the consent as tick-box perhaps because of its incongruity with the previous talk and the triviality of its imposition. Claire's orientation is manifest in the downplaying and distancing entailed in the request, Jack's in his grudging but emphatic granting of consent. Claire has used a consent exchange in order to deal with an ambiguous institutional requirement. She uses tick-box consent talk in order to fulfill institutional needs.

The next excerpt similarly followed a report of an extremely minor crime that centered on the misdelivery of some items of post (mail), yet this excerpt illustrates something rather different in both the formulation of the information regarding Victim Support, by Carol, the call taker, and the response by Bob, the caller:

Excerpt 2: As you're a victim of crime

1	Carol	okay um as you're a victim of crime we're
2		passing your details on to Victim Support?
3		which means they will be looking at the
4		crime report and posting any services to
5		you? =
6	Bob	= u:::gh =
7	Carol	= would you be happy with
8		that at all?
9	Bob	(.) um well- well you can do but it- it's not
10		necessary =
11	Carol	= okay =
12	Bob	= because I'm- um it's not
13		as if I'm um =
14	Carol	= yeh =
15	Bob	= a victim of crime or
16		anything is it
17	Carol	[laughs] ((that's it))

In her first turn, Carol offers a circumscribed summary of Victim Support's provision (lines 3 to 5). This indicates that contact with Victim Support will be by post, but gives no indication of what will be posted and through the use of "any" (line 4) makes it unclear whether materials will be posted at all. Carol's introduction of Victim Support initially takes up the gist of the "Questions to Ask" document by presenting the passing of details to Victim Support as automatic so as not a matter for consent. If we think back to the characteristics of consent, offered earlier, this attempt to elicit consent does not seem particularly robust in terms of allowing *voluntariness* in an *informed* way, giving Bob an opportunity to *express* consent through *dialogue* so that he can influence *outcome*. The tick-box impetus here is so strong that it seems that Carol had decided against even using a consent exchange.

Bob's response, which can be described only as a gasp of dismay (line 6) is the trigger for Carol's consent question, "would you be happy with that at all." His evident lack of happiness seems to cause Carol to reframe what she initially presented as information about Victim Support (lines 3 to 5) as a consent question (lines 7–8). The dirty work of circulating Bob's details, given that he is calling about an issue with the postal service, presents Carol's work as more dirty than it might have at first appeared and she responds by using the consent question.

Bob replies by grudgingly consenting to the contact ("you can do", line 9) but immediately casts this contact as "not necessary" (lines 9 and 10). He is ultimately willing to question his status as a victim of crime (lines 12 to 16), asserting "it's not as if I'm a victim of crime or anything." This risks Carol dismissing his crime report because if he is not a victim, he cannot be reporting a crime. It also risks upsetting Carol, the gatekeeper to police services, by threatening her positive face (Brown and Levinson 1987: 13) in suggesting that she has misclassified him. This all seems to create considerable confusion about whether Bob is, in fact, consenting to his details being passed to Victim Support. Yet, the combination of Bob's ambivalence and Carol's failure to probe that indifference results in the details being passed along anyway. Here, the impetus created by tick-box consent talk enabled both to simply move on to the next topic, despite Bob's apparent discomfort with this. The consent talk misfires as it does not provide for establishing whether Bob genuinely consents.

In this section, then, we have seen how tick-box consent talk looks when mundane, low-risk matters are consented about. In the next section, we see how tick-box talk can take on quite a different significance when the stakes are higher.

Tick-Box Consent Talk with Consequences

We now move to consent-seeking at the beginning of interviews with suspects. Specifically, we examine points in the police-suspect interviews when suspects consent (or not) to proceed with those interviews without legal advice. Despite the seriousness of such exchanges, they have a tick-box quality for two main reasons: first, suspects will have been asked whether they wish to speak to a solicitor several times before reaching the interview (implying the consent exchange in interview is redundant); and second, once the interview begins, it might seem too late to do much about wanting a solicitor (implying the consent exchange is ineffectual). Thus, this consent request might appear, to one or both participants, merely as an opportunity to put consent on record. The consent procedure itself derives from the Police and Criminal Evidence Act (PACE) Code C, which advises that normally:

> The interviewer should remind the suspect of their entitlement to free legal advice and ... the interview can be delayed for legal advice to be obtained ... It is the interviewer's responsibility to make sure all reminders are recorded in the interview record.
>
> (Home Office 2014, Section 11.2, p. 36)

Attention to the recording of reminders (lines 3 to 5) gives the procedure a tick-box quality from its outset. Note 11.2 might not immediately seem to concern consent. However, police forces tend to recontextualize their requirements into a consent routine. Just as we saw individual officers using consent procedures in the previous section, here the process operates at a messo-institutional level as the police force itself draws on ethicization by seeking consent both to neutralize its dirty work (cf. Dick 2005: 1366) and to get things done. Data for this section are from a police force that codifies the consent procedure in a standardized form of words to which officers can add free-form explanation. Reciting a standardized wording further invokes the tick-box quality by conveying the impression that the question is not directed at the individual and has not been created for the particular instance in question.

The consent questions themselves, for there are two, appear simultaneously logical and illogical. The first question, with its preceding information, is:

> You are entitled to free and independent legal advice, which includes the right to speak to a solicitor on the telephone and this interview can be delayed for you to obtain such legal advice. Do you want to have a solicitor present at the interview and/or speak to one on the telephone?

Unlike many institutional questions, this one expects a "no" response insofar as a "yes" at this point would require the interview to be halted: "no" means "yes, we can get on with the interview." Yet this expectation of a "no" is odd given the number of studies, from different disciplines, which note that when asking questions, questioners expect to hear "yes" and answerers find it easier to say "yes" than "no" (for a summary, see Rock 2007: 207). Additionally, the question is asked at a time when the value of obtaining support might be crystalizing for suspects as they confront the reality of police interview so they might be beginning to recognize the value of saying "yes." Thus this is a self-defeating way for the institution to ask this question. Despite all this, the question might appear, to the bureaucrat, to offer a reliable way to ensure that suspects decline legal advice on record because it asks directly about intentions and desires. This question is followed by a second that, presumably, seeks to elicit evidence of the suspect's willingness to be interviewed without a legal advisor. This question begins by summarizing events so far:

> You have continued to decline legal advice. What are your reasons for this?

Again, this question might appear sensible because it can elicit proof from the suspect's own mouth of his or her willingness to be interviewed without legal advice. However, as the data will show, far from eliciting answers that tick the box, it frequently provides space for problematic exchanges that discourage rather than support ethicization. This second question, about reasons for declining legal advice, is not easily answered. Suspects evidently struggle to provide a single, delineated reason for their decisions and, as I have shown elsewhere, often appropriate this turn to indicate their orientation to the interview (e.g., an intention to tell the truth) (Rock 2007: 128–133). The question is also troublesome because suspects seemingly overlook its tick-box aspects. They orient to the question as a genuine request for information rather than a hoop that they and the officer must together pass through in order to move on. This results in a mismatch with each participant understanding the question differently. It is this mismatch that causes problems, as the data will show. Officers receive suspects' answers about their reasons for declining legal advice but seemingly lack the resources or impetus to address those answers, particularly if suspects appear unsure of their motivations for declining legal advice. Officers seem to view the questions as tick-box but without knowing what ticking the box might look like. This creates an impression that some officers ignore suspects' concerns.

We join Excerpt 3 as the police officer, Ben, delivers the standardized wording for question 1.

Excerpt 3: I've already spoke to one

1	Ben	you are entitled to free and independent legal advice . . . do you want to have a solicitor present at the interview or speak to one on the telephone?
2	Dave	well I've already spoke to one on the telephone
3	Ben	right and that's prior to this interview?
4	Dave	yes
5	Ben	did you un- fully understand what the solicitor's advice was?
6	Dave	yes I did yeah
7	Ben	and you're perfectly satisfied that you're happy for this interview to go ahead?
8	Dave	yeah
9	Ben	okay [clears throat] you've continued to- er you've accepted your legal advice?
10	Dave	yeah

The tick-box consent exchange in turn 1 asks Dave, the suspect, whether he wants to exercise a right that he has, in fact, already exercised. This is reminiscent of the victims of minor crimes in the previous section being offered support for "what they were going through," despite having experienced only minor crimes that they did not orient to as distressing. The question makes sense from the perspective of institutional record-keeping but not in the local context. It is classic tick-box incongruity. Dave, addressing the last part of the question (cf. Eades 1994: 243), notes this oddity through stress on "spoke" (turn 2). In so doing, he orients to the question as a genuine request for information rather than a tick-box police procedural that merits only confirmation. The question asks whether he wants legal advice at that moment, but, by viewing it as information seeking, he takes it to be about general access to legal advice. This all causes him to sidestep the consent issue entirely. In response, at turn 3, Ben notes the irrelevance of Dave's answer to his tick-box question, by presenting Dave's answer as concerning something "prior to" the interview and thus outside their joint focus. Ben also uses this turn and the next to get on record that legal advice was given (turn 3) satisfactorily (turn 5).

In turn 7, Ben follows up on the abortive consent exchange in turn 1, by improvising a new one. Turns 1 to 6 asked whether Dave wanted to have a solicitor present. Now he instead seeks Dave's consent for the "interview to go ahead" (turn 7). The original question in turn 1 offered legal advice, which this question does not. However, we can view turn 7 as recasting the initial consent question with more contextual relevance. This gets to the central issue of whether the interview can felicitously continue and, for good measure, incorporating the strong formulation "perfectly satisfied." Taking this view, we recognize Ben orienting to ticking the box and working on bringing Dave with him through the hoop of consent. Moreover, we see that when one consent exchange fails, Ben "draws on" a consent exchange to manage what comes next (cf. Stevens and Harper 2007).

In turn 9, Ben begins to returns to his usual interview script and to the first part of the second question of the scripted consent exchange, "You've continued to decline legal advice. Can I ask your reasons for this?" In view of the preceding talk, this question has become nonsensical and accordingly Ben self-corrects before even finishing the question. However, he does not disregard consent but instead converts the aborted second question into a new tick-box, reversing the polarity of the scripted, recommended question noting acceptance rather than decline of legal advice. This is not simply talk about receiving legal advice, ticking the box of consent is the guiding principle.

In Excerpt 3, then, Ben, when confronted with an interview that was troublesome because his interviewee failed to orient to tick-box consent as such, constructed a new tick-box and employed serial questions, combining scripted and spontaneous talk, to draw the witness through this new hoop of consent. Other officers, having entered the dangerous area opened up by the scripted sequence of tick-box questions, were less successful in managing jumping through the hoop of consent. Excerpt 4 presents a disturbing exchange:

Excerpt 4: I don't know

1	Brian	do you want to have a solicitor present at this interview and or speak to one on the telephone?
2	Derek	(2.0)
3	Mary	you need to answer that
4	Derek	no
5	Brian	you've continued to decline legal advice what are your reasons for this?
6	Derek	[tearfully] I don't know
7	Brian	what do you mean by that Derek?
8	Derek	[sniffs] I don't know I just want to get the interview done
9	Brian	okay okay because I'm investigating a criminal offence I must caution you and that caution is

This exchange does not begin well; Derek apparently freezes when confronted with the initial consent question and answers only when prompted by Mary, his "appropriate adult," there to support him because he was under 18. Brian's subsequent question makes matters worse for Derek, who begins to cry and cannot offer any explanation for his rights waiver. This is risky for Brian because if his interviewee does not know why he has waived his right to legal advice, the waiver appears infelicitous (Navarro-Reyes 2010). Certainly Derek's consent does not appear very *informed*.

Brian attempts to move toward consent through a request for clarification in turn 7. However, Derek's response makes matters worse. Derek reiterates that he does not know why he has agreed to an interview without legal advice and is going ahead only to "get the interview done" (turn 8). Shuy problematizes the "meaning conveyed by uncertainty" (1997: 192), which is exemplified in the first part of turn 8. He also raises the possibility that suspects might agree to interview without legal advice in the hope of "getting the interrogation over with" (1997: 183), exemplified in the second part of turn 8. This latter theme is developed by Ehrlich, who notes that in rape cases, acquiescence can be a signal "not ... of consent" but a way to prevent something more "prolonged" or "extreme" (2013: 195). Although Derek's turns are ambiguous, they do not prompt Brian to really unpack them or to explain to Derek what legal advice is. Instead, unable to align Derek with ticking the box of consent, Brian simply abandons this line and moves on to the next phase of the pre-interview routine, introducing recitation of the police caution (turn 9). Brian seems strikingly ill-equipped to accomplish the eliciting of genuine consent. He and Derek both orient to the consent exchange as tick-box; something to get through in order to "get the interview done" and move on. This leaves Derek in apparent confusion about this key right. Brian appears very focused on the paperwork and the required formulas in that his first turn features the phrase "and or" echoing, in talk, their written appearance on his crib sheet ("and/or"). He seems unable to escape the ritualistic aspects of the interview opening. Ultimately, unlike the officer in the previous excerpt, he does not accomplish the aims of the script by adapting the eliciting of consent to the context. The concomitant impact on Derek's rights is an *outcome* that the linguist cannot measure. However, his rights appear to have been adversely affected by the way that tick-box consent talk makes it possible to simply dismiss matters that have been raised.

The final excerpt here, too, sees the suspect not recognizing the question about legal advice as procedural:

Excerpt 5: That's absolutely fine

1	Belinda	do you want to have a solicitor present ... or ... on the telephone?
2	Dan	[carefully] I don't think I require a solicitor?
3	Belinda	you have continued to decline legal advice and we'll now have to ask the question what were your reasons for this it's just (.) to clarify
4	Dan	u:::m (5.6) ur I'm not clear how a solicitor would help me=
5	Belinda	=yep understand that's absolutely fine

For Dan, the suspect, lack of clarity about the solicitor's function makes it impossible to felicitously decline legal advice. He flags his uncertainty with stress on "think" and invites clarification through rising intonation (turn 1). He thus orients to Belinda's first turn not as box-ticking but as a genuine opportunity to discuss the topic raised. Belinda, on the other hand, seems to be very much in a tick-box frame in that she takes what could be seen as two consecutive requests for information about legal advice (turns 2 and 4) not as requests but as consent. Logically, informed consent to an interview without legal advice cannot come from a suspect confused about legal advice. Legally, this does not look like a safe, *voluntary* and *informed* rights waiver, and morally, the suspect might have been better understood as asking for help than waiving his rights.

It is notable that neither Excerpt 4 nor 5 features explicit consent on the part of the suspects, yet the interviewing officers in both cases continue regardless, as if they have no idea how to orient to the exchanges except as tick-boxes. These examples recall Ness, Kiesling, and Lidz's (2009: 358) lost opportunities to communicate about consent decisions in that instead of opening up a space to explore facts and implications of legal advice, the tick-box frame is restrictive, closing down opportunities for information exchange and confusing officers and detainees. The result is that officers ultimately look, at best, uncompassionate but potentially even manipulative or coercive. In these examples, the procedure misfires because it neither ensures nor provides evidence of consent to interview without legal advice.

Conclusion

Her Majesty's Inspectorate of Constabulary points out that "a major and enduring strength of British policing is that it is undertaken with the consent and support of the public at large" (2007: 2). For this consent to be maintained at the societal level, individual consent exchanges must function in particular ways at the interpersonal level. In this chapter I have considered both the micro-level situatedness of individual consent exchanges in relation to participants' immediate, localized encounters but also messo-level situatedness (Blommaert 2005) in relation to the ethicized framing of social life through consent exchanges that can be seen to mitigate unpalatable aspects of policing (Dick 2005: 1369).

Tick-box consent talk does not have a single, unified realization or even definitive formal characteristics, although certain features do recur, such as laughter and minimization, and there are patterns in the occurrence of tick-box consent talk in openings and closings, for example. In any case, the notion of tick-box consent is not intended as a diagnostic but rather is most useful in showing tensions and contradictions in the ways that consent works in policing. For example a tick-box quality seems to be in play both when the institution attends disproportionately to the consented-about issue (drawing excessive attention to something seemingly trivial such as passing contact details to a support service) yet conversely also when it trivializes important matters (such as consent to interview without legal advice).

In the data presented here, we have seen how tick-box consent can function, as in Excerpt 1, quite smoothly. There, both participants recognize that they are "going through the motions," that consent concerns something so unimportant that the consent request can contain much minimization and downplaying. Yet, even when the matter for consent is inconsequential, like agreeing to receive a leaflet, the quality of tick-box consent can provide for unwilling people to "go along with" consent. This can be so coercive, as in Excerpt 2, that those who have stated their unwillingness, fairly unambiguously, still find themselves consenting, with their stated lack of consent unexplored. In Excerpt 3, we saw that even when the stakes were higher, concerning legal advice, some participants could build on tick-box consent talk. In that excerpt, the officer devised a new consent routine when the institutionally mandated one became problematic. In the final two excerpts, the coerciveness of tick-box consent was explored. In both excerpts, suspects seemed to be doing something other than consenting yet their words were taken as consent and their interviews went ahead. I have argued that the potential of tick-box consent made this possible.

To close, I return to the five key elements of consent outlined at the opening of this chapter and show how the examination of tick-box consent presented here has illuminated them. To say that the exchanges presented here were not *informed* and thus not *voluntary* would be an overstatement. Yet there are clearly problems with these exchanges, and one underlying issue seems to be the way that the tick-box quality seems to suggest to participants that consenting is a fait accompli, either for the callers, who simply agree to their details being passed on, or to the police officers, who do not always seem able to break out of their rituals during interview openings. The more cynical reader might feel that tick-box consent talk has been deliberately exploited to downplay the significance of what is being consented to, although this is beyond the scope of linguistic analysis. The data here showed that sometimes, in *expressing* consent, emphatic repetition co-occurs with signs of reluctance such as sighing and that even apparent requests for information or statements of confusion can be taken to index consent (cf. Ehrlich 2001, 2013; Eades 2008). It has been suggested that consent might be best expressed in institutional settings in highly formal register using "Yes, I do" for example (Berk-Seligson 2009: 137). In Excerpts 3, 5 and 6, not only did emphatic answers not appear, but the laypeople's answers did not seem to matter at all, as consent was assumed irrespective of them. Turning to *involvement*, an alternative possible reason for recruiting consent is to manage potentially interpersonally or institutionally compromising moments, such as those when dirty work must be accomplished. Just as rituals are "sanctuaries" in which "we are freed from personal responsibility for the acts we are engaged in" (Labov 1972: 168), consent is a powerful resource that creates similar protection and license. Yet consent is not a way to ensure that policing is fair, as a narrow concern with consent in social debate can overlook or even conceal more substantive issues (Leith 2007: 1031); ethicization does not guarantee morality. Although we cannot know whether the resulting communicative and instrumental *outcomes*, the sending of information and the continuation of interview, were undesirable for the laypeople in these encounters, the consent moves suggest discomfort, of various forms, with consenting. Finally, looking to *situatedness* and *context*, we have seen the complex of factors that shape consent exchanges, and I have suggested that the cultural proliferation of tick-box consent, driven in part by increasing concerns with ethicization, might have a cumulative effect on our orientations to consenting.

Appendix: Transcription Conventions

<u>Underlining</u>	Indicates stress signaled by the speaker through a change in pitch and volume
(.)	A micropause of 0.9 seconds or less
(1.2)	A pause of 1.0 second or more, the duration appearing within the brackets. In this case, for example, the pause lasted for 1.2 seconds
// //	Simultaneous or overlapping talk. Words within the double slashes on consecutive lines are simultaneous
hhh	Audible out-breath
=	Latching on
-	Self-correction or speaker breaking off
[ ]	Comments (for example, [coughs])
(( ))	Unclear speech (double brackets either contain an attempt to decipher the unclear speech or, where that is not possible, an estimation of the number of inaudible syllables)
:	The preceding segment was prolonged
. . .	Indicates that words have been removed from an excerpt, to increase intelligibility through brevity

References

Ashford, Blake and Glen Kreiner. 1999. "How can you do it?": Dirty work and the challenge of constructing a positive identity. *The Academy of Management Review* 24(3): 413–434.

Barton, David, Mary Hamilton and Roz Ivanič. 2000. *Situated Literacies*. London: Routledge.

Barton, Ellen and Susan Eggly. 2009. Ethical or unethical persuasion? The rhetoric of offers to participate in clinical trials. *Written Communication* 26(3): 295–319.

Baxter, Jacqueline and John Clarke. 2013. Farewell to the tick-box inspector? Ofsted and the changing regime of school inspection in England. *Oxford Review of Education* 39(5): 702–718.

Berk-Seligson, Susan. 2009. *Coerced Confessions*. Berlin: Mouton de Gruyter.

Bhui, Hindpal. 2009. Prisons and race equality. In Hindpal Bhui (ed.) *Race and Criminal Justice*. London: Sage Publications Ltd. 83–101.

Blommaert, Jan. 2005. *Discourse*. Cambridge: Cambridge University Press.

Bogner, Alexander and Wolfgang Menz. 2010. How politics deals with expert dissent: The case of ethics councils. *Science, Technology & Human Values* 35(6): 888–914.

Brecher, Bob. 2010. The politics of professional ethics. *Journal of Evaluation in Clinical Practice* 16(2): 351–355.

Brown, Penelope and Stephen Levinson. 1987. *Politeness*. Cambridge: Cambridge University Press.

Butler, Judith. 1990. *Gender Trouble: Feminism and the Subversion of Identity*. New York: Routledge.

Cameron, Deborah. 2000. Styling the worker: Gender and the commodification of language in the globalized service economy. *Journal of Sociolinguistics* 4(3): 323–347.

Camiciottoli, Belinda. 2012. Downplaying the downturn: A critical analysis of interdiscursivity in earnings calls. In Paul Gillaerts, Elizabeth de Groot, Sylvain Dieltjens, Priscilla Heynderickx and Geert Jacobs (eds.) *Researching Discourse in Business Genres: Cases and Corpora*. Bern: Peter Lang. 163–180.

Dick, Penny. 2005. Dirty work designations: How police officers account for their use of coercive force. *Human Relations* 58(11): 1363–1390.

Eades, Diana. 1994. A case of communicative clash: Aboriginal English and the legal system. In John Gibbons (ed.) *Language and the Law*. London: Longman. 234–264.

Eades, Diana. 1995. Aboriginal English on trial: The case for Stuart and Condren. In Diana Eades (ed.) *Language in Evidence: Issues Confronting Multi-Cultural Australia*. Sydney: University of New South Wales Press. 147–174.

Eades, Diana. 2008. *Courtroom Talk and Neocolonial Control*. Berlin: Mouton de Gruyter.

Ehrlich, Susan. 1998. The discursive reconstruction of sexual consent. *Discourse and Society* 9(2): 149–171.

Ehrlich, Susan. 2001. *Representing Rape: Language and Sexual Consent*. London: Routledge.

Ehrlich, Susan. 2013. Post penetration rape: The decontextualization of witness testimony. In Chris Heffer, Frances Rock and John Conley (eds.) *Legal-Lay*

Communication: Textual Travels in the Law. Oxford: Oxford University Press. 189–205.

Erickson, Frederick and Jeffrey Schultz. 1982. *The Counselor as Gatekeeper: Social Interaction in Interviews*. New York: Academic Press.

Fairclough, Norman. 2001. *Language and Power* (2nd ed.). Harlow, U.K.: Longman.

Gee, James. 2005. *An Introduction to Discourse Analysis: Theory and Method* (2nd ed.). London: Routledge.

Granero-Molina, José, Cayetano Fernández-Sola and Gabriel Aguilera-Manrique. 2009. Applying a sociolinguistic model to the analysis of informed consent documents. *Nursing Ethics* 16(6): 797–812.

Grant, Lynn. 2011. The frequency and functions of *just* in British academic spoken English. *Journal of English for Academic Purposes* 10(3): 183–197.

Green, Julie, Rony Duncan, Graeme Barnes and Frank Oberklaid. 2003. Putting the "informed" into "consent": A matter of plain language. *Journal of Paediatrics and Child Health* 39(9): 700–703.

Her Majesty's Inspectorate of Constabulary. 2007. *Beyond the Call: A Thematic Inspection of Police Contact Centres' Contribution to Incident Management*. London: HMIC.

Homan, Roger. 1991. *The Ethics of Social Research*. London: Longman.

Home Office. 2014. *Police and Criminal Evidence Act (PACE) Code C*. London: Home Office.

Kärreman, Dan and Mats Alvesson. 2009. Resisting resistance: Counter-resistance, consent and compliance in a consultancy firm. *Human Relations* 62(8): 1115–1144.

Kulick, Don. 2003. No. *Language & Communication* 23(2): 139–151.

Labov, William. 1972. Rules for ritual insults. In David Sudnow (ed.) *Studies in Social Interaction*. New York: Free Press. 120–169.

Leith, Valerie. (2007). Consent and nothing but consent? The organ retention scandal. *Sociology of Health and Illness*, 29(7): 1023–1042.

Lichtenberg, Illya. 2004. The impact of a verbal warning on police consent search practices. *Journal of Criminal Justice* 32(1): 85–87.

McFee, Graham. 2014. Ethical considerations. In Lee Nelson, Ryan Groom and Paul Potrac (eds.) *Research Methods in Sports Coaching*. London: Routledge. 98–108.

McNamee, Mike, Stephen Olivier and Paul Wainwright. 2007. *Research Ethics in Exercise, Health and Sports Sciences*. London: Routledge.

Meyer, Anneke. 2010. "Too drunk to say no": Binge drinking, rape and the *Daily Mail*. *Feminist Media Studies* 10(1): 19–34.

Nadler, Janice and J. D. Trout. 2012. The language of consent in police encounters. In Peter Tiersma and Lawrence Solan (eds.) *The Oxford Handbook of Language and Law*. Oxford: Oxford University Press. 326–339.

Nash, Kate. 2012. Telling stories: The narrative study of documentary ethics. *New Review of Film and Television Studies* 10(3): 318–331.

Navarro-Reyes, Jesús. 2010. Speech acts, criteria and intentions. *Lodz Papers in Pragmatics* 6(1): 145–170.

Ness, David, Scott Kiesling, and Chares Lidz. 2009. Why does informed consent fail? A discourse analytic approach. *Journal of the American Academy of Psychiatry and the Law Online* 37(3): 349–362.

Nielsen, Mie, Søren Nielsen, Gitte Gravengaard and Brian Due. 2012. Interactional functions of invoking procedure in institutional settings. *Journal of Pragmatics* 44(11): 1457–1473.

Olufowote, James. 2008. A structurational analysis of informed consent to treatment: Societal evolution, contradiction, and reproductions in medical practice. *Health Communication* 23(3): 292–303.

Oxford English Dictionary. 2014. Oxford: Oxford University Press.

Petersen, Alan. 2005. Securing our genetic health: Engendering trust in UK Biobank. *Sociology of Health and Illness* 27(2): 271–292.

Reich, Marissa. 2003. United States v. Drayton: The need for bright-line warnings during consensual bus searches. *Journal of Criminal Law and Criminology* 93(4): 1057–1093.

Reyes-Rodriguez, Antonio. 2008. Discursive strategies in Chavez's political discourse: Voicing, distancing, and shifting. *Critical Discourse Studies* 5(2): 133–152.

Rock, Frances. 2007. *Communicating Rights: The Language of Arrest and Detention*. Basingstoke, U.K.: Palgrave Macmillan.

Sarangi, Srikant. 2001. On demarcating the space between "lay expertise" and "expert laity." *Text* 21(1/2): 3–12.

Sarangi, Srikant and Celia Roberts. 2002. Discoursal (mis)alignments in professional gatekeeping encounters. In Claire Kramsch (ed.) *Language Acquisition and Language Socialization: Ecological Perspectives*. London: Continuum. 197–227.

Shrader-Frechette, Kristin. 1994. *Ethics of Scientific Research*. London: Rowman and Littlefield.

Shuy, Roger. 1997. Ten unanswered language questions about Miranda. *Forensic Linguistics* 4(2): 175–196.

Shuy, Roger. 1998. *The Language of Confession, Interrogation, and Deception*. Thousand Oaks: Sage Publications Ltd.

Solan, Lawrence and Peter Tiersma. 2005. *Speaking of Crime: The Language of Criminal Justice*. Chicago: University of Chicago Press.

Stevens, Peter and David Harper. 2007. Professional accounts of electroconvulsive therapy: A discourse analysis. *Social Science and Medicine* 64(7): 1475–1486.

Stokoe, Elizabeth and Derek Edwards. 2008. "Did you have permission to smash your neighbour's door?" Silly questions and their answers in police-suspect interrogations. *Discourse Studies* 10(1): 89–111.

Stokoe, Elizabeth and Derek Edwards. 2009. Asking ostensibly silly questions in police-suspect interrogations. In Alice Freed and Susan Ehrlich (eds.) *Why Do You Ask? The Function of Questions in Institutional Discourse*. Oxford: Oxford University Press. 108–132.

Terms of Service; Didn't Read (ToS;DR). 2014. Home page. Retrieved November 21, 2014, from http://tosdr.org.

Thurlow, Crispin and Katherine Bell. 2009. Against technologization: Young people's new media discourse as creative cultural practice. *Journal of Computer-Mediated Communication* 14(4): 1038–1049.

Tiersma, Peter. 2007. The language of consent in rape law. In Janet Cotterill (ed.) *The Language of Sexual Crime*. Basingstoke, U.K.: Palgrave Macmillan. 83–103.

Victim Support. 2014. Home Page. Retrieved November 21, 2014, from http://www.victimsupport.org.uk.

Wiles, Rose, Vikki Charles, Graham Crow and Sue Heath. 2006. Researching researchers: Lessons for research ethics. *Qualitative Research* 6(3): 283–299.

Young, Amanda, Loel Kim, Shu Li, Justin Baker, Michael Schmidt, Jonathan Camp and Raymond Barfield. 2010. Agency and communication challenges in discussions of informed consent in pediatric cancer research. *Qualitative Health Research* 20(5): 628–643.

Zoller, Heather. 2003. Health on the line: Identity and disciplinary control in employee occupational health and safety discourse. *Journal of Applied Communication Research* 31(2): 118–139.

6

Transparent and Opaque Consent in Contract Formation

Lawrence M. Solan

Introduction

In this chapter I address whether people have really agreed to terms in U.S. form contracts. Of course, hardly anyone reads these documents before signing or clicking. By taking our chances we get leases, mobile phone service, internet service, home videos, software licenses, insurance policies, loans for the purchasing of cars and homes, credit cards, and many other things that we value greatly. For the most part, such documents are enforceable under law, subject to scrutiny for fraud, unconscionable terms (see Corbin 2014 vol. 7: §§ 28.13 and 29.1), and, in some cases, compliance with regulatory standards.

I argue that the notion that one has consented to terms with which one has no familiarity is licensed by a peculiar ambiguity in the relationship between verbs of psychological content (such as *consent, agree, believe, want*) and their objects. In particular, when the object of an agreement is stated as a definite description, such as "the terms of this agreement," rather than by naming the terms themselves, we can alternatively understand that description as shorthand for a list of things that the speaker had in mind or simply as a nonspecific characterization. Following the terminology used in some of the philosophical literature, I refer to these understandings respectively as *transparent* and *opaque* consent to contractual terms. This ambiguity is

---

The author is the Don Forchelli Professor of Law, Brooklyn Law School. My thanks to Janet Ainsworth, Jaap Baaij, Randy Barnett, Brian Bix, Neil B. Cohen, Ted Janger, Bailey Kuklin, Donna Jo Napoli, Stephen Neale, Barbara Partee, Craige Roberts, and Gideon Rosen for valuable suggestions. Earlier versions were presented at workshops at John Marshall Law School, the University of Hamburg Law School (sponsored by DAJV), and the Pacific McGeorge School of Law. I benefited from helpful comments at each of these presentations. I also wish to thank Teisha Ruggiero and Elliott Siebers for their excellent work as research assistants. This work was supported by a Dean's Summer Research Stipend from Brooklyn Law School.

harmless and goes unnoticed when the terms are simple. For example, "I agree to buy your car for $2,500" and "I agree to your terms," amount to the same thing when the terms are that I will buy your car for $2,500. However, the ambiguity makes a great deal of difference when we consider more complex contracts. "I agree to your terms" can mean that either I agree to each member of the list of terms or, as a general matter, I agree to be bound by the terms, whatever they are and whether or not I know what they are.

As commercial life has moved more and more from transparent to opaque agreement, the law has not adequately responded. Rather, it has accepted opaque consent as adequate to form a contract without adjusting contract doctrines to respond to this historical development. Radin (2012) refers to this shift in the nature of consent as "normative degradation." I argue here that this degradation is licensed (although by no means required) by the ambiguity in the concept of consent.

Judges assume that their only two options for interpreting consent are the following: to agree to your terms I must agree to each of them specifically, that is, transparently, or to agree to your terms, I may agree to all of them opaquely. Missing is the option of construing the agreement as, say, specific agreement to certain key terms (terms that should be brought to the consenting party's attention), and as a general agreement to other terms, which, perhaps, are less salient. The all-or-nothing concept of consent has made judges hesitant to restrict opaque contractual terms to those that meet the reasonable expectations of the consenting party. The resistance to the possibility of a hybrid form of consent, or to insisting upon enforcing only those opaque contractual terms that meet peoples' reasonable expectations, leaves American contract law with very few devices for responding to the realities of modern commerce. This article describes the operative ambiguity and its ramifications for the law governing consumer transactions. It further compares the American legal doctrines to those of the European Union, whose consumer law includes some of the protective legal devices that American law has rejected.

Opaque Contexts in Natural Language

Depending on how we understand *consent*, it is legitimate to say that a consumer signing a form contract has manifested consent, and it is possible to say that the same consumer has not manifested consent. The ambiguity stems from the fact that words like *consent* and *agree* create what philosophers and linguists call an *opaque* context, a phenomenon that has produced substantial literature (see, e.g., Quine 1960: 138–156). Consider the following example, adapted from an article by the linguist-philosopher Barbara Partee (1974):

Tom believes that a student in my class is a spy.

This sentence has two distinct meanings, elaborated below:

Tom believes that a student in my class, say Frances, is a spy.

Tom believes that some unidentified student in my class is a spy.

The first meaning is called the referential, or transparent, one. The phrase "a student in my class" is used to refer to a particular student in my class. The second meaning is the opaque meaning. The identity of a student in my class is opaque to my description.

Note that the same ambiguity holds when we produce a sentence with a definite description, instead of the indefinite "a student in my class." (See Partee 1974; Ludlow and Neale 1991; Chierchia and McConnell-Ginet 1996: 244; Ludlow and Neale 2006.) Consider this example:

Bond believes that the author of this letter is a spy.

On one reading, the speaker refers to a particular author, whom Bond believes to be a spy. On the other, Bond believes there to exist an individual who is both the author of this letter and a spy.

Significantly, as Partee points out, contexts in which opaque readings are possible also allow for transparent readings. The converse, however, is not true. This suggests that transparency is the general case, and that opacity occurs only in certain linguistic contexts. Everyday experience reinforces this view. If I say,

A student in my class is frequently disruptive.

I most likely mean this in the transparent, referential sense. Even if I do not know that student's name, I do have a particular student in mind, and I am most likely conveying the fact that I have a particular student in mind. But it is also possible to understand this sentence to mean that with some frequency, some unidentified student in my class is disruptive. This is the opaque reading.

Significantly, the following syllogism holds for the transparent reading, but not the opaque one:

Bond believes that the author of this letter is a spy.

O'Leary is the author of this letter.

Therefore, Bond believes that O'Leary is a spy.

On the opaque reading, in which Bond does not know who wrote the letter—only that whichever person did write it must be a spy—the syllogism is false. The sentence says nothing about Bond's belief about O'Leary—only that there is a spy among the students in the class.

Now consider the following:

Tom consented to the terms of the cardholder agreement.

This sentence has both a transparent and an opaque reading. In the transparent reading, the speaker is saying that Tom has agreed to $T_1, T_2, \ldots T_n$ for each term in the contract. But it can also be understood opaquely to mean that whatever the terms, Tom agreed to abide by them even if they were not identifiable to him at the time. Thus, like *belief, consent* creates an opaque context. Both readings seem natural enough, and context is likely to determine which of the two is intended.

The examples discussed above point to an observation made by Russell (1905): definite descriptions (e.g., "the author of this letter" and "the terms of the cardholder agreement") are not the same as names, even though we sometimes use them as descriptions of individuals whom we are able to identify. Philosophers Ludlow and Neale (1991: 173) develop this point further: "So on Russell's account, where we have a thought *about* a particular individual, we entertain a singular proposition; where we only have a thought to the effect that a unique individual satisfies some description, we entertain a general proposition." See also Ludlow and Neale (2006) for discussion of differing explanatory accounts of these and related phenomena.

Furthermore, the opaque contexts discussed above create ambiguity—not vagueness. The distinction between ambiguity and vagueness can be important in legal settings (Solan 2010; Poscher 2012). While vagueness is about borderline cases with fuzzy boundaries, ambiguity is an all-or-nothing affair—as the distinct meanings of *bank* (river bank vs. savings bank) illustrate. This suggests that judges who wish to remain loyal to the notion that *consent* is at the core of contract formation will choose one or the other of the two understandings of the term as seems adequate in any given case.

With these two distinct choices available to them, judges have had difficulty finding some middle ground between transparent and opaque contract formation. This is because opaque contexts do not create a continuum of understanding, which is the hallmark of vagueness. If, for example, a publishing contract includes the distribution of pamphlets, but not books, we might have trouble deciding whether a particular volume is one or the other because it seems to be on the borderline. Such instances of vagueness invite us to make judgments at the margin in a way that is not possible with the ambiguity generated by opaque contexts.[1]

THE AMBIGUOUS NATURE OF CONSENT

Now, let us turn to the law of contracts. I agree with Barnett's position that the essence of contract law is consent (see Barnett 1986; Solan 2007; Barnett 2012).

Bell (2010: 20) observes that about half of the sections in the Second Restatement of Contracts concern the concept of consent. (For readers not familiar with American contract law, the Restatement is a multivolume treatise that has no special legal standing, but is enormously influential on judges making common-law rulings in contract cases; see American Law Institute 1981). Consenting is to commit oneself voluntarily to act in accordance with the terms of the contract, or to subject oneself to whatever consequences the law imposes. What counts as consent in contract law is much the same as what counts as a valid speech act in other legal contexts: one must act in a way that leads the other party to believe that one has consented. Intention to bind oneself legally does not matter as long as one acts in a way that causes the other party to reasonably infer such intent.

Other legal acts work the same way. The law of contracts uses both "agreement" and "assent" in addition to "consent." Their meanings differ in subtle ways not relevant to this chapter, and they are all subject to the ambiguity I describe. Criminal acts, such as "threats," work similarly in this respect. If you are held up at an ATM machine at gunpoint, the mugger cannot successfully defend himself by claiming that he never intended to shoot you. You had a right to feel threatened by virtue of the way he behaved (see Tiersma and Solan 2012).[2]

Returning to the ambiguity between transparent and opaque consent, commercial life has become commodified to a point where actual consent to individual terms occurs much less frequently than does blanket consent to a group of unread terms, especially in consumer contracts (see Burke 2000; Hillman and Rachlinski 2002). The law governing contract formation, in turn, has accommodated this change by shifting from the transparent notion of consent to the opaque notion of consent—without announcing or even noticing the shift. The availability of both readings is clear enough: on one reading, the parties have agreed to the specific terms themselves; on the other reading, they have not. My argument here is that this ambiguity is what has licensed the law to quietly shift away from enforcing agreements consented to transparently to enforcing agreements consented to opaquely.

Thus, as in the earlier example, the following syllogism is true only under the transparent reading of *consent*:

> Max agreed to the terms of the contract.
>
> The contract requires Max to arbitrate any disputes in Guam.
>
> Max agreed that he would arbitrate any disputes in Guam.

Under the transparent interpretation, Max agreed to arbitrate any disputes in Guam only if Max read and understood the contract before signing it, noticed the arbitration clause, and agreed to it (perhaps because he didn't think anything important would depend upon it). If he did not read and accept that specific term, then he did not agree to it in this transparent sense. But there is another reading—the opaque reading—in which Max agreed only generally to the terms of the contract without knowing what the terms were. Under this reading, Max indeed did consent, and therefore may well be legally bound to arbitrate in Guam by virtue of having agreed to the terms of the contract, whether or not he even knew that such a clause existed. For that matter, he may not know what arbitration is. Significantly, all consent clauses in which an individual is asked to agree to a general description (i.e., to "the terms of the user agreement") are ambiguous in this sense.

Many doctrines in contract law assume transparency. For example, Section 201 of the Second Restatement, the basic rule governing contract interpretation, states: "Where the parties have attached the same meaning to a promise or agreement or a term thereof, it is interpreted in accordance with that meaning." Not only is this provision subjective in nature, but it also contemplates that the parties actually know and comprehend the terms of the agreement. That is, the Restatement assumes transparency. Doctrines such as "offer," "acceptance," and "consideration" also assume transparency.[3] In fact, almost all classic contract cases studied in American law schools are cases concerning transparent contracts. Although form contracts are nothing new (see Rakoff 1983 for some history), students study opaque consent in the context of what it means for a contract to be unconscionable,[4] but not in the context of core contract doctrines. Those are all motivated by cases in which the actual terms are articulated.

Were the legal system to require transparent consent in all contracts, virtually all consumer form contracts would be unenforceable. The consumer would correctly testify that he did not know what the contract required of him. The drafter, in turn, would either know that the consenting party did not read the agreement, or have no idea one way or the other whether he did, which would leave the consumer's testimony uncontroverted. As currently formulated, however, contract law makes these inquiries largely irrelevant. Signing a document may constitute a manifestation of the required state of mind—namely, opaque consent—and courts so hold.

Once courts accept opaque consent, a signature constitutes adequate manifestation of assent no matter what the signer's state of mind. To some extent, such a stance is inevitable. How can the law possibly require that the terms of your internet service not apply unless you take and pass a comprehension test to prove your transparent consent at the time you subscribe to the service? The commodification of the provision of goods and services may therefore come at the cost of transparency, but it has also resulted in the provision of inexpensive and largely efficient services, including at-home internet shopping in a competitive marketplace.

Thus, while I sympathize with some of the suggestions of writers who criticize current contract law as perverting the nature of contract formation, I do not agree that opaque consent is no consent (see, e.g., Meyerson 1993: 1265; White and Mansfield 2002). On the contrary, opaque consent is an actual state of mind, subject to manifestation (i.e., through a signature or a click of a mouse). But it is not agreement to individual terms, as some courts hold. Rather, it is agreement to delegate the statement of contractual rights and obligations to the other party, the drafter of the agreement. Thus, I would accept both Bix's (2010) characterization of transparent consent as consent "in the robust sense," and Radin's (2012) characterization of opaque consent as "normatively degraded."[5]

My argument here is not, then, that consent in contract formation should be limited to transparent consent. My argument, instead, is that contract doctrines, in general, have continued under the assumption—no longer justified—that consent to terms continues to mean consent to specific terms. Consequently, the shift from transparent to opaque consent invites a reexamination of a number of doctrines within the law of contract. In a world where you know that the used car you bought from your neighbor for $800 is a clunker, it is reasonable for contract law to set the bar high for undoing the transaction based on the subsequent claim that you overpaid, assuming you were not deceived in some way. Thus, courts rarely hold that a contract is unconscionable merely because the price is too high; and arguing a failure of consideration is even less likely to succeed in such cases. But in a world in which you have no real understanding of what you have committed to—nor could you without not only reading and understanding a very long document, but also devising a series of hypotheticals about what might go wrong to your disadvantage—stronger regulation may be in order. I return to this below.

THE OBJECTIVE THEORY OF CONTRACTS AND THE DUTY TO READ

As noted above, American contract law does not generally require actual psychological agreement for a contract to be formed. Instead, it requires a reasonable manifestation of assent. This is what is meant by the "objective theory" of contracts. Courts evaluate the actions of the parties from the perspective of a reasonable person, and make no serious inquiry into the parties' actual states of mind.[6] Because a signature is the prototype of manifested assent, it may be tempting to try to explain the acceptance of opaque consent as an application of the objective theory to consumer form contracts. This argument is fallacious because, as discussed below, opaque consent would be valid under either subjective or objective standards.

The objective theory developed in the middle of the 19th century largely as a means of providing stability in contract interpretation, taking away from litigants the opportunity to argue that they did not mean what they said or signed.[7] Holmes (1899: 417–418) had earlier espoused the objective approach:

> [Even a whole contract] does not disclose one meaning conclusively according to the laws of language. Thereupon we ask, not what this man meant, but what those words would mean in the mouth of a normal speaker of English, using them in the circumstances in which they were used, and it is to the end of answering this last question that we let in evidence as to what the circumstances were. But the normal speaker of English is merely a special variety, a literary form, so to speak, of our old friend the prudent man. He is external to the particular writer, and a reference to him as the criterion is simply another instance of the externality of the law.

The expression "objective theory of contract" was not itself, however, put into use in American legal discourse until Williston (1922: 2731, 2795) published his treatise on contracts. Law journal articles soon followed, in part anticipating the publication of the first *Restatement of the Law of Contracts* under Williston's stewardship.

While opacity and objectivity go hand in hand, they are not the same thing, as Table 6.1 shows. If transparency were a result of the objective theory, we would expect the columns to align. Instead, it is the rows that align.

A person who signs an unread contract has given opaque consent that is both subjective and objective. Subjective consent arises from the fact that the consenting party knew he was binding himself to the agreement when he signed it—whatever the terms. Objective consent arises from the fact that the drafting party has a right to believe that the consenting party has opaquely agreed to the terms based on his signature. Thus, objectivity is irrelevant when consent is opaque. The party is bound under either an objective or a subjective approach.

Now consider whether there is transparent consent in such a case. By definition, there is not. Transparency requires that the consumer knew the contract's terms and agreed to them. While one may argue that the person who signs a form contract has transparently consented under an objective (but not a subjective) theory because the drafting party has the right to assume that the contract was read and understood, such an approach would introduce a legal fiction totally at odds with everyday experience. The contract was not, in fact, read and understood. Yet, the objective theory and opaque consent

TABLE 6.1

Did you legally consent to the terms of a contract that you signed, but didn't read?

	Objective	Subjective
Transparent	No	No
Opaque	Yes	Yes

are related, because both doctrines eschew the requirement that the consenting party actually understood and consented to the individual terms of the contract. Occasionally, judges do indeed refer to the objective theory as the reason that an individual should be bound by an agreement that she did not read. Consider the following quote from a federal court applying the law of Connecticut:

> The general rule is that where a person of mature years, who can read and write, signs or accepts a formal written contract affecting his pecuniary interests, it is his duty to read it, and notice of its contents will be imputed to him if he negligently fails to do so.[8]

This duty to read rule derives from the objective theory of contracts, under which one party to a contract must be permitted to rely on the manifested assent demonstrated by the other party's signature (or action) without fear that the latter may subsequently void the contract by claiming failure to read or understand. The judge clearly got the law right: If you did not read your contract but signed it anyway, you are likely to be bound by its terms regardless. But the judge's reasoning is faulty because the same result would have held under a subjective theory of contract, assuming that the policyholder was aware that he had signed something binding him to the terms of his policy.

Instead of resorting to the objective theory, most judges engage the following justification for enforcing unread agreements: the consenting party had every opportunity to read the contract, which would have led either to transparent consent or to rejection of the terms. But the party did not exercise that right. Therefore, it is fair enough to enforce the terms of the contract anyway. Judges generally have very little sympathy with those who claim not to be bound by contracts that they have signed, but did not read. The principle is sometimes called the "duty to read" rule (Slawson 1996: 21). The aversion to such claims goes so far as to hold both illiterate (White and Mansfield 2002) and non-English speakers (Miller 2009) responsible for the content of whatever contracts they sign. As one federal court of appeals has put it, "In the absence of fraud, the fact that an offeree cannot read, write, speak, or understand the English language is immaterial to whether an English-language agreement the offeree executes is enforceable."[9]

Using the Lexis state and federal court library, I conducted a search of cases that contain various expressions that judges use to indicate an obligation to read a contract or suffer the consequences. Table 6.2 tallies the occurrences of the phrase "did not read," "failed to read," and "duty to read" within three words of "contract or agreement," for the past four decades.

These expressions are not the only ones that describe cases of this type, but the trends over time are clear enough. While the somewhat more derogatory "failed to read" is used less often, the patterns of usage are largely the same. The significant increase in the usage of these expressions since 1980

TABLE 6.2

Federal and state cases containing "contract or agreement" within three words of "did not read" and "failed to read" and "duty to read"

	"Did not read"	"Failed to read"	"Duty to read"
1970–1979	77	14	11
1980–1989	149	46	30
1990–1999	228	59	61
2000–2009	428	90	134

demonstrates a growing judicial reluctance to engage in serious inquiry into the terms of a contract that is signed by both parties. Moreover, this increase comes at a time when more and more contracts are consented to only opaquely.

If all that matters is whether one has shown a reasonable manifestation of assent, and opaque consent is good enough for that purpose, then it should make no legal difference whether the person read or understood the contract at all, as the Third Circuit makes clear. What the "duty to read" cases accomplish, then, is to enable courts to lash out at the consenting party for not performing his or her duty as a contracting party, while absolving the legal system of moral responsibility for enforcing contractual terms under such circumstances. Judges ridicule consumers for not taking advantage of their opportunity to consent transparently, and then hold them to what they have consented to opaquely. What the courts do not say is that, in most cases, the individual would not have benefited from reading the contract. Without knowing what is likely to go wrong, and keeping these inferred pitfalls in mind—and without feeling some power to negotiate—there is really no point to reading the contract in the first place. Judges also do not announce in open court that they do not read their form contracts either, although some refreshing acknowledgments are reported from time to time.[10]

Courts, legislatures, and scholars are aware of the inadequacy of requiring a party to read the terms of form contracts, and have developed some doctrines in response. However, as we shall see, the growth of the combination of opaque consent and the objective approach to contracts has made attempts to reform contract law through common law decision making largely ineffective.

Can the System Both Require Consent and Be Fair to Consumers?

Scholars and legislators have proposed two approaches to the issues raised in this chapter: first, provisions that do not meet the ordinary expectations of the consenting party should be considered unenforceable; second, sufficiently important terms should be consented to transparently in order for them to be enforced by a court. The first of these solutions is contained in the Second Restatement, and the second of them appears a few times in the Uniform Commercial Code. Neither, however, has received a friendly reception from judges. I suggest that this is so because both solutions appear to challenge the primacy of consent as the core concept in contract formation.

Before discussing the American law, though, it is worth pointing out that European law has contained for the past two decades a hybrid of transparent and opaque consent, further tempered by outlawing unfair terms. Directive 93/13/EEC states as follows:

> 1. A contractual term which has not been individually negotiated shall be regarded as unfair if, contrary to the requirement of good faith, it causes a significant imbalance in the parties' rights and obligations arising under the contract, to the detriment of the consumer.
> 2. A term shall always be regarded as not individually negotiated where it has been drafted in advance and the consumer has therefore not been able to influence the substance of the term, particularly in the context of a pre-formulated standard contract . . .
> 3. The Annex [to the Directive] shall contain an indicative and non-exhaustive list of the terms which may be regarded as unfair.[11]

Among the provisions contained in the Annex as presumptively and illustratively "unfair" and thus unenforceable are: "enabling the seller or supplier to terminate a contract of indeterminate duration without reasonable notice except where there are serious grounds for doing so"; and "enabling the seller or supplier to alter unilaterally without a valid reason any characteristics of the product or service to be provided."[12] By virtue of another provision, the price and the goods or services to be provided do not count as subject to analysis for unfairness so long as these terms are in "plain intelligible language."[13] Thus, it is assumed that when people sign a contract for mobile phone service they know what they are buying and how much they are paying. But the boilerplate language (called "general terms" in European law) is subject to regulation.

Note that the way to escape the prohibitions of the directive is through transparency. The directive applies only to provisions that are opaque (at least that is almost the case). As for opaque provisions, the "unconscionability" of American law is replaced by "unfairness" in European law, with many illustrations to guide judges in determining what is fair and what is unfair. Thus, sellers and service providers can weigh transparency against the likelihood that an opaque term will be considered unfair. This combination—valuing transparency and prohibiting unfair provisions in form contracts—has some roots in American law as well. But, as noted, neither has caught on with the judiciary.

THE REASONABLE EXPECTATIONS OF THE CONSENTING PARTY

Given the possible understandings of what constitutes an agreement, it should not be surprising to see some courts speak of assent in opaque terms, finding no difference between form contracts and any other contract. For example, in *Rory v. Continental Insurance Company*, decided in 2005, the Supreme Court of Michigan held:

> [U]nless a contract provision violates law or one of the traditional defenses to the enforceability of a contract applies, a court must construe and apply unambiguous contract provisions as written. We reiterate that the judiciary is without authority to modify unambiguous contracts or rebalance the contractual equities struck by the contracting parties because fundamental principles of contract law preclude such subjective post hoc judicial determinations of "reasonableness" as a basis upon which courts may refuse to enforce unambiguous contractual provisions.[14]

In that case, an insurance policy provided for a one-year limitations period for filing an uninsured motorist claim against the insurer. The statute of limitations for filing a tort suit against the party who allegedly caused the accident in Michigan is three years, and the statute for bringing a contracts claim is six years. The lower courts had ruled in favor of the policyholder, in part because it would be unreasonable to expect an accident victim to discover the insurance status of the other party quickly enough to bring a lawsuit well within the first year after the accident, which is what he would have had to do in order to leave time to file a claim against the insurer, thereby undermining the three-year tort deadline.

The Michigan Supreme Court left open traditional contract defenses such as fraud, duress, and unconscionability, but closed the door on analyses that would question the reasonableness of the shortened limitations period contained in the contract. The court based its opinion on freedom of contract: "Courts enforce contracts according to their unambiguous terms because doing so respects the freedom of individuals freely to arrange their affairs via contract" (*Rory*: 30).

In contrast, some courts also driven by concerns of individual autonomy, have accepted the position that the Supreme Court of Michigan rejects. These courts have held that terms in form contracts that do not conform to the reasonable expectations of the consumer should not be enforced. These courts do not require transparent assent, but give additional protection to those who have assented only opaquely. The doctrine, first articulated by Keeton (1970: 963–965), has been applied principally in the context of disputes over the scope of exclusions in insurance policies (Stempel 1998).[15] In his insightful book, Slawson (1996: 44–73) describes this principle as having broader application than has generally been appreciated, and suggests that courts analyze form contracts more generally to determine whether a reasonable consumer would be aware of and agree to its various terms.

A version of the reasonable expectations doctrine is stated in Section 211 of the Second Restatement:

> **§ 211 Standardized Agreements**
>
> (1) Except as stated in Subsection (3), where a party to an agreement signs or otherwise manifests assent to a writing and has reason to believe that like writings are regularly used to embody terms of agreements of the same type, he adopts the writing as an integrated agreement with respect to the terms included in the writing.
> (2) Such a writing is interpreted wherever reasonable as treating alike all those similarly situated, without regard to their knowledge or understanding of the standard terms of the writing.
> (3) Where the other party has reason to believe that the party manifesting such assent would not do so if he knew that the writing contained a particular term, the term is not part of the agreement.[16]

Section (1) holds standard form contracts to be valid, provided that the party signing the contract understands it to be a standard contract. It recognizes the validity of opaque assent. Parties who sign contracts are bound to their terms if it reasonably appears that they intended to bind themselves, regardless of whether they understood or even read the contract's provisions.

But the Restatement also pays some deference to transparency. Subsection (3) can be understood as disallowing terms that the drafter knows the consumer does not accept, but it can also be understood as disallowing terms that a reasonable business would assume that a consumer would not accept, because no reasonable person would accept such terms. The provision brings a degree of transparency back into form contracts. Sellers have an obligation to write provisions that an attentive buyer would be likely to accept in the transparent sense, even if the buyer has already opaquely consented.

In recent years courts have not embraced the reasonable expectations doctrine as espoused in the Second Restatement. Like Michigan, some states reject the doctrine outright.[17] Others use the doctrine to resolve ambiguities.[18] Still others, like Arizona, adopt a version that applies in limited circumstances:

> There are a limited variety of situations in which Arizona courts will apply the reasonable expectations doctrine to defeat unambiguous boilerplate insurance terms: (1) where the contract terms, although not ambiguous to the court, cannot be understood by the reasonably intelligent consumer who might check on his or her rights, the court will interpret them in light of the objective, reasonable expectations of the average insured; (2) where the insured did not receive full and adequate notice of

> the term in question, and the provision is either unusual or unexpected, or one that emasculates apparent coverage; (3) where some activity which can be reasonably attributed to the insurer would create an objective impression of coverage in the mind of a reasonable insured; and (4) where some activity reasonably attributable to the insurer has induced a particular insured reasonably to believe that he has coverage, although such coverage is expressly and unambiguously denied by the policy.[19]

Like the Second Restatement, Arizona's approach attempts to balance transparency and opacity: it allows opaque assent in general, but it limits the extent to which businesses may take advantage of it. A business may not insert terms that an aware consumer would not have agreed to under ordinary circumstances.

Yet concern about the reasonableness of the terms of form contracts persists, often under the rubric of unconscionability. Even courts that enforce form contracts to the letter are willing to examine the contract to determine whether its terms are unconscionable.[20] The Supreme Court of Michigan specifically noted that the plaintiff in *Rory v. Continental Ins. Co.* had failed to plead traditional contract defenses, including unconscionability, when it granted judgment to the insurance company.[21] Typically, some combination of procedural and substantive unconscionability is necessary to justify the avoidance of a clear contractual term.[22] What combinations will suffice, however, span a wide gamut. Yet to the extent that unconscionability doctrine purports to deny the enforcement of unreasonable terms in form contracts, the doctrine acts as a substitute for the reasonableness analysis that accompanies the recognition of transparency.

REQUIRING THAT CERTAIN TERMS BE TRANSPARENT

An attractive approach to this problem has been developed by Korobkin (2003). Writing in the law and economics tradition, Korobkin first notes that courts are most prone to refuse to enforce a term because it is unconscionable in consumer form contracts. When should courts invalidate contractual provisions? The provisions least justifiable are those that are both inefficient and not salient to consumers who must decide whether to enter into the contract. While price is virtually always a salient provision of a consumer contract, provisions such as dispute resolution procedures and limitations on damages are not. Korobkin advocates for adjustments to be made in the law governing unconscionability analysis to take questions of saliency and efficiency into account.

Saliency and efficiency also serve as reasonably good measures for identifying terms of a contract that were probably not reached through mutual assent, at least in its transparent sense, either because one of the parties was totally unaware of them, or because this party failed to understand their significance. To use some of Korobkin's examples, it may well be efficient to eliminate consequential damages in the sale of an inexpensive product when their inclusion would lead to a significant increase in the product's price. On the other hand, efficiency is probably reduced when a manufacturer can insulate itself from any responsibility for a poorly made product by including in a contract an arbitration clause that makes dispute resolution too expensive given the value of the product.

Whether one accepts Korobkin's approach to form contracts or some other approach, it is important to note that form contracts are not standard agreements in at least one legally relevant sense. Barnett, for example, explains why being bound to an agreement to which one has consented only opaquely creates difficulty for those who regard consent as the core of contractual liability: "Or perhaps the better formulation is that, if most reasonable persons would not have agreed to such a term, then the other party cannot assume consent to be bound to such a term unless it is made visible. In this way, hypothetical consent is perhaps the best way we have to determine actual consent to unread terms" (Barnett 2002: 638). As noted, contract law generally assumes the parties' transparent assent to a transaction, whereas form contracts generally are based upon an opaque notion of assent. As such, it is not unreasonable to insist that significant terms in form contracts be made transparent. Rakoff (1983: 1250–1255) referred to distinguishing between terms that must be *visible* and those that may remain *invisible*, buried in the boilerplate.

For purposes of this chapter, what is particularly interesting about this entire discussion is the inability of the concept of *consent* itself to handle the problem. Let us assume, consistent with the views of both Korobkin and Barnett, that a fair contract law regime should require that important terms be specifically brought to the attention of the individual who will be bound by them. In other words, opaque consent suffices for the most part, but with respect to such things as price, duration of an obligation, penalties for early cancellation, and perhaps waiver of consequential damages, transparency is required.

Consider, for example, your mobile phone service agreement. You should know that you are paying $50 per month; what that $50 includes and does not include; how long you must keep the service you have without being penalized for canceling; and the fact that if you are on an important business call and the cell phone service fails, causing you to lose a deal, the company providing the cell phone service cannot be held responsible for your business loss. Rather, you can recover only part of your monthly fee that went to paying for the time during which you did not have the service.

Note that this approach requires actual consent of one form or the other. The reasonable expectations doctrine, in contrast, is somewhat more of a challenge, even to opaque consent. Once a party has consented, courts are stepping in and protecting one side over the other. The argument there must be, then, as Slawson (1996) puts it, that the manifestation of assent cannot be reasonable if the terms themselves are not reasonable and were not brought to the party's attention. This, to my mind, is an entirely sensible argument, but it does require more probing into the actual terms of the contract, a probing in which courts are reluctant to engage once they have already accepted opaque consent as sufficient. I do not defend this reluctance to probe, but it does explain why, decade after decade, courts have been willing to examine form contracts only with respect to whether their formation and terms violate such doctrines as unconscionability, a standard that is hard to meet, and which courts are reluctant to expand.

None of this, however, explains why proposals such as those by Korobkin and Barnett have not been adopted as part of the organic development of common law doctrine. If I am right that both transparent and opaque consent are indeed consent, one would expect those who see consent as the essence of contract law to be comfortable with a mix-and-match approach between the two: transparent consent when it appears necessary to achieve adequate knowledge to support the vision of autonomy in contract law, and opaque consent the remainder of the time, such as with respect to all of the boilerplate language in form contracts. Simply initialing four or five places, or checking a few boxes specifically while online, would be sufficient to accomplish this goal.

It is easy enough to attribute this reluctance to the conservative nature of the judiciary, especially in the past few decades, but I do not regard that as much of an explanation. Not all judges are politically conservative, yet judges of all political stripes adhere to the doctrinal positions described in this chapter. My sense is that the stability of the adherence to opacity in contract law stems from an observation I made earlier: consenting to a definite description of a contract is ambiguous; this ambiguity lends to two notions of consent (opaqueness and transparency); and these two readings are distinct. Consistent with the way we interpret other ambiguous terms, we conceptualize consent only one way at a time. As Chomsky (2000) points out, it is very difficult to switch from one meaning to another when words can be used in distinct senses. That is why it seems very odd to say such things as "Barnett wrote an extremely interesting book. It weighs 14 ounces." I've switched from using "book" to refer to the book's intellectual content using "book" to refer to the book as a physical object. Or consider this: "London, which takes up about 611 square miles, loves its Indian restaurants." Here, I have switched from using "London" to refer to political boundaries, to using "London" to refer to the population (or at least a characterization of some representative part of the population). Thus, we can use such words one way or the other, but not both ways at the same time, even though we understand them to mean both things.

What makes this fact particularly interesting is that unlike London, when it comes to consent, it is possible to understand transparency as a continuum. Just as a person can be more or less tall, an agreement can be more or less transparent depending on how much of it was transparently agreed upon. In other words, "transparent" is a "graded adjective" (Kennedy 2007 and references cited therein). That is true not only with respect to the rather technical linguistic issue upon which this chapter is built, but with respect to other uses of the term "transparent." Nonetheless, while we *can* understand transparency as a continuum, we do not do so in ordinary life. Transparency in the sense discussed here is not a graded category. Rather, it is one of two possible but distinct relationships between the act of consenting (or assenting or agreeing) on the one hand, and a description of the object of consent on the other. The ambiguity does not arise when the term of the agreement is specified, as in an agreement that Buyer will purchase Seller's used Toyota Camry for $5,000. But it does arise, as Russell first discussed a century ago, when we use a definite description like "the terms of the contract" in lieu of the terms themselves.

This fact, I believe, is what has allowed courts to shift the doctrine of consent from transparent consent to opaque consent over the course of a century, without requiring a hybrid version of consent that falls somewhere between transparency and opacity, and that would comport with what so many people writing about the issue would deem to be a fair resolution. The hybrid solution is inconsistent with our understanding of consent as an all-or-nothing proposition.

This inconsistency should not, however, stop the legal system from making the small adjustment that I suggest. Requiring some combination of transparent and opaque consent in the case of form contracts is a far cry from abandoning the concept of consent altogether, even if we typically do not think of consent in this mixed form in everyday life. While courts have not yet been willing to adopt this approach, there is at least some support in the legislatures. For example, the Uniform Commercial Code requires that a provision in a contract for the sale of goods that excludes the right to modify or rescind the contract except in a written agreement must itself be separately signed.[23] It also requires that if the offeree includes on a form that an offer is to be held open for a particular amount of time, it must be "separately signed by the offeror."[24]

It is precisely this type of blend of transparent and opaque consent that the law should develop through various legal institutions. If transparent consent is valid consent and opaque consent is valid consent, then it will do little damage to the values underlying the law of contracts to require some combination of the two when fairness so demands.

Conclusion

I have argued in this chapter that the relationship between consent and the thing being consented to is ambiguous in contexts important to the law. Consenting to terms can either be shorthand for consenting to the individual terms themselves, or it can refer to blanket consent, regardless of whether the consenting party even knows what the terms are. Using terminology from the philosophy of language, I refer to these as transparent and opaque consent, respectively.

This chapter also reinforces a point made by others in various contexts: while insights from the philosophy of language can help to elucidate the cognitive foundation of longstanding disagreements in the law of contracts, the ultimate answer of how to deal with form contracts must be a legal one. Others have commented on the limited use of particular philosophies of language in the determination of legal rules (see Patterson 1995; Bix 2003; Green 2003; Rosen 2011; Bix 2012). Nonetheless, advances in such fields as linguistics, philosophy, and psychology can provide important insights into cognitive sources of disagreements and biases that may explain the prevalence of various legal rules.

Contract law is heavily dependent upon the concept of consent, making transparent and opaque meanings available for judges who construe contractual terms. Crucially, the ambiguity permits us to construe consent one way or the other, but not both ways at the same time. This fact causes judges to overlook opportunities to create hybrid rules, requiring, for example, that important terms be made transparent, while allowing other terms to remain opaque.

In a world in which so much of commerce is accomplished through various forms that people cannot be expected to read, courts should come to an understanding that a blended approach to transparency does not do serious harm to the consent requirement, since both transparent and opaque consent are species of consent. However, if the judges continue to enforce lengthy form contracts on those whose consent is opaque, even with respect to crucial terms, they will eventually minimize the importance of consent as a practical matter, undermining their initial reasoning. For this reason, if judges are unwilling to effect change, legislators and regulators should step in to reintroduce transparency to the law of contracts.

Notes

1. It is worth noting that the kind of ambiguity discussed in this section does arise in various legal contexts. See generally (Rodes 1998). For specific examples, see Anderson

(2008) (Americans with Disabilities Act); Yaffe (2011) (state of mind in connection with criminal act).

2. I do not address in this chapter the important issue that arises when one gave the appearance of consent, but did so under duress or undue influence. In such cases, one can say that the person did not consent at all, or that the person consented, but the consent was involuntary, and thus legally null. See Bix (2010) for discussion such cases.

3. The classic case on consideration is *Hamer v. Sidway*, 27 N.E. 256 (1891). There, a promise to pay a teenaged nephew for refraining from smoking, drinking, swearing, or playing billiards for money until the age of 21 was enforced. It is almost universally included in casebooks. Offer and acceptance cases by definition involve discussion of the actual terms.

4. See, e.g., *Williams v. Walker-Thomas Furniture Co.*, 350 F.2d 445 (D.C. Cir. 1965).

5. Radin (2012: 96–97) argues that Bix (2010) lets the system off the hook too easily by accepting less than fully robust consent as adequate for contract formation in contemporary life. My sense is that I am also more comfortable with the notion of opaque consent constituting actual consent of some sort than is Radin, although she and I seem to be in accord about the normative consequences and the need for doctrinal adjustment.

6. At least this is the standard story. In fact, the actual state of mind of a party plays a more significant role than is advertised. For example, if it is clear that neither party intended to enter into a contract, but it would seem to a reasonable observer that they had, courts will not impose the contract upon them (see Barnett 1986, 2012; Solan 2007).

7. See Horwitz (1977). There is disagreement about this history. Perillo (2000) argues that objective approaches had been the norm through the history of the common law, with a brief flirtation with subjectivity in the early 19th century, creating the false impression that the objective turn in the late 19th and early 20th centuries was more radical than it really was.

8. *Ursini v. Goldman*, 118 Conn. 554, 562 (1934).

9. *Morales v. Sun Constructors, Inc.*, 541 F.3d 218, 222 (3d Cir. 2008).

10. Perhaps most famously, Judge Richard A. Posner, one of the leading legal intellectuals in the United States, admitted not having read the papers he signed to refinance his house. See "Judge Posner Admits He Didn't Read Boilerplate for Home Equity Loan," *ABA Journal*, Posted by Debra Cassens Weiss, June 23, 2010, available at http://www.abajournal.com/news/article/judge_posner_admits_he_didnt_read_boilerplate_for_home_equity_loan/.

11. Council Directive 93/13/EEC of April 5, 1993, on Unfair Terms in Consumer Contracts.

12. Id. at Annex (g) and (k).

13. Id. at Article 4(2).

14. *Rory v. Continental Ins. Co.*, 703 N.W.2d 23, 26 (2005).

15. The classic case is *C & J Fertilizer, Inc. v. Allied Mut. Ins. Co.*, 227 N.W.2d 169, 176 (Iowa 1975).

16. Restatement (Second) of Contracts § 211.

17. See, e.g., *Allen v. Prudential Property & Cas. Ins. Co.*, 839 P.2d 798 (Utah 1992).

18. See, e.g., *O'Donnell v. Blue Cross Blue Shield*, 76 P.3d 308, 315 (Wyo. 2003) ("Where insurance contract terms are clear and unambiguous, the reasonable expectations of the contracting parties are irrelevant to contract construction issues. A rule of construction that considers the reasonable expectations of the parties is of no assistance where

the policy terms are clear and unambiguous."); *Shepard v. Calfarm Life Ins. Co.*, 5 Cal. App. 4th 1067, 1076 (Cal. Ct. App., 1992) ("It is a basic principle of insurance contract interpretation that doubts, uncertainties and ambiguities arising out of policy language ordinarily should be resolved in favor of the insured in order to protect his reasonable expectation of coverage. [Citations.] It is also well established, however, that this rule of construction is applicable only when the policy language is found to be unclear."). For analysis, see Stempel (1998: 193).

19.*Gordinier v. Aetna Casualty & Sur. Co.*, 154 Ariz. 266, 273 (1987).

20. See *Brower v. Gateway 2000, Inc.*, 676 N.Y.S.2d 569 (App. Div. 1998).

21. 703 N.W.2d 23, 43 (2005).

22. Examples abound. For recent cases, see, e.g., *Society of Lloyds v. Reinhart*, 402 F.3d 982, 997 (10th Cir. 2005); *Nagrampa v. MailCoups, Inc.*, 401 F.3d 1024, 1027 (9th Cir. 2005); *Jenkins v. First Amer. Cash Advance of Ga.*, 400 F.3d 868, 875 (11th Cir. 2005); *Lovey v. Regent Blueshield of Idaho*, 72 P.3d 877, 883 (Idaho 2003).

23. UCC 2–209(2) (2012).

24. UCC 2–205 (2012).

References

American Law Institute. 1981. *The Restatement (Second) of Contracts*. Washington, D.C.: American Law Institute.

Anderson, Jill. 2008. Just semantics: The lost readings of the Americans with Disabilities Act. *Yale Law Journal* 117: 992–1069.

Barnett, Randy. 1986. A consent theory of contract. *Columbia Law Review* 86: 269–321.

Barnett, Randy. 2002. Consenting to form contracts. *Fordham Law Review* 71: 627–645.

Barnett, Randy. 2012. Contract is not promise: Contract is consent. *Suffolk University Law Review* 45: 647–665.

Bell, Tom. 2010. Graduated consent in contract and tort law: Toward a theory of justification. *Case Western Reserve Law Review* 61: 1–68.

Bix, Brian. 2003. Can theories of meaning and reference solve the problem of legal determinacy? *Ratio Juris* 16: 281–295.

Bix, Brian. 2010. Contracts. In Franklin Miller and Alan Wertheimer (eds.) *The Ethics of Consent: Theory and Practice*. Oxford: Oxford University Press. 251–279.

Bix, Brian. 2012. Legal interpretation and the philosophy of language. In Peter Tiersma and Lawrence Solan (eds.) *The Oxford Handbook of Language and Law*. Oxford: Oxford University Press. 145–155.

Burke, John. 2000. Contract as commodity: A nonfiction approach. *Seton Hall Legislation Journal* 24: 285–325.

Chierchia, Gennaro and Sally McConnell-Ginet. 1996. *Meaning and Grammar: An Introduction to Semantics*. Cambridge, Massachusetts: MIT Press.

Chomsky, Noam. 2000. *New Horizons in the Study of Language and Mind*. Cambridge: Cambridge University Press.

Corbin, Arthur. 2014. *Corbin on Contracts* (revised edition, Joseph Perillo, ed.). Lexis Electronic Resource.

Green, Michael. 2003. Dworkin's Fallacy, or what the philosophy of language can't teach us about the law. *Virginia Law Review* 89: 1897–1952.

Hillman, Robert and Jeffrey Rachlinski. 2002. Standard-form contracting in the electronic age. *New York University Law Review* 77: 429–495.

Holmes, Oliver Wendell. 1899. The theory of legal interpretation. *Harvard Law Review* 12: 417–420.

Horwitz, Morton. 1977. *The Transformation of American Law 1780–1860*. Cambridge, Massachusetts: Harvard University Press.

Keeton, Robert. 1970. Insurance law rights at variance with policy provisions. *Harvard Law Review* 83: 961–985.

Kennedy, Chris. 2007. Vagueness and grammar: The semantics of relative and absolute gradable adjectives. *Linguistics and Philosophy* 30: 1–45.

Korobkin, Russell. 2003. Bounded rationality, standard form contracts, and unconscionability. *University of Chicago Law Review* 70: 1203–1295.

Ludlow, Peter and Stephen Neale. 1991. Indefinite descriptions: In defense of Russell. *Linguistics & Philosophy* 14: 171–202.

Ludlow, Peter and Stephen Neale. 2006. Descriptions. In Michael Devitt and Richard Hanley (eds.) *The Blackwell Guide to the Philosophy of Language*. Malden, Massachusetts and Oxford, U.K.: Blackwell Publishing. 288–313.

Meyerson, Michael. 1993. The reunification of contract law: The objective theory of consumer form contracts. *University of Miami Law Review* 47: 1263–1333.

Miller, Lauren. 2009. Breaking the language barrier: The failure of the objective theory to promote fairness in language-barrier contracting. *Indiana Law Review* 43: 175–206.

Partee, Barbara Hall. 1974. Opacity and scope. In Milton Munitz and Peter Unger (eds.) *Semantics and Philosophy*. New York: New York University Press. 81–101.

Patterson, Dennis. 1995. Against a theory of meaning. *Washington University Law Quarterly* 73: 1153–1157.

Perillo, Joseph. 2000. The origins of the objective theory of contract formation and interpretation. *Fordham Law Review* 69: 427–477.

Poscher, Ralf. 2012. Ambiguity and vagueness in legal interpretation. In Peter Tiersma and Lawrence Solan (eds.) *The Oxford Handbook of Language and Law*. Oxford: Oxford University Press. 129–144.

Quine, Willard Van Orman. 1960. *Word and Object*. Cambridge, Massachusetts: MIT Press.

Radin, Margaret. 2012. *Boilerplate: The Fine Print, Vanishing Rights, and the Rule of Law*. Princeton, New Jersey: Princeton University Press.

Rakoff, Todd. 1983. Contracts of adhesion: An essay in reconstruction. *Harvard Law Review* 96: 1174–1284.

Rodes, Robert, Jr. 1998. De re and de dicto. *Notre Dame Law Review* 73: 627–636.

Rosen, Gideon. 2011. Textualism, and the law of the contract. In Andrei Marmor and Scott Soames (eds.) *Philosophical Foundations of Language in the Law*. Oxford: Oxford University Press. 130–164.

Russell, Bertrand. 1905. On denoting. *Mind* 14: 479–498.

Slawson, David. 1996. *Binding Promises: The Late 20th-Century Reformation of Contract Law*. Princeton, New Jersey: Princeton University Press.

Solan, Lawrence. 2007. Contract as agreement. *Notre Dame Law Review* 83: 353–408.

Solan, Lawrence. 2010. *The Language of Statutes: Laws and Their Interpretation.* Chicago: University of Chicago Press.

Stempel, Jeffrey. 1998. Unmet expectations: Undue restriction of the reasonable expectations approach and the misleading mythology of judicial role. *Connecticut Insurance Law Journal* 5: 181–293.

Tiersma, Peter and Lawrence Solan. 2012. The language of crime. In Peter Tiersma and Lawrence Solan (eds.) *The Oxford Handbook of Language and Law.* Oxford: Oxford University Press. 340–353.

White, Alan and Cathy Mansfield. 2002. Literacy and contract. *Stanford Law and Policy Review* 13: 233–266.

Williston, Samuel. 1922. *The Law of Contracts* (vol. 3). New York: Baker, Voorhis & Company.

Yaffe, Gideon. 2011. Trying to kill the dead: De dicto and de re intention in attempted crimes. In Andrei Marmor and Scott Soames (eds.) *Philosophical Foundations of Language in the Law.* Oxford: Oxford University Press. 184–216.

7

The Empty Performative?

INFORMED CONSENT TO GENETIC RESEARCH

John Conley, R. Jean Cadigan, and Arlene Davis

In this chapter we analyze the linguistic and discursive aspects of a specialized form of consent: *informed consent* given by people who contribute DNA samples to genomic biobanks, which are repositories of genetic material and derived data stored for present and future research. Our particular focus is on the understandings of informed consent expressed by research subjects. Our principal finding is that subjects express limited understanding of informed consent, and the understandings they do express have little in common with those of the research establishment.

Throughout the developed world, informed (or voluntary, as it was originally known) consent by individual medical research subjects has been a fundamental requirement since the 1947 Nuremburg Declaration, which was developed in response to the exposure of Nazi "medical" atrocities. In the United States, the doctrine of informed consent began to take on its current form following reports in the 1960s and 1970s by Henry Beecher (1966) and others who revealed the unethical treatment of research subjects in this country, most infamously in the 40-year Tuskegee Syphilis Study. These revelations punctured the illusion that researchers themselves, acting as moral agents, could be trusted as the arbiters of ethical research conduct. In response, a government-sponsored 1976 initiative called the Belmont Report (National Commission for the Protection of Human Subjects of Biomedical and Behavioral Research 1979) enshrined three ethical principles for human

---

The authors' professional titles are William Rand Kenan, Jr. Professor of Law; Research Assistant Professor of Social Medicine; and Associate Professor of Social Medicine at the University of North Carolina at Chapel Hill, and all are affiliated with the University's Center for Genomics and Society. The authors thank Josh Lance and Amanda Sherrin, students at the UNC School of Law, for their excellent research assistance.

subjects research: respect for persons, beneficence, and justice. These principles were operationalized in the 1991 Common Rule (US Department of Health and Human Services 1991), which governs nearly all federally funded research, with informed consent as its core premise. Under the Common Rule, all research involving human subjects must be approved and supervised by Institutional Review Boards (IRBs), and their mandate includes ensuring that all subjects give informed consent.

The informed consent requirement has proven especially difficult to implement in the genomic biobanking context. Medical research has traditionally involved single researchers or existing groups of researchers obtaining and using tissue samples for defined purposes, with appropriate disclosures to and the specific consent of the participants. With genomic biobanks, by contrast, the future uses of the samples may be unknown at the time of collection—indeed, unknowable, given the pace at which genetic research evolves—and, accordingly, traditional informed consent may be illusory if not impossible. In simplest terms, if you cannot inform subjects about what may be done with their DNA in the future, how can they give informed consent?

The Indeterminate Nature of Informed Consent to Research

Linguists and philosophers of language have long been interested in the nature of consent generally. Cowart (2003: 496–497), a philosopher, emphasizes that "there is still little agreement concerning how consent should be defined"; moreover, in legal contexts, "[u]nderstanding what it means to consent is further complicated by the fact that current legal conceptions are not necessarily grounded in argument; they typically depend on appeals to authority and precedent." In view of these levels of ambiguity and complexity, she suggests that "[a] possible starting point for developing an analysis of consent is speech act theory, since it offers a systematic approach for uncovering the complex relationship between uttering words and what one does by uttering them."

Taking up Cowart's suggestion, linguists have sometimes analyzed the giving of legal consent as an example of an illocutionary speech act. In the easy case, a person uses the performative "I consent." In harder cases, the speaker's utterance is ambiguous, and intent—or lack thereof—must be inferred from the pragmatic context, and then evaluated against a legal standard that may be ill-suited to take pragmatic complexity into account. Solan and Tiersma (2005), for example, examine the criminal law problem of "consensual" searches, where a court must determine whether a suspect effectively communicated consent to a police officer's request. In one case they discuss, "an officer asked [the defendant] if he 'minded if we looked in the trunk,' in response to which the man said nothing but opened the trunk"

(Solan and Tiersma 2005: 47). Just as in Cowart's framing of the problem, a judge faced with such facts must reach conclusions about the defendant's intent not by reference to a coherent definition of consent but by "appeals to authority and precedent"—that is, by lining up the "facts" (an immensely problematic concept in its own right) of the current case against those of prior cases decided by authoritative courts.

Informed consent to medical research illustrates the entirety of Cowart's dilemma, and more. Neither the law nor the applied ethics of medical research offers a definition of informed consent, let alone one "grounded in argument." Even "appeals to authority and precedent" are largely unavailing, as there is little to be found. Moreover, speech act theory may be of limited value. By signing an informed consent document, the subject nominally utters a performative akin to "I consent." However, as we shall see, available evidence about the pragmatic context suggests that those involved on the researcher side are ambivalent about just what illocutionary force is actually intended, while the subjects themselves express limited understanding of what they may be consenting to.

From the legal and research perspectives, informed consent to medical research is an elusive and unstable concept. Like many things in law (obscenity being the classic example), it has a "you know it when you see it" quality: the concept itself has no clear and concise definition, although it does have some identifying attributes. For example, the human subjects regulatory guidance issued by the US Department of Health and Human Services (2009), which reflects expert thinking at the intersection of law and medical ethics, provides an eight-part "Basic elements of informed consent" list that must be communicated to prospective subjects. These elements include a description of the research, "a description of any reasonably foreseeable risks or discomforts to the subject," "a description of any benefits to the subject," a statement about confidentiality, "an explanation as to whether any compensation and an explanation as to whether any medical treatments are available if injury occurs," and "a statement that participation is voluntary." Despite this specificity, such fundamental questions as what it means to consent and how concepts such as "voluntary" are understood are left unexamined. The case law provides little further help on these issues.

Informed consent to medical research is usually memorialized in an informed consent document that the prospective subject signs after an opportunity to read it and ask questions. However, neither statutes, regulations, nor case law explain just what the legal status of that document is. To the lawyer members of our group (Conley and Davis), an informed consent document looks like a written contract. The classic legal definition of a contract is an agreement by which the parties agree to obligate themselves to do (or, in some cases, not to do) specified things, with each party receiving an inducement, or "consideration." The typical informed consent document seems to track this definition. In exchange for the promise of some benefits, tangible (a very small payment, sometimes disclosure of clinically significant findings) and intangible (a sense of contributing to medical progress), subjects agree to turn over something of value to the researchers (their specimens); for their part, the researchers commit to providing the tangible benefits as well as to protecting the subjects in specified ways (e.g., by endeavoring to preserve their confidential participation). If the document is a contract, then the promises made therein—mostly by the researchers—are presumably binding. Yet, precisely because of its fear of this binding effect, the research community almost universally takes the position that it is *not* a contract. The public websites of many medical research organizations state explicitly that "informed consent is not a contract" (e.g., that of the National Institutes of Health, n.d.). Similarly, IRBs routinely forbid researchers to refer to payment as an "inducement" or even a "benefit" in their research proposals—even though to subjects it is a primary inducement (Conley, Mitchell, Cadigan, Davis, Dobson and Gladden 2012).

While we understand why researchers would like to avoid characterizing informed consent documents as contracts, we have no legal explanation for this view, nor have we seen any plausible legal defense of the researchers' position. The odd reality is simply that a document that apparently states the terms of a bilateral agreement, and promises consideration (which can be anything that a party views as having value), is widely assumed not to be a contract.

The consensus view is illustrated by the consent document used by one of the two biobanks that are the subject of this chapter (the government-run biobank described in the Methods section below; the consent form used by the other biobank is very similar in substance, though longer). This provision appears at the end of the form, immediately above the subject's signature:

> **Subject's Agreement**
>
> I have read the information provided above. I voluntarily agree to participate in this [biobank]. My signature below signifies that my blood sample may be used for this research purpose.

The "agreement" is apparently that the subject's blood sample may be used for "this research purpose," which—again apparently—incorporates the description of the project set out in earlier portions of the form. Among other things, subjects may withdraw, in which case their physical blood or DNA samples will be destroyed, but derived data will be retained and ongoing analyses will continue. But the Subject's Agreement provision (consistent with the whole form) is especially interesting for what it does *not* say: there is no reference to this being a contract with binding mutual obligations. On the contrary, while the subject agrees—indeed, *voluntarily* agrees—to participate, and to permit use of his or her sample in the research project, there is no reference to any reciprocal agreement on the part of the researchers. Nor can any such agreement be discerned from the body of the consent form, with the exception of several statements about the researchers' efforts to protect subjects' privacy, and another that says that the subject "will receive $20 for participating." These statements might be deemed to be enforceable promises, but only if the whole document were deemed to be a contract.

A logical next question is: if the informed consent document is not evidence of a contract, what is it? The few courts that have even approached the issue have tended to side with the researchers. For example, an Ohio court dealing with a lawsuit brought by a person who was injured by an experimental medical procedure concluded, "Construing the informed consent statement as a whole and applying the ordinary meaning to the language employed in the document, we conclude the document at issue serves merely as written notice that plaintiff gave her informed consent to participate in the medical research study" (Ohio Court of Appeals 2004). Another court (U.S. Court of Appeals for the Eighth Circuit 2008) has treated a biospecimen contribution as a gift. If this is the case, then perhaps the informed consent document amounts to a kind of deed. Otherwise, from a legal perspective, these documents seem to be nothing at all: a set of vague consumer disclosures that are mandated by federal regulations but that give injured consumers no privately enforceable rights.

This chapter reflects our effort to explore how the vague and elusive concept of informed consent is understood from the subjects' side. We find that, to the extent that the explicit written assent to the terms of the informed consent document—"I voluntarily agree," in the example given above—is a performative, it is an empty one.

The Literature on Informed Consent

There is a small but revealing literature that focuses on the linguistic and other behavioral aspects of informed consent Most relevant to our work are two studies that focus on the consent appointment as ritual or ceremony. Lipworth and colleagues analyzed semistructured interviews of 12 "stakeholders" (including patient/donors, parents of child patients, and health advocates) in an Australian biobank to examine the concept of public trust in research. They find that securing consent functions "as a means not only of allowing [donors] to exercise their autonomy but also as a 'ceremony' that can help to 'secure trust'" (Lipworth, Morrell, Irvine and Kerridge 2009: 130). Continuing in this anthropological vein, they further argue that this trust "needs to be seen as an emergent property of good social relationships that are built up over time" (Lipworth et al. 2009: 130, quoting Levitt and Weldon

2005: 320). In a similar study also done in Australia, Allen and McNamara (2011: 162) find that research participants "express a degree of autonomy that moves beyond its association with a self-sufficient and self-realizing individual to encompass a relational framework based on inter-subjectivity." They, too, focus on the formal consent ceremony, finding that "the actual act of giving consent through the signing of a document ritualizes the process, thus allowing the participants to declare themselves as moral beings" (Allen and McNamara 2011: 163). One would think that the same could be said of the researchers.

Consistent with the ceremony model, medical research practice treats informed consent as an event. Linguistically, researchers use *consent* as a transitive verb, routinely speaking of researchers *consenting* subjects, and, when the scope or purpose of the research changes, *reconsenting* them. Medical ethicists have criticized this event or ceremony model, implying that the ceremony may be an empty one and suggesting that consent needs to approached as a discursive process. For example, Barton and Eggly (2009) have analyzed offers to participate in clinical trials as persuasive processes, while Allen and McNamara (2011) have described the giving of consent to participate in a biobank as a decision-making process with ongoing social significance. There is also a growing body of empirical literature that argues that research subjects often do not read consent forms and in fact choose whether to participate for reasons that have little or nothing to do with the information contained in a consent form (Hoeyer 2003; Barr 2006; Cadigan and Davis 2009; Hoeyer 2010). Exploring this problem through qualitative discourse analysis, Dixon-Woods and colleagues have found that "misunderstanding" is not, as many researchers believe, a communication problem caused by the complexity of the subject matter, but is rather "likely to be an incorrigible and persistent feature of people's reading" of informed consent documents—that is, a problem that derives from subjects' tendency to read into consent documents features that simply are not there (Dixon-Woods et al. 2007: 2219). This finding casts doubt on the very principle of informed consent.

Methods

We have conducted and analyzed semistructured interviews with 57 people who were asked to contribute to either of two genetic biobanks (about half of them joined and half declined). One of the biobanks is federally funded and government-run; the other is foundation-sponsored and community-based. The former is linked with a university medical center and many of its recruits have a university affiliation, whereas the latter is based in an economically distressed small city and its recruits tend to be less affluent and less educated.

The former study pays subjects $20 in cash; the latter gives them a $10 gift card to Walmart or Target.

Interviews lasted approximately 60 minutes and followed a topic outline that included questions about how people decided whether to join the biobank; and their perceptions of the benefits and risks of the biobank to themselves, their family, their community, and society. Additionally, subjects were asked about their understanding of certain features of the biobank, such as what types of data and specimens are collected and how long they are stored, the possibility of recontact by the biobank, the potential for return of individual research results, and the ownership of the specimens. Having raised these general topics, the interviewers encouraged the subjects to go on in whatever specific direction, and at whatever length, they chose. All interviews were transcribed. Because our primary focus has been on issues of content, the transcripts reproduce all of the words spoken during the interviews, using standard English spellings, but they do not generally capture pauses, nonverbal utterances, stress, and other features of conversation that are often reproduced in linguistic transcripts.

Our analytic method involves reviewing the recorded interviews as a group, with each member noting and raising for discussion issues that were of interest to him or her. We gave close attention to the specific ways in which subjects expressed themselves, though our primary interest was in topic and content rather than interactional details. In the tradition of linguistic anthropology, we see "subjects ... that is, speakers, first and above all as social actors" (Duranti 1997: 3)—in our case, as social actors in the enterprise of genetic research. Our approach is probably best described by the umbrella term discourse analysis.

Analysis of the Interviews

THE CEREMONY

Generally, the recruits who joined either of the biobanks analyzed their decision in ways that were consistent with the event/ceremony model. They remembered the event, and that a form was involved, but little about the form's content, and such memories as they had were often at odds with what the form actually said. Most also recalled the compensation, with some viewing it as a welcome windfall, while others complained about the researchers' stinginess. The speaker in Text 1 ("J" indicates someone who joined; "D" someone who declined to join) emphasized the simplicity of the event, although he did infer from it that he would be "treated with respect and dignity and appreciation":

Text 1

J-1: What does someone have to do to participate?

I: Yeah.

J-1: Get up, drive over. Well, first of all sign a form to get in the study, be there on time, go over what the brief information, be prepared to have fun, in and out, treated with respect and dignity and appreciation, and go on and do whatever you're going to do the rest of the day.

Looking ahead to future studies, this subject would retain the same attitude:

Text 2

I: Okay. If you're contacted about participating in a study, can you envision what kind of questions you may have about it?

J-1: At this point I'm so pleased with what I've seen so far it would just be 'Well, yeah. Where do you want me to be when?'

I: Okay. Fair enough. Just logistical questions.

J-1: Yeah.

Another person who joined was even more emphatic about just how "easy" the ceremony was. Note especially the response to the question about going over the form: "No," followed by the enigmatic "Just the person who presented it."

Text 3

I: Okay. What do you remember about the logistical process of joining the study? Kind of how difficult was it to-

J-2: It was easy. I mean I just came here and had some conversation with—you know more information. I think I signed something and gave some blood.

I: Okay. So you did it here at the hospital.

J-2: Yeah.

I: Okay. Great. Did you go over the consent form with anyone?

J-2: No. Just the person who presented it.

I: Okay. Did you feel comfortable with it?

J-2: Yeah. Sure.

I: Have any questions about it?

J-2: No.

A more elaborate recollection of the ceremony came from another person who joined, and whose recollection may have been enhanced by the difficulty of the blood draw. This subject's recollection of her visit to the research site embodied several things that might be characterized as ceremonial: hearing a "preamble," receiving "some literature to read," signing "some releases," and then the "nurses trying to do something with me." But even here, the recollection amounts to little more than a memory of an event at which something significant—and apparently uncomfortable—was done. In particular, there is no evidence here or in any of our interviews of subjects viewing the ceremony as an opportunity "to declare themselves as moral beings" (Allen and McNamara 2011: 163).

Text 4

I: And when you actually went to join here in your building, can you—what do you remember about sort of the process? I know we talked a little bit about how they stuck you so many times, but can you tell me anything about your meeting with people there?

J-3: They went over kind of the same kind of preamble you did as far as being voluntary, reassuring confidentiality. It's been a while back. Again I can't remember all the particulars, but I do know they gave me some literature to read while I was there, and I believe I had to sign some releases, and then they started the team of different nurses trying to do something with me. That's what I remember most about it.

It is also interesting that this subject characterized the signed forms as "releases." In law, a release is contractual in nature, an agreement to discharge another from liability or duty in exchange for a payment or other consideration. For example, a plaintiff who is being paid to settle a lawsuit is always required to sign a form releasing the defendant from further liability, and someone taking ski lessons may be required to sign a release in consideration of being allowed to participate. While medical researchers might be pleased to receive signed releases, the concept is rarely employed in consent forms; neither of the biobanks we studied includes a release in its form. This interview thus illustrates a pattern we observed throughout our interviews: subjects rarely recalled the specific content of the consent document, and when they did they were often wrong.

EMERGENT UNDERSTANDINGS

But even as our interviews confirmed that subjects remember the informed consent process as a more or less meaningless ceremony, they also suggested the ethical inadequacy of treating informed consent as a one-time event. Given the opportunity to reflect on their participation decisions, subjects tended to develop a discursive model of informed consent as an emerging understanding that could evolve over time in response to interactions with a variety of interlocutors. Some even expressed a kind of buyer's remorse at having forgone the chance to make the consent ceremony more useful.

This subject, who joined the government-run biobank, initially answered a question about later-developing concerns with a simple negative: "Well, no." But she turned immediately and spontaneously to a reflection on the interview—"as I'm sitting here." She then verbalized her thought process, first posing the question that came into her mind about possible "negative things," and then (after the interviewer interjected an apology) developing a theory about genetic discrimination:

Text 5

I: And, since joining have you thought of any additional negative things for yourself or others that you hadn't thought of during the decision making period?

J-4: Well, no. But, as I'm sitting here, I'm thinking, 'What kind of negative things could be?'

I: That's not the purpose of our interview. Sorry.

J-4: I know. But, hum. Then, the only thing I think of is 'Well, I guess if you were had found to have a certain gene that indicated something negative. And, it got out. Then, I guess there could be a possible perception of prejudice against people with this type of gene or something.'

The same subject continued this process of reflection several minutes later in the interview. In response to the question, "[H]ow would you describe the biobank and what someone has to do as a participant?" she made some comments about how easy it was, and then, with respect to "possible implications or whatever," said, "I would tell them to probably go and read it on the website or something." But then she shifted, unbidden, into further rumination on the consent process, this time wondering if "really quick" might in fact have meant "a little rushed":

Text 6

J-4: I really don't remember all the—and, as I said, I wasn't thinking of any negative consequences at the time. But, like I said, if they were just 'Hey. What about this? Is it easy?' 'Yeah. It's real easy. Very quick.' Well, I'm not going to say that yet. Maybe you'll ask me at some point. So, I'm not going to.

I: Go ahead.

J-4: I was just going to say that it's really quick. And, that—I was going to say in fact I felt a little rushed through the process.

I: So, we've covered a lot of topics in this interview. We're now at the end. But, we realize that we may not have covered everything that you feel is important to know about genetic research or genetic information more generally. Is there anything else that you'd like to share?

J-4: No. Just that it certainly has made me think a lot. For the time being, I don't know how much I'll think about it. And, I am more interested in knowing what can actually be known about a person from genetic information. And, I see how much media plays a part in my perceptions of DNA and genes. And, I just remember—I think I was asking about, 'Do they know what everything is on it? And, what it does?' And, I'm like, 'Wait a minute. I remember reading a little something about mapping the genome. Or, mapping.' And, I'm like, 'Well, what does that really mean? Does it mean that they know the gene that causes eye color? And, the, this little place that causes this little thing. Or, that kind of thing. Does that mean they know all that stuff now?' So, I think this has been a good experience. And, like I said, it certainly made me think more about my genetic information.

The subject's references to time are especially interesting. She recalled that everything was good "at the time" of the consent interview; she "wasn't thinking of any negative consequences." She next repositioned herself back in the present of our interview with her, declining to reaffirm the quick-easy-no-negative-consequences narrative "yet." She then looked ahead in the interview, speculating that we might ask her about potential problems "at some point." When the interviewer prodded her ("Go ahead"), she took a second look back at the consent interview, this time noting the downside of it having been "quick." Finally, invited to sum up, she commented on the discursive value of the interview, which was almost over: "[I]t certainly has made me think a lot." Situating herself back in the present and looking into the short-term future ("For the time being"), she expressed doubt about whether she would continue to reflect on genetic research. But she resumed doing so immediately, launching into a detailed performance of a thought process—apparently triggered by her interaction with the media—that jumped back and forth between past and present.

We believe that the significance of these complex temporal references is to underscore the inadequacy of treating informed consent as a one-time event. It should instead be viewed as a process, one that is potentially lengthy, unbounded, and fundamentally discursive. The ceremony of consent and the performative it generates may be empty, but an individual subject's understanding of informed consent may be anything but. That understanding is likely to be emergent and evolving, with its specifics at any given point in time strongly influenced by the discursive opportunities that the individual has encountered. The consent ceremony, with its accompanying documentation, is one of those opportunities, but only one, and perhaps not a very important one.

SEPARATING "INFORMED" AND "CONSENT"

Interviews with prospective subjects who declined to join a biobank illustrate some of the realities of this process of evolution and emergence. These interviews show that when the informed consent ceremony does take on substance, it is likely to be because of its place in a larger discursive context. A critical aspect of this discursive context has to do with the relationship between *informed* and *consent*. The two words are invariably used together in the literature and practice of medical research, suggesting that they express a unitary concept, but this may mask how active and complex their relationship is. It became clear in our interviews that a subject's attitude to *consent* at any point in time is relative to, if not determined by, the way in which he or she is *informed*. Subjects who joined a project typically recalled paying little attention to the information provided at the informed consent ceremony and (consequently?) consenting quickly (see Texts 1 to 4). But as the discursive process plays out, before, during, and after the ceremony, and as the subjects experience changes in the extent to which they are *informed*, their understanding of the *consent* they are giving may change in tandem (see Texts 5 to 8). For joiners, this process may occasion buyer's remorse; for others, it may tip the balance against joining.

The subject quoted in Text 7 declined to join the government-run biobank. In this account given at the start of the interview, she described two phases of the discursive process. Her first interaction was with a TV ad, which seemed to pique her interest. She then called an information number and had an unsatisfactory interaction with the woman who answered. The subject brought a good deal of knowledge to this initial call—she asked about reviewing a consent form. When the person on the phone "wasn't very forthcoming," the subject began to "feel really nervous" and failed to show up for the consent interview that she had set up.

Text 7

I: Why did you decide not to join the [biobank]?

D-1: Well, I called.

I: From the TV ad.

D-1: Right. And, the lady on the phone gave me a very brief description. 'We're collecting blood samples for this [biobank]. And, you get paid this amount. And, this is the location we do it.' Which was someplace in [the area]. And, I said 'Well, am I able to review a consent form or anything like that?' And, she said 'No.' That wasn't available. I'd need to come to the appointment. And so, I asked her a few more questions. And, she was—probably this is the person I happened to get on the phone. But, she wasn't very forthcoming with information. Which made me feel really nervous about exactly what I was giving my blood to. So, I made the appointment. And then, I didn't go.

Later in the interview, the subject emphasized the importance to her decision of the dynamics of the phone conversation, saying, "It was like I don't really know sort of like exactly what it's all about. Because, that lady couldn't give me any information. And, that was my basis for not joining." She even provided a script for how the call should have gone (she had learned about and visited the biobank's website after the call):

Text 8

D-1: And, it seems like even for someone on the phone who was like 'Oh. I've got all these calls to make.' They could have said, 'Well, you know we have a website. Let me give that to you. You can go there. You can read everything that's on it. Give me a call back if you have any other specific questions. Or, you know you want to schedule. Or, whatever.'

In this instance, the problem was not that, having been *informed*, the subject declined to *consent*. Rather, because the discursive process revealed the biobank's seemingly evasive attitude about information, the subject refused even to consider the possibility of giving consent. It is also interesting that the critical factor in this decision was neither the informed consent document nor the ceremony, but something that plays no role in the IRB supervision and approval process: it was the attitude conveyed by the person who answered the phone that "probably" (Text 7) determined the outcome. And, as Text 8 confirms, it might have gone the other way.[1]

Text 9 presents a final example and a particularly elaborate account of this discursive process. Like the previous subject, this woman first heard about the biobank in a TV ad. She was enthusiastic at that point, and went to the recruitment center for an informed consent interview, at which point she declined to join. But then her church and the NAACP urged her and other members of the local African American community to join, and, having been thus "coerced," she was at the time of our interview reconsidering her initial decision to decline. (Earlier in the interview, the interviewer had referred to this pending reconsideration as a decision to "re-enter"; in the portion reproduced in Text 9 the subject clarified that she had not "re-joined." In both instances the "re-" seems inaccurate, since it appears that she had never joined in the first place.)

Text 9

D-2: I think so. Yeah. But why did I decide to go back and re-enter?

I: Yeah.

D-2: My church and the NAACP, and they admonished us to go because we are presuming there are not going to be a significant number of African Americans involved in the study. To that end we need to make sure that we're involved so that any information coming out of the study can reflect some of the issues that we have.

I: Sure. I can understand that.

D-2: So it was coerced.

I: By the church.

D-2: By the church.

I: Well, yeah. So again some of these questions are going to seem repetitive, but don't worry about it. Excuse me. So you said your initial impression though when you heard about it or on the TV—was it a negative, positive, neutral impression?

D-2: No. I really wanted to do it.

I: Oh. So when you first heard, you were interested.

D-2: Yeah. That's why I voluntarily went over to [name of city] to the—

I: Right. To the center.

D-2: Yeah.

I: I forget what it's called. Right. And so you said initially you were interested. You then decided that after having this interview process that you weren't, that it didn't go so well, but then you said you ultimately did join?

D-2: No.

I: You still haven't joined.

D-2: I haven't, but I didn't, we just had this at church a couple of Sundays ago.

I: Oh, I see.

D-2: And then when you called, I said 'Well, it might be an opportunity for me to join.'

I: I see. I see, but you haven't joined yet. Okay. That's just, just want to make sure we're, clarify that.

D-2: No, I haven't joined. I haven't re-joined.

I: Right. I got you. So yeah. Have you heard or read more about the study you know during this period since you initially were interested? I mean you said the church.

D-2: Now they, a group of women came, and they gave a presentation, and they had literature, and they were able to answer all the questions that I wanted that were not answered before.

I: Okay. And again we'll get to that a little bit more. So initially when you went to that interview, why did you decide not to join? Can you elaborate about that interview process?

D-2: I had some specific questions. One of them was privacy, and the second one was the length of the involvement, and the other one was when you volunteer for a study like this you don't expect any compensation, but I was not under the impression that I would get any feedback from the study. So you know if I'm in a study, and you can't tell me any kind of aggregate information that you're obtaining and how it pertains to me, maybe I don't want to you know.

Several aspects of this text are striking. The first is the most obvious: that her decision remained uncertain even after a three-step discursive process. At the time of our interview, that process had involved seeing a TV ad, going through an informed consent interview, and then interacting with a group of women (and apparently the NAACP) at church. Each of these interactions yielded a different result. After the TV ad, she "really wanted to do it." But the informed consent interview made her concerned about privacy and the lack of "feedback from the study." But then the women at church "were able to answer all the questions," opening up the possibility of "re-joining." In fact, she came to her interview with us thinking, "[I]t might be an opportunity for me to join" (which it was not, as our project has no affiliation with the biobank). This interview is also a rare instance of the consent ceremony performing its intended purpose: this subject went into the interview as an enthusiast and emerged a skeptic, dissuaded by what she had learned. The ceremony itself informed her in such a way that she decided to decline to consent. As anthropologists and ethicists we are not in the business of drawing statistical inferences. It is nonetheless interesting that our clearest example of ceremony-with-substance came from the account of a decliner.

Equally interesting is the ironic quality of the subject's respective discursive relationships with the regulatory apparatus, as represented by the biobank's consent "center," and the group of women at her church. As anyone who has ever sought IRB approval will attest, research ethicists are very concerned about the possibility of researchers practicing subtle coercion in the consent interview and other aspects of the recruitment process. Conversely, IRBs tend to favor—or even demand—community involvement in recruitment for public health studies. But here the subject felt "coerced" (after having been "admonished," another strong word) not by the formal recruitment regime, but by an agent of her community: her church.

Discussion

For most of those who *joined* either of the two biobanks we studied, the informed consent interview and everything it entailed was mere ceremony. Like the subjects quoted in Texts 1 to 4, most of those who joined came to the interview with considerable enthusiasm for joining and paid little attention to the opportunity to read the consent form and ask questions about it. This widely expressed attitude was captured succinctly by the comment in Text 3 about the subject's comfort with the consent form—"Yeah. Sure." As we have reported elsewhere (Mitchell, Conley, Cadigan, Davis, Dobson and Gladden 2011; Conley et al. 2012), the chance for easy money was perhaps the most significant source of subjects' enthusiasm. One of the subjects we quoted in an earlier paper (Conley et al. 2012: 620) spoke for many when, in response to the question "Why did you join?" he responded, "I thought it would be an easy twenty-five dollars."

By signing the consent form and assenting to a proposition such as "I voluntarily agree to participate," those who joined engaged in a kind of written performative. As we noted above, the full legal and ethical consequences of these words—just what the subject voluntarily agrees to—are uncertain. Researchers do not believe that these words create a contract, yet think at the same time that the subject has somehow waived future rights. It is nonetheless clear that the words do have some illocutionary force that is generally consistent with the researchers' understanding: three different American courts have held, for example, that a research subject cannot claim a property interest in a tissue sample that has been provided pursuant to an informed consent agreement.[2]

At least from this limited legal perspective, then, this performative effectively ends the informed consent process. By signing, the subject brings to a climax whatever might have gone before and renders moot much of what might come after. "I voluntarily agree to participate" is to subject recruitment what "I do" is to courtship. In both cases, the respective performatives fundamentally alter the relationship; it will still be possible to get out, but it will be harder to do so and some consequences of the relationship will be permanent. For example, just as a divorcing spouse cannot simply carry off whatever furniture he or she chooses, a research subject will not be able to demand the return of a DNA sample.

So the ceremony and its culminating performative comprise an *event* of great significance for those who join. But, as we have tried to demonstrate, there are two major problems with this oversimplified conception of consent. First, our evidence suggests that the giving of informed consent in any meaningful sense is better viewed as a discursive process, unfolding over time and contexts, and likely to have many twists and turns. To freeze it at a single point—the signing—is arbitrary; the information necessary to make an informed decision about whether to consent is just as likely to be apprehended at any number of other points. Recall the comment in Text 6 about the ceremony being a "little rushed"; the subject in Text 5 feeling buyer's remorse "as I'm sitting here"; and the speaker in Text 9 changing her mind twice as she went through a three-step discursive process.

This leads to the second problem, the emptiness of the performative. Not only is the chosen decision point arbitrary, but those who have joined say almost uniformly that they gave their consent at a time when they were not well informed. Most were swept up by initial enthusiasm, often fueled by the promise of easy money. Many of those we interviewed had no qualms about their participation, with neither our interview nor anything else providing a discursive trigger to information-gathering and reflection. For others, however—such as the speaker in Text 5—there was such a trigger, which they sometimes wished had come earlier.

For those who *declined*, that trigger usually did come earlier in the discursive process. In the case of the speaker in Texts 7 and 8, it was the perceived attitude of "the person [she] happened to get on the phone" that made her "feel really nervous" and caused her to rethink her initial enthusiasm. As a result, she never got to the ceremony. Text 9 is the rare example of the ceremony actually being the key point in the process, the moment at which the prospective subject raised concerns, got unsatisfactory answers, and decided (at least for the moment) not to join. Even here, though, the subject had done substantial and sophisticated preparation in advance of the interview, developing "specific questions" about privacy, length of the study, and return of results. So the ceremony apparently took on meaning precisely because it was a step in this subject's discursive process.

Conclusion: What Can Be Done?

We come away from our analysis with two general conclusions. First, those who consent to join genomic biobanks typically do so without being well informed. They begin the discursive process that might lead them to becoming better informed only after they have consented, sometimes to their chagrin. Second, and on the other hand, those who decline to consent have usually begun a discursive engagement with biobanking before entering upon the ceremony of the informed consent interview. In other words, those who ultimately utter a performative such as "I voluntarily agree" may have little understanding of what they are agreeing to and little sense of the import of the phrase, whereas those who decline have probably developed their concerns in contexts other than the ceremony. In either case, the ceremony and the document it yields have added little value.

Medical ethicists have been concerned about the quality of informed consent to genomic biobanking for some time, usually for other reasons (Rothstein 2005; Greely 2007). One issue is that, because of the pace at which genetic science changes, it may be simply impossible to inform prospective subjects about the future uses of their DNA samples. In addition, advances in the technology for identifying individuals in large DNA samples have cast doubt on customary assurances about protection of identity through anonymity or confidentiality. As the ethicists have recognized, the problem of ill-informed subjects cuts two ways: some people may be joining biobanks on the basis of limited or incorrect understandings of what they are getting into, but others may be staying away on the basis of invalid concerns. As a result, the ethics community has issued a call for "new ethical paradigms for research involving biobanks," approaches that respect both "the public interest in protecting the rights of human subjects" and the public's "substantial interest in facilitating research and eliminating unnecessary impediments to bringing to market new products" (Rothstein 2005: 99).

In response, we have proposed what we call a "trade secret model" for informed consent (Mitchell et al. 2011; Conley et al. 2012) that respects both subject autonomy (itself a contested concept; see Hoeyer 2008: 436) and the discursive nature of informed consent. It was inspired by several subjects describing their DNA in terms evocative of the legal concept of a trade secret: for example, "a piece of their essence," "such a personal thing," and "it's who you are." Many subjects then went on to lay out the terms and conditions on which they might give researchers access to this trade secret. This is precisely how a trade secret license (a specialized kind of contract) works in the commercial world. The conditions proposed varied from subject to subject, but typically included compensation, protection against certain kinds of uses, a right to opt out, and time limits—all of which are common in trade secret licenses. The basic premise of our model is that the giving of informed consent should be treated *explicitly* as an enforceable contract on the model of a commercial trade secret license in which the subject contributes a genetic sample (in effect, discloses a trade secret) in exchange for compensation and various promises made by the researchers.

We have outlined a "menu" of three contractual models in which the more compensation the subject receives, the more control the researchers gain over the sample. For example, at the highest level of compensation, the subject would give up all rights in the sample, and the researcher would promise only reasonable efforts to maintain confidentiality; at a lower payment level, the subject (and his or her heirs) would retain the right to withdraw from the research and have the sample destroyed, and the researchers would promise to notify the subject of any clinically significant findings and to use any income derived from their use of the sample only for research purposes.

At first glance, the trade secret model looks generally similar to the present system. There is a significant difference, however: while the present system may *look* like a contractual exchange, no one in a position of power treats it as such. With our model, researchers will announce to subjects that they are entering into a binding contract—and will acknowledge that the researchers will be bound to keep their promises as well. Moreover, the payments made to subjects will be characterized as what they are, at least from the subjects' point of view: inducements to participate. Finally, our model does not directly resolve all of the issues raised by medical ethicists. Neither it nor any other approach can solve the problems posed by the rapid advance of genetic science, nor cannot it prevent hackers from staying a step ahead of the security specialists. What it does do, however, is create an environment where problems should be disclosed more frankly. If researchers are bound by their promises and assurances, they are likely to take greater care in making them. And subjects, for their part, will be encouraged by the need to make menu choices to pay closer attention to those choices and their implications.

The point to be emphasized in this chapter is that we developed this model in response to the discursive characteristics of informed consent that we report here. It is in a very real sense an exercise in applied linguistics. We recognize, of course, that people sign contracts every day without reading or understanding them. But in the case of our model, the subject cannot simply sign an unread form, but must make choices about how much money they want to receive and, in consequence, how much control they will give up. The menu is limited, but it must be attended to. We have tried, in other words, to treat informed consent as a discursive process, and to insert a discursive trigger before rather than after the climactic but heretofore empty performative. We hope thereby to ameliorate that present disjunction between *informed* and *consent* in genomic biobanking.

Notes

1. To complete the story: After the phone call, and shortly before her interview with us, the subject found and read the biobank's website. She found some aspects of the project to be objectionable. In hindsight, taking into account what she had read on the website, her ultimate conclusion was, "Had I called on a different day and talked to someone else who was more forthcoming with information, I probably still wouldn't have participated."

2. *In Washington University v. Catalona* (U.S. Court of Appeals for the Eighth Circuit 2008) the court (which hears federal appeals from seven Midwestern states) held that neither a former Washington University researcher nor the donors of biospecimens he had collected had any property rights in the biospecimens and therefore could not compel their transfer to the researcher in his new position. Applying Missouri state law, the court found that the biospecimens had been a gift to Washington University. In *Greenberg v. Miami Children's Hospital Research Institute, Inc.* (U.S. District Court for the Southern District of Florida 2003), a federal trial court in Miami held under Florida law that donors had no property right in biospecimens they had contributed. The *Greenberg* court cited *Moore v. Regents of University of California* (California Supreme Court 1990), in which the California Supreme Court reached a similar result under California law.

Cases Cited

California Supreme Court. 1990. *Moore v. Regents of University of California*, 51 Cal.3d 120; 271 Cal. Rptr. 146; 793 P.2d 479.

Ohio Court of Appeals. 2004. *Harden v. University of Cincinnati Medical Center*, 2004 WL 2341713 (October 19, 2004).

U.S. Court of Appeals for the Eighth Circuit. 2008. *Washington University v. Catalona*, 437 F.Supp.2d 985 (E.D. Mo.), *aff'd*, 490 F.3d 667 (8th Cir. 2007), *cert. denied*, 128 S. Ct. 1122 (2008).

U.S. District Court for the Southern District of Florida. 2003. *Greenberg v. Miami Children's Hospital Research Institute, Inc.*, 264 F.Supp.2d 1064.

References

Allen, Judy and Beverley McNamara. 2011. Reconsidering the value of consent in biobank research. *Bioethics* 25: 155–166.

Barr, Michael. 2006. "I'm not really read up on genetics": Biobanks and the social context of informed consent. *BioSocieties* 1: 251–262.

Barton, Ellen and Susan Eggly. 2009. Ethical or unethical persuasion? The rhetoric of offers to participate in clinical trials. *Written Communication* 26: 295–319.

Beecher, Henry. 1966. Ethics and clinical research. *New England Journal of Medicine* 274: 1354–1360.

Cadigan, R. Jean and Arlene Davis. 2009. Deciding whether to participate in a biobank: The concerns of healthy volunteers. In Jane Kaye and Mark Stranger (eds.) *Governing Biobanks: What Are the Challenges?* Farnham, Surrey, U.K.: Ashgate Publishing. 117–133.

Conley, John, Robert Mitchell, R. Jean Cadigan, Arlene Davis, Allison Dobson and Ryan Gladden. 2012. A trade secret model for genomic biobanking. *Journal of Law, Medicine and Ethics* 40: 612–628.

Cowart, Monica. 2003. Understanding acts of consent: Using speech act theory to help resolve moral dilemmas and legal disputes. *Law and Philosophy* 23: 495–525.

Dixon-Woods, Mary, Richard Ashcroft, Clare Jackson, Martin Tobin, Joelle Kivits, Paul Burton and Nilesh Samani. 2007. Beyond "misunderstanding": Written information and decisions about taking part in a genetic epidemiology study. *Social Science & Medicine* 65: 2212–2222.

Duranti, Alessandro. 1997. *Linguistic Anthropology.* Cambridge: Cambridge University Press.

Greely, Henry. 2007. The uneasy ethical and legal underpinnings of large-scale genomic biobanks. *Annual Review of Human Genetics* 8: 343–364.

Hoeyer, Klaus. 2003. "Science is really needed—that's all I know": Informed consent and the non-verbal practices of collecting blood for genetic research in northern Sweden. *New Genetics and Society* 22: 229–244.

Hoeyer, Klaus. 2008. The ethics of biobanking: A critical review of the literature. *Biotechnology and Genetic Engineering Reviews* 25: 429–452.

Hoeyer, Klaus. 2010. Donors' perceptions of consent to and feedback from biobank research: Time to acknowledge diversity? *Public Health Genomics* 13: 345–352.

Levitt, Mairi and Sue Weldon. 2005. A well placed trust? Public perceptions of the governance of DNA databases. *Critical Public Health* 15(4): 311–321.

Lipworth, Wendy, Bronwell Morrell, Rob Irvine and Ian Kerridge. 2009. An empirical reappraisal of public trust in biobanking research: Rethinking restrictive consent requirements. *Journal of Law & Medicine* 17: 119–132.

Mitchell, Robert, John Conley, R. Jean Cadigan, Arlene Davis, Allison Dobson and Ryan Gladden. 2011. Genomics, biobanks, and the trade-secret model. *Science* 332: 309–310.

National Commission for the Protection of Human Subjects of Biomedical and Behavioral Research. 1979. The Belmont Report. Available at http://www.hhs.gov/ohrp/humansubjects/guidance/belmont.html.

National Institutes of Health. n.d. NIH clinical trials and you—the basics. Available at http://www.nih.gov/health/clinicaltrials/basics.htm.

Rothstein, Mark. 2005. Expanding the ethical analysis of biobanks. *Journal of Law, Medicine & Ethics* 33: 89–101.

Solan, Lawrence and Peter Tiersma. 2005. *Speaking of Crime: The Language of Criminal Justice.* Chicago: University of Chicago Press.

US Department of Health and Human Services. 1991. Federal policy for the protection of human subjects ("Common rule"). Available at http://www.hhs.gov/ohrp/humansubjects/commonrule/index.html.

US Department of Health and Human Services. 2009. General requirements for informed consent. Code of Federal Regulations, Title 45, §46.116.

SECTION 3

The Influence of Discursive Practices

8

Promoting Litigant Consent to Arbitration in Multilingual Small Claims Court

Philipp Sebastian Angermeyer

Introduction

In institutional talk, the notion of consent is often invoked when lay participants have a choice between alternative courses of action and are asked to choose a particular one that is institutionally preferred. Within the institution, such conditions frequently give rise to routinized consent procedures, which are designed to manage the lay participants' behavior and steer them toward the preferred option. "Giving consent" is then manifested through an individual's signature on a consent form by which she or he enters into a legally binding agreement, often waiving rights and protecting the institution from future legal claims. Through such routinized consent procedures, institutions manage to exert control without overtly denying the lay participants' right to make their own decision. The analysis of this process thus represents a fruitful site for the investigation of power in institutional talk.

This chapter investigates an example of such a ritualized consent procedure in the legal sphere, specifically in small claims court in New York City. In these courts, disputants (litigants) have the choice to have their case heard by a judge or by a volunteer arbitrator. This choice has both legal and procedural implications: in contrast to a trial by judge, arbitration hearings can be scheduled on short notice and lead to a final decision that cannot be appealed. For various reasons that are outlined below, the courts steer litigants toward arbitration, and this chapter explores the process by which this is done, beginning with the information court officers provide during the so-called calendar call, and focusing on the actions of arbitrators and

This paper is based upon work supported by the National Science Foundation under Grant No. BCS-0317838. I'm grateful to the editors for their careful reading and insightful observations.

interpreters at the beginning of arbitration hearings, when litigants are asked to give written consent. By signing the consent form, litigants waive their right to appeal the eventual decision.

Many litigants in court have limited proficiency in English and rely on the services of a court interpreter during the hearing, as well as during the consent procedure. In such cases, interpreters take on an important role in the negotiation of rights and responsibilities. The potential impact of interpreters on consent briefings has been demonstrated by Meyer (2003, 2004), who investigated doctor-patient interviews in which patients were asked to give consent to proposed medical procedures. He found that patients who relied on an interpreter received far less information than those who did not, and often appeared to consent to medical procedures without being aware of all potential side effects or of alternative treatment methods. In doctor-patient interaction, interpreting is often provided by nonprofessional ad hoc interpreters, such as patients' family members. By contrast, legal institutions often insist on the use of professional court interpreters, who are employed by the institution. This is done not only to enforce standards of translation practices, but also because of ethical concerns. While nonprofessional interpreters are often suspected of siding with a party rather than remaining neutral, court interpreters are bound by professional norms and legal guidelines that emphasize neutrality and impartiality as essential components of ethical and professional behavior. This notion of neutrality relates primarily to the dispute between the parties involved in the case, but not to negotiations involving the institution. As employees of the court, interpreters may not be neutral if the interaction is between a layperson and another representative of the court. As will be shown below, interpreters are found to interfere in the consent procedure in ways that demonstrate their alignment with the goals of the court system, while at the same time contravening professional norms for court interpreting.

NYC Small Claims Court

This study draws on a corpus of 60 audio-recorded small claims proceedings, as well as on ethnographic fieldwork in three courthouses in New York City (Angermeyer 2015). Small claims court has been characterized as "informal justice" (Conley and O'Barr 1990) because it provides low-cost, simplified access to legal recourse in disputes with a limited monetary value (up to $5,000 in New York at the time of fieldwork). Typical cases in small claims court involve disputes between tenants and landlords, merchants and customers, or workers and their former employers. Claimants and defendants are not required to hire an attorney and most do appear *pro se*, in other words, presenting their own case. Rules of procedure and evidence are relaxed, and many courts offer alternative forms of dispute resolution, such as mediation or arbitration.

In New York small claims courts, litigants are given a choice between two types of proceedings: namely, a trial conducted by a civil court judge or an arbitration hearing conducted by a volunteer arbitrator (arbitrators are trained attorneys who volunteer as a form of community service). The two procedures of trial and arbitration differ in several important ways, especially in the legal status of the decision, and in the qualification, experience, and accountability of the legal decision maker. Trials are audio-recorded to create a court record, whereas no record is made of testimony in arbitration hearings. As a consequence, a judge's decision can be appealed, but that of an arbitrator is final. Because of the absence of a court record, arbitration hearings also tend to be relatively informal compared to trials. The difference in formality is apparent for example in the seating arrangement, as many arbitrators sit at a table together with the litigants, whereas trials are always marked by a physical distance between the participants, with the judge sitting up on the bench, the litigants sitting at tables in the courtroom below, and an armed court officer passing documents between them. This different degree of formality also extends to the amount of time spent on hearings. All the trials that I observed lasted at least 30 minutes, often much longer. By contrast, most arbitration hearings were much shorter, often lasting only 10 to 15 minutes. In fact, the ability to conduct hearings quickly was a primary factor by which court staff evaluated the arbitrators whom they assigned cases to.[1]

While some arbitrators gave litigants ample time to argue their case, others were found to cut litigants short after only a few minutes of testimony, declaring that they had heard enough to make a decision. By agreeing to arbitration, litigants thus risk receiving only very cursory attention, depending on what type of arbitrator they face. This is especially detrimental for claimants who have to present a convincing narrative in order to be successful in court (Conley and O'Barr 1990). A survey of legal outcomes over a sample period suggests that judges are more likely to decide in favor of the claimant than are arbitrators (Angermeyer 2015).

Despite the fact that trials may better serve the interests of claimants, the reduction in costs and processing times make arbitration the preferred choice from the perspective of the court system, as cases can be processed more quickly and in greater numbers. In fact, the court system does not allocate sufficient resources to small claims court to have all cases go to trial, and therefore tries to steer as many litigants as possible toward arbitration. However, this requires the litigants' written consent. Specifically, litigants have to sign that they agree to have their case decided in arbitration and waive the right to an appeal. In the following, I show how court staff, arbitrators, and interpreters work to promote arbitration and discourage litigants from choosing to go to trial, focusing in particular on litigants who speak a language other than English.

Prior to the Hearing: The Calendar Call

The choice between procedures is made when both parties in a lawsuit come to court for a scheduled appearance. Upon arriving in the courthouse, litigants are first asked to go to a large courtroom for the so-called calendar call at the beginning of the court session. As the docket includes typically between 80 and 120 cases, a considerable crowd assembles in the courtroom's gallery, comprised of litigants and people accompanying them. Before the actual calendar call begins, a clerk or court officer reads an announcement that instructs litigants on how to respond when their case is called. For most litigants, the difference between judges and arbitrators is first introduced in this announcement. This text is sometimes also displayed in writing at the entrance to the courtroom. An excerpt is shown in Example 1, reproducing formatting choices of original text.

Example 1

SMALL CLAIMS INFORMATION

PLEASE READ BEFORE ENTERING COURTROOM

GOOD EVENING LADIES AND GENTLEMEN.
BECAUSE OF THE LARGE NUMBER OF CASES ON TONIGHT'S CALENDAR, IT WOULD BE IMPOSSIBLE FOR THE JUDGE TO TRY ALL OF THE CASES. THEREFORE, IN ADDITION TO THE JUDGE, WE HAVE **MANY ARBITRATORS** AVAILABLE TO ASSIST THE COURT AND TRY THESE CASES.

THE ARBITRATORS ARE COURT APPOINTED, EXPERIENCED ATTORNEYS WHO HAVE VOLUNTEERED THEIR TIME TO TRY SMALL CLAIMS CASES. MOST CASES ARE HEARD BY ARBITRATORS.

WHEN THE CALENDAR IS CALLED, **PLEASE STAND AND REPEAT YOUR NAME**.

IF BOTH PARTIES ARE PRESENT, YOU WILL GET AN IMMEDIATE TRIAL TONIGHT IF BOTH PARTIES AGREE TO HAVE AN ARBITRATOR TRY THE CASE. HOWEVER, **IF YOU CHOOSE TO HAVE YOUR CASE HEARD BY THE JUDGE**, SAY 'READY BY THE COURT.' KEEP IN MIND, **YOU MAY HAVE TO RETURN TO COURT SEVERAL TIMES BEFORE YOUR CASE CAN BE REACHED FOR TRIAL BY A JUDGE.**

WHEN YOUR CASE IS SENT TO AN **ARBITRATOR**, THERE IS A CARD WHICH YOU WILL BE ASKED TO SIGN. YOUR SIGNATURE ON THIS CARD WILL INDICATE THAT YOU UNDERSTAND THAT THE ARBITRATOR'S AWARD IS FINAL AND BINDING ON BOTH SIDES AND THAT THERE'S NO APPEAL. HOWEVER, IF YOUR CASE IS TRIED BY THE JUDGE, **IT IS POSSIBLE TO APPEAL FROM A JUDGE'S DECISION. PLEASE NOTE THAT AN APPEAL MAY BE EXPENSIVE AND TIME CONSUMING.** [. . .]

As is evident in the text shown in Example 1, the court administration tries to steer litigants toward arbitration by presenting it as the default option ("Most cases are heard by arbitrators"), and typographically emphasizing the word *arbitrator* in the displayed text. In the litigants' response to the calendar call, simply repeating one's name (or answering "Ready") is taken as agreement to arbitration, whereas a trial by the judge has to be explicitly requested with the formulaic and nontransparent phrase "Ready by the court" (see Example 6). Moreover, the announcement draws attention to several downsides of trials, especially the need to "return to court several times," as well as the expense and effort required for an eventual appeal (note that all of these aspects are emphasized through underlining in the displayed text shown in Example 1). That is, arbitration is presented as an equivalent choice, except for the fact that the decision cannot be appealed.[2] No reference is made to other differences between trial and arbitration such as those discussed above. The text shown in Example 1 is in English, as are corresponding announcements. However, many litigants whom I observed were native speakers of other languages and had only limited competence in English. In two of the courthouses where I conducted fieldwork, a Spanish interpreter was sometimes given the opportunity to make a comparable announcement in Spanish, instructing litigants how to respond in English during the calendar call. Speakers of other languages never had such information made available to them.

When the calendar call begins, a clerk reads the names of the litigants from the docket, one by one. Litigants respond and are then told to go to another room in the courthouse to wait for their hearing. This calendar call is conducted in English only. Litigants do not have access to official court interpreters at this stage, nor can they rely on ad hoc interpreting by a family member or acquaintance, as court officers insist on perfect silence during the calendar call, unless the language needing interpreting is American Sign Language. As a consequence, litigants with limited proficiency in English ordinarily cannot be expected to have understood the difference between trial and arbitration, and their default response to the calendar call should therefore not be regarded as constituting informed consent to arbitration. In fact, on several occasions I observed litigants who found themselves in front of an arbitrator only to state that they had meant to opt for a trial (see Example 6). However, as will be shown below, many arbitrators nevertheless act on the assumption that litigants have already decided in favor of arbitration by the time that they come into their courtroom.

Requesting Consent: Variation among Arbitrators

After the calendar call, litigants who have not explicitly requested a trial are sent to other parts of the courthouse, until they eventually find themselves in a small courtroom or deliberation room in front of an arbitrator. Before the hearing can begin, the arbitrator asks the litigants to sign a statement in which they consent to arbitration and waive the right to an appeal. Among the arbitrators recorded for this study, there is considerable variation in how they approach this request for consent. Some arbitrators provide litigants with information about the differences between the procedures before asking them to sign the waiver. Other arbitrators assume that litigants have already made an informed decision prior to this interaction, and these arbitrators do not engage in further explanations. This is illustrated in the following examples. In Example 2, the arbitrator does little more than ask for the litigants' signatures.[3] By contrast, the arbitrator in Example 3 produces a lengthy monologue that describes some of the legal and practical aspects that litigants need to consider in order to make an informed decision.[4] Both transcript excerpts are from interpreter-mediated interaction, but any intervening or overlapping turns by interpreters are omitted to facilitate the comparison of arbitrator approaches.

Example 2 (see appendix for transcription conventions)

1	Arbitrator:	Okay, my name is Bob Brown (.) I'm an arbitrator for the
2		court +//.
3		By your coming here, you agree to have an arbitrator
4		decide this case +//.
5		All decisions (.) made by an arbitrator will be final +//.
6		Mister Green +//.
7		Sign here please.

Example 3

Arbitrator: Okay before I can begin (.) You have to understand
(.) that I'm an attorney and not a judge.
Actually I'm an attorney, that's true +//.
but I'm a- an arbitrator tonight.
I'm an attorney and I can here decide this case for you. tonight
If you both consent to have me do so.
I'll hear your case out tonight (.) I'll render my decision
and you'll receive it in the mail within a week to ten days.
Because arbitrators are not given court reporters
(.) there is no record (.) so you can't take an appeal.
So therefore my decision, win or lose, is final.
You do have a right to go before a judge.
(.) That's a much longer, slower process.
Most (of) the people signing in tonight (.) were signing in
for the judge (.) and the judge hears the cases in the order of age.
So you might have to come back several times
until your case is the oldest and judge-ready case of the night.
A judge does have a court reporter=
Lawyer: =Tape recorder
Arbitrator: A tape recorder now?
Okay the judge has a record anyway. So you /can take appeal.
But only on the grounds that the judge applied the wrong law.
in order to take an appeal you need to purchase a transcript
(.) you need to write a brief (.) you need to know what the law /is
(.) and of course there are filing fees
and for most people this requires them hiring an attorney.
(.) So while it is a right to appeal, it is actually a very limited right.
Now I've explained you the trade-offs between going between-
before a judge and going before an arbitrator.
Do you consent to arbitration?

The excerpts in Examples 2 and 3 illustrate fundamental differences between arbitrators in their approach to eliciting consent from litigants. In Example 2, the arbitrator acts as if the litigants' consent is already established ("By your coming here, you agree," line 3) and merely needs to be formally recorded through the signing of the consent form. By contrast, the arbitrator in Example 3 does not presume any prior decision by the litigants, nor any knowledge about court procedures on their part. Instead she presents the litigants with information about legal and procedural aspects of arbitration hearings and trials by the judge. In doing so, she focuses on the court's scheduling practices and on the process of appealing a judge's decision, suggesting that protecting the right to appeal is the only reason why one would want to have a trial by a judge (however, her claim in lines 14 to 15 that "Most [. . .] people [. . .] were signing in for the judge" is not accurate). Finally, the arbitrator proclaims to have "explained" (line 28) the differences between the two types of hearings and the "trade-off" between legal rights and procedural convenience that is involved in making the decision. Only then does she ask for consent to arbitration, in other words, for the litigants' signatures on the consent form.

While both arbitrators in Examples 2 and 3 speak about consent to arbitration in general terms, other arbitrators personalize the request in a way that equates consent to arbitration with agreement to have a specific person act as arbitrator, as shown in Example 4. (This example includes turns by a court interpreter who is translating the arbitrator's turns into Haitian Creole.) The arbitrators' wording corresponds to the actual text on the consent form, where the arbitrator is personally named. However, this personalization of the request can also be seen as further discouraging litigants from opting for a trial by the judge, because doing so would amount to a face-threatening act against the arbitrator who is requesting this consent. If a litigant responds negatively, they could be heard as saying "I don't want *you* to decide my case" rather than as "I don't want my case to be decided by an arbitrator."

Example 4

1	Arbitrator:	Okay, my name is Nancy Black, I'm the int-	
2		[I'm the arbitrator today.]	
3	Interpreter:	[(xxx)]	
4	Arbitrator:	Uhm, I am here to listen	[to your case and decide
5			your case] +//.
6	Interpreter:		[(Li ye la pou ka-)]
7		Li ye la pou deside ka-a.	
		{'She is there to decide the case'}	
8	Arbitrator:	Is that okay with both of you?	
9	Interpreter:	Eske ou vle ke (fè) ka-ou?	
		{'Do you want her (to do) your case?'}	

While there are thus considerable differences between arbitrators, individual arbitrators were found to be consistent in their approach across hearings (most arbitrators were observed in multiple hearings, and several were observed on multiple dates). For example, I recorded the arbitrator in Example 3 on another occasion, when she conducted the consent procedure in a very similar way, using many of the same or similar phrases found in Example 3, such as "You do have a right to go before a judge. (.) That's a much longer, slower process" (compare lines 12 and 13), "So you might have to come back several times until your case is the oldest and judge-ready case of the night" (compare lines 16 and 17), or "Now I've explained you the trade-offs between going [. . .] before a judge and going before an arbitrator" (lines 28 to 29). (Compare also Example 5 for further examples from this arbitrator.) These parallels between different episodes create the impression that the arbitrator's consent briefing is a preformulated text. While the arbitrator did not read from a written manuscript, her monologue exemplifies the "instruction as legal text" paradigm of legal/lay communication that is common in formal courtrooms (see Heffer 2006 on jury instructions). Such spoken texts are characterized by a "presumption of comprehension" (Heffer 2006: 167) and an absence of attempts to elicit addressee feedback or verify uptake, in other words, following what Reddy (1979) has termed the conduit metaphor of communication. While the arbitrator in Example 3 thus intends to provide the litigants with a basis for giving informed consent, it does not follow that her explanations have actually been communicated successfully, particularly if they are then translated by an interpreter, as will be discussed below.

This distribution of the arbitrators' approaches to the elicitation of consent is comparable to findings from previous studies of the discourse of legal decision makers, where variation across the group was paired with consistent behavior in individuals. For example, in their study of US small claims courts, Conley and O'Barr (1990) distinguish five different types of judges, based on their approach toward decision making. And in a study of guilty plea procedures in Arizona courts, Philips (1998) similarly identifies systematic differences in the strategies that judges use to take defendants' pleas. With guilty pleas, judges are required by law to determine that a defendant is pleading guilty knowingly and voluntarily, and they ask questions of defendants in order to do so. Some judges, whom Philips characterizes as "procedure-oriented," seek to "personally establish the defendant's knowingness and voluntariness" (1998: 49). Their behavior contrasts with that of "record-oriented" judges who are concerned primarily with producing a court record that would not be overturned upon appeal. Philips (1998: 50) notes, "When record-oriented judges look . . . for evidence that the defendant was informed of his due process rights, they are looking for evidence that others (i.e., lawyers or even police) informed the defendant of these rights, and as they do so they are also sharing their responsibility to the defendant with others rather than taking it entirely onto themselves as the procedure-oriented judges do." The differences among small claims arbitrators can be explained along similar lines. The arbitrators in Examples 2 and 4 resemble record-oriented judges in that they focus entirely on the written record of the litigants' consent, in other words, their signature on the form, while assuming that others have already provided the necessary information. By contrast, the arbitrator in Example 3 resembles procedure-oriented judges in that she takes responsibility for informing the litigants of their rights before asking them to sign a waiver of these rights. However, in contrast to the judges in Philips's study, she does not check whether the litigants have actually understood her explanation of their rights.

In previous analyses (Angermeyer 2009, 2015), I placed arbitrators along a continuum of "fast" and "slow," drawing on categories used by the court clerks who assign cases to arbitrators. This designation is based on the average time arbitrators spent per hearing, but corresponds also to differences in discursive practices. "Fast" arbitrators frequently cut short litigants' testimony and announced that a decision had been made, whereas "slow" arbitrators gave litigants ample time to testify and attempted to mediate between them, instead of looking to make a quick decision. The variation found in the treatment of the consent procedure lends further support to this distinction. Not only does the amount of time devoted to the consent procedure differ significantly, but arbitrators who rush through the consent procedure, as in Examples 2 and 4 are also displaying "fast" behavior at other times during the hearing. Similarly, in Philips's (1998: 51, 54) data, the two judges whom she characterizes as the most record-oriented are found to have spent the least amount of time per plea, while the most procedure-oriented judge took the longest time on average.

Interpreters

In hearings with litigants who use a language other than English, the interaction between the participants is mediated by court interpreters. Interpreters in small claims court are employed by the court system, most of them as full-time employees who are on staff at a particular courthouse. Court clerks prefer to assign cases with interpreters to arbitrators whom they view as working "fast," in order to compensate for the extra time that they believe is taken up by interpreting.[5] Nevertheless, interpreters were observed in hearings with both types of arbitrators, and were found to translate requests for consent to arbitration in ways that reflected the individual arbitrator's approach.

Most court interpreters in the sample have undergone training and testing to become accredited full-time court interpreters, and as such they are expected to adhere to professional norms of court interpreting, like those of the National Association of Judicial Interpreters and Translators (NAJIT), an organization of which many are members.[6] Such codified norms of legal interpreting require interpreters to faithfully render all parts of the source speech in their translation while refraining from any activities that are unrelated to the translation task. However, as will be seen in the following, these norms are followed only selectively, in ways that reflect the interpreters' alignment with the court system.

Example 5 is taken from a hearing with the same arbitrator as in Example 3, who was shown to provide litigants with a relatively detailed explanation of the legal differences between trials and arbitration hearings. Example 5 shows only an excerpt of the consent briefing, but includes also intervening and overlapping speech by the interpreter, who translates the arbitrator's talk into Russian for the benefit of a Russian-speaking claimant. As can be seen, the arbitrator pauses for the interpreter, but the pauses are not frequent enough or long enough to enable the interpreter to translate in consecutive interpreting mode. The interpreter is thus forced into simultaneous mode at times (lines 15 to 23), which requires her to translate the arbitrator's prior speech while processing her concurrent speech at the same time. Evidently and not surprisingly, the interpreter is unable to fulfill this task consistently, as she falls behind in line 20, where she produces a false start.[7]

As a consequence, several of the arbitrator's utterances remain untranslated (see boldface type in lines 15, 19, and 22). As shown in line 24, the interpreter does not list the individual conditions for an appeal (know the law, write a brief, pay filing fees, and possibly hire an attorney), but rather summarizes them as *vsë èto*, "all this."[8]

Example 5

1	Arbitrator:	A judge's ahm (.) sessions are recorded,
2		so you /can appeal [from a judge's decision] +//.
3	Interpreter:	[to čto proisxodit pered] sud'ëj
4		zapisyvaetsja,
		{'what happens before a judge is recorded'}
5		i vy možete appelirovat' rešenie [sud'i.]
		{'and you can appeal the decision of a judge'}
6	Arbitrator:	[but only] on the grounds
7		that
8		the judge applied the wrong [law] +//.
9	Interpreter:	[no tol'ko] liš' v tom slučae,
10		esli vy sčitaete,
		{'but really only in that case, if you think'}

11		čto sud'ja primenil nepravil'no zakon.
		{'that the judge has misapplied the law.'}
12	Arbitrator:	(.) in order to do this, you need to purchase a tran [script] +//.
13	Interpreter:	[Dlja togo]
14		čtoby èto sdelat' – to est' [appelirovat',]
		{'In order to do this, that is to appeal'}
15	Arbitrator:	[you need to **know what]**
16		**[the law is]** +//.
17	Interpreter:	[vam nužno]
18		[kupit' transkript,]
		{'you need to buy a transcript'}
19	Arbitrator:	[you have to **write a] brief** (.) there [are **filing** fees] +//.
20	Interpreter:	[vam nužno- vam-]
		{'you need to- you-'}
21		[uh]
22	Arbitrator:	**[and for] most people this [requires hiring an attorney]** +//.
23	Interpreter:	[dlja togo, čtoby vsë èto sdelat'],
		{'for that, to do all this'}
24		vam nužno za vsë èto platit'.
		{'you need to pay for all this.'}
25	Arbitrator:	(.5) So while there is a right to appeal, it's a very limited [right.]
26	Interpreter:	[I]
27		poètomu, daže nesmotrja na to, čto vy imeete pravo appelirovat',
		{'And therefore, despite the fact that you have the right to appeal,'}
28		èto očen' limitirovano.
		{'it is very limited'}

The incompleteness of the translation in Example 5 is in part to blame on the arbitrator's failure to produce adequate pauses; however, the interpreter could have solved this problem by asking the arbitrator to slow down or to repeat certain utterances. Court interpreters in the study are found to alert and interrupt other participants when such translation problems occur, though they are much more likely to interrupt a litigant than an arbitrator (see Angermeyer 2009: 21). Nevertheless, the interpreter's decision to "skip" part of the arbitrator's consent briefing could also result from a belief that the omitted utterances are not important enough to warrant an interruption.[9]

This idea is supported by the fact that interpreters were observed to routinely translate "fast" requests (as in Examples 2 and 4) without showing any sign that they objected to this practice. This contrasts with other observed situations in which interpreters monitored the arbitrators' adherence to court practices. For example, in another routine sequence during arbitration hearings, arbitrators asked litigants to write their name and address on an envelope, which would then be used to mail the decision to them. Occasionally, an arbitrator forgot to do this, only to be reminded of it by the interpreter. As staff members at the court and routine participants in arbitration hearings, many court interpreters are more familiar with relevant small claims court practices than are the arbitrators, many of whom volunteer only a few times per year. Consequently interpreters feel entitled to point out procedural requirements, even though this could be viewed as a violation of the norms of court interpreting. The fact that interpreters were not observed to interfere in the consent procedure suggests that they did not view "fast" requests as problematic. The only exception to this tendency was found in one case with a freelance interpreter who interrupted the arbitrator and provided the litigants with additional information about the differences between arbitration and trials (e.g., specifying the time period during which a judge's decision could be appealed). Unlike all the other interpreters in the sample, he was not a full-time employee of the court system, but a freelancer who filled in only occasionally when staff interpreters were unavailable. Due to these exceptional circumstances, this case is excluded from further analysis in this discussion.

Litigant Hesitation

The fact that the court interpreters and most arbitrators aligned with the court's goal of steering cases to arbitration became particularly apparent whenever litigants hesitated to agree to arbitration once they learned from the arbitrator that the decision could not be appealed. The occurrence of such incidents demonstrates that many litigants did not understand the rules of the calendar call and "ended up" in front of an arbitrator without having consciously chosen to do so. This is shown in Example 6, with an English-speaking claimant. Note that the reverse does not happen, in other words, litigants don't find themselves in front of a judge and then decide that they prefer arbitration.

Example 6

1 Claimant: But I didn't (.) call for an arbitrator. That's the problem.
2 Arbitrator: You didn't call 'by the court' either, did you?
3 Claimant: (.) 'By the court'? By the- No he didn't- he didn't ask me,
4 he just said, [am I here].

Arbitrator: [I'm the-]
Claimant: he just said if- answer if you're here and I said [yes].
Arbitrator: [No],
he says to answer 'by the court' if you wanted (.) the [court].
Claimant: [He didn't-]
He didn't say that =
Arbitrator: =Ah.
Claimant: (1.3) I prefer going to the judge.
Arbitrator: Okay (.) go.
Claimant: Alright. So what do I do? Just bring the papers =
Arbitrator: =To five o
nine {*room*}
You're gonna sit all night.

Here the arbitrator reacts to the claimant's hesitation and eventual rejection of arbitration first by arguing about the meaning of the calendar call, and then by sending him off with a warning "You're gonna sit all night" (line 17). This final comment frames the claimant's decision to go to the judge as an irrational choice that is taken against the recommendation of the legal professionals in the room.

While the claimant in Example 6 refused to consent to arbitration, other hesitant litigants were usually persuaded that arbitration was preferable. Arbitrators reacted to litigants' doubts by providing them with some additional information, most commonly focusing on the delay that litigants would have to expect when opting to see a judge instead (as in line 17 of Example 6). This is also evident in the following Example 7, which further shows the involvement of a court interpreter (the same Russian interpreter as in Example 5). Here, the defendant, a Russian-English bilingual, expresses doubts about her choice of procedure. Unlike in Example 6, the arbitrator initially does not seem intent on discouraging the defendant from choosing a trial by judge (lines 2 and 6). However, the interpreter, who had previously translated the arbitrator's speech into Russian, now ceases to act as an interpreter and volunteers additional information ("/But you have to keep in mind that it's costly" in line 9), which is arguably designed to influence the litigant, but also informs the arbitrator about habitual court practices. Her subsequent turn continues in English, now addressing the arbitrator specifically, speaking about litigants in the third person and referring to a court clerk by his first name. In doing so, she hedges her intervention by deferring to the authority of the clerk, whom arbitrators turn to when they have procedural questions. By demonstrating her own alignment with the court administration and its goals, she is able to mitigate the potentially face-threatening acts of correcting the arbitrator and of breaking interpreting norms by speaking on her own behalf. The interpreter's intervention is particularly remarkable, given the absence of comparable comments when interpreters translate "fast" arbitrators, as in Examples 2 and 4. Interpreters do not intervene when arbitrators fail to provide litigants with complete information about their rights, but here the interpreter does interfere when the arbitrator fails to mention facts that may dissuade a hesitant litigant from going before a judge.

Example 7

1	Defendant:	What's the ah alternative?
2	Arbitrator:	=The other alternative is to go downstairs and speak
3		with a judge.
4	Interpreter:	=Vy možete pojti vniz i vas-
		{'You can go downstairs and you --'}
5		vaše delo budet slušat' sud'ja.
		{'a judge will hear your case'}
6	Arbitrator:	And the judge's decision is appealable.
7	Interpreter:	=I rešenie sud'i vy možete apellirovat'.
		{'And you can appeal the judge's decision'}
8	Defendant:	(2.2) {*sighs*}
9	Interpreter:	/But you have to keep in mind that it's costly.
10	Arbitrator:	(.7) It takes /a:ll night to wait for the judge
11		and the judge may not see you tonight.
12	Interpreter:	(.6) No, and- and appeal expensive,
13		it's- usually Bill {*clerk's name*} tells them
14		(.) you know so they /do know
15		because sometime they think it's for /free.
16		(.) But it's not.
17	Arbitrator:	(.) Uhum.
18	Defendant:	So I have to pay for the judge as well?
19	Interpreter:	(.7) For if- esli vy budete delat' appeal
		{'if you will make an appeal'}
20	Defendant:	Ahum?
21	Interpreter:	to appeal možet vam stoit' stol'ko,
		{'this appeal can cost you so much'}

22 skol'ko (.) ili bol'še skol'ko stoit vaše delo
{'as much or more than your case'}
23 potomu čto vy dolžny (.) budutu vzjat' plënku
{'because you will have to take the recording'}
24 transcribe sdelat' [eë.]
{'have it transcribed'}
25 Defendant: [Ahum.]
26 Interpreter: =i: za èto vy dolžny zaplatit' [den'gi za appeal.]
{'and for that you have to pay money for the appeal'}
27 Defendant: [a č'ja storona] platit?
28 kotoraja [podaët?]
{'And whose side pays – that which files?'}
29 Interpreter: [Vy platite.]
{'you pay'}
30 Defendant: Ili ja tože dolžna platit'?
{'or I also have to pay?'}
31 Interpreter: Tot, kto delat appeal, tot [platit.]
{'whoever makes the appeal, pays'}
32 Defendant: [Vot] (.) ja- devuška platit.
{'So, I- the girl pays'}
33 Interpreter: Ona soglasna (.) na arbitra.
{'She agrees to the arbitrator'}
34 Defendant: (1.4) A značit esli ona ne soglasna ja ne mogu.
{'And so if she doesn't agree I cannot'}
35 Interpreter: (0.7) Ona soglasna na arbitra. Esli /vy ne soglasny,
36 vy idëte k sud'e.
{'She agrees to the arbitrator, if you don't agree, you go to the judge'}
37 (0.9) Ona soglasna, čtoby arbitr slušal delo.
{'She agrees for the arbitrator to hear the case'}
38 Defendant: Uhm (1.3) okay (1.2) Ja- it's okay.
{'I'}
39 Arbitrator: Can I ask you to sign here?

Following the interpreter's comments to the arbitrator, the defendant self-selects in line 18, in English, to ask a question about court costs. In asking "So I have to pay for the judge as well?" it appears that she has been confused by the interpreter's earlier comment ("keep in mind that it's costly"), which she has evidently taken to refer to the act of requesting a trial by judge, rather than to the act of appealing a judge's eventual decision. It is not clear whom she addresses with this question, but judging from her language choice of English and from the context, her turn is more likely addressed to the arbitrator than to the interpreter. However, it is the interpreter who responds, switching to Russian, with a more detailed explanation of the costs of filing an appeal (lines 19 to 26), which is followed by further interaction in Russian between the interpreter and the defendant (lines 27 to 37). This sequence is highly unusual in the data set, in that it consists of talk in a language other than English that is neither a translation of prior English talk, nor serves as input for a translation into English. As a consequence, those participants who do not speak Russian (including the arbitrator) are relegated to the status of nonratified participants. Meanwhile, the arbitrator never responds to the defendant's question in line 18, even though it has been asked in English (and must thus have been understood). Instead of clearing up the confusion, the arbitrator relies on the interpreter to provide the requested information in Russian. It is not clear though whether the defendant's apparent misunderstanding is actually resolved by the interpreter's response. By focusing solely on what happens in the event of an appeal (*esli vy budete delat' appeal*, "if you will make an appeal," line 19), the interpreter does not explicitly reject the defendant's suggestion that a trial by judge has to be paid for. Subsequently, the defendant asks in Russian who would pay, her or the claimant (lines 27, 28, 30). When the interpreter explains that the fees are paid by the party that appeals (line 31), the defendant takes this to refer to the claimant (*devuška platit*, "the girl pays," line 32), suggesting that she continues to confuse the trial and the potential appeal (or, specifically, confusing the roles of appellant on appeal and claimant in the initial trial).

Apart from failing to fully clear up an apparent misunderstanding, the arbitrator and interpreter also show a bias in the information that they do provide to the hesitant litigant, as they are emphasizing disadvantages of opting for a trial by a judge. As in Example 6, this corresponds in part to the information that "slow" arbitrators provide routinely from the start. Like the slow arbitrator in Example 3, the arbitrator emphasizes the inconvenience associated with trials (notice the vowel lengthening in "a:ll night" in line 10) and the interpreter points out that it costs money to appeal a judge's decision. However, the interpreter goes beyond a mere statement of this fact to introduce an evaluation that is clearly designed to discourage the defendant from protecting her right to appeal. As shown in lines 21 and 22, she notes that the costs of filing an appeal could actually exceed the monetary value of the lawsuit. Throughout the excerpt, the defendant is thus presented with information that makes the choice of a trial by judge appear undesirable. She finally agrees to proceed with the arbitrator and waive her right to an appeal (line 38). This turn is marked by hesitation and takes the form of a second-pair part that acquiesces to a prior speaker's request ("okay, yeah, it's okay"), suggesting that she has been persuaded, and is not consenting on her own initiative.[10]

As mentioned above, many of the interpreter's utterances in Example 7 violate legal norms for court interpreting. For example, the NAJIT code of ethics contains the provisions that court interpreters "are to remain impartial and neutral" and "shall abstain from comment on matters in which they serve" ("Canon 2") and that they "shall limit their participation in those matters in which they serve to interpreting and translating, and shall not give advice to the parties or otherwise engage in activities that can be construed as the practice of law" ("Canon 4"). The interpreter in Example 7 arguably violates both of these, first by commenting to the arbitrator on the legal information that should be given to claimants (lines 9 and 12 to 16), then by explaining court procedure to the defendant (lines 19 to 26), and finally by responding to the defendant's questions in Russian (lines 29 to 37), instead of translating them into English to be answered by the arbitrator. Ironically, these violations of the norms of court interpreting occur when the interpreter is acting in support of the court administration's goals. As discussed above, such violations do not occur when "fast" arbitrators refrain from explaining the differences between trials and arbitration hearings (see Example 4), that is, when interpreters could in theory violate the norm of impartiality in order to serve the interests of claimants as opposed to the institution.

As noted, ethical guidelines for legal interpreters emphasize in particular the need to be neutral and impartial in the legal matters at hand (see Berk-Seligson 1990; Inghilleri 2012). This notion of impartiality is inherently linked to language ideologies about translation, specifically the assumption that competent interpreters produce "verbatim" translations that are referentially equivalent to their source (Haviland 2003). As noted by Inghilleri (2012: 40), "Impartiality is believed to work simultaneously to ensure the possibility of semantic and pragmatic equivalence between utterances, to guarantee mutual understanding or agreement between interlocutors, and to position interpreters as neutral participants in deliberative contexts." This notion of impartiality forbids the interpreter from taking sides for or against the other-language speaker, but it does not automatically prohibit actions on behalf of the legal institution. Courts in particular view themselves as neutral and impartial by definition, so interpreters are able to align themselves with the court without compromising the perception that they are neutral in the legal dispute. However, this alignment prevents them from remaining neutral in a negotiation between a layperson and a representative of the institution, as in the case of the consent procedure in small claims court. In this regard, it is relevant to note the case of a freelance interpreter that was mentioned above. Unlike the full-time court interpreters in the sample, he took an active role in informing the litigants of their rights and checked their understanding (see

Angermeyer 2009). This comparison suggests that the interpreters' stances toward the institution and toward the participants are greatly influenced by their employment status, as full-time interpreters are loyal to their institutional employer, while freelance interpreters may see their role primarily as a service to their fellow LOTE (languages other than English) speakers.

In her investigation of the ethics of interpreting, Inghilleri (2012: 53) draws on the philosophical notion of "role morality," which is distinct from ordinary morality and holds that "actions taken in the name of an institutional practice are justified and can be evaluated only by standards internal to the practice." Exploring the role of interpreters in British asylum hearings, Inghilleri describes situations in which their role morality converges with the interests of the state bureaucracy that views asylum seekers with suspicion and aims to reduce the number of successful applicants (2012: 87). Similarly, the court interpreters' involvement in the consent procedure can be taken as evidence that their role morality is aligned with the interests of the court, which aims to reduce the number of cases that are decided by judges. These findings are reminiscent of those by Davidson (2000), who argues that the hospital staff interpreters in his study act as institutional gatekeepers. They are found to interpret selectively, often omitting patients' questions or answering them in place of the doctor, thereby reducing the amount of time spent on patients' visits. Davidson (2000: 400) notes, "There is no evidence . . . of interpreters putting forth the patient's agenda vigorously. . . . This is not the inevitable role that interpreters must take in hospital discourses, however, and the reasons they act in this way . . . [are] largely a result of their position within the hospital hierarchy." Similarly, interpreters in small claims court act as gatekeepers when they support the court's agenda of steering litigants to arbitration, but also, for example, when they prevent litigants from speaking out of turn (Angermeyer 2009: 20–21). As Wadensjö (1998: 69) notes, in "institutional interpreter-mediated talk, . . . gatekeeping is, in effect, doubled."

Conclusion

Focusing especially on cases with litigants who speak a language other than English, this chapter has explored how small claims courts in New York City influence litigants to choose arbitration instead of a trial by the judge. As shown above, litigants give consent to arbitration by signing a legal document that states that they agree to having their case decided by an arbitrator and that they waive their right to appeal the eventual decision. However, this act has to be seen in the context of the litigants' overall experience in court, prior to the arbitrator's request for consent. Policies set by the court administration and actions taken by court officers, volunteer arbitrators, and staff interpreters all converge on creating the expectation that litigants opt for arbitration.

This is done by withholding information or presenting it selectively, and especially by presenting arbitration as the default option: rather than choosing arbitration from two equally acceptable choices, litigants are put in a position where they have to actively "opt out" of arbitration and assert their preference for trial by judge. This is evident during the so-called calendar call, when court officers read aloud the names on the docket and expect litigants to respond with an indication of their procedural preference. Litigants who merely note that they are present (i.e., calling "ready" or repeating their name, rather than responding "ready by the court") are sent to arbitration. As demonstrated above, many litigants (especially those with limited fluency in English) do not understand the significance of the calendar call and find themselves in front of an arbitrator without having consciously chosen to do so. Litigants are then further steered toward arbitration by arbitrators who ask for their signature on the consent form without giving an explanation, acting as if litigants have already made an informed decision. Other arbitrators do provide such information, but emphasize the negative aspects of trials and the cost and difficulty involved in appealing a judge's decision. Arbitrators and interpreters also emphasize these aspects in situations when they attempt to dissuade a hesitant litigant from opting for a trial by judge. Litigants who want their case to be heard by a judge thus need to actively assert this preference with court officials, arbitrators, and even interpreters, all of whom are likely to present them with arguments against this decision. In addition, litigants may have to assert this preference in opposition to the other party in their dispute, who has likely agreed to arbitration.

These findings raise questions about the notion of consent in institutional interaction. In principle, consent implies a voluntary decision, in which a person chooses one of several options available. However, the choice is presented by representatives of the institution who often display a clear preference for one particular option and may request consent in such a way that choosing an alternative course of action amounts to a face-threatening act against them. In such circumstances, requests for consent involve an inherent conflict of interest. In this, the circumstances of arbitration hearings are parallel to those of doctor-patient interviews, when doctors ask patients for their consent to a proposed medical procedure. As Meyer (2003: 2) points out, "[D]octors do not adopt an impartial stance regarding the patient's decision-making." They "inform the patient and, at the same time, maintain the patient's compliance." Such a conflict of interest is even more evident in interaction involving police, when police officers ask suspects to speak to them without an attorney being present, or to agree to a police search without a warrant. When interpreters are present in these types of interactions, their stance may not be impartial either, especially if they are affiliated with the institution. Berk-Seligson (2009) shows particularly clear cases of this, with police officers acting as interpreters undermining suspects' invocations of the so-called Miranda rights, for example, by responding to them in Spanish rather than translating them. In such situations, participants who do not speak the language of the institution are systematically hindered from asserting their preference in a way that accomplishes a performative speech act. The findings of this study converge with this research in showing that institutional agents (including court-employed court interpreters) are able to exploit linguistic differences as a resource to achieve legal outcomes desired by the institution.

Appendix: Transcription Conventions

(.)	Brief, untimed pause
(1.1)	Pause with length in seconds
/but	Emphasis
(fè)	Unclear segment
(xxx)	Inaudible segment
<u>appeal</u>	English element used by LOTE speaker
[No]	Overlap
I-	Cut-off or self-interruption
+//.	Utterance is paused to facilitate consecutive interpreting and resumed later
=No	Quick uptake
{'Yes'}	English gloss
{*room*}	Author comment or explanation
a:ll	lengthened vowel

Notes

1. Because arbitrators' decisions cannot be appealed, they receive relatively little scrutiny from supervising court officers. Whenever I observed court officers comment on an arbitrator's performance, it was with regard to the arbitrator's ability to process cases quickly, not with regard to the legal decisions they made.

2. Note also that the text of the court notice that is reproduced in (1) refers to arbitration hearings as *trials*, which serves to further downplay the distinction between the two types of hearings ("[Y]ou will get an immediate trial tonight if both parties agree to have an arbitrator try the case"). By contrast, American legal usage generally reserves the terms *try* (a case) and *trial* for judge-led proceedings, and this is how I use them in this chapter. Similarly, the arbitrators whom I observed almost invariably spoke of *arbitration* and of *hearing a case*, rather than of *trial* or *trying a case* (see example 3).

3. All names are pseudonyms.

4. Example 3 is from a hearing in which one litigant was represented by an attorney. Lawyers were present in approximately one third of all hearings, most commonly to represent insurance companies in cases about car accidents. It is not clear whether the

presence of a lawyer has an influence on the consent procedure, as the styles found in (2) and (3) were observed both with and without a lawyer present.

5. The belief that interpreting slows down proceedings is widespread in the legal system, but it has not been empirically validated. At the least, this delay would be limited to portions of the trial that are conducted in consecutive interpreting, such as the testimony of minority language speakers. By contrast, the simultaneous interpreting used for other portions of the trial would likely not prolong proceedings in any way.

6. See http://www.najit.org/about/NAJITCodeofEthicsFINAL.pdf (accessed August 31, 2012).

7. While court interpreters are generally able to interpret short passages in (near-) simultaneous mode, they do not have the specialized training nor the working conditions required for sustained simultaneous interpreting. By comparison, simultaneous interpreters in conferences work in soundproof booths, take frequent breaks, and interpret only into one language, not both.

8. Utterances in Russian are written in Roman script, transliterated from standard Cyrillic orthography according to the ISO system (Cubberley 1996: 351).

9. The untranslated utterances in Example 5 provide information that makes the choice of trial by judge less attractive. The fact that the interpreter omits these from translation would seem to contradict the argument that interpreters support the court's goal of steering cases to arbitration. However, in contrast to Example 7, the litigants in Example 5 show no sign of objecting to arbitration, making the inclusion of this information less crucial from the court's point of view.

10. The corresponding request is absent from the excerpt and indeed from the recording, but it can be surmised to consist of the arbitrator's initial request for consent, comparable to those shown in Examples 3 and 4.

References

Angermeyer, Philipp Sebastian. 2009. Translation style and participant roles in court interpreting. *Journal of Sociolinguistics* 13: 3–28.

Angermeyer, Philipp Sebastian. 2015. *Speak English or What? Codeswitching and Interpreter Use in New York City Courts*. New York: Oxford University Press.

Berk-Seligson, Susan. 1990. *The Bilingual Courtroom: Court Interpreters in the Judicial Process*. Chicago: University of Chicago Press.

Berk-Seligson, Susan. 2009. *Coerced Confessions: The Discourse of Bilingual Police Interrogations*. Berlin and New York: Mouton de Gruyter.

Conley, John and William O'Barr. 1990. *Rules versus Relationships: The Ethnography of Legal Discourse*. Chicago: University of Chicago Press.

Cubberley, Paul. 1996. The Slavic alphabets. In Peter Daniels and William Bright (eds.) *The World's Writing Systems*. New York: Oxford University Press. 346–355.

Davidson, Brad. 2000. The interpreter as institutional gatekeeper: The social-linguistic role of interpreters in Spanish-English medical discourse. *Journal of Sociolinguistics* 4: 379–405.

Haviland, John. 2003. Ideologies of language: Reflections on language and U.S. law. *American Anthropologist* 105: 764–774.

Heffer, Chris. 2006. Beyond "reasonable doubt": The criminal standard of proof instruction as communicative act. *The International Journal of Speech, Language and the Law* 13: 159–188.

Inghilleri, Moira. 2012. *Interpreting Justice: Ethics, Politics and Language*. New York: Routledge.

Meyer, Bernd. 2003. *Bilingual Risk Communication*. Hamburg: Universität Hamburg.

Meyer, Bernd. 2004. *Dolmetschen Im Medizinischen Aufklärungsgespräch: Eine Diskursanalytische Untersuchung Zur Wissensvermittlung Im Mehrsprachigen Krankenhaus*. Münster: Waxmann.

Philips, Susan. 1998. *Ideology in the Language of Judges: How Judges Practice Law, Politics, and Courtroom Control*. New York and Oxford: Oxford University Press.

Reddy, Michael J. 1979. The conduit metaphor: A case of frame conflict in our language about language. In Andrew Ortony (ed.) *Metaphor and Thought*. Cambridge: Cambridge University Press. 284–324.

Wadensjö, Cecilia. 1998. *Interpreting as Interaction*. London and New York: Longman.

9

Consent and Compliance in Youth Justice Conferences

Michele Zappavigna, Paul Dwyer, and J. R. Martin

Background: NSW Youth Justice Conferencing

This chapter considers some of the ways in which young people consent to, and comply with the expectations of, a diversionary legal process known as youth justice conferencing. In the state of New South Wales, Australia, where the fieldwork for this research was undertaken, a program of youth justice conferencing (with close parallels to programs in other Australian jurisdictions) has been in operation since the late 1990s. These conferences are an alternative to dealing with juvenile criminal offenses by a children's court magistrate. They involve bringing a young person who has admitted an offense into a face-to-face meeting with his or her victim (or a victim's representative). Also in attendance are support people for the young person and the victim (e.g., family, friends, a social worker, a teacher) as well as police (typically a youth liaison officer but also, on occasion, the arresting officer) and, where relevant, an ethnic or indigenous community liaison officer. Importantly, the convener of the conference has no direct judicial or law enforcement role. He or she is a citizen acting in a private capacity, tasked with facilitating a "structured conversation" (Moore and McDonald 2000: 14) about the young person's offending behavior, its repercussions and possible consequences.

While conferences are an attempt to divert offenders away from formal court proceedings, it is important to remember that they operate within, rather than outside, the juvenile justice system. Under the provisions of the NSW Young Offenders Act (1997), a youth justice conference (YJC) can take place only where a young person (YP) has already admitted an offense to the police. A referral to conferencing may then be made either by the police, before the matter goes to court, or else by a magistrate as an alternative to judgment in court. The Young Offenders Act defines the purpose of a YJC, in a narrow sense, as determining an "outcome plan" according to which the YP agrees to undertake various reparative actions (such as a formal apology to victims or perhaps unpaid work in a community organization). These outcome plans are then submitted to the children's court magistrate for ratification before they are implemented. Failure to complete an approved plan also leads back to the children's magistrate who would, in such an instance, deal with the offense through a conventional court hearing.

However, in addition to the narrowly defined purpose of brokering an outcome plan that is acceptable to all conference participants, the Young Offenders Act also refers to broader principles that are meant to underpin YJCs. These include promoting acceptance by the YP of "responsibility for his or her own behaviour," "strengthening the YP's family or family group," helping the YP to "become a fully autonomous individual," enhancing "the rights and place of victims in the juvenile justice process," and so on (Young Offenders Act, section 34[1]). These strong aspirational statements in the legislation tie in with what we will refer to as a "discourse of integration" running through YJCs. They also point to the close links between YJCs and a range of processes in other jurisdictions (e.g., family group conferencing in New Zealand, victim-offender mediation in the United States and Europe, circle sentencing in Australian and Canadian indigenous communities) that have been widely promoted in recent decades as part of a more general "restorative justice" reform movement. For proponents of such reforms, crime is conceived not simply as lawbreaking but as "a violation of people and relationships," hence justice is considered less a matter of retribution/punishment and more an effort to involve "the victim, the offender and the community in a search for solutions which promote repair, reconciliation, and reassurance" (Zehr 1990: 181).

Kathleen Daly (2001) has argued that this distinction between retributive and restorative forms of justice, despite its strong rhetorical appeal, is much harder to maintain when one looks closely at how restorative justice principles are applied in practice. She also sounds a note of caution with regard to the way restorative justice advocates often portray these practices as a rediscovery of traditional dispute resolution processes in many indigenous communities:

> To say that conferences are "like" indigenous justice practices is to re-engage a white-centred view of the world. It erases the many histories of indigenous justice practices, some of which would not be comprehensible or acceptable in the modern world. And, as Blagg (1997) suggests, it may lead to a "double failure" for indigenous groups: not only will they have failed to act in a law-abiding fashion [. . .] they will appear to have "failed" to act appropriately as indigenous people according to a white-centred justice script. (Daly 2001: 66)

Foreshadowing the conclusion to our chapter, we suggest that Daly is right to question whether conferencing is really such a close cultural fit for disenfranchised indigenous youth or, indeed, for any young person without the appropriate "cultural capital" (including the necessary linguistic resources) to engage in it. Nevertheless, like Daly, we remain sympathetic to the social justice ideals that underpin many reforms undertaken in the name of restorative justice and we acknowledge the findings from numerous studies of conferencing programs that suggest many participants do find the process satisfying and procedurally fair (see, for example, Palk, Hayes and Prenzler 1998; Strang, Barnes, Braithwaite and Sherman 1999; Trimboli 2000).[1]

Criminologists and social psychologists have made a number of claims regarding the nature of the social interaction that "restores justice" in conferencing, invoking such concepts as the management of "social bond threats," the experience of "collective vulnerability," or the salutary effects of "reintegrative (rather than stigmatizing) shaming" (Retzinger and Scheff 1996; Braithwaite 1989; Ahmed, Harris, Braithwaite and Braithwaite 2001; Moore and McDonald 2001). From our point of view as discourse analysts, perhaps the most surprising thing about this literature on conferencing is its seeming indifference to the fact that the democratically toned discourse of integration in YJCs is embedded within (or, as we will explain below, "projected" by) a hierarchical, regulative discourse. To put this bluntly, the invitation to the YP who agrees to participate in a YJC is often couched in a language of empowerment and community ("Just tell us in your own words what happened," "This has affected all of us, including you") whereas the tacit expectation of the more powerful participants in the conference is that the YP will take up this offer in quite particular ways, by enacting a preferred "genre identity" (suitably deferential, remorseful, etc.). Not all young people are willing or able to "pull off" this kind of linguistic performance, and this, in turn, may have consequences for the way consent operates in YJCs. For instance, while it is true that a YJC can proceed only if the YP gives his or her consent (and this consent may be withdrawn at any stage during the process), it is also the case that victims (should they attend the conference) have input into, and a right of veto over, the conference outcome plan. In short, while the legislation requires only the YP's consent, his or her interlocutors require more (and more than they themselves perhaps realize). In the analyses below, we focus on aspects of genre and exchange structure that bear upon the negotiation of not only formal, legal consent but also the performance by YPs of a compliant genre identity.

Youth Justice Conferencing as a Macrogenre

This chapter explores consent and compliance across a sample of youth justice conferences that were observed and videotaped between 2008 and 2010.

TABLE 9.1

Summary of youth justice conferences in our sample

YJC	Offense
Affray	The YP committed an affray offense, chasing a rival gang member, threatening him, throwing bricks across the road at him, causing damage to property and apparently terrifying a number of bystanders.
Guidedog	The YP stole the wallet of a blind woman.
Mobile Phone	The YP swapped his mobile phone for a stolen mobile phone.
School Library	Two YPs entered a school library and "roughed up" a student.
Shopping Trolley	The YP threw a shopping trolley near railway tracks.
Train Tracks	The YP stole a packet of chips from her local service station and ran away onto train tracks when pursued by police.

Table 9.1 gives a brief summary of these conferences (each conference has been given a shorthand title that we will use throughout the chapter when labeling transcript excerpts in order to remind the reader of the matters being dealt with).

One limitation of the fieldwork undertaken for this study is the fact that we were not able to observe any of the preconference briefings that conveners hold with key participants.[2] However, our experience of having attended conference convener training workshops, along with the descriptions of conferencing in pamphlets produced by the NSW Department of Juvenile Justice, does offer some insight into the kind of expectations with which participants may approach this relatively novel genre of legal interaction. One point to note is that the printed materials provided to participants before they come to a YJC tend to treat the main roles and activities within conferencing ("the young person," "the victim," "tell[ing] the story of what happened") as more or less transparent, given categories (NSW Department of Juvenile Justice 1999). Similarly, in our field observations of convener training, the ideal-typical role to which conveners were encouraged to aspire was that of an almost transparent, neutral cypher: "Ideally the convenor 'disappears' after starting the conference. [It's] not an active management [of the other participants]" (field note, September 11, 2005). Such images belie the complexity of the genre as we have observed it in actual conferences. A fuller description of YJCs needs to account for the many smaller steps involved beyond the (never so straightforward) telling of stories and needs to consider, alongside the ideational content of the discourse, the (sometimes very active) management of interpersonal meanings.

To this end, the analysis in this chapter takes a systemic functional linguistics (SFL) approach, based on a model of social meaning-making that conceives of genres "as staged, goal oriented social processes" (Martin and Rose 2008: 5). Genres can be thought of as recurrent patterns of meanings that occur in texts (in some disciplines, these are referred to as "text types"). Figure 9.1 outlines the structure of YJCs as we have observed them in our fieldwork, suggesting that they be seen as a "macrogenre" (Christie 2002) comprising six functional genres, which each comprise configurations of elemental genres (that is, smaller genres which are linked together). These elemental genres are staged, because they take more than one step to achieve their social purpose. We see this in the movement of YJCs from an initial introduction and legal framing, through a retelling of the offense and exploration of its impact, toward the generation of a plan for how the young person will make amends for their action and concluding with the closing of the conference (see Figure 9.1).

Conferences begin with a Mandate genre, which institutionalizes the conference as a legal proceeding. This is followed by Testimony, through which the offense is recounted. In the ensuing Rejoinder, support persons and police officers evaluate the impact of the offense. This may be followed by a Caution, in which (typically) a police youth liaison officer (YLO) looks forward and comments on the choices open to the YP as far as reintegration into the community is concerned.[3] The Caution is followed by the Outcome Plan, where agreement on reparation is reached, and then by Reintegration, through which legal proceedings are brought to a close and participants have an opportunity to mingle as members of the community. As is evident from this description of the genres, initial capital letters are used for genre labels.

Formal, legal consent is elicited at the beginning of the conference in the Mandate genre and again near the very end of the conference when the outcome plan is endorsed during the Reintegration genre. Typically involving a yes/no response to a formulaic question, the negotiation of consent in these moments that bookend the conference relates to strongly classified (Bernstein 1990) criteria defined in section 36c of the Young Offenders Act. By contrast, the YP's compliance (or not) with what we see as the preferred genre identity in YJCs is a less obvious negotiation over the duration of the whole conference. This compliance involves a largely implicit agreement by YPs both to be a part of the conferencing macrogenre and to engage in the linguistic processes or patterns that constitute this genre. It means conforming to the kinds of identity or subject position that the genre makes available to YPs. In the discussion below, we sometimes refer to this as a kind of "prosodic" compliance to reflect the way that it is a *process* that "ebbs and flows" across the entire conference rather than the *product* of a particular moment when the YP is formally asked to state his or her agreement. Prosodic compliance is largely a matter of evaluative language, involving the use of various appraisal resources (in SFL terms, these are language choices that construe affect, appreciation, and judgment, and/or which suggest the force or focus of an evaluation, as well as the choices we make to reference other people's evaluations or not—see Martin and Rose 2007 for details).

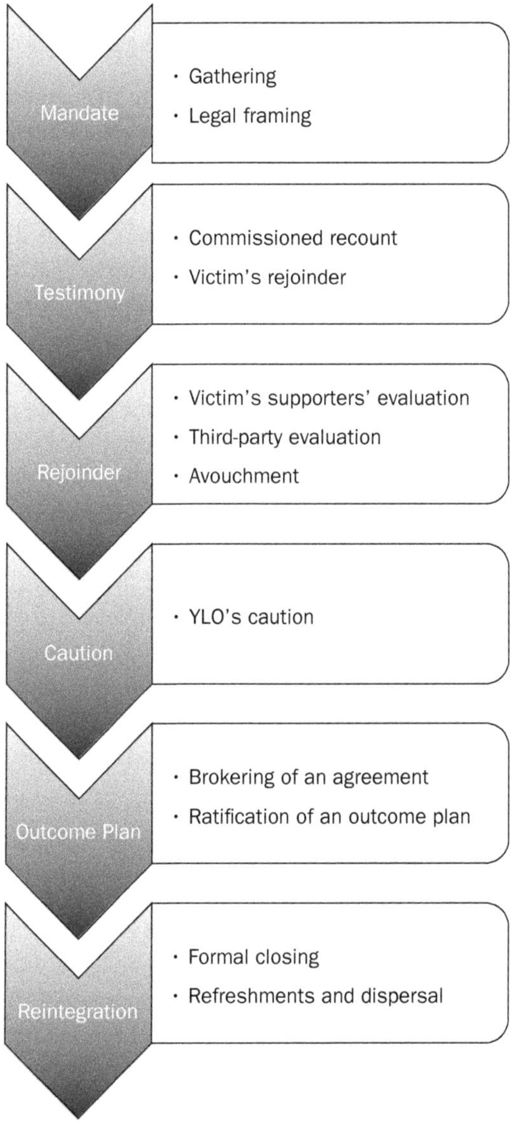

FIGURE 9.1 Canonical structure for youth justice conference macrogenre

As we will see below, some of this evaluative language comes from YPs themselves but, more often, YPs are responding to evaluations of their behavior that other speakers have offered. Martin and Rose explain the link between prosody and genre:

> Appraisal resources are used to establish the tone or mood of a passage of discourse, as choices resonate with one another from one moment to another as a text unfolds. The pattern of choices is thus "prosodic." They

> form a prosody of attitude running through the text that swells and diminishes, in the manner of a musical prosody. (Martin and Rose 2007: 59)

The significance of all this for the way in which YPs engage in conferencing emerged several times during the fieldwork phase of our research. In one particularly memorable instance, after the conclusion of a conference, the researcher was offered a lift back to the university by police officers who had been present. When asked by the researcher "What did you make of the YP's demeanour?" one of the officers commented that the YP's apology came far too early and was therefore insincere ("He was too polished, too well rehearsed"). Bearing in mind that this officer was the victim of offenses for which the YP had been charged (abusing a police officer and resisting arrest) and therefore held a right of veto over the outcome plan, we can see how formal, legal consent may be influenced by participants' assessment of the YP's compliance with the genre.

Of course, the genre also places expectations on participants other than the YP in relation to the kinds of identity they enact. Our fieldwork observations suggest, for instance, that victims generally refrain from vindictive attitudes (including the police officer in the example above who did not exercise his right of veto). The following discussion focuses almost exclusively, however, on the experience of consent and compliance from the perspective of YPs since their attempts to enact a suitably remorseful identity are complicated by the fact that they have such limited control over the genre.

Negotiating Formal Consent

As noted, YPs are called upon to provide formal consent at two main points in the conference: during the Mandate genre, which we will explore in this section, and during the ratification of the outcome plan in the Reintegration genre at the end of the conference, explored later in this chapter. The Mandate genre, which occurs at the beginning of a YJC, has a very recognizable configuration of meanings and predictable staging (in the following notation, ^ signals sequence and · freedom of sequence—that is, that the genre following this midline period can occur at any part of the sequence):

> [Official welcome ^ Legal invocation ^ Role declaration ^ Goal affirmation] · Housekeeping

During this stage participants are brought together and seated in a circle configuration and introduced to one another. The Young Offenders Act is invoked as the relevant legal framework for the conference, and the aims of the conference are outlined by the convener. Even though some participants may have already introduced themselves upon arrival, conveners will offer an official welcome once everyone is seated, as a way of formally marking the start of proceedings. Participants are asked, one by one, to state their name and role. This stage can sometimes appear quite stilted. While the conveners prefer the term "young person" to "young offender," since it avoids a potentially stigmatizing label (Braithwaite 1989), we have yet to hear a formula such as "I'm X and I'm the young person who did Y" spontaneously produced by a YP at the start of a conference. Similarly, we have observed reluctance on the part of police officers, who have sometimes been punched, kicked, or spat upon by a YP, to introduce themselves as a "victim" unless prompted very explicitly to do so by the convener. The convener then offers a brief overview of what the conference is meant to achieve (Goal affirmation). Finally, Housekeeping covers such matters as the convener pointing out to people where the nearest toilets are, offering people a glass of water, and so on. Overall, this period in a conference tends to involve frequent shunting back and forth by the convener between talk that emphasizes the formal legal status of proceedings (where participants have roles and obligations) and talk that seems to be more about "knocking the sharp edges off the law," intimating that conference participants have assembled with the common goal of achieving consensus regarding how the YP can make reparation for the harm caused.

The YP's formal consent is elicited during the Legal framing stage of the Mandate, when the convener makes sure that the YP has admitted to the offense, since this admission is a prerequisite for a legitimate conference (Young Offenders Act, section 36b). The following is an example taken from the Mandate of a YJC involving a YP who had stolen the purse of a blind woman seated on a public bench along the main street of a country town:

Extract 1: Guidedog YJC

CONVENER: Thanks all for making the effort to attend. It's a difficult matter. Your presence here will help us deal with it successfully. The conference will focus on an incident that happened at [Location X] on date X about 10 o'clock in the morning. It involves YP and Victim X. The Young Offenders Act 1997 requires that the young person has admitted the offence and agreed to the conference. YP do you confirm your admission to the offence of stealing?

YP: Yes.

CONVENER: And do you give your consent for the- this conference to proceed?

YP: Yes.

CONVENER: Do you understand that at any time you can elect to have this matter to be dealt with by the court?

YP: Yes.

CONVENER: Thanks. OK. Now let's proceed.

The convener may attempt to determine that the YP is attending voluntarily, presumably by way of helping to ensure genuine consent to the proceedings, as in the following exchange from the "affray" YJC:

Extract 2: Affray YJC

CONVENER: Ok, YP, one of the conditions of a juvenile conference is that you admit to the offence in front of all of us here today and that you tell us that you are here of your own free will. So did you commit the offences you were charged with?

YP: Yes.

CONVENER: And are you here of your own free will?

YP: Yes.

CONVENER: OK. Thank you. OK, what we are going to do now is just go around the table and were going to start with YP. YP, what I'd like you to do is to tell everybody what happened on that particular day. . . .

The kind of consent in play during the Mandate functions as a formal legal consent—a binary agreement by the YP with statements made by the convener. This form of consent may theoretically be withdrawn during any stage of the conference by the YP, thereby diverting the matter to a magistrate, though we do not have any instances in which this has occurred in our recorded conferences or observations. Of course, the apparently straightforward way in which YPs consent to having the matter dealt with by means of a YJC does not mean that they are always sure of what, exactly, they are agreeing to in terms of the ensuing process.

Prosodic Compliance and Regulative Discourse

As suggested earlier, in addition to the formal consent required by law as a precondition for the conference to proceed, YPs are expected to demonstrate a less obvious form of compliance in which the language of evaluation is often critical. However, it is not only a matter of how participants evaluate, for example, the nature of the YP's offending behavior; it is also a matter of when and where the macrogenre encourages such evaluations and from whom. YPs must fit in with a "prosody of attitude" that unfolds across the whole macrogenre, but perhaps the clearest example of the challenge they face can be seen in the special role that evaluative language plays in the Commissioned recount. To prepare the ground for an analysis of the Commissioned Recount genre, we begin with some comments about the regulative discourse that features prominently in YJCs and which impacts upon the kinds of subject position that the YP is able to take up within the conferencing macrogenre.

As the exchanges between the YP and the convener in the Mandate extract introduced in the previous section suggest, determining the issue of consent is convener "driven" during that initial part of the conference in terms of exchange structure, with the convener making all of the initiating moves and the YP responding a word at a time. This process of obtaining formal consent resembles what Basil Bernstein, British sociologist of education, termed a regulative discourse operating within a pedagogic discourse. For Bernstein (1990: 183), a pedagogic discourse is "the rule which embeds a discourse of competence (instructional discourse) into a discourse of social order (regulative discourse)." What he is exploring here is the relation between the discourse of the subjects being taught in school (e.g., science, history, mathematics) and the discourse used to teach them (including control of student behavior and the pacing, sequencing and evaluation of what is learned). Fundamental to his argument is the idea that "the regulative discourse is the dominant discourse [. . .] because it is the moral discourse that creates the criteria which give rise to character, manner, conduct, posture" (Bernstein 1996: 48). As a consequence, the discourses of the subjects being taught are always recontextualized discourses, taken out of the contexts in which they are routinely produced and deployed and subsequently reworked into the moral order of schools. In Bernstein's terms, the purpose of the "pedagogic device," that is, the rules and social relationships that enable and regulate pedagogic communication, is "to provide a symbolic ruler for consciousness" (Bernstein 1996: 50). Christie develops this work in her analysis of classroom discourse, focusing on variables of register in the discourse and preferring Halliday's notion of "projection" to Bernstein's "embedding": "The first order or regulative register, it will be argued, 'projects' a second order or instructional register" (Christie 2002: 25). She explains her metaphorical use of the grammatical term "projection":

> A clause that projects in some sense takes something said or thought before and reinstates it. Hence the notion of projection is used metaphorically to refer to the relationship of the two registers in the pedagogic discourse. A field of knowledge and its associated activity is taken, relocated and in some sense therefore "projected" for another purpose and another site. (Christie 2002: 25)

Pedagogic discourses are not restricted to school settings, however, as Muntigl shows in his extension of these ideas to the study of relationship counseling discourse:

> I shall argue that the narrative counselling discourse interview [. . .] includes both a regulative and instructional register. Regulation involves the degree to which the client's social actions are managed by the counsellor [. . . t]he instructional register [. . .] involves [. . .] the ways in which

> the clients are meant to construe experience [. . .] it is by regulating clients' verbal behaviour that a certain view of problems and their influences becomes possible. (Muntigl 2004: 124)

In a similar vein, we suggest that youth justice conferencing can be seen as a pedagogic discourse that includes elements of regulative discourse and elements of what we have been calling a discourse of integration, intended to realign the YP with the values of his or her family, ethnic group, and community and diminish the relatively malign influence of peers. This duality is hardly surprising given that the design of this evolving macrogenre has its origins in the concerns of both the criminal justice and social work systems (Cunneen and White 2007). Again, however, as Bernstein and Christie would have it, it is the regulative discourse that is dominant, "projecting" and thereby recontextualizing the discourse of integration.

The regulatory dimension of conferencing as a pedagogic discourse reveals itself, in part, through the realization of the interaction by conveners (and sometimes other professionals in the room, such as police youth liaison officers) as an occasion for "linguistic servicing" (i.e., requests for verbal performances of various kinds that can be double-coded as requests for both knowledge and action) (see Ventola 1987 on the role of linguistic servicing in service encounters).

Tables 2 to 4 present a simplified version of the kind of exchange structure analysis we have adopted in our work in order to keep track of both regulative and integrative moves in conferencing discourse (for more detailed analysis and explanation of notation see Martin, Zappavigna and Dwyer 2009b). This approach to exchange analysis considers dialogue in terms of what is being negotiated by speakers, that is, whether they are initiating or responding to information or knowledge (K) (for instance, asking what the time is), or whether they are offering or demanding action (A) (for instance, asking for a drink of water) (Martin and Rose 2007). It builds on the IRF (initiation, response, and feedback) model of classroom discourse developed by Sinclair and Coulthard (1975) and extended by Berry (1981a, 1981b), Ventola (1987), and others.

In Tables 2 and 3, we have edited a portion of the transcript from near the start of an actual conference so as to artificially separate out, for a moment, the regulative moves from the integrative moves in the discourse. In Table 9.2, where the convener is demanding a specific (verbal) action from the YP, the hierarchical relationship between them is very clear. In Table 9.3, the convener is asking a question that, however formulaic, is at least premised on the notion that the YP has better knowledge of his or her "own free will" than the convener does. To the extent that this exchange endows the YP with some sense of agency, it launches the process by which

TABLE 9.2

Regulative moves in an exchange between a convener and YP

Speaker	Talk	Regulative
Convener	So what I need you to do is admit you're guilty.	A2 (command)
YP	OK. [nods]	A1 (undertaking)

TABLE 9.3

Integrative moves in an exchange between a convener and YP

Speaker	Talk	Integrative
Convener	You've already admitted your guilt to this offence and you're here of your own free will?	K2 (question)
YP	Yep. [nods]	K1 (answer)
Convener	Yep?	K2f (follow up)

TABLE 9.4

Regulative and integrative moves in an exchange between a convener and a YP

Speaker	Talk	Regulative	Integrative
Convener	So what I need you to do is	A2 (command)	
	<<you've already admitted your guilt to this offence	A1 (undertaking)	K2 (question)
	and you're here of your own free will?>>		
YP	Yep. [nods]		K1 (answer)
Convener	Yep?		K2f (follow up)
	OK	A2f (follow up)	

the YP can begin to establish him- or herself as a candidate for reintegration into family and community networks.

Table 9.4 presents the actual transcript from which the edited talk in Tables 9.2 and 9.3 was taken. Here, we see how closely the regulative and integrative dimensions of the discourse work together, to the point where some exchanges in youth justice conferences can be interpreted as offering or demanding action just as much as they are initiating or responding to information. Regulative and integrative work is happening at the same time.

Compliant YP Identities and Evaluation of the YP's Story

Throughout the conference, the convener has the dual role of managing compliance at the level of exchange structure, as seen in the examples above where she is interacting specifically with the YP, and compliance in terms of the overall macrogenre, where she must assist all conference participants in moving through the different parts of the conference toward a successful resolution in a working outcome plan. To assist this process, the pressure of the conferencing macrogenre seems to be propelling YPs toward adopting a particular subject position: a forthcoming, remorseful young person (Martin, Zappavigna and Dwyer 2009a). Often, however, we have observed a "small target" YP, that is, a YP who appears to want to say as little as possible to avoid becoming a target of criticism. Consequently, details and evaluation regarding the offense often have to be extracted from the YP by the convener (or sometimes other participants, for example, the police youth liaison officers) during the Commissioned Recount (Martin et al. 2009b). In this section we will explore some typically minimalist recounts of offending behavior that, nevertheless, support the construction of a compliant YP "genre identity" since both the young people involved willingly submit to an extension of their brief recount by answering additional questions proposed by the convener. (This kind of compliance will be contrasted, in the next section of the chapter, with a much less common, noncompliant genre identity produced by YPs who are markedly resistant to some of the things said about them in the conference.)

The Commissioned Recount is the genre during which the YP relates the offense and its impact on those around them.[4] Our first example of this genre is developed below. Given the floor by the convener, the young person begins as follows:

Extract 3: Mobile phone YJC

I was walking to a mate's house
And ( ) and I was walking with him.
This guy just came up to me
and he goes "Do you want to buy this phone?"

At this point the convener interrupts him, in order to ask him to speak louder (for the benefit of the police liaison officer who, she says, has a cold, and perhaps also for the benefit of our recording process). He then resumes, in a slightly louder voice (stages within the genre are shown in bold subtitles):

Extract 4: Mobile phone YJC

Orientation

Yeah, I was, I was walking to a mate's house.

Record of events

This guy just came up to me
and goes 'Do you want to buy a phone?'
and I go 'No'
and I go 'Do you want to swap?'
( ) want to swap with my phone
and he looked at my phone
and he goes 'Yeah' and we swap
and I went and stayed at my mate's house
and when it came to night time I was going back home,
and we was walking, was walking up the road
and the police just came and got us.

The convener at this point nods encouragingly, in case the young person wishes to expand on his statement—an invitation the young person declines:

Extract 5: Mobile phone YJC

Reorientation

. . [as convener nods] That's it.

In terms of genre staging, this is a typical recount (Martin and Rose 2008), beginning with an Orientation (in Extract 4), establishing the Record of Events (also in Extract 4) and closing with a Reorientation (Extract 5). However, the level of detail provided is minimal and there is no self-evaluation or assessment of the offense (e.g., was it a bad thing to do?). The convener thus scaffolds an Extension to the recount (in Extract 6 below), covering events at the police station, and elicits more details from the YP about how the offense has affected people in his family, all with a view to exploring how the YP might reintegrate back into his family network.

Extract 6: Mobile phone YJC

Extension

CONVENER: And then what happened? They came and got you. They found the phone. What did they say to you?

YP: They go that this phone was stolen.

CONVENER: OK. What did you say?

YP: I go, you know, I swapped it. Yeah, they just took- took me.

CONVENER: Took you where?

YP: Police station.

CONVENER: And who did they ring when they brought you to the police station?

YP: My dad.

Our second example of a Commissioned Recount has a longer Record of Events, as the young person recounts what happened when he went to back up a mate who had arranged to fight someone one-on-one. We hear how the "duel" gets out of hand: someone is stabbed; the young person responds by chasing the rival gang member who did the stabbing, threatening him, throwing bricks across the road at him, causing damage to property and apparently terrifying a number of bystanders. He has pleaded guilty to a charge of affray (though at the conference he initially introduces himself as "the victim"[5] and has to be corrected by the convener).[6] His account begins as follows:

Extract 7: Affray YJC

Orientation

It was up there –
It was—( ) on a Tuesday yeah. ( )

Record of events

and I got a call from my friend, [Person X], ( ) to come down to [name of suburb].
Something going on;
but when I went down with them to [name of different suburb] station
and jumped on the train ( )
and the train we got it straight to [name of suburb],
we got off at [name of suburb]
( ) [Person Y] and other—his other two friends.
And they had a one on one
and I jumped in
and I turn around.
I was having a go with his friends
and the (one) next to me got stabbed
and he ( ) goes 'Chase him!'
and I went and chased him,

started chucking stuff at him,
hitting him.
I couldn't stop him.
He still had the knife in his hand
and after that I walked back to the station to see [Person X]
and I see the policeman coming as I walked away
and ( ) happened to him
and I said to the two officers 'Assault me, search me.'
They took out all my stuff
and they found out I was involved
and they took me back to the police station.
And my ( )
and I had an interview
and they took my pants, my hat, my jacket
and I was released.

As the notation above shows, his recount once again begins with an Orientation and continues with a Record of Events; there is, however, no formal closing (i.e., Coda).[7] The convener then scaffolds a long Extension stage, exploring why the young offender went to back up his mate, and establishing that he was also charged with possession of a knife:

Extract 8: Affray YJC

Extension

CONVENER: And when you- when you decided you would go down and help your friend, what did he actually say to you?

YP: He was going to see [Person X].

CONVENER: And why was he going to see [Person X]?

YP: Because [Person X] offered him out.

CONVENER: Offered what?

YP: Nah ( ) two of us have a go like one on one.

CONVENER: To fight?

YP: Yeah.

CONVENER: And so why did he need you there if he was going to fight him one on one?

YP: Because I'm closer ( ). He trusts me like in case anything happens because I've known him since primary.

CONVENER: And why did he think something would happen?

YP: In case.

CONVENER: And when you went to this location you had something on your person. You had something with you. What was that?

YP: The knife.

CONVENER: So you want to tell us about the knife?

YP: ( ) didn't know I even had it on me. Forgot I had it on me the whole time and then I couldn't remember I had it until they ( ) and pulled it out and showed them. It doesn't even work. You can't even use it.

CONVENER: But it's not actually a knife.

YP: No.

CONVENER: A knife is included in it isn't it?

YP: Yes.

CONVENER: What else is it?

YP: A can opener, screwdriver.

CONVENER: And so when the police, um, searched you and found the um, what are they, a Leatherman? Is that what they're called?

Arresting Officer: A Leatherman sort of tool.

CONVENER: When they found that what did you say to them?

YP: Said it's for work.

CONVENER: Tell everybody what you did for work back then.

YP: Panel beater.

CONVENER: So, as I explained to you the other day, why do you think the police charged you with having that weapon in your possession?

YP: ( ) They thought I got ready for a fight . . . to use it

CONVENER: And what else did they say to you? Do you remember?

YP: Nup.

CONVENER: Did they say anything to you about the fact that it, you know, as a panel beater you probably don't need a knife?

YP: Yes.

CONVENER: Is that—do you think that's reasonable?

YP: Yes.

CONVENER: So you accept the fact that you got charged with the possession of the knife.

YP: Yes.

CONVENER: Alright and then when you chased after [Person X] what were you going to do when you caught him?

YP: Wasn't going to fuck with him. Was going to bring him back.

CONVENER: Bring him back to where?

YP: The station . . . Well I couldn't, he had the knife in his hand still.

CONVENER: What did you think when you saw [Person Y] with the knife?

YP: I didn't want to get—I didn't want to get (next to him) in case I got stabbed. If I only had the knife I would have pulled it out on him too but I didn't have it. I forgot I had it on me.

CONVENER: So what did he say to you when you—when you caught up with him?

YP: He just goes 'What did I do? I didn't do nothing.'

CONVENER: And then what did you do to him?

YP: I chased him until he went in—inside a shop.

CONVENER: Yeah. And then what did you do?

YP: I went back to the station and I went back down and that's when I got stopped.

In both the YJCs cited above, we can see that the YP's recounts are very "flat" and ideationally focused (that is, they are focused on the "topic" e.g., the specific events leading to the YP's arrest). This is in contrast to personal recounts in young people's everyday conversations in which there is usually an ongoing prosody of evaluation (that is, instances of evaluative language that unfold sporadically throughout the text, that add to the bare bones of a story by giving the speaker's "take" on these events, suggesting what it means for them and inviting listeners to bond with the speaker in relation to these meanings). In terms of the discourse of integration that is so important to the designers of YJCs, there is clearly an expectation that the YP's recount is already a step toward redemption, a sign that the YP is starting to take responsibility for his or her actions. However, as the excerpts above show, the integrative aspect of these recounts is, once again, framed or projected by the regulative discourse in which the convener's role is paramount. This is why we describe the recounts in YJCs as "commissioned." They are a linguistic service that the YP agrees to provide. The limited *self*-evaluation by YPs during the Commissioned Recount arguably detracts from their value in terms of integration but, as the examples above also demonstrate, a compliant engagement by the YP with the evaluations provided by other conference participants who help extend the recount usually offsets this deficit.

Noncompliant YP Identities and Disruption to the Macrogenre

In one of the conferences from our sample, however, we did encounter young persons who resisted what was said about them by other participants. In terms of prosodic compliance, their aberrant resistance underscores the compliant nature of YP behavior in all the other conferences we observed. These young persons were quite open about what had happened, but made excuses, blamed others, and were generally unconvincing as far as showing remorse was concerned. Below, in the Rejoinder phase of the school library YJC, the convener pushes against this stance, reminding the YPs that the offense has seriously affected the victim's life. This conference involved two young offenders (YP1 and YP2), who have roughed up a student in a school library; YP1 has excused their behavior on the grounds that the victim has allegedly been picking on a female friend of theirs ("It's not right for a guy to pick on a girl and I've just been brought up to stand up for girls and guys shouldn't do it. If a guy's got a problem do something to a guy not to a girl.")

Extract 9: School library YJC

Rejoinder

CONVENER: It's affected his life.

YP1: Yeah I know it has. That's what I am saying. It's changed a lot. I- I do realise what we've done=

CONVENER: =Well the snickering and the smiling doesn't make me think that-

YP1: ( ) Yeah well I'm not a rat from [Location X].

CONVENER: W- I know that.

YP1: I'm not one of those friggin' retarded people that just say 'oh yeah I done that. I w- I'll do it again'. [pause] I'll do everything that I can to change everything that's happened. Seriously. Walk the streets, mate. Go have fun. Go get drunk. Do whatever. Party on. ( )

By suggesting, in this exaggerated manner, that the victim is now free to get drunk and party without any fear of being roughed up, YP1 is eschewing the "small-target" persona that most other YPs in our sample adopted. The excessive posturing of YP1 draws a rebuke from the attending police youth liaison officer (YLO), who likens the YPs to farmyard roosters:

Extract 10: School library YJC

Rejoinder *(continued)*

YLO: See you two guys are a bit like the old farmyard rooster.

YP1: The what?

YLO: All farmyard roosters are all fluffed up and want to impress people. So you go into the school grounds all fluffed up ready to go

YP1: No.

YLO: and then you want to impress people so you barge through and just 'I'm here. I'm here to do what I like. No one's going to stop me'

YP2: ( ) [shakes head then folds arms]

As far as the design of YJCs is concerned, this talk of the YLO is fairly transgressive behavior in itself, since it is considered important, when communicating disapproval of an offender's behavior, not to directly attack them as a person (Ahmed et al. 2001). The YLO's labeling of the YPs as "roosters" is accompanied by a clearly negative evaluation (these roosters are dismissed as "old" and inappropriately "fluffed up") and even, as the video recording of this YJC shows, an element of physical parody as the YLO starts puffing out his own chest and embodying the image he has conjured up of these YPs. He has thus considerably "ramped up" the criticism of the YPs from the convener's earlier mild rebuke about their "snickering and smiling"). The upsurge of bad feeling in the prosody of this YJC soon erupts as YP1's sister, who has attempted to respond on her brother's behalf, breaks down and leaves the conference circle in tears. YP1 responds to her departure as follows:

Extract 11: School library YJC

YP1: Happy now?

YLO: Pardon?

YP1: Happy now?

YLO: Mate, I've been doing the job for 22 years and there's people that have different sides to them. There's the side you portray to your family, there's the side you portray by yourself, and then when you get together as a group, there's another side that comes out again.

YP2: A fluffed up rooster.

YP1: Yeah. Maybe you're the fluffed up rooster. ( )

YP2: A bad way to describe me.

YLO: Well, we're not here to sling comments at ya.

YP2: You slinged one.

YP1: ( )

YLO: It was an analogy- an analogy I drew—that's all—to try and portray what it looks like.

=YP1: Yeah. I see. I see, mate.

This characterization of YP1 and YP2 as farmyard roosters, and their reaction to it, was a pivotal moment. The YPs are, in effect, threatening to renege on the implicit agreement, established in earlier stages of the conference, that they will comply with the prosody of evaluation anticipated by the genre.

They explicitly challenge the claims made by the YLO, sarcastically quoting his words and throwing them back at him in the following moves:

YP2: A fluffed up rooster.

YP1: Yeah. Maybe you're the fluffed up rooster. ( )

YP2: A bad way to describe me.

This degree of disrespect for authority is unique in our corpus and has no doubt been enabled by the YLO himself stepping out of line by labeling the YPs in this way. The YLO attempts to recover the situation by commenting metalinguistically on what is going on, suggesting that he was not intending to insult the YPs:

YLO: Well, we're not here to sling comments at ya.

YP2: You slinged one.

YP1: ( )

YLO: It was an analogy- an analogy I drew—that's all—to try and portray what it looks like.

However, the YPs also resist the YLO's conversational repair work here. The video recording of the conference shows YP1 slouching back in his chair, with his hand on his chin as he skeptically considers the YLO and replies sarcastically, "Yeah. I see. I see, mate." Clearly, the YPs' inability or unwillingness, at this point, to produce a compliant genre identity is a major disruption. The fact that this conference did ultimately resume its macrogeneric progress, resulting in an outcome plan that was consented to by both YPs and the victim, owed a great deal to the "hyper-compliant" genre identity produced by YP1's sister, his main support person in the conference. Upon returning to the room, she explained her distress in terms of the anxiety she felt about YP1 getting into serious trouble with the police and about the stresses of her role as primary caregiver for YP1 in the wake of their mother having left the family home. Without the ability of YP1's sister to bond with the victim's mother and the victim's support person in relation to their evaluations of the impact the YPs' offending behavior had on the victim, consent to an outcome plan may have been very difficult to achieve.

Consenting to Reintegration and the "Outcome Plan"

The informal prosodic compliance discussed in the previous sections is condensed in the culminative Reintegration genre that occurs at the end of the conference. This genre involves the conference participants negotiating the reparation that the young person will undertake. It has the following structure:

> [Brokering a collective agreement ratification of outcome plan ^ (Apologies and acknowledgments)[8] ^ Formal closing (Shared refreshments) ^ Dispersal]

During the Reintegration the participants must come to an agreement regarding the outcome plan under the terms of which a YP commits to certain tasks (a formal apology, payment of some monetary compensation, volunteer work in a community organization, etc.) as a way of "putting things right." As noted above, both the YP and the victim (if one is present) must formally consent to the outcome plan in order for it to be ratified and implemented. Conveners will also typically enquire whether other conference participants more generally are "happy with" its terms:

Extract 12: School library YJC

CONVENER: OK. Alright, what we're going to do now is, um, we're gonna have a quick break and I'm going to write up the outcome plan, so, is everybody happy with the ten hours community service, and the apology letter?

In most conferences the convener draws up the written outcome plan during the break for refreshments after the verbal discussion of the plan has occurred:

Extract 13: Mobile phone YJC

CONVENER: What we are going to do now is have a little break. OK? And I am going to write up the outcome plan, and that's the community service and the school issues, OK?

The convener will usually follow up by reading out this outcome plan to ensure that it represents the terms discussed:

Extract 14: Traintracks YJC

CONVENER: OK, thanks guys. I'll just quickly read out the outcome plan so that everybody knows what it says before everyone signs it, OK. The young person will complete ten hours community service at [Location X] Police Citizen Youth Centre. The young person will write a letter of apology to the CEO of [Organisation X] and send it to [Person X] at [Location X]. That's easy isn't it. OK? So there will be no doubt about where you got to send that letter, OK. Alright, his monitor is [Person X] and the start day will be the twenty-first of this month. There'll be a review date on the fourth of November and you'll finish it on the eighteenth of November, so that gives you plenty of time.

The convener then explicitly asks, one last time, whether the outcome plan is deemed satisfactory by those present, by implication checking that they consent to its implementation:

Extract 15: Traintracks YJC

CONVENER: Does that sound fair enough to everybody? Okeydokey. So if I could please have you sign it, YP, just there where it says "Young Person," for me, and pass it over to mum, and get mum to sign it where it says "Carer," just over there un- above my signature there.

MOTHER: [( )]

CONVENER: Car—carer. Thank you. And then just for you, thank you [Victim X], as the Victim, ta. Thanks [Person Y]. Ah, you're gonna sign victim, there. Excellent, thank you very much. OK, now (give) everyone their copies. There you go. That one's for you, that one's for you, and can you give that to YLO for me please? Thank you, alright. OK, well that wraps up the business end of the deal.

The oral presentation of the written plan echoes the way conveners sometimes read aloud when invoking the Young Offenders Act during the Mandate at the beginning of the conference. The delivery suggests that participants are intended to perceive the agreement as binding, legal and formal in nature. The signing of this written document is a codifying of the consent which has, in no small measure, been enabled through the enactment of compliant genre identities throughout the conference.

Conclusion

This chapter has investigated consent and compliance by young persons involved in NSW youth justice conferencing: strongly classified, legal consent in the Mandate and Outcome Plan stages of the conference, and a more prosodic, weakly classified genre compliance throughout the proceedings. In considering compliance we have explored the kind of identities that the young person is able to enact within the constraints of the macrogenre, noting the dominance of a "small-target" YP, though the potential for a more resistant, less amenable YP also exists. Considering conferencing as a macrogenre, we have investigated the exchanges that occur between conveners and YPs, emphasizing the regulative function of the discourse. To conclude, we want to touch briefly on some of the broader implications of the arguments advanced in this chapter.

We have stressed that the participation of YPs in conferencing is heavily scaffolded by conveners and other powerful participants, to the point where YPs can find it difficult to comply with expectations regarding genre and identity. It is not so easy for YPs to present themselves as forthcoming, sincere, and remorseful when they have little control over the genre. That said, we do not mean to suggest that scaffolding is necessarily a bad thing. On the contrary, given that youth justice conferencing is still an emerging macrogenre and a novel, typically one-off experience for most participants (not to mention the low levels of literacy and fluency in English of some YPs), some form of scaffolding is clearly essential. Furthermore, while the regulative discourse in conferencing inscribes hierarchical power relations among participants, this is often paired with close and certainly negotiable relations of solidarity with respect to the values of family, ethnicity, religion, or other community affiliations invoked as part of the integrative discourse of conferencing. Indeed, many times in our fieldwork observations, we have been impressed by the sensitivity with which conveners and, in particular, Indigenous or ethnic community liaison officers have steered YPs through the demands of the macrogenre.

It remains a concern for us, however, that there is widespread misrecognition among theorists and advocates of restorative justice of the extent to which regulative discourse drives conferencing. To ignore this is to render conferencing a kind of "invisible pedagogy" (Bernstein 1990) in which relations of power are masked while YPs and other "lay" participants are loaded up with responsibility for the success of the process. It is also to understate, as various critics have argued in relation to disenfranchised indigenous youth in particular (Daly 2001; Cunneen, 2002; Dickson-Gilmore and La Prairie 2005; Blagg 2008), the extent to which the experience an individual has of conferencing will relate to the wider social struggles of communities that are frequently subjected to racial discrimination and aggressive over-policing. While conferencing can be practiced in ways that are "flexible and accommodating toward cultural differences," as Daly (2001: 65) acknowledges, it would be naïve to think that the relative informality of conferencing talk could be, in and of itself, sufficient to persuade "at-risk" YPs, from "targeted" communities, that they can (or would want to) have a voice in it.

The ability to perform well in this complex macrogenre seems, in many respects, a product of what Bourdieu (1990) would define as "habitus": the whole gamut of habitual thoughts, actions, and ways of being in the world to which social agents become heavily predisposed through family upbringing, schooling, and other formative life experiences and which, while not class-determined, are definitely class-related. In the case of YJCs we have observed and documented, it is clear that some YPs are much better equipped to deal with the genre than others. They "just seem to know" (in other words, they learned long ago) when to look down, when to look at the person who's talking, how to speak with a deferential tone, and, most important, how to put across a metanarrative that suggests they've learned from the past. The genre suits them. We don't see these more gifted performers as necessarily insincere, but to argue that such a gift comes naturally is to perpetuate a form of additional symbolic violence (Bourdieu 1991) against those for whom the genre is less straightforward and for whom conferencing has often been most zealously promoted as a less alienating, more rehabilitative framework than formal court proceedings.

Notes

1. Most evaluations of conferencing programs carried out by criminologists have been focused on four issues: the percentage of participants who report being satisfied with the process; the percentage of participants who see conferencing as procedurally fair; the costs of settling matters by means of conferencing compared to court disposal; and the possibility that juvenile offenders who go through a conference are less likely to reoffend compared to offenders who go to court. While there is considerable variation in findings (see Daly 2001), most surveys report very high levels of satisfaction (sometimes as high as 90%). Some studies have found that rates of satisfaction are lower for victims than offenders, but, even in these cases, there is still a clear majority of victims who report being satisfied. Perceptions of procedural fairness are similarly high. The issues of cost and recidivism rates have, perhaps not surprisingly, attracted most attention from legislators and bureaucrats. Advocates of restorative justice have perhaps raised higher than reasonable expectations in this regard. Smith and Weatherburn (2012) have found that the introduction of conferencing in NSW has made no significant difference to recidivism rates. They conclude, nevertheless, that conferencing serves a valuable purpose insofar as it "gives victims of crime some measure of closure and relief while at the same time restraining the public appetite for expensive and ineffective punishments" (2012: 17).

2. The ethics protocol for our research, approved by the University of Sydney and the NSW attorney general, allowed us to observe and document YJCs but not the pre-conference briefings. This protocol also requires us to present transcript materials in a way that protects the anonymity of participants: we have omitted the names of participants and any other details that might make it possible to identify the case for which the YJC was convened.

3. We use the label "YLO Caution" somewhat tentatively here. This genre is not part of the design of YJCs outlined in the NSW Young Offenders Act, but we sense that it has become a part of the macrogenre as a result of the fact that police youth liaison officers regularly attend conferences. The Young Offenders Act does authorize YLOs to conduct a formal, legal caution (which YPs attend at a police station, accompanied by an adult carer) as a lower level intervention for lesser offenses (the act presents "on the spot" warnings, formal YLO cautions, and YJCs as the three options in a scale of graduated responses). We suspect that YLOs carry across into YJCs the discourse patterns they have practiced in running police cautions.

4. For a detailed analysis of regulative and integrative discourse in YJC in relation to exchange structure, see Martin et al. (2009b).

5. It is possible that the YP was unfamiliar with the term "victim" or was confused due to the nature of the offense which involved two offenders and he may have seen himself as the victim of the second offender.

6. The NSW Crimes Act (section 93C) defines the charge of affray as follows: "A person who uses or threatens unlawful violence towards another and whose conduct is

such as would cause a person of reasonable firmness present at the scene to fear for his or her personal safety is guilty of affray and liable to imprisonment for 10 years." It's obviously closely related to assault charges, the difference being to do with the presence of, and impact upon, terrorized bystanders.

7. As the use of terms like "Orientation" and "Coda" suggest, the work of Labov and Waletzky (1967) on narratives of personal experience was one of the early influences on the way SFL theorists began describing and analyzing a range of genres in school classrooms and other contexts from the late 1980s onward. See Martin and Rose (2008) for details.

8. The parentheses here indicate optionality.

References

Ahmed, Eliza, Nathan Harris, John Braithwaite and Valerie Braithwaite. 2001. *Shame Management Through Reintegration*. Cambridge: Cambridge University Press.

Bernstein, Basil. 1990. *Class, Codes and Control: The Structuring of Pedagogic Discourse* (vol. 4). London: Routledge.

Bernstein, Basil. 1996. *Pedagogy, Symbolic Control and Identity: Theory, Research, Critique*. London: Taylor and Francis.

Berry, Margaret. 1981a. Systemic linguistics and discourse analysis: A multi-layered approach to exchange structure. In Malcolm Coulthard and Martin Montgomery (eds.) *Studies in Discourse Analysis*. London: Routledge. 120–145.

Berry, Margaret. 1981b. Towards layers of exchange structure for directive exchanges. *Network* 2: 23–32.

Blagg, Harry. 1997. A just measure of shame? Aboriginal youth and conferencing in Australia. *British Journal of Criminology* 37(4): 481–501.

Blagg, Harry. 2008. *Crime, Aboriginality and the Decolonisation of Justice*. Sydney: Hawkins Press.

Bourdieu, Pierre. 1990. *The Logic of Practice*. Cambridge, U.K.: Polity Press.

Bourdieu, Pierre. 1991. *Language and Symbolic Power*. Cambridge, U.K.: Polity Press.

Braithwaite, John. 1989. *Crime, Shame and Reintegration*. Cambridge: Cambridge University Press.

Christie, Frances. 2002. *Classroom Discourse Analysis*. London: Continuum.

Cunneen, Chris. 2002. Restorative justice and the politics of decolonization. In Elmar Weitekamp and Hans-Jürgen Kerner (eds.) *Restorative Justice: Theoretical Foundations*. Cullompton, Devon, U.K.: Willan Publishing. 32–49.

Cunneen, Chris and Rob White. 2007. *Juvenile Justice: Youth and Crime in Australia*. Oxford: Oxford University Press.

Daly, Kathleen. 2001. Conferencing in Australia and New Zealand: Variations, research findings, and prospects. In Allison Morris and Gabrielle Maxwell (eds.) *Restorative Justice for Juveniles: Conferencing, Mediation & Circles*. Oxford, U.K.: Hart Publishing. 59–83.

Dickson-Gilmore, Jane and Carol La Prairie. 2005. *Will the Circle Be Unbroken?: Aboriginal Communities, Restorative Justice, and the Challenges of Conflict and Change*. Toronto: University of Toronto Press.

Labov, William and Joshua Waletzky. 1967. Narrative analysis: Oral versions of personal experience. In June Helm (ed.) *Essays on the Verbal and Visual Arts*. Seattle: University of Washington Press: 12–44. [Republished in 1997 in *Journal of Narrative and Life History* 71(4): 33–38].

Martin, J. R. and David Rose. 2007. *Working with Discourse: Meaning Beyond the Clause*. London: Continuum.

Martin, J. R. and David Rose. 2008. *Genre Relations: Mapping Culture*. London: Equinox.

Martin, J. R., Michele Zappavigna and Paul Dwyer. 2009a. Negotiating narrative: Story structure and identity in youth justice conferencing. *Linguistics and the Human Sciences* 3(2): 221–254.

Martin, J. R., Michele Zappavigna and Paul Dwyer. 2009b. Negotiating shame: Exchange and genre structure in youth justice conferencing. In Ahmar Mahboob and Caroline Lipovsky (eds.) *Studies in Applied Linguistics and Language Learning*. Newcastle upon Tyne, U.K.: Cambridge Scholars Publishing. 41–72.

Moore, David and John McDonald. 2000. *Transforming Conflict in Workplaces and Other Communities*. Sydney: Transformative Justice Australia.

Moore, David and John McDonald. 2001. Community conferencing as a special case of conflict transformation. In Heather Strang and John Braithwaite (eds.) *Restorative Justice and Civil Society*. Cambridge: Cambridge University Press. 130–148.

Muntigl, Peter. 2004. *Narrative Counselling: Social and Linguistic Processes of Change*. Amsterdam: Benjamins.

NSW Department of Juvenile Justice. 1999. *A Guide to Youth Justice Conferencing* [Pamphlet]. Sydney: NSW Department of Juvenile Justice.

Palk, Gerard, Hennessey Hayes and Timothy Prenzler. 1998. Restorative justice and community conferencing: Summary of findings from a pilot study. *Current Issues in Criminal Justice* 10(2): 125–137.

Retzinger, Suzanne and Thomas Scheff. 1996. Strategy for community conferences: Emotions and social bonds. In Burt Galaway and Joe Hudson (eds.) *Restorative Justice: International Perspectives*. Monsey, New York: Criminal Justice Press. 315–336.

Sinclair, John McHardy and Malcolm Coulthard. 1975. *Towards an Analysis of Discourse: The English Used by Teachers and Pupils*. Oxford: Oxford University Press.

Smith, Nadine and Don Weatherburn. 2012. Youth justice conferences versus children's court: A comparison of re-offending. *Crime and Justice Bulletin* 160. Sydney: NSW Bureau of Crime Statistics and Research.

Strang, Heather, Geoffrey Barnes, John Braithwaite and Lawrence Sherman. 1999. *Experiments in restorative policing: A progress report on the Canberra Reintegrative Shaming Experiments (RISE)*. Canberra: Research School of Social Sciences, Australian National University.

Trimboli, Lily. 2000. *An Evaluation of the NSW Youth Justice Conferencing Scheme*. Sydney: NSW Bureau of Crime Statistics and Research.

Ventola, Eija. 1987. *The Structure of Social Interaction: A Systemic Approach to the Semiotics of Service Encounters*. London: Pinter.

Zehr, Howard. 1990. *Changing Lenses: A New Focus for Criminal Justice*. Scottsdale, Pennsylvania: Herald Press.

10

Nonconsent and Discursive Resistance

RADICAL REFORMULATION IN A POST-STING POLICE INTERVIEW

Philip Gaines

What Happened in the Lindbergh Terminal

On June 1, 2007, just after noon, US senator Larry Craig of Idaho entered a restroom in the Minneapolis–St. Paul International Airport where, unbeknownst to him, Dave Karsnia, a Metropolitan Airport Commission police officer, was seated, working undercover in one of the restroom stalls, investigating reports of sexual solicitation.[1] In Minnesota, sexual solicitation falls under the purview of a more general law, Statute 609.72, which states that whoever does the following in a public place, "knowing, or having reasonable grounds to know that it will, or will tend to, alarm, anger or disturb others ... is guilty of disorderly conduct, which is a misdemeanor":

> ... (3) Engages in offensive, obscene, abusive, boisterous, or noisy conduct or in offensive, obscene, or abusive language tending reasonably to arouse alarm, anger, or resentment in others.

Karsnia's written report gives the following account of what he observed:

> At 1213 hours, I could see an older white male with grey hair standing outside my stall.[2] He was standing about three feet away and had a roller bag with him. The male was later identified ... as Larry Edwin Craig. ... I could see Craig look through the crack in the door from his position. Craig would look down at his hands, "fidget" with his fingers, and then look through the crack into my stall again. Craig would repeat this cycle for about two minutes. I was able to see Craig's blue eyes as he looked into my stall.
>
> At 1215 hours, the male in the stall next to the left of me flushed the toilet and exited the stall. Craig entered the stall and placed his roller

> bag against the front of the stall door. My experience has shown that individuals engaging in lewd conduct use their bags to block the view from the front of their stall. From my seated position, I could observe the shoes and ankles of Craig seated to the left of me. He was wearing dress pants with black dress shoes. At 1216 hours, Craig tapped his right foot. I recognized this as a signal used by persons wishing to engage in lewd conduct. Craig tapped his toes several times and moved his foot closer to my foot. I moved my foot up and down slowly. The presence of others did not seem to deter Craig as he moved his right foot so that it touched the side of my left foot, which was within my stall area.
>
> At 1217 hours, I saw Craig swipe his hand under the stall divider for a few seconds. The swipe went in the direction from the front (door side) of the stall back towards the back wall. His palm was facing towards the ceiling as he guided it all [*sic*] the stall divider. I was only able to see the tips of his fingers on my side of the stall divider. Craig swiped his hand again for a few seconds in the same motion to where I could see more of his fingers. Craig then swiped his hand in the same motion a third time for a few seconds. I could see that it was Craig's left hand due to the position of his thumb. I could also see Craig had a gold ring on his ring finger as his hand was on my side of the stall divider.

Convinced that he had seen enough, Karsnia showed Craig his police identification under the divider and motioned for him to leave the stall. After a response of "No!" from Craig, Karsnia pointed to the stall door again, and Craig exited the stall without flushing the toilet. Not wanting to "make a scene," Karsnia told Craig that they would speak in a private police operations room. Craig, anxious and resistant, refused to go. Karsnia told Craig that he was under arrest, and Craig finally complied, submitting to custody at 1222, nine minutes after entering the restroom.

Surveillance, Stings, and Decoys

Larry Craig had been the subject of an undercover *covert investigation*—a "concealed or secret" (Buckwalter 1983: 2) investigation "of which the suspect is assumed to be unaware. . . . Primarily this means some form of active surveillance" (Harfield and Harfield 2008: 2), which "includes . . . monitoring, observing or listening to persons, their movements, their conversations or their other activities or communications" (Harfield and Harfield 2008: 50). One type of covert investigation is the *sting operation*—"any effort by the authorities to encourage wrongdoing, with the intention of punishing the offenses that result" (Hay 2003: 4). Hay uses "encourage" "very broadly, to encompass any action designed to create apparent opportunities for crime, or to make its commission easier or more attractive" (Hay 2003: 7). Thus, in a sting operation, "authorities induce, or tempt, an individual to commit a crime or comparable rule violation" (Hay 2003: iii). In so doing, they "create, or facilitate, the very offense of which the defendant is convicted" (Hay 2003: 2)—giving the suspect "a government-provided opportunity to break the law" (Marx 1988: 65). Sting operations are not only covert but deceptive (Marx 1988: 12). In one type of sting, the authorities set up a *decoy* by having "an agent pose as a prospective victim of unlawful activity" (Hay 2003: 5). Here, the decoy becomes a "target of opportunity for victimization" (Marx 1988: 65), a "sort of bait" (Hay 2003: 12).

Karsnia's procedure illustrates many of the principles and methods of police surveillance and covert investigation. His detail was, in virtually all respects, a classic sting operation to investigate public solicitations of sex. Karsnia, as "decoy" (Gallo, Mason, Meisinger, Robin, Stabile and Wynne 1966: 690), took up a position in a setting where sexual solicitation was known to have occurred and where arrests had been made. Since his feet were placed below the door and divider of the stall, he was visible to users of the restroom. His presentation in the stall was deceptive, inasmuch as his location and position suggested that he was a user of the toilet. At the same time, his presence in a restroom known to be frequented by men seeking sexual encounters deceptively suggested that he might be available for such an encounter; as a decoy, he was presenting himself as a target of opportunity in a facilitative operation.

The Ethics and Effects of Surveillance

Legal precedent in the United States has clearly established the right of governments to conduct covert investigations, including stings. Moreover, conducting decoy operations does not constitute an unwarranted invasion of privacy. As Marx (1988: 44) puts it:

> [B]y targeting an undercover operation toward a given milieu where a pattern of crime occurs and by structuring it to permit self-selection rather than reselection of particular suspects, the operation becomes entirely consistent with Fourth Amendment values that preclude the government from intervening in the private affairs of its citizens without grounds for suspicion.

According to what Marx cites as the "social contract" view of the world, "undercover work is ethical because citizens grant to government the right to use exceptional means, such as coercion and deception, in order to be protected" (Marx 1988: 91). In spite of its hiddenness, however, a covert investigation, whether or not it results in an arrest, inevitably "infringes on the private life of the suspect" (Harfield and Harfield 2008: 2)—albeit only to an extent allowable by law. Further, sting operations in which an arrest is made turn targets into "sting victims" (Hay 2003: 4). Such a sting victim was Larry Craig, whose surveillance initiated either the actuality or the risk of being:

- Observed covertly and unknowingly
- Deceived as to the identity of the person in the stall
- Provided an opportunity and tempted to violate the law
- Exposed to behavior consistent with a positive response to a solicitation of sex
- Allowed to initiate and continue illegal behavior
- Self-incriminated
- Arrested
- Embarrassed in public
- Interrogated
- Convicted of a crime
- Fined
- Identified in court documents as a violator of the disorderly conduct statute
- Exposed publicly to ridicule and condemnation
- Negatively affected in a range of life situations

The risk of such a trajectory put Craig in a very problematic position, to say the least. The most consequential effect—and the one whose implications will be focused on in this chapter—is that he was discovered clearly violating the law. A decoy operation "produces evidence that is often considered to be incontrovertible" (Harfield and Harfield 2008: 5) since "the fact that participants [are] observed doing what they [are] doing cannot be contradicted" (Harfield and Harfield 2008: 6). Craig had been caught in the act, and the evidence was among the strongest of types: the eyewitness testimony of a police officer. Being unknowingly observed and monitored in a successful sting operation generally results in virtually irrefutable self-incrimination. Suspects tend to have no plausible defense and find themselves essentially helpless in the face of the charge.

The culmination of a sting operation is the production of a body of knowledge of events shared by the officer and the suspect. This situation makes the post-sting interview fundamentally different from the typical interview in which the officer seeks to elicit facts from the suspect in order to confirm to her- or himself that the suspect is guilty of the crime in question. In such cases, the degree of confidence in the suspect's guilt varies depending on how much the officer already has to go on. Thus, "[t]here may be two objectives of legal questioning. One is a genuine process of elicitation of information. Another is to obtain confirmation of a particular version of events that the questioner has in mind" (Gibbons 2003: 95, cited in Newbury and Johnson 2006: 218). The task is to "elicit the facts from the suspect in order to establish the events that had taken place"—to "procur[e] previously withheld information" (Carter 2008: 168). Thus, the police interview becomes "a species of information-seeking dialogue" (Walton 2003: 1773). In most cases, the officer is seeking confirmation of—and thereby consent to—what Auburn, Drake, and Willig (1995) call the "preferred version" of events: "The preferred version is . . . one version of events . . . which is privileged by the police. Nevertheless, gaining agreement to this version, as an intersubjectively agreed version of 'what happened' will, more often than not, require negotiation and argumentation by the participants" (Auburn et al. 1995: 357). In such a context—one in which the officer is aggressively seeking a confession and the suspect is acting on powerful self-protective impulses—the interview can turn into a "tug of war to get or conceal . . . information" (Walton 2003: 1779).

The post-sting interview begins under very different circumstances. Because the target has been the unknowing object of eyewitness observation, the officer is not at a knowledge deficit. There is no information-seeking required. In fact, the suspect is not a suspect at all in the mind of the officer—rather, a known violator. The preferred version of events, the one the officer has in mind, is not *presumed* to be true but rather *known* to be so and requires no confirmation, making consent to the truth of the preferred version practically a foregone conclusion. There is no withheld information that the officer must elicit in order to establish the events that had taken place—no tug of war to get or conceal information. This makes the work of the interviewing officer relatively simple and straightforward: get the perpetrator to consent to the truth of what the officer already knows, obtain a formal confession, and set it motion the necessary institutional protocols for finalizing the process—a guilty plea before a judge, a conviction, and a fine. The officer can reasonably expect the perpetrator to be cooperative and compliant, which is what Karsnia claimed during the Craig interview to have been his normal experience following sexual solicitation sting arrests. Decoy officers are regularly in the position of being able to conduct what Heydon calls "the perfect interview," consisting of "the formal police statements at the beginning and end, and a suspect-produced monologue forming a confession in the middle" (2005: 31).

This is not how things turned out in the Craig case, however. In the face of a police eyewitness claim that he had violated the law prohibiting disorderly conduct, Craig denied any wrongdoing. Although shared knowledge of what had happened meant that he was in a position of total exposure, legal disadvantage, and discursive helplessness—and that there was no reasonable hope of convincing Karsnia of his innocence—Craig chose to contest the claim of disorderly conduct and, in the interview, to render an account of his and—crucially, as we will see—Karsnia's action that contradicted the officer's assertions of what had taken place in the bathroom. To do so, Craig employed a process of radical reformulation.

Strategies of Reformulation

The notion of the reformulation, by both questioner and answerer, of accounts of "what happened" in disputed events was first articulated from a conversation analytic perspective by Drew in his detailed study of discursive construction in courtroom cross-examination. Drew explicates the various mechanisms recruited by both attorney and witness to produce what he variously calls "alternative description" (1985: 141), "competing characterizations" (1985: 143), "repair" (1990: 45), the "reformulating" of "depictions" (1990: 49), "contrasting versions" (1992: 516), and "alternative and competing versions" (1992: 516), which the "attorney, and then the witness, produce to describe the 'same' action, event, or scene" (1992: 516). In the courtroom, reformulation typically occurs in the next-turn question or answer and offers an account that differs—to varying degrees—from that presented in the previous turn.

Auburn et al. (1995) present a case in which a suspect being interviewed as to his involvement in a bar fight constructs a favorable "reformulation of the action" following the police officer's formulation of him as the "perpetrator of an intentional action designed to cause injury to the victim" (Auburn et al. 1995: 375). Using a variety of mechanisms, the suspect's reformulation "conveys its unintentional and accidental quality and removes the perpetrator as the person responsible for causing the event and any harm which ensued" (Auburn et al. 1995: 375). This involves "an acknowledgement of the actions, but with different versions of their agency" (Auburn et al. 1995: 369).

OPTION A: MITIGATING REFORMULATION

One type of reformulation process that can be observed in suspects' responses to questions in police interviews involves an account of events that mitigates the seriousness of the suspect's behavior. With such a discursive strategy, the suspect consents to a certain generalized core proposition offered by the interviewing officer but proceeds to reformulate the proposition in a way that that downplays its severity. In these examples adapted from Auburn et al. (1995: 370), a UK police officer (O) is questioning an assault suspect (S):

O: Have you ever been violent to your current wife prior to yesterday?

S: No, we've had ups and downs, but we've never had any— no great problem, no.

O: Have you ever assaulted your previous wife?

S: We've had a few problems, but my present wife was involved in that.

In the first example, the suspect reformulates being "violent to your current wife" as the two of them having "ups and downs" that were "no great problem." In the second, having "assaulted your previous wife" is reformulated as the two of them having "had a few problems" that his current wife "was involved in." Both reformulations are classic mitigation tactics by which the suspect consents to the officer's claims that he had behaved in inappropriate ways but describes a considerably less serious situation ("no great problem, no," "a few problems") than is put forward by the police officer. The suspect is able to characterize his actions as considerably less violent than the question suggests—thus admitting to improper behavior of a markedly lesser degree of seriousness.

As the victim of a sting operation, a mitigating reformulation of events was not a viable option for Craig. Due to the incontrovertible nature of Karsnia's eyewitness evidence, Craig could not consent to any formulation asserted by Karsnia that implicated him in improper behavior; it was essential that he systematically and exhaustively contradict Karsnia's interview account of events. His resistance to Karsnia's formulation required an alternative account that admitted no questionable behavior.

OPTION B: COMPETING REFORMULATION

As mentioned above, Drew has identified a reformulation process that produces alternative, competing, or contrasting versions of events. In this strategy, the answerer does not consent at all to the proposition offered by the questioner. The following example adapted from Drew (1992: 486) illustrates the pattern. Here, a rape defense attorney (A) is questioning a witness (W), the alleged victim:

A: You had some fairly lengthy conversations with the defendant, didn't you, on that evening of February fourteenth?

W: Well, we were all talking.

A: Well, you knew at that time that the defendant was interested in you, didn't you?

W: He asked me how I'd been.

The witness performs two reformulations of the propositional content of the attorney's questions. In the first, she reformulates having "some fairly lengthy conversations with the defendant" as "[W]e were all talking." Engaging in lengthy conversations with the accused would have suggested a familiar and possibly intimate relationship. In the second, she reformulates the defendant being "interested in [her]" as "He asked me how I'd been." Knowing that the defendant had been interested in her would suggest that her willingness to converse at length with him signaled an openness to that interest. In both cases, the purpose of the reformulation is to counter the suggestion that there was a significant level of relational intimacy between the defendant and herself. This is accomplished by characterizing (1) the conversation as only one element of a larger group interaction and (2) the defendant's attentions as nothing more than the asking of a friendly question. In this case, the reformulation does not seek to mitigate the degree of seriousness of improper behavior but rather denies the reality of *any* improper behavior, thus advancing a competing version of events. Larry Craig's strategy adopts this approach of competing reformulation. What is distinctive about it, however, is its global, rather than merely local, scope.

SOLUTION: RADICAL, GLOBAL REFORMULATION

Both the courtroom examination and police interview examples above illustrate an interactional process that has been the focus of the literature on reformulation: reformulation occurring in quite local conversational contexts—specifically in yes/no question-and-answer turns. In this interactional work, turn-by-turn reformulation involves a kind of antagonistic negotiation between questioner and answerer: the interviewer asks a question with a damaging implication or presupposition, and the interviewee responds with a reformulation that serves either to cast doubt on the implication or presupposition or to mitigate its power. Of course, the questioner is the person in the position of greater power whose agenda is to pressure the answerer toward consent to her or his "preferred version" of events (Auburn et al. 1995: 357).

A striking aspect of the Larry Craig interview is the nearly total absence of the kind of yes/no questions that tend to elicit responses of reformulation. Instead, Craig's reformulation work operates on a larger scale, drawing its alternative propositional content not from immediately preceding questions but from a wider array of discursive data either supplied by Karsnia or found elsewhere in the interactional context. His method is to construct, during the interview, a *radical reformulation* of both (1) the actual events at the scene and (2) the identities of the participants in both the investigative process and the police interview. The effect of this reformulation was to generate a profile of himself as an innocent commuter whose actions while using a restroom were either misperceived, misunderstood, or misinterpreted.

The Radical Reformulation of Events: Facts and Questions

From their FBI experience as suspect questioners, Navarro and Schafer (2001: 11) observed, "Liars prefer concealing the truth rather than fabricating an entirely fictitious story." Such concealment is an advantage in the tug of war for information between questioner and suspect; the fabrication of a different story out of whole cloth is difficult to maintain consistently and runs the risk of being contradicted on many points through astute interrogation. For a victim of a sting operation, however, concealment is not an option. In Craig's case, Karsnia directly observed everything that happened in the restroom. Craig's only resort was reformulation—but reformulation into an account that was plausible: in other words, that would not seem ridiculous in comparison to Karsnia's.

Since Craig chose to maintain his absolute innocence of any wrongdoing, it was necessary to formulate an account of events that supported that claim. It would not do for him simply to deny Karsnia's assertions wholesale; Karsnia, a police officer whose report would be accepted as accurate, had been an eyewitness to Craig's behavior, making his evidence virtually irrefutable in a court proceeding. Craig's strategy was to acknowledge and foreground a limited set of facts about the events in question and then formulate an entirely new explanation for these events. Craig's approach embodies what Grace calls the linguistic construction of a *conceptual event*:

> [T]he event, as an event, is actually a conception of the speaker. It is the speaker who, first of all, identifies the parts of the event which he/she reports as together constituting a unity and, secondly, decides how to characterize the structure of the event ... and its various elements. (Grace 1987: 33)
>
> It is a single "event" because the speaker has attributed unity to it—has abstracted certain happenings out of a possibly very extensive context and represented them as constituting a unity. In short, the unity, and therefore the event as an event, is in the eye of the beholder; what constitutes an event is whatever the speaker is able to interpret as one. (Grace 1987: 32)

The answer to the question "What happened?" in any given context allows for—indeed, requires—as many alternatives as participants and/or witnesses involved by virtue of unique individual conceptions. Each reporter conceptualizes both the global nature/meaning—Grace's "unity"—of the event as well as which parts are salient or relevant in support of it. Craig's conceptual event was that of a commuter using an airport restroom, and the unity of the event is constituted by the facts he stipulates. "[I]t is the speaker who chooses what *kind* of event he/she will represent it as being. The choice is not dictated (except in a quite general way ...) by what actually happened" (Grace 1987: 33).

TABLE 10.1

Restroom Activities

Domain of Activity	Larry Craig's (LC's) "Facts"	Dave Karsnia's (DK's) Formulation	LC's Reformulation
Use of restroom	LC used the restroom in the Lindbergh Terminal	in order to solicit sex	to go to the bathroom
Activity outside stall	LC stood outside DK's stall	in order to establish contact with DK as a potential sex partner	while waiting for a stall to become available
	LC waited	for DK's stall—specifically—to become available	for any stall to become available
	LC looked at DK's stall	in order to establish eye contact with DK for the purpose of showing interest in having sex	in the process of seeing which stall would become available first
Choice of stalls	LC used the stall next to DK's	in order to position himself next to a potential sexual partner	because it was the first stall to become available
Foot activity	LC moved his foot toward DK's	as an indication of interest in having a sexual encounter	to accommodate his need to have his pants not slide
	LC's foot touched DK's	as a further indication of interest in having a sexual encounter	as an accidental event due to his positioning actions—possibly facilitated by DK's "entrapment" activities
Hand activity	LC's hand went below the level of the bottom of the stall divider	to rub his hand along the bottom of the stall divider as a further indication of interest in having a sexual encounter	to pick up a piece of paper off the floor

THE REFORMULATION OF RESTROOM ACTIVITIES

In Table 10.1 is a list of activities that occurred in the restroom—and that Craig agreed occurred—followed by the formulations of Karsnia and Craig, respectively. As can be seen, these formulations provide different motivations or explanations for the activities in question. For example, with respect to activity outside the stall, Craig agrees that after he entered the restroom, he stood outside Karsnia's stall. In Karsnia's formulation, Craig did this in order to be in a position to establish contact with a potential sexual partner. In Craig's formulation, this just happened to be the position he took up while waiting for a stall—any stall—to become available.

Missing, of course, in Table 10.1 are many of Craig's activities alleged by Karsnia but *not* agreed to by Craig, at least not in the form that Karsnia represented them:

1. Craig looked at Karsnia repeatedly through the crack of Karsnia's stall.

2. He waited for the stall next to Karsnia's when others were already available.
3. He used the stall next to Karsnia's when others were available.
4. He put his roller bag against his stall door.
5. He tapped his right foot repeatedly.
6. He could not have picked up a piece of paper because there wasn't one on the floor.
7. He put the fingers of his left hand under the stall divider.
8. He swiped his hand, palm up, along the bottom of the stall divider three times.
9. He was wearing a gold ring on the hand that Karsnia saw.
10. He responded with "No!" when Karsnia's presented his police ID under the stall divider.
11. He resisted exiting his stall when first told to do so.
12. He did not flush the toilet when he exited his stall.

Activities 4 to 6 and 10 to 12 are asserted only in Karsnia's official report and did not come up in the interview; thus Craig did not have the opportunity to incorporate them into his reformulation. Most of the remaining activities—1 to 3 and 7 to 8—constitute extremely damaging evidence and thus required reformulation by Craig, which he provides by incorporating them into an alternative explanatory framework or interpretive scheme, as can be seen in the rightmost column of Table 10.1. Activity 9 was impossible for Craig to argue for as misunderstanding or misinterpretation on Karsnia's part since it was a simple case of visual observation. Craig's only recourse was to suggest that Karsnia was either lying or that his eyes were deceived:

DK: Was your gold ring on your right hand at anytime to[day.]
LC: [Of course not. Try to get it off. Look at it.
DK: Okay. Then it was your left hand. I saw it with my own [eyes.]
LC: [Alright, you saw something that didn't happen.

REFORMULATION BY QUESTION

One of Craig's distinctive moves in his alternative explanatory framework is the construction of questions that reformulate the focus of the inquiry. In addition to one occurrence of the actual reformulation of a question by Karsnia, there are several instances in which Craig formulates his own "interview questions"—in which he assumes the persona of someone questioning him—and then gives answers that affirm certain elements of his larger reformulation. Reference to the literature on the reformulation of questions will help provide context for understanding this distinctive move.

In a study of the discursive interview conventions of journalists and public figures, Clayman identifies a practice he calls "reformulating the question" (1993: 161), by which the interviewee may either "indicate how a complex question will be initially dealt with" or "sidestep or avoid some aspect of the question." Clayman's treatment of the latter purpose of this practice is germane to the analysis undertaken here. Clayman observes that question reformulations "represent a class of objects that paraphrase ... or re-present ... the prior question or some aspect of it" (1993: 163–164). Such reformulations tend to appear in contexts where a direct reply to the information sought in the question would likely create problems for the interviewee; the solution is "furnishing a version of the question to which the ensuing talk can be seen as responsive"; thus, "the talk following a [reformulated] question is presented as indeed 'answering' the question" (1993: 165). For example, in a television interview with former US senator and presidential candidate Gary Hart, a journalist asked the question, "Did you have an affair with Miss [Donna] Rice?" Hart's response was, "If the question is in the twenty-nine years of my marriage, including two public separations have I been absolutely and totally faithful to my wife, I regret to say the answer is no" (1993: 168). For Clayman, "the advantages of such a transformation are obvious. It enables Hart to appear 'forthcoming,' but in response to a question that, by virtue of its generality, is much less pointed" (1993: 168). A key element of question reformulation is its ability to "propose ... that what follows is responsive to the underlying spirit, if not the actual letter, of the original question" (1993: 170).

As we will see, there is only one example in the Craig interview of the sort of question reformulation identified by Clayman. In the process of developing his reformulation of events, Craig performs instead an ingenious variation on the theme of question reformulation: he constructs reformulations (which I call "reformulations-by-question") in which he (1) engages with an assertion or suggestion by Karsnia—either in the immediately preceding co-text or the larger context of the interview, (2) produces from its elements a fact to which he is willing to agree, (3) re-represents the fact in terms that neutralize its damaging implications, and then (4) asks whether the fact is true. Thus, he takes a complex of assertions/suggestions by Karsnia and proposes what appears to be the essential question—Clayman's "underlying spirit"—in the process removing the implication of anything improper happening and allowing him to answer unequivocally, as though he is being cooperative, forthcoming, and honest. As Haworth puts it, this sort of reformulation "allows [the suspect] to usurp [the police officer's] role as questioner: [the suspect] simply sets his own question and answers that [one] instead" (Haworth 2006: 750). Following are all instances of this practice and a discussion of the distinctive elements of each.

65 DK: Okay. Um, I just want to start off with uh your side
66 of the story, okay? So, uh=
67 LC: =Well, I go into the bathroom here as I normally do. I'm a
68 commuter through here.
69 DK: Okay.
70 LC: I sit down um to go to the bathroom, and uh
71 you said our feet bumped. I believe they did uh
72 because I reached down and scooted over, and uh the
73 next thing I knew under the bathroom divider
74 comes a card that says police. Now uh
75 ((sigh; source uncertain, likely LC)) that's about as far as
76 I can take it. I don't know of anything else uh your foot
77 came toward mine, mine came toward yours, was that
78 natural? I don't know. **Did we bump?** Yes, I think we
79 did. You said so.=
80 =((throat clearing; source uncertain but not LC))=
81 LC: =I don't disagree with that.

Craig here constructs a formulation of events involving foot movements—both his and Karsnia's. Since this is the first mention of feet in the interview, Craig's assertion that Karsnia "said so" (line 79) must refer to a statement by Karsnia prior to the recorded dialogue. The formulation (1) posits the foot-touching as mutual, each party being responsible in part for the touching, and (2) characterizes the touching as the two of them having "bumped," a typically accidental activity; people don't generally bump intentionally. Later, as we will see, Karsnia formulates Craig's foot movement as the only foot activity and presents it as an intentional act performed for a purpose prohibited by law; Craig's reformulation-by-question posits the spirit of the apparently unasked "question" as whether the innocent act of mutual bumping occurred—to which he can easily and safely answer in the positive.

120 DK: I will say that every person I've had so far has told me
121 the truth. We've been respectful to each other
122 and then they've gone on their way.
123 LC: Yeah.=
124 DK: =And I've never had to bring anybody to jail because
125 everybody's been truthful to me.=
126 LC: =I don't want you to take me to jail, and I think

127 [(unintelligible)]
128 DK: [I'm not going to take you [to jail as long as you'll be
129 LC: [Alright]
130 DK: cooperative, but I— I'm not going to lie. I— we— we—
131 LC: **Did my hand come back below the divider?** Yes, it did.
132 DK: Okay. Sir. We deal with people that lie to us
133 every day.

Here Craig (1) gives agency to his hand rather than to himself, (2) has his hand "coming" rather than "going"—a process perhaps less overt and directive, and (3) characterizes his hand as coming "back below" rather than "under"—"below" being a consequence of reaching back behind him. Rather than deal with the many details contained in Karsnia's formulation of Craig's hand actions, Craig abstracts from them the most general and unarguable element: that his hand went below the level of the bottom of the stall divider. Since he has an explanation for why this occurred, he is able to answer unproblematically the spirit of the question—again, one which was never asked directly.

157 DK: Alright, so let's start from the beginning. You went in
158 the bathroom.
159: LC: I went in the bathroom.
160 (1.2)
161 DK: And then what did you do when you [(unintelligible)]
162 LC: [I stood
163 beside the wall waiting for the stall to open.
164 I got in the stall, sat down, I [started to go
165 DK: O[kay.]
166 LC: to the bathroom. [Uh] **did our feet come together?**
167 DK: [Okay.
168 LC: Apparently they did bump; [I won't dispute that.
169 DK: When [I]
170 Okay, when I got out of the stall, I noticed
171 other stalls were open . . .

In a formulation in the same domain of activity as that in line 78, Craig (1) depersonalizes the agency from "we" to "our feet," (2) reformulates the activity as "coming together" rather than "bumping"—an even less concrete result of movement, and again (3) represents the action as mutual. In Karsnia's formulation, their feet did indeed come together as a result of Craig moving his foot toward and ultimately into contact with his. Following Craig's reformulation-by-question, he is able to answer that he does not disagree that this accidental touching of feet occurred. Karsnia never asked if their feet came together; the question is Craig's.

180 DK: Were you looking at me while you were waiting? I could
181 see your eyes. I saw you playing with your fingers and then
182 look up, play with your fingers and then [look up.]
183 LC: **[Did I glance**
184 **at your stall?** I was glancing at a stall right
185 beside yours waiting for a fella to empty it. I saw him
186 stand up, and therefore I thought it was gonna empty.

This is the sole instance of an actual question reformulation along the lines discussed by Clayman. In his immediately preceding turn, Karsnia had asked, "Were you looking at me while you were waiting?" Karsnia goes on to assert that Craig looked repeatedly at him, even making eye contact. Craig (1) reformulates this as "glancing" rather then "looking"—a far less intentional action and one taking less time, and (2) makes the object of his glance the stall that Karsnia was in, not Karsnia himself. Further, his choice of verb aspect reformulates the action as a one-time act versus an ongoing activity. Craig's reformulation suggests either a mistaken observation on Karsnia's part, in other words, that Craig's glance at the stall "right beside" Karsnia's might have appeared to Karsnia to be a glance at his stall, or the possibility that Craig had indeed glanced at Karsnia's stall—one of two glances that innocently occurred in the process of seeing which stall would become available first. Craig does not answer his own question directly, but the implication of his discussion is that neither a "yes" nor "no" answer would be incriminating.

190 DK: Okay. And you went in the stall, and then what?
191 (1.1)
192 LC: Sat down.
193 DK: Did you do anything with your feet?
194 (1.5)
195 LC: Positioned them. I don't know. I don't know at the time.
196 (2.6) I'm a fairly wide guy. I uh
197 DK: I understand. [(unintelligible)]
198 LC: [I tend– I tend to spread my legs

199 DK: Okay.=
200 LC: =when I lower my pants so they won't slide.
201 DK: Okay.
202 (1.2)
203 LC: **Did I slide them too close to yours?** Did I– I looked down
204 once, your foot was close to mine . . .

Karsnia never asked this question, nor did he ever say that Craig "slid" his feet. Craig also indicates that he slid "them," in other words, his feet, which is consistent with him having positioned his feet while spreading his legs rather than moving only one foot, which would be more suspicious. (Note that he does admit elsewhere to special movement with his right foot resulting from him scooting over to pick up a piece of paper back behind him.) "Too close" suggests the possibility that the sliding of his feet went beyond appropriate social boundaries—critically not intentionally so; he has already explained the innocent actions that caused the movement. With what follows, Craig's suggestion is that if it appeared that he had slid his feet too close to Karsnia's, it is possible, if not likely, that the reason was that Karsnia's foot was already close to his. Also possible is that they did not actually bump but that because Karsnia's foot was close to his, a situation was created that could be misinterpreted as them having bumped. Again foregoing a direct answer, Craig provides himself the safety of a "yes" or "no" due to the nature of his reformulation-by-question.

204 LC: . . . **Did we**
205 **bump?** Uh you said so. I don't recall that, but
206 apparently we were close.

In an echo of his question in line 78, Craig invokes again the mutual touching of their feet. This time he supports the representation by having pointed out that Karsnia's foot was close to his. Craig's answer this time, however, does not assert that they bumped but that he was willing to take Karsnia's word for it; if they didn't actually bump, they were close—mainly because Karsnia's foot was close to his.

281 DK: . . . I'm [experienced at this.
282 LC: [Did I]
283 O[kay]
284 DK: [I'm trained in [this, and I know what I'm doing.
285 LC: [Did I turn]

286 LC: **Did I tur[n]**
287 DK: [And I saw you put your hand under there and you're
288 going to sit there [and]
289 LC: [I admit I put my hand down.
290 DK: You put your hand and rubbed it on the bottom of the stall
291 with your left hand.
292 LC: Now wait a moment.
293 DK: And I'm– I'm not dumb. You can say "I don't recall" . . .

After an unrelated colloquy, Craig returns to the matter of his hand movement. While it is not clear where this false-start question was headed, a distinct possibility is that he is simplifying and reformulating Karsnia's assertions about what he did with his left hand by suggesting that, while he did not put his left hand below the divider, his movement to pick up the piece of paper might have caused him to turn in such a way that would explain why Karsnia claims that Craig used his left hand. Although this explanation would be highly implausible, of course, it does tangentially address Karsnia's claim. While the question suggests a harmless turning, Craig later (line 295) indicates that "turning sideways" was not a likely action for him to have taken, being more extensive and (perhaps) intentional than simply "turning"; it involves a significant reorientation of the body. In any case, an answer of "yes" to this reformulation-as-question would be nonproblematic for Craig.

76 . . . I don't know of anything else uh your foot
77 came toward mine, mine came toward yours, **was that**
78 **natural?** I don't know . . .

Although this question appears earlier in the interview than the other reformulations-as-questions discussed above, it is treated last due to its distinctive nature. Rather than reformulating either a question, assertion, or suggestion of Karsnia's, Craig here constructs a conceptual event that does not engage with any specific element of Karsnia's discourse at all. Instead, he raises a new issue—that of the naturalness/non-naturalness of the two men's foot movements—thus suggesting an interpretive scheme for understanding them. Since Craig maintains that he did not make any movements that were motivated by an interest in having a sexual encounter and that, in his view, Karsnia had solicited him, it is most likely that a "no" answer to his question would suggest the possibility of a non-naturalness of foot movement consistent with entrapment. Alternatively, a "yes" answer would simply reconfirm that his foot movement was an incidental effect of his appropriate positioning activities in the toilet stall, in other words, that it *was* natural. In the case of this question, Craig's reformulation can be thought of as an exploration of the abstract ontological property of the concrete action of foot movement.

The Radical Reformulation of Participants' Identities

Craig's reformulation of events through the selection of nondamaging facts and the construction of a competing version of events is only one of two moves in developing a radical global reformulation. His other move is to reformulate the very nature both of the investigative process occurring in the bathroom and its participants and of the interview itself. Important to constructing a plausible record that represents him as an innocent party in an unfortunate situation, Craig must not only deny the assertions made by Karsnia but also formulate a profile of the entire context in which he is presented in the best possible light and Karsnia in the worst. Craig does this in three ways: by (1) reformulating Karsnia's account of him as a lawbreaker and sexual predator into one characterizing him as a harmless person going about his normal business, (2) reformulating Karsnia's profile as a competent police officer on a legitimate surveillance assignment into one that reveals him as deceptive and dishonorable, and (3) reformulating the interview situation itself as not a routine confession-elicitation procedure but rather a confrontation and conflict between a false accuser and a man defending his honor.

CRAIG AS INNOCENT COMMUTER

Following an invitation from Karsnia to tell his "side of the story" (line 65), Craig explains how he happened to be in the restroom in the Lindbergh Terminal:

67 LC: . . .Well, I go into the bathroom here as I normally do. I'm a
68 commuter through here.

Craig represents his use of that particular bathroom—one that had developed a reputation as a place for sexual encounters—as a place that he frequents for its legitimate purpose, one emerging naturally from his role as a regular commuter through the Minneapolis Airport to and from his home in Idaho. Later, following Karsnia's presupposition-heavy question as to whether Craig had been "successful in these bathrooms here before" (line 265), Craig replies (in an answer indicating that he either misunderstands the question or feigns doing so),

267 LC: I go to that bathroom regularly. . .

Far from being a solicitor of sex, according to Craig, he is someone who simply uses this restroom for its intended purpose—which he claims to have done in this instance:

164 LC: I got in the stall, sat down, I started to go...
166 ...to the bathroom...

The more general support that Craig gives for his claim of normal, innocent use of the restroom is that he is a respectable heterosexual man who would never do the things he is being accused of:

86 LC: I don't- uh uh uh I- I- I am not gay. I don't do these
87 kinds of things
...
235 LC: I don't do those things.
...
270 LC: Absolutely not. I don't seek activity in bathrooms.
...
313 LC: I'm a respectable person and I don't do these kinds of...

Craig, a US senator, presents himself as having a character that would not permit the kind of behavior that he is being accused of. He makes an appeal to ethos similar to that of Harold Shipman, a physician, in a police interview following his arrest for the murder of a female patient. Newbury and Johnson see such professional self-presentation as key to countering allegations of wrongdoing: "For the suspect—especially one as skillful and articulate as Shipman—we see a struggle to resist ... control and to avoid giving damaging information. His struggle is for identity, for Shipman. He struggles to preserve his image as a caring doctor in the face of accusations which claim to contradict that persona" (2006: 231). Just as a caring doctor would never harm a patient, a respectable—and straight—public servant would never solicit gay sex in an airport restroom. In summary, Craig reformulates Karsnia's account of him as a solicitor of sex and violator of a law against disorderly conduct into one of a respectable man going about his normal business.

KARSNIA AS UNETHICAL ENTRAPPER

For Craig, Karsnia is a different kind of person. Even before Karsnia formally begins the questioning, Craig offers the following:

16 LC: You solicited me

Craig represents Karsnia's decoy actions in the restroom as constituting the appearance of the solicitation of sex, an act that Craig believes to be wrong. It is hardly likely, of course, that Craig is accusing Karsnia of actually soliciting sex, yet Craig's statement does not include the qualification that it was the *appearance* of solicitation, in other words, giving the false impression, as a decoy, that he was soliciting sex. While the context makes it certain that this is what he meant, the unqualified statement grammatically identifies Karsnia as the agent of the process—an illegal activity. Later, Craig does directly accuse Karsnia of entrapment:

99 LC: But you shouldn't be out to entrap people either.

Since Craig here invokes the entrapment defense, a brief discussion of entrapment is appropriate to contextualize LC's claim. Hay notes that "[s]ting operations ... are controversial because the police participate in, or even orchestrate, the very crime for which the defendant is convicted" (Hay 2003: 2), yet, according to Marx, "[a]uthorities have great leeway in the setting of traps" (Marx 1988: 78). Users of a public restroom expose themselves to the possibility that their actions will be observed because "citizens grant to government the right to use exceptional means, such as ... deception, in order to be protected" (Marx 1988: 91). For Harfield and Harfield, "[c]overt investigation is necessary to prosecute any criminal activity evidence of which cannot be secured by normal, overt means" (Harfield and Harfield 2008: 3)—usually the case in the sorts of crimes that covert investigation is used for. Here, the goal is to "identify those who are engaged in, or likely to engage in, criminal activity. A target's response to the temptations held out by the government may signal his propensity to commit the offense in question" (Hay 2003: 8). This notion was explicated in an early entrapment case, in which the Supreme Court opined,

> Artifice and stratagem [*sic*] may be employed to *catch those engaged in criminal enterprises*. The appropriate object of this permitted activity ... is to reveal the criminal design; ... *to disclose the would-be violators of the law*. (*Sorrells v. United States*, 287 US [1932], cited in Hay 2003: 19; emphasis Hay's)

In sum, the fact that the government has provided an opportunity for illegal behavior and, further, has facilitated that behavior is not, in itself, grounds for a successful entrapment defense. There must be overt inducement. As Dworkin puts it, "Entrapment occurs when government agents procure the commission of a criminal act by someone who, except for the solicitation, persuasion, or enticement, would not have committed the crime" (1985: 21). It is not clear what the complete range is of Karsnia's behaviors that Craig has in mind as constituting entrapment; candidates might include sitting for an extended period of time in the stall, establishing eye contact, not moving his foot away when Craig's foot came close, moving his foot up and down slowly, and not reacting negatively or exiting the stall when Craig put his hand under the stall divider. Of course, to point these out would be to implicate himself in sexual solicitation, so Craig limits himself to an account of one specific behavior on LK's part that is consistent with solicitation and thus, in his estimation, entrapment: the movement and position of Karsnia's foot:

76 LC: . . . I don't know of anything else uh your foot
77 came toward mine, mine came toward yours. . .

203 LC: Did I slide them too close to yours? Did I– I looked down
204 once, your foot was close to mine. . .

In summary, Craig reformulates Karsnia's profile of himself as an experienced, competent professional into a deceptive, unethical police officer who victimizes innocent people.

THE INTERVIEW AS A FIGHT

Craig's representations of himself as an innocent commuter and of Karsnia as an unethical entrapper create a natural setup for the police interview to be characterized as oppositional and confrontational—and indeed this is what it becomes. Three times during the interview, Craig uses the word "fight" in reference to the interaction between himself and Karsnia. Here is the first instance on the audio recording:

1 LC: ((recording begins mid-utterance)) . . . not gonna fight you
2 in court?

Here, Craig indicates that the interaction is one of conflict—or at least has the potential to be. The implication is that he has been put into a position where he must forcefully defend himself against a false accusation of wrongdoing. Later in the interview, Craig uses "fight" again:

247 LC: Well, we can dispute that. I'm not gonna fight you in court.
. . .
273 LC: Well, it's embarrassing for both— I'm not gonna fight you.

Although he says here that he is "not gonna fight" Karsnia, the implication is clear that Craig sees the situation as confrontational and hostile. People who are subject to entrapment are victims, of course, and Craig the victim must fight to defend his honor and innocence.

Conclusion

In a typical police interview, one of the decisions a suspect must make is the degree of consent to be given to the account of events offered by the interviewer. In this "tug of war" for information, the suspect tends to conceal as much as possible. When concealment is not feasible, an alternative strategy is reformulation—either mitigation of the seriousness of certain behaviors or construction of an alternative or competing account. The Larry Craig interview is a story of absolute nonconsent to an account that would either implicate him directly in behavior inappropriate to any degree or that would allow for an interpretation that would suggest the likelihood or even possibility of such behavior. The record being made on tape must be free of any such consent in order to exculpate him. To make a record that supported a claim of innocence, Craig could not consent to the accuracy of any of Karsnia's incriminating observations. It certainly would not do to reformulate Karsnia's account in order to mitigate the seriousness of any of his claims. Such mitigation would leave intact an interpretation of events that would still potentially suggest improper behavior. Even a reformulation to construct a competing account offering an explanation of a behavior that removed any interpretation allowing for impropriety would not be sufficient—for example, waiting for the next-door stall to become available because of not noticing that others were empty, looking repeatedly at the decoy because he was suspicious that he was soliciting sex, sliding his foot into contact with the decoy through clumsiness, running his hand along the bottom of the stall divider to stabilize or reposition himself, and so on. To attempt an innocent interpretation of such inherently suspicious behaviors would strain plausibility. Thus, Craig's reformulations posited actions that would tend to be interpreted as prima facie innocent.

Craig's move was to perform a global, radical reformulation of both the series of events in the restroom and the identities and purposes of the individuals involved in the interaction. The reformulation was global in that it encompassed, on the one hand, the entirety of the activity in the restroom and, on the other hand, the overall identities and purposes of both actors in the scene. The reformulation was radical in that it reconceptualized the activity in the restroom within a completely different explanatory framework to Karsnia's and presented fundamentally different personae for himself and Karsnia. This combination of the global and the radical in reformulation distinguishes the Craig interview from the typical police interview in which negotiation and argumentation tend to be locally managed, in other words, where the officer focuses on extracting an item of information and the suspect focuses on concealing it. Rarely does the untruthful suspect "fabricat[e] an entirely fictitious story" (Navarro and Schafer 2001: 11), as Craig does here. Rather, attention is paid to resisting the interviewer's efforts to extract information in a series of question-and-answer turns.

Craig's use of reformulation-by-question can be seen as a novel approach to taking control of interview discourse in the context of police-suspect interrogations. Rather than consent to the centrality and relevance of Karsnia's questions, Craig himself assumes the role of questioner, presenting questions that purported to probe the essential matters under consideration (*Did we bump? Did my hand come back below the divider? Did our feet come together? Did I glance at your stall?*) and whose presuppositions established the factual foundation from which any further elucidation should be seen to be derived. This dual move of assuming the interviewer position and reconceptualizing the questioning agenda is a striking reversal of both the roles and their inherent power asymmetry in the typical police interview. In these instances, Craig consents to neither the questioning authority of the officer nor the validity of the officer's questioning regimen.

I mentioned earlier that it is difficult to imagine that Craig's reformulation work in the police interview was an attempt to win the "tug of war" for information with Karsnia. With the latter as an eyewitness to Craig's actions, it is nearly inconceivable that Karsnia would consider the possibility that Craig was innocent, no matter how carefully crafted his alternative account. Thus, this case can be understood as Craig's *word* against Karsnia's *knowledge*. However, the interview was audio-recorded, where "talk is knowingly produced for a third party" (Heydon 2005: 39): "In the police interview, the tape recorder represents the future listeners of the tape, an audience (also referred to as the silent participant and the overhearing audience) that comprises members of the criminal justice system such as supervisory officers, legal advisors, members of the court and jury" (Carter 2008: 87). Since Craig was a US senator and thus a very public figure, the circle of potential—and, as it turns out, actual—future listeners should be enlarged to include the media and the public. For this reason, it was critical for Craig to produce an account for the record that made the interaction his *word* against Karsnia's *word*. Since the risks associated with media exposure of socially sanctioned behavior were great, it was incumbent on Craig to cast doubt on Karsnia's account. He ended up pleading guilty to the charge of disorderly conduct but several months later petitioned (unsuccessfully) to have his guilty plea withdrawn. Arguably this was Craig's only act of consent in the entire affair—one that ultimately proved to be his undoing. Around the same time, the unthinkable happened for Craig: the audio interview appeared on YouTube for all the world to hear, inviting derision and mockery for what were perceived to be his outrageous explanations for what happened in the restroom. Nevertheless, Craig's reformulated account provided a rhetorical foundation for his unswerving insistence on his innocence.

The intricate analysis undertaken here is meant to exhibit the sophisticated discursive mechanisms available to an interactant compelled to such a degree of extremity and their distinctive use in a particular situation. For the vast majority of individuals who unknowingly subject themselves to a sting, the resulting helplessness almost invariably predicts surrender. For a public figure, however, whose career and standing in society depend so heavily on maintaining a reputation that satisfies certain broadly held moral standards of conduct, the stakes are usually too high to allow surrender as a viable option. Craig could consent to nothing without dire consequences. Instead, his response was to enact resistance through a radical reformulation of events, agents and their motivations, and the nature of the interview itself. As Newbury and Johnson have it, "[I]t is in these moments [of confrontation with the authority of the police] that interviewees assert their right to resist institutional control and determine what is agreed and confirmed in the interview" (2006: 231). In the case of the Larry Craig interview, resistance and determination were thoroughgoing—if not absolute.

Appendix: Transcription Conventions

______	emphatic stress
= =	latched utterances
[ ]	overlapping talk
( )	length of pause in seconds
( )	transcriber doubt as to utterance content
(( ))	scenic detail
:	lengthened sound
...	transcriber-omitted talk
—	false start

Notes

1. The analysis in this chapter was based on a transcript, produced by the author, of an audiotape of the interview released by the Minneapolis–St. Paul Police Department in response to media interest in its content. The written police report by Karsnia was also released to a number of media outlets.

2. Most public restrooms in the United States have a design in which the door of the stall does not contact a jamb to provide complete visual privacy. When the door is closed and locked, there remains between the door and the partition immediately adjacent to it a small gap through which one can look into and out of the stall.

Cases Cited

Sorrells v. United States, 287 US 435 (1932).

References

Auburn, Timothy, Sue Drake and Carla Willig. 1995. "You punched him didn't you?": Versions of violence in accusatory interviews. *Discourse and Society* 6: 353–386.

Buckwalter, Art. 1983. *Surveillance and Undercover Investigation*. Boston: Butterworth.

Carter, Elizabeth. 2008. Policing talk: An investigation into the interaction of the officer and suspect in the police interview. Unpublished PhD dissertation. Essex, U.K.: University of Essex.

Clayman, Steven. 1993. Reformulating the question: A device for answering/not answering questions in news interviews and press conferences. *Text* 13: 159–188.

Drew, Paul. 1985. Analyzing the use of language in courtroom interaction. In Teun Van Dijk (ed.) *Handbook of Discourse Analysis* (vol. 3). London: Academic Press. 133–147.

Drew, Paul. 1990. Strategies in the contest between lawyer and witness in cross-examination. In Judith Levi and Anne Graffam Walker (eds.) *Language in the Judicial Process*. New York: Plenum. 39–64.

Drew, Paul. 1992. Contested evidence in courtroom cross-examination: The case of a trial for rape. In Paul Drew and John Heritage (eds.) *Talk at Work: Interaction in Institutional Settings*. Cambridge: Cambridge University Press. 470–520.

Dworkin, Gerald. 1985. The serpent beguiled me and I did eat. *Law and Philosophy* 4: 17–31.

Gallo, Jon, Stefan Mason, Louis Meisinger, Kenneth Robin, Gary Stabile and Robert Wynne. 1966. The consenting adult homosexual: An empirical study of enforcement and administration in Los Angeles County. *UCLA Law Review* 13: 647–832.

Gibbons, John. 2003. *Forensic Linguistics: An Introduction to Language in the Justice System*. Oxford: Blackwell.

Government of Minnesota. 2007. Minnesota Statute §609.72, subd. 1.

Grace, George. 1987. *The Linguistic Construction of Reality*. London: Croom Helm.

Harfield, Clive and Karen Harfield. 2008. *Covert Investigation* (2nd ed.). Oxford: Oxford University Press.

Haworth, Kate. 2006. The dynamics of power and resistance in police interview discourse. *Discourse and Society* 17: 739–759.

Hay, Bruce. 2003. Sting operations, undercover agents, and entrapment. Discussion paper No. 441, John M. Olin Center for Law, Economics, and Business, Harvard Law School, Cambridge, Massachusetts.

Heydon, Georgina. 2005. *The Language of Police Interviewing: A Critical Analysis*. London: Palgrave Macmillan.

Marx, Gary. 1988. *Under Cover: Police Surveillance in America*. Berkeley: University of California Press.

Navarro, Joe and John Schafer. 2001. Detecting deception. *FBI Law Enforcement Bulletin* 70: 9–13.

Newbury, Phillip and Alison Johnson. 2006. Suspects' resistance to constraining and coercive questioning strategies in the police interview. *International Journal of Speech, Language, and the Law* 13: 213–240.

Walton, Douglas. 2003. The interrogation as a type of dialogue. *Journal of Pragmatics* 35: 1771–1802.

SECTION 4

The Coercive Force of Cautions

11

Totality of Circumstances and Translating the Miranda Warnings

Susan Berk-Seligson

Suspects in custody are generally assumed to have given free and voluntary consent to being questioned by the police if they acknowledge that they have understood the police explanation of their rights in custody—which include the right to remain silent—and they then proceed to answer interrogators' questions. However, as considerable research has shown, many suspects' understanding of what they have agreed to is far from complete. The problem is especially acute, as we know, when the suspects are immigrants whose proficiency in English is limited. In the United States today, however, translations of these rights (known as Miranda rights) have become widely available in the languages of the major immigrant groups. In the case of the largest linguistic minority, Hispanics, the Miranda rights are frequently communicated in Spanish. Nevertheless, when those rights are read by non-native Spanish-speaking police officers, they are all too often so garbled and mispronounced that they are rendered defectively (Rogers, Correa, Hazelwood, Shuman, Hoersting and Blackwood 2009). Since there is no standard English version of the Miranda warnings in the United States, Spanish translations abound, and given the lack of quality control over these translations, they vary in their fidelity to the English language source. Therefore, even when the police officer reading the Miranda translations is a native Spanish speaker, he or she can convey the rights inaccurately if the written translation is a poor one. This chapter will review the literature on several distinct factors that can affect the comprehensibility of Spanish translations of Miranda, and will demonstrate with a case study that even when a police district utilizes a Spanish translation of the Miranda warnings, *and* they are delivered by a native Spanish speaker, there can still be problems for a Spanish-speaking suspect to understand those rights, and thus to give free and willing consent.

Comprehensibility will be shown to partly involve linguistic characteristics of the Miranda warnings, and the educational background of the suspect. Furthermore, when the detainee comes from a country that has no equivalent of the Miranda warnings, as is the situation in the case study analyzed in this chapter, the lack of familiarity with Miranda further reduces the prospects of accurate comprehension. In this chapter I treat such cases as instances of lack of cultural equivalence, and suggest that this is a further factor impeding comprehension.

This chapter examines police interrogations conducted in Spanish, as well as studies of Spanish translations of the warnings to demonstrate the variety of ways in which English and Spanish versions of the Miranda warnings fail to line up. In the case study focused on here, I consider reasons that one Hispanic suspect is unlikely to have understood one of those Spanish renditions. Beyond the issue of comprehensibility, the chapter uses a sociolegal theoretical perspective to explore some of the elements that can be considered relevant to the question of whether the decision of a suspect in police custody to answer the questions of interrogators was an "uncoerced choice" or not (see US Supreme Court's decision in *Moran v. Burbine*). In legal terms, these elements are referred to as the "totality of circumstances," and reflect the law's recognition that more than linguistic comprehension is involved for suspects to be considered to have chosen to waive their Miranda rights in an uncoerced way.

The Miranda rights, the outcome of a 1966 US Supreme Court decision, specifically guarantee suspects two of their constitutional rights, namely the Fifth Amendment right that "[n]o person . . . shall be compelled in any criminal case to be a witness against himself," and the Sixth Amendment right to a defense attorney. Thus, suspects must be warned (1) that they have the right to remain silent, and that they need not answer any questions; (2) that if they do answer questions, their answers can be used as evidence against them; (3) that they have the right to consult with a lawyer before or during the questioning of them by the police; and (4) that if they cannot afford to hire a lawyer, one will be provided for them without cost to them. Furthermore, if suspects indicate at any time or in any way that they do not want to talk, the interrogation has to stop. The interrogator does not have the right to attempt to persuade a suspect out of his or her refusal to talk (Inbau, Reid and Buckley 1986: 220).

This chapter, then, will (1) review empirical studies on (a) difficulties associated with the use of police as interpreters for limited English proficient (LEP) suspects and (b) the comprehensibility of the Miranda warnings; (2) examine the issue of "totality of circumstances," giving special attention to cultural barriers to comprehending the Miranda warnings; and (3) analyze the Mirandizing segment of the interrogation of a Mexican murder suspect by a native Spanish-speaking detective.

Review of the Scholarly Literature

INADVISABILITY OF USING THE POLICE AS INTERPRETERS AT CUSTODIAL INTERROGATIONS

The need for interpreting services in the justice system has blossomed, partly because of the ever-increasing immigrant population now living across a broad section of the United States, including areas that have up until the recent past been relatively homogeneous from a linguistic standpoint—namely, rural parts of the Midwest and the Southeast. The courts (which in the United States operate at three levels: federal, state, and municipal) to various degrees have made important strides in providing trained interpreters to LEP speakers (Berk-Seligson 2002). However, when it comes to pretrial phases of the judicial process, the justice system continues to fall short of doing so.

Berk-Seligson (2009) reviewed appellate cases involving the problematic use of persons having no professional training as interpreters for the police—both at arrests and during custodial questioning. The study reveals that the police enlist a heterogeneous mix of bilingual people who happen to be present at a crime scene or in the police station, and have them serve as ad hoc, "on-the-spot," interpreters. Often these interpreters are relatives or friends of the suspect, and sometimes even confederates in the crime, and only rarely do they have any formal training in legal interpreting. In fact, some of these interpreters themselves may have only limited proficiency in English. Yet the police regularly and systematically rely on such ad hoc interpreters, for lack of a sufficient number of qualified bilingual police officers.

This problem is particularly acute in the setting of police interviews. Primarily because of a lack of budget for professional interpreting services, police precincts rely heavily on police officers who have some, but often limited, proficiency in languages other than English (LOTE), many of whom are given "crash courses" in Spanish, for example, to give them some degree of bilingual ability. These crash courses, often called "survival skills Spanish," can amount to as little as 16 to 24 hours of instruction, given over a two- to-three-day period.

Even when the police interrogator is a fluently bilingual Spanish/English speaker, the outcome can be bad for an LEP immigrant Latino, Berk-Seligson (2009) finds. In one such case the suspect was also a fluent bilingual Latino. The police officer conducted the interrogation entirely in English, in the presence of a monolingual English-speaking detective. However, whenever the suspect was invited to narrate his version of events on the day of the murder he would switch to Spanish; in other words, he would engage in "code-switching." Yet the interrogating detective would respond exclusively in English, which in the United States is an unusual way of responding to a fellow Latino's switch to Spanish. Following typical interactional patterns between interlocutors who are bilingual and who share ethnicity, we would expect the bilingual police officer to continue in Spanish. It is hypothesized that the reason for the failure of the bilingual detective to switch to Spanish on every occasion of the suspect's code-switching is that this would have placed him in the role of interpreter for the monolingual police officer present during the speech event, and to act simultaneously as interpreter and interrogator is untenable. This would amount to cognitive overload, and would have adversely affected the quality of both roles. Interestingly, the detainee was very sensitive to the detective's failure to switch to Spanish, because several times he made metalinguistic comments about this to the police officer.

In sum, the failure of police precincts to provide independent, trained interpreters at custodial interrogations makes for various sorts of poor outcomes for detainees. Even when both police interrogator and suspect are fluently bilingual, suspects are often denied the right to express themselves in the language that at the moment is easiest to access for the purpose of the discourse function at hand.

Comprehensibility of the Miranda Warnings

Most of the empirical studies of the comprehensibility of the Miranda warnings in the United States have been conducted over the past decade, whereas studies of a similar nature in other countries that have comparable warnings go back further, into the mid-1990s. The United Kingdom, for example, has a standardly worded police "caution," a set of warnings that are roughly similar to the Miranda warnings in their intent and purpose.[1] An empirical study of the UK caution by Shepherd, Mortimer, and Mobasheri (1995: 1) finds that of 109 people who were asked to listen to the caution, "About one in four actually understood the first element, one in eight the second, and one in three the third," and on average about half of it made sense to them. Particularly disturbing is the finding that over half of the people who participated in the study considered the caution to in fact be a way of pressuring or threatening them. In the United States, where there is no standardized written version of the Miranda warnings, every jurisdiction has the right to use the wording it chooses. Thus, in the state of New Jersey alone, for example, there are at least 31 different versions of Miranda warnings used by state police (Helms 2003) and sixteen different versions used at the county level (Greenfield, Dougherty, Jackson, Podboy and Zimmerman 2001), according to Rogers, Harrison, Shuman, Sewell and Hazelwood (2007: 179). The lack of standardization in the warnings is one source of variability in their comprehensibility.

An additional factor contributing to variability in the comprehensibility of the Miranda warnings is that police officers do not have to read the rights from a printed card at all. They are allowed to paraphrase them. Even in the United Kingdom, where the wording of the caution is standardized, the police often paraphrase the warnings, and in so doing, often make them less comprehensible than they are in the printed version that appears on the "caution card," according to Cotterill (2000). Shuy (1998: 53), working in the United States, finds that even when the police read directly from the card, their performance as readers is often so poor that comprehension of the Miranda warnings is adversely affected. Even if the warnings are read well, Shuy (1998: 55) finds that "their sequencing has a strange illogicality," so that persons being read their rights do not realize that the first decision that they have to make is whether to ask for a lawyer, and that the decision to speak or remain silent should be made after that decision, rather than before.

For several decades, quantitative studies of the comprehensibility of the Miranda warnings have been carried out by psychologists and psychiatrists, using a standardly accepted statistical tool: the Flesch-Kincaid Readability Level or Grade Level and Flesch-Kincaid Reading Ease measures. Both are based on word length and sentence length. The Flesch-Kincaid approach to readability and comprehensibility, which has its counterparts in similar statistical tools such as the Gunning Fog Index, the Dale-Chall Readability Index, and SMOG (Simple Measure of Gobbledygook). The courts have accepted the product of statistical tools such as Flesch-Kincaid, considering them to be scientifically valid measures. But they have come under heavy criticism by linguists, who rightfully point out that syntactic complexity and syntactic features such as multiple negation are entirely overlooked by these measures, and that therefore the "cookbook approach" that underlies this automated, blind method of determining the comprehensibility of a text is a wrongheaded one (Charrow and Charrow 1979; Campbell and Holland 1982; Tiersma 1999; Stygall 2002). Charrow and Charrow (1979), for example, discovered that nominalizations, vague and uncommon prepositional phrases, double or triple sets of negative words and phrases within a single clause, passive constructions (especially in subordinate clauses), and strings of closely related words connected by *and* or *or* reduce the comprehensibility of a text. Tiersma (1999) found that impersonal constructions, often through the use of nouns rather than the pronouns *I* or *you*, and complex syntactic construction (e.g., embedded clauses) add to comprehension difficulties, as does technical legal jargon with its use of archaic, formal, and unusual vocabulary. Stygall's (2002) analysis of the language of American immigration application forms includes the findings of psycholinguists, who have shown that the more embedded clauses there are in a text, the more difficult it is to comprehend that text, and the longer it takes to process its meaning. Furthermore, "clauses without their immediately visible subjects, such as infinite clauses, present additional processing difficulties as readers search for the proper subject" (Stygall 2002: 44).

Despite finding various flaws in the use of readability formulas, Tiersma (1999) points out that scholars involved in the Plain English movement, such as Benson (1985) and Klare (1974–1975), find utility in them. Benson believes that "readability formulas, with all their shortcomings, perform a valuable function in promoting plain legal language" (Tiersma 1999: 227), and Klare has pointed out that while "word length and sentence length do not *cause* difficulty in reading, ... they are reasonable *indices* of difficulty" (Tiersma 1999: 227). Tiersma, himself, concludes that "as a rough indicator, readability tests work fairly well," noting for example that "although sentence length is not *directly* related to complexity, long sentences *generally* tend to be more complex" (Tiersma 1999: 227).

Comprehensibility of the warnings becomes a separate issue when translation is involved. Perhaps the most comprehensive empirical study of Miranda warnings is Rogers et al.'s (2009) study of 121 Spanish translations and their English originals, obtained from prosecutors, public defenders, and sheriffs across 33 states.[2] The Spanish translations were often inaccurate versions of their English originals in various ways, some more significantly inaccurate than others. The authors found problems in general understandability in three categories (Rogers et al. 2009: 63):

> (a) minor variations in the translation that were unlikely to affect the general meaning, (b) awkward translations that may contribute to problems in comprehension, and (c) mistranslations that inaccurately reflect the meaning. Beyond understandability, content differences were also categorized. They included (a) missing Miranda components, (b) substantially dissimilar content in explaining Miranda components, and (c) substantive errors in describing Miranda components.

Rogers et al.'s (2009) study shows that among the most serious discrepancies between the English Miranda warnings and their translations is the complete omission of a warning (what Rogers et al. 2009 refer to as "missing component"). That is, missing from such translations are one or more of the following: (1) the right to silence, (2) that anything you say can be used against you, (3) the right to talk to an attorney, (4) the right to a free, court-appointed attorney if the detainee is indigent, and (5) the right to stop the questioning at any time. In the examples of "dissimilar content," in the Spanish translations of the right to silence, the warning has been reduced dramatically from the English original, and is left vague ("You have the right not to say anything"), whereas the English source is much more specific, stating that the detainee "cannot be compelled to answer" and has "the right to refuse to answer any questions asked of you while you are in custody." Thus, in these examples the English is far more informative than is its translation. In the example of one's right to a free court appointed defense attorney, the English specifies "One will be provided free," whereas some Spanish translations do not include the point that the attorney will be appointed free of charge. In the example that refers to one's continuing right to stop the questioning at any point, the

English source refers twice to the presence or absence of an attorney; by contrast, some Spanish renditions make no reference to any attorney at all. In the category "substantive error," referring to one's continuing rights, the English source says, "To exercise these rights and not answer any questions or make any statement," but some Spanish translations substantially change the meaning of the original, saying merely, "To finish the interview," thus omitting any reference to specific rights.

On the whole, Rogers et al. find that "Spanish warnings provided less information than their English counterparts" (2009: 65). They conclude:

> Because many Hispanic offenders have some working knowledge of English ... or can infer the intended meaning, the effects of awkward usage and even mistranslations must be evaluated on a case-by-case basis. Some mistranslations (e.g., "remain silent" as "shut up") still communicate the gist of the information, whereas others may confuse or mislead Spanish-speaking suspects. Consistent with the *totality of circumstances* (emphasis added), forensic clinicians must evaluate the cumulative effects of mistranslations, grammatical errors, ambiguous wording, and confusing statements.

From the standpoint of forensic psychologists such as Rogers et al. (2009), empirical evidence of the sort that they uncover leads to the conclusion that limited-English-speaking suspects need to be evaluated comprehensively, taking into account "the *combined effects* of language, situational factors, cognitive abilities, and psychological impairment" (emphasis added), as well as acute intoxication, "on the understandability of translated warnings" (Rogers et al. 2009: 68). In sum, the comparison between English-language Miranda warnings and their Spanish back translations presents a highly disturbing picture. Suspects in police custody are given distorted versions of the warnings. If they start off the interrogation not receiving accurate renditions of their rights, then how could they possibly be said to have understood those rights? The following discussion will demonstrate that there are additional factors affecting comprehension of the Miranda warnings—factors referred to above as the "totality of circumstances."

Totality of Circumstances: Issues Relevant to the Comprehension of the Miranda Warnings

While the English and Spanish versions of the Miranda warnings can be analyzed for their comprehensibility, the question as to whether any given person in custody understood the warnings that were read to them and voluntarily waived their rights is another issue. Factors beyond the comprehensibility of the wording of the warnings come into play. These factors have been subsumed under the rubric of "totality of circumstances," a principle set forth by the US Supreme Court in 1986 under *Moran v. Burbine*. Rogers et al. (2009) explicitly use this term in referring to the combined effects of the various factors that need to be taken into account in determining whether or not a given suspect understood the Miranda rights. Typically, according to legal scholars, the totality of circumstances includes the suspect's "age, education, background and intelligence and ... whether he has the capacity to understand the warnings given to him, the nature of his Fifth Amendment rights, and the consequences of waiving those rights" (*Fare v. Michael C.* 1979). For other legal scholars (Ramirez, Kay and Weber 1994–1995: 2), the totality of circumstances also includes "length of detention, the coerciveness of the police/suspect encounter, and the accused's knowledge of the right to refuse consent." As the Supreme Court argued in *Moran v. Burbine* (as cited in Solan and Tiersma 2005: 75–76):

> First, the relinquishment of the right must have been voluntary in the sense that it was the product of a free and deliberate choice rather than intimidation, coercion, or deception. Second, the waiver must have been made with a full awareness of both the nature of the right being abandoned and the consequences of the decision to abandon it. Only if the "totality of circumstances surrounding the interrogation" reveals both an uncoerced choice and the requisite level of comprehension may a court properly conclude that the *Miranda* rights have been waived.

From Solan and Tiersma's (2005: 75) standpoint, not only should the age and cognitive ability of a suspect be taken into account in considering the totality of circumstances, but his or her ability to speak and understand English should be considered as well. Some trial courts have taken language proficiency into account in determining the voluntariness of a suspect's statements to the police. Ramirez et al.'s (1994–1995: 6) review of case law finds in *US v. Fung and Chen* a trial court's decision to consider inadmissible the statement of a Chinese defendant whose proficiency in English was minimal, and who was Mirandized by being asked to read aloud a card on which the Miranda warnings were printed in Chinese. According to Ramirez et al. (1994–1995: 6), "The court held that the defendant was not properly advised of her rights given her poor language skills, her lack of knowledge of the American legal system, and the stress of the situation, which likely interfered with her comprehension."

Ramirez (2007), who reviews the cultural issues that have been raised by defense attorneys in criminal defense cases, including matters related to the Miranda warnings, also finds that some trial court judges do suppress interrogation evidence based on linguistic factors. Specifically, they suppress evidence resulting from the suspect's being read the warnings in English, when he was later found to understand English poorly or hardly at all; and the suspect being read the warnings by a person who was not an interpreter by profession, but by someone with limited proficiency in the language other than English. While problems in comprehending the waiver of the Miranda rights are often a cause of suppression of evidence, judges at the appellate level sometimes overturn trial court decisions that favor the defendant in cases of this type (Ramirez 2007).

Despite this broad sweep of factors included under the "totality of circumstances" rubric, in American courts cultural differences between non-US nationals and Americans generally have not been included. There are a number of cultural arguments that can be made and that have been made (Renteln 2004), but these have usually failed at the level of appellate courts. One cultural argument that affects the voluntariness of the Miranda waiver is fear of the police, an issue raised in *US v. Zapata* (1993), in which the district court judge held that "[b]ecause of his upbringing in Mexico, Defendant believed that he must acquiesce to all police requests because failure to do so could result in dire consequences, including physical harm," and that the defendant "reasonably felt intimidated by the presence of the officers, and reasonably interpreted (the Agent's) 'requests' as commands or demands" (*US v. Zapata* 1993: 755). However, the lower court's opinion was rejected by the appellate court, which reversed the trial court's decision. The appellate court "thought the objective reasonable person test had to be applied, meaning that Zapata's 'own subjective attitudes toward the police encounter ... are irrelevant,'" and considered the lower court to have "erred in taking his background into account" (Renteln 2004: 91).

This chapter argues that the feelings of fear and mistrust of the police held by defendants who are of Mexican origin, such as Zapata, derive from concrete situations, which are well-documented, well-founded feelings that belong to the realm of Mexican culture. A recent ethnographic study (Tello 2012) of Mexico City police, found that "when circumstances allow, they exercise every ounce of power they can, be it legitimate or abusive," and know that their image among the citizenry is highly stigmatized (2012: 20). The case study described later in this chapter deals with a Mexican national who had grown up in Mexico. It is relevant, therefore, to take note that the police in Mexico City are so universally disliked that they become the objects of verbal abuse and physical assault, including lynching (Azaola 2006 in Tello 2012: 20). In short, "There is a collective image of the police, their corruption, arrogance, their abuse and inefficiency" (Tello 2012: 21). (See also Weiner 2002, as well as Arteaga Botello and López Rivera's 1998 two-year undercover ethnographic study of the police in Mexico, which shows that the current state of affairs goes back to corruption practices dating to the 19th century.)

Another element in the totality of circumstances affecting Miranda comprehension, one especially important in the case of Mexican nationals, is the cultural phenomenon of gratuitous concurrence. As Liberman (1981, 1985), Eades (1994, 2008), Mildren (1999), and Walsh (1994) first noted in the speech of Aboriginal Australians, gratuitous concurrence is a pattern of agreeing with one's interlocutor, and it is undoubtedly more prevalent in situations of power asymmetry (Eades 2008: 94). Liberman (1985: 234) sees gratuitous concurrence in court as a form of accommodation, a protective device used by Australian Aboriginals to keep their talk harmonious, a "strategy of acquiescing to the suggestions of their court interrogators." Eades (2008) considers gratuitous concurrence to be a strategy used by other sociocultural groups as well, a strategy of acquiescence out of fear, or in the case of second language speakers, out of a lack of understanding.[3] In the particular case of the Miranda warnings, when suspects are asked, "Do you understand this?" they might answer with a variety of affirmative types of responses (e.g., "Yeah," "Mhm," "Yes"), yet this does not necessarily mean that they have understood the warnings. They might be engaging in gratuitous concurrence.

Miranda Warnings in Spanish: A Case Study

In the case study I outline here, I focus on a police interrogation that would seem to be ideal in terms of the suspect's ability to understand his rights. It is a case in which the Miranda rights were read from a card, and thus were presumably professionally prepared, and were administered by a native Spanish-speaking police officer. Yet, as I demonstrate, the presence of a native Spanish-speaking police detective as an interrogator, using a printed Spanish-language translation of the Miranda warnings, is no guarantee of a comprehensible rendition of the warnings. Specifically, as I point out, (1) the interviewee's level of formal education was significantly below what would have been required to understand the warnings, (2) the interviewee was not read the cautionary statement that precedes the reading of the rights, (3) the police officer made numerous errors in reading him the rights, including the addition of features generally associated with legal language, and (4) the interviewee's responses to the questions and statements of the officer suggest that he did not understand the warnings. It should be noted that these four factors are not specific to the situation of second language speakers; they might equally be present in monolingual speech contexts.

The case involves the interrogation of a 26-year-old Mexican man by a police officer speaking a Caribbean variety of Spanish. It reveals a number of defects in the printed "official" translation, as well as a greater number of defects in the detective's oral rendition of that translation. The English and

Spanish versions of the Miranda warnings, as printed on cards and distributed to police officers in this particular precinct, are reproduced below.[4] The man in custody was suspected of being an accessory to murder. Working as a bouncer in a bar, one of his friends, a coworker, apparently decided to kill a mutual young friend of theirs whom the coworker suspected of informing the police about his cocaine-trafficking activities. The suspect adamantly insisted to the interrogating officer that he had no idea that his friend had intended to kill the youth when he and the coworker went looking for him on the night of the murder.

The case was brought to my attention by a defense attorney looking for a linguistic expert, in preparation for a suppression of evidence hearing. I was sent a video recording of the police interrogation, along with photocopies of the English-language Miranda warnings used by the police, together with a Spanish translation of the warnings used in that precinct. I was also sent an English translation of the interrogation, although no transcription of the original Spanish was made available to me (there may not have even been one). I transcribed the Spanish Mirandizing portion of the interrogation based on the video recording.

Printed Miranda Warnings Used by the Police Precinct

GIVE THIS WARNING TO ANY SUSPECT DETAINED PRIOR TO ANY QUESTIONING, IDENTIFY YOURSELF AND STATE:

"I am required to warn you before you make any statement that you have the following constitutional rights:

(1) You have the right to remain silent and not answer any questions.

(2) Any statement you make must be freely and voluntarily given.

(3) You have the right to presence and representation of a lawyer of your choice before you make any statement and during any questioning.

(4) If you cannot afford a lawyer, you are entitled to the presence and representation of a Court appointed lawyer before you make any statement and during any questioning.

(5) If at any time during the interview you do not wish to answer any questions, you are privileged to remain silent.

(6) I can make no threats or promises to induce you to make a statement. This must be of your own free will.

(7) Any statement can be and will be used against you in a court of law."

Spanish Translation of the Miranda Warnings Used by the Police Precinct

DE ESTE AVISO O ADVERTENCIA A CUALQUIERA, PERSONA SOSPECHOSA DETENIDA ANTES DE ALGUN INTERROGATORIO IDENTIFIQUESE A SI MISMO Y EXPONGA: Estoy obligado a prevenirle antes de que usted haga algún relato o declare de que usted tiene los siguientes derechos constitucionales:

(1) Usted tiene el derecho de quedarse callado o silencioso y no contestar cualquier pregunta.

(2) Cualquier relato o declaración que usted haga debe ser libre y voluntariamente dado.

(3) Usted tiene el derecho de la presencia de un abogado de su preferencia o selección antes de que usted haga algún relato o declaración y durante cualquier interrogatorio.

(4) Si usted no tiene los medios de proveerse o proporcionarse con los servicios de un abogado, tiene el derecho a la presencia de un abogado de oficio asignado por la Corte antes de que usted haga algún relato o declaración y durante cualquier interrogatorio.

(5) Si en algún momento durante la entrevista usted no desea contestar alguna pregunta o preguntas es su privilegio de quedarse callado o silencioso.

(6) No puedo amenazarle o prometerle nada para persuadirle o inducirle a que haga un relato o declare. Esto debe ser por su propia cuenta y libre voluntad.

(7) Cualquier relato o declaración puede ser y será usado en contra suya en una Corte de leyes.

We saw above that linguists have generally eschewed readability formulas. But following Tiersma's concession (also discussed above) and the fact that the judicial system has widely accepted readability evidence from expert witnesses, it is worthwhile putting the Spanish version of the Miranda warnings presented above to a readability test. Because of problems discussed earlier in this chapter (see note 2) with the Huerta Reading Ease test (which is a Flesch Reading Ease test modified for Spanish texts), the Spanish warnings were subjected to a readability test that is designed to be language neutral, the Coleman-Liau test. The numbers produced by the test represent school grade level. The results of the test are as follows: warning 1 = grade 14; warning 2 = grade 15.9; warning 3 = grade 13.2; warning 4 = grade 12.2; warning 5 = grade 15.2; warning 6 = grade 11; warning 7 = grade 9.1. Every year beyond the completion of high school (12th grade in the United States), is assigned an additional grade. Thus, 14th grade would be the equivalent of second year of university studies completed. The decimal points indicate partial completion of a grade.

The suspect in the case being analyzed here had attained ninth-grade education in Mexico, which is likely to be equivalent to a lower-than-ninth-grade education in the United States (see Organization for Economic Co-operation and Development 2012 for comparative ratings). Thus a higher grade level on a readability score such as Coleman-Liau would be required for people educated in Mexican public schools. When considering that Mexican education levels are far below those in the United States, this suggests that the chances of this suspect understanding any of the warnings are slim. Even without adjustment, he might possibly have understood the seventh warning, but it is unlikely that he would have understood the remaining six. The fact that the first, third, and fourth warnings are grammatically complex sentences (see turns 13, 21, and 23, respectively, in the transcript that follows) provides one explanation for why they would be difficult to understand. Further, while the readability test results apply to the (Spanish) translation as it appears on the card, the way in which these warnings were actually administered orally diverged from what was written on the printed cards given to the police (as we will see). Thus, in this case, in addition to syntactic complexity is the manner in which the detective read the rights, which included a number of disfluencies. It is likely, therefore, that her oral rendition of the rights was less comprehensible than the readability scores for the card would predict. Here are the Spanish source language question/answer sequences and their English translations:

1 Detective A: What's up bud?
2 Luis Rojas: Hola.
[Hello.]
3 Detective A: You're all right?
4 Luis Rojas: Perdón, yo estaba durmiendo.
[Yeah. I'm sorry, I was sleeping.]
5 Detective B: Huh?
[Huh?]
6 Luis Rojas: Estaba durmiendo. Perdón.
[I was sleeping. I'm sorry.]
7 Detective B: ¿Por qué? ¿Tienes sueño?
[Why? Are you sleepy?]
8 Luis Rojas: Sí.
[Yeah.]

9 Detective B: ¿Estoy tan aburrida?
[Am I so boring?]
10 Luis Rojas: No::! (inaudible) que no.
[No. No, no, (inaudible) of course not.]
11 Detective B: Te voy a leer esto. ¿Okey?
[I'm going to read this to you. Okay?]
12 Luis Rojas: Okey.
[Okay.]
13 Detective B: Tienes el derecho – Te voy a hacer unas preguntas, y por ley cuando uno está en la jefatura tengo que leerte tus derechos para hacerte unas preguntas acerca lo que pasó en la esquina ésa.
[You have the right – I'm going to ask you some questions, and by law when you're at the station I have to read you your rights to ask you some questions about what happened on that corner.]
14 Luis Rojas: Mhm.
[Uh-huh.]
15 Detective B: Entonces con eso,
[So, with that.]
16 Luis Rojas: Mhm.
[Uh-huh.]
17 Detective B: Usted tiene el derecho de quedarse callado y silencioso y no contestar ningunas preguntas. ¿Tú entendiste eso?
[You have the right to remain quiet and silent and not answer any questions. Did you understand that?]
18 Luis Rojas: Mhm.
[Uh-huh.]
19 Detective B: Cualquier relato o declaración que usted haga tiene que ser por su libre y voluntariamente dado.
[Any account or statement that you give must be by your -- freely and voluntarily given.]
20 Luis Rojas: Mhm.
[Uh-huh.]
21 Detective B: Usted tiene el derecho de la presencia de un abogado de su preferencia o selección antes de cualquier interrogatorio o declaración y durante cualquier interrogatorio. ¿Tú entendiste eso?
[You have the right to have an attorney of your preference or selection present before any interrogation or statement and during any interrogation. Did you understand that?]

22 Luis Rojas: Mhm.

[Uh-huh.]

23 Detective B: Si usted no tiene los medios de provenerse o proporcionarse con los servicios de un abogado, usted tiene el derecho a la presencia de un abogado de oficio asignado por la Corte antes de cualquier declaración y durante cualquier interrogatorio. ¿Tú entendiste eso?

[If you don't have the means to – to procure or provend (not a word in Spanish) yourself the services of an attorney you have the right to the presence of a public defender assigned by the court before any statement and during any interrogation. Did you understand that?]

24 Luis Rojas: Mhm.

[Uh-huh.]

25 Detective B: Si en algún momento durante la entrevista usted no desea con-, con-contester alguna pregunta tien-, tiene el privilegio de quedarse callado, o silencioso. ¿Entendiste?

[If at any time during the interview you don't wish to -- an-, an-, answer any question you you ha-, have the privilege of remaining quiet or silent. Did you understand?]

26 Luis Rojas: Sí.

[Yes.]

27 Detective B: ¿Entendiste?

[Did you understand?]

28 Luis Rojas: Okey.

[Okay.]

29 Detective B: Cualquier, ah – No puedo amenazarte ni prometerte que haga ninguna, o presurirle que haga, o inducirle que haga un relato o declaración. Esto debe ser por su libre, por su propia cuenta y su libre voluntad. ¿Entendiste?

[Any, uh – I can't threaten you or promise you to do any, or to presurirle (not a word in Spanish)[5] or lead you to give any account or statement. This ought to be of your free – of your own account and your free will. Did you understand?]

30 Luis Rojas: Okey.

[Okay.]

31 Detective B: Cualquier relato o declaración puede ser usuado en contra suya en una Corte de leyes. ¿Entendiste eso?

[Any account or statement can be usuado (not a Spanish word) against you in a court of law. Did you understand that?]

32 Luis Rojas: Mhm.
[Uh-huh.]

33 Detective: Okey, fírmame aquí, que lo entendiste. ¿Tú quieres un refresco? ¿Tienes sed?
[Okay. Sign here that you understood it. Do you want a soda? Are you thirsty?]

34 Luis Rojas: Mhm.
[Uh-huh.]

Language Problems Not Specific to the Second-Language Situation

A number of problems are apparent in the detective's delivery of the Miranda warnings. Several of these problems are not specific to the fact that the warnings were given in translation: these are issues that—independent of the language of the interview—would make it difficult for many suspects to understand their rights. For example, the detective did not read to the suspect the prefatory warning, which cautions the suspect that he has constitutional rights that will be read to him. She not only did not read it from the Spanish language card, nor did she paraphrase it, but she omitted it in its entirety. Instead of telling him that she is *cautioning* him, and that she will read him his rights *before he makes any statement*, she conveys to him unequivocally that she will in fact be asking him questions (turn 13). From the way in which she phrases the introduction to the reading of the rights, she gives the unmitigated impression that he will not have a choice in the matter: the questions will, without a doubt, be asked.[6] This is presupposed in the final clause of the sentence ("to ask you some questions about what happened on that corner"). Perhaps if she had preceded this clause with the verb "to be able to," it would have left open the possibility to the suspect that asking him questions would not necessarily follow. By not reading the prefatory caution, the detective was adversely affecting the detainee's ability to understand it.

Another factor that had to have contributed to diminishing the suspect's comprehension is the manner in which the detective read the rights: she was speaking at lightning speed, often slurring over her words (a police practice reported in other studies of the caution, including Shuy 1998: 53; Rock 2007: Chapter 8; Leo 2008: 127). This, of course, is obvious from the video of the interrogation, and anyone watching the video would note it. But even in the transcript this becomes obvious. In her reading of the seventh right (turn 31), in her rapid pace, she slurs the boundary between the words *ser y será usado*, producing the blend, *ser usuado*, omitting the future tense verb *será* ("will be"). My listening to this phrase in the video recording well over

15 times confirmed for me that the phrase *ser y será usado* was not uttered; the resulting participle *usuado* does not exist as a word in Spanish.

A further problem is the use of high register vocabulary, which must have constituted a problem for someone who has completed only middle school (i.e., ninth grade education). This is seen in the English original with words such as "presence," "representation," and "privileged." The fourth warning, in particular, evidences such vocabulary. For example, the word *medios* ("means"), meaning "money," may not be clear at all to a person with a middle-school level of attainment. The word *medio* in its other senses is common enough (e.g., "half," or in the expression *por medio de*, "by means of"), but in a monetary sense it is not commonly used by poorly educated persons. Similarly, *proveerse* ("provide") and *proporcionarse* are words belonging to a high register and are associated with higher levels of educational attainment. Furthermore, the noun phrase *abogado de oficio* ("court-appointed lawyer" or "public defender") is a term of art, a Spanish phrase that belongs to legal jargon. Similarly, the term *asignado* ("assigned") does not necessarily include the semantic feature "free of charge"; that the suspect would not be required to pay for the services of a court-appointed lawyer is not at all obvious from the combination of the terms "court-appointed lawyer" and "assigned," especially if he is a recent immigrant and has not had previous experience with the American criminal justice system.

Language Problems Specific to the Second-Language Situation

Several problems are specific to the fact that the warnings were given in translation. Mainly because the detective speeds through the rights, she makes a number of substantive changes in their meaning. One of the more serious substantive errors the detective makes in reading the Spanish version of the Miranda warnings is her omission of the phrase *que usted haga algún relato* ("you give any account" or "you give any report," or "you relate any narrative"), in the third warning. In substituting *cualquier interrogatorio* ("any questioning") in turn 21 for the phrase that appears on the Miranda card, she produces what is now a difficult-to-understand sentence: "You have the right to have an attorney of your preference or selection present before any questioning or statement and during any questioning." The warning does not say whose statement this would be (i.e., the interrogating detective's or the suspect's) or what the word "statement" refers to, as this is a legal term in the context of a police interrogation, but then the translation on the card does not make this clear either, whereas the English version specifies the agent of the verb, "you" ("before you make any statement and during any questioning"). The Spanish translation of this phrase is further obscured in that it refers to *algún relato o declaración*, ("any account [narrative] or statement"), distinguishing between the two, whereas the English refers only to the suspect's making "any statement," clearly connecting such a statement to him (the use of the pronoun of address *usted*), whereas the phrase "any questioning" (*cualquier interrogatorio*) is not tied to him. This is one of several phrases containing conjoined similar words connected by "or" or "and," a feature of legal language, and one that the detective repeatedly uses.

Further, both the Spanish translation of the first right and the detective's reading of it are misleading. Whereas the card reads *quedarse callado o silencioso* ("remain quiet or silent"), giving the addressee a choice, the English-language card specifies only one: "remain silent." Furthermore, in turn 17 the detective changes *callado o silencioso* to *callado y silencioso* ("quiet and silent"), which is confusing, since the two adjectives then appear to have a distinct meaning; but if in fact they do, then how could the suspect simultaneously carry out both actions?

In one instance, the detective improves upon the Spanish translation. Whereas the English-language card says, in the second warning, "Any statement you make *must be* freely and voluntarily given," the Spanish card erroneously says *debe ser libre y voluntariamente dado*. The phrase "must be" indicates obligation and should be translated as *tiene que ser*; the phrase *debe ser*, however, indicates desirability, as in "ought to" or "should," and thus has a weaker illocutionary force than the English source language modal verb. Interestingly, in reading the warning (turn 19), the detective changes the wording on the card to *tiene que ser*, thereby correcting the translator's error.

Probably the most incomprehensible warning uttered by the detective is the sixth one. While the card reads *No puedo amenazarle o prometerle nada para persuadirle o inducirle a que haga un relato o declare*, the detective uttered the following (turn 29): *No puedo amenazarte ni prometerte que haga ninguna, o presurirle que haga, o inducirle que haga un relato o declaración* ("I can't threaten you or promise you to do any, or to presurirle [not a word in Spanish; see note 5] or lead you to give any account or statement"). First of all, it is a good example of legalese, as characterized by Tiersma (1999), in that it contains a number of phrases conjoined by "or." In addition, the detective's reading, as is evident, is filled with backtracking and contains two coinages. The first phrase makes no sense, in other words, the detective cannot promise the suspect that he should give an account (a speaker can promise only something that they themselves can fulfill; the speaker cannot make a promise about the interlocutor's actions, if this is to have the illocutionary force of a true promise). Finally, the warning displays features considered to be typical of legal language, features that increase the difficulty of comprehending it. Specifically, it contains a string of closely related words connected by "or" (the word *o* is repeated three times), and in addition contains three negative markers within the same clause (*no, ni, ninguna*). Spanish, in contrast to

English, does not use the grammatical rule that two negative words produce a positive meaning. In fact, in Spanish any number of negative markers will convey negative meaning. It is possible that the processing of a string of negatives in Spanish is not as laborious cognitively as it would be in a language such as English; however, psychological experimenting would be needed to determine whether or not this is the case.

Finally, as the police officer was speaking in a Caribbean variety of Spanish, she constantly deleted syllable-final /s/ (which in word-final position can function as a plural marker on nouns, adjectives, and determiners; it also acts as the second-person singular informal verb morpheme). As a result of its morphemic functions, /s/ occurs very frequently in ordinary conversation. In addition, the detective pronounced certain instances of /r/ as the lateral /l/, in the infinitival form of verbs, another characteristic feature of Caribbean Spanish. Mexican Spanish as spoken nearly everywhere except in certain coastal areas does not exhibit these variable phonological features. For a Mexican immigrant not from the coast, who has had little contact with any of the Caribbean Spanish varieties, hearing it suddenly in the middle of the night upon waking up was likely to have been an additional barrier to comprehension.

Further Problems

Beyond the issues of the comprehensibility of the Spanish translation on the card and the detective's rendition of that translation are the remaining totality of circumstances. The suspect had been living in the United States for only five years in an almost entirely Spanish-speaking social network (he lived with Mexican relatives—all immigrants such as himself—in a city having a large Spanish-speaking population; all of his friends were Spanish-speaking; his place of work at the time of arrest was a Mexican bar; and his previous employment consisted of blue-collar work involving manual labor, where many of his coworkers were Spanish-speaking). Furthermore, this was the first time that he had ever been Mirandized. Coming from Mexico, which has nothing comparable to the Miranda rights, he most likely would have been unfamiliar with them at the interrogation. Beyond that, he was given the warnings orally, rather than in writing, and so he did not have the opportunity to process them at his own pace (e.g., to reread phrases that were difficult for him to grasp on the first reading).

Also relevant is an issue that would be expected to have an impact on any suspect, regardless of linguistic or cultural background: the interrogation took place, at 4:30 a.m., and the suspect had fallen asleep by the time the detective returned to the interrogation room to begin the questioning. On awakening, he was groggy when the interrogation began, and fell back to sleep immediately after the detective left the room.

From the video recording alone it is impossible to determine precisely the extent to which the detainee had problems understanding the Miranda warnings. However, there is evidence in the video that his comprehension must have been limited, varying from one warning to another, depending upon the degree to which the Spanish renditions were problematically rendered. He responded to most of the detective's comprehension checks with the paralinguistic affirmation token "Uh-huh." One of these "Uh-huh" tokens was used unequivocally to answer in the affirmative to an offer of something to drink and to the question as to whether he was thirsty (turn 34). Yet, two other of his utterances of "Uh-huh" are clearly back channel responses and not affirmative responses: turn 16, which is a response to the preface to a statement, not even to a statement of a right; and turn 20, in answer to a statement of the right that is not followed by a question regarding his understanding of it. Furthermore, he twice responded inappropriately with "okay" to the question "Did you understand?" (turns 28 and 30), a sign of gratuitous concurrence, and in turn 30, oddly enough, his "okay" in response to the detective's comprehension check followed the most mangled of the detective's readings of the rights (turn 29), suggesting another instance of gratuitous concurrence. Only twice did he answer with the truly affirmative response "Yes" (*Sí*) (in turn 8, after being asked if he was sleepy, and turn 26, a comprehension check). With respect to the detainee's remaining utterances, it is impossible to know which of them represent true instances of affirmation and which ones are merely tokens of gratuitous concurrence. However, the factors—both linguistic and extralinguistic—reviewed above suggest that gratuitous concurrence is likely to be happening in this interview, especially since the suspect was trying to be pleasant in his interaction with the detective (smiling a great deal, responding in kind to the detective's joking—in short, trying to be *simpático*, a cultural trait valued very highly among Mexicans and Mexican-Americans).

Conclusions

Consent to questioning by the police relies on understanding the meaning of the Miranda rights. The fact that there is no standardized wording of the Miranda warnings in the United States, a country whose judicial structure is highly decentralized and localized, guarantees that there can be no standardized translation of them. In short, there is a great deal of variation among the numerous translations of the warnings, and many serious defects in these translations, as Rogers et al. (2009) have shown. Furthermore, if the translation is rendered orally by a police officer, depending on whether that police officer is a native speaker of Spanish or simply a fluent non-native speaker, the suspect's comprehension of the warnings will vary. If the dialect of Spanish spoken by the fluent Spanish-speaking officer diverges substantially from that of the suspect (e.g., Caribbean varieties of Spanish versus Mexican or highland Andean Spanish), and the suspect has had little or no contact with the variety spoken by the police detective, there will be ample room for poor comprehension, in the realms of both phonetics and lexicon, particularly in informal registers. A suspect who is a relatively recent immigrant to the United States and whose social network consists largely of people from his or her country of origin is unlikely to understand the Miranda rights if it is the first time he or she is hearing them and if such rights do not exist in his or her country of origin.

To conclude, any consideration of whether suspects have voluntarily consented to answering the questions of police interrogators entails issues connected to the understanding of the Miranda rights. These issues include the totality of circumstances, which, for suspects who have limited proficiency in English and who are in police custody, must include linguistic factors as well as cultural factors. This chapter has shown that simply providing the rights in the suspect's first language, even if this is done by a native speaker of this language, does not necessarily guarantee comprehension of the rights.

Notes

1. One important difference between the Miranda warnings and the British caution is that as of 1994, as a result of the enactment of section 34 of the Criminal Justice and Public Order Act (CJPOA), the caution was modified in such as way as to allow the courts to draw inferences from a detainee's failure or refusal to answer police questions (Rock 2007: 139). As Rock demonstrates, however, since the passage of that act, "A body of case law and appellate opinion in Britain and Europe has restricted *s*34" (Rock 2007: 139).

2. Although one part of this study was the application of a statistical readability tool, it is not dealt with in this chapter because the mathematical formula in the particular test used (Huerta Reading Ease) has been found to be erroneous (Law 2011).

3. Liberman (1985) points out an important reason for this pragmatic pattern being particularly prevalent in Australian Aboriginal interactions with non-Aboriginal people—not only in relation to fear or lack of understanding—namely, "the widespread cultural norm that harmony and agreement should be preserved at an immediate level, and differences can be worked out in due time" (Eades 2010: 91).

4. To protect the identity of the persons whose speech is analyzed, throughout this chapter all personal names, place names, and dates have been either changed or left unspecified.

5. The detective coined a verb, *presurir*, which appears to be based on the English verb *to pressure*. She probably intended to utter the Spanish equivalent of "persuade you" (*persuadirle*), but either did not know the Spanish word or was simply in the habit of using Spanish/English contact forms.

6. Ironically, if she had read the warning directly from the card, she would have uttered the word *prevenirle* ("prevent you"), producing the clause, "I am required to prevent you before you make any statement," which makes no sense.

Cases Cited

Fare v. Michael C., 442 US 707, 725 (1979).
Moran v. Burbine, 475 US 412, 421 (1986).
US v. Fung and Chen, 780 F. Supp. 115 (E.D. N.Y. 1992).
US v. Zapata, 997 F.2d 751 (1993).

References

Arteaga Botello, Nelson and Adrián López Rivera. 1998. *Policía y corrupción: El caso de un municipio en México*. Mexico City: Plaza y Valdés.

Azaola, Elena. 2006. *Imagen y autoimagen de la policía de la Ciudad de México.* Mexico City: Ediciones Coyoacán.

Benson, Robert W. 1985. The end of legalese: The game is over. *N. Y. U. Review of Law and Social Change* 519: 547–550.

Berk-Seligson, Susan. 2002. *The Bilingual Courtroom: Court Interpreters in the Judicial Process*. Chicago: University of Chicago Press.

Berk-Seligson, Susan. 2009. *Coerced Confessions: The Discourse of Bilingual Police Interrogations*. Berlin and New York: Mouton de Gruyter.

Campbell, Leo and V. Melissa Holland. 1982. Understanding the language of public documents because readability formulas don't. In Robert DiPietro (ed.) *Linguistics and the Professions: Proceedings of the Second Annual Delaware Symposium on Language Studies*. Norwood: Ablex. 157–172.

Charrow, Robert and Veda Charrow. 1979. Making legal language understandable: A psycholinguistic study of jury instructions. *Columbia Law Review* 79(7): 1306–1374.

Cotterill, Janet. 2000. Reading the rights: A cautionary tale of comprehension and comprehensibility. *Forensic Linguistics* 7(1): 4–25.

Eades, Diana. 1994. A case of communicative clash: Aboriginal English. In John Gibbons (ed.) *Language and the Law*. London and New York: Longman. 234–264.

Eades, Diana. 2008. *Courtroom Talk and Neocolonial Control*. Berlin and New York: Mouton de Gruyter.

Eades, Diana. 2010. *Sociolinguistics and the Legal Process*. Bristol, UK: Multilingual Matters.

Greenfield, Daniel, Edward Dougherty, Ryno Jackson, John Podboy and Marc Zimmerman. 2001. Retrospective evaluation of Miranda reading levels and waiver competency. *American Journal of Forensic Psychology* 19: 75–86.

Helms, Jeffrey. 2003. Analysis of Miranda reading levels across jurisdictions: Implications for evaluating waiver competency. *Journal of Forensic Psychology Practice* 3(1): 25–37.

Inbau, Fred, John Reid and Joseph Buckley. 1986. *Criminal Interrogation Confessions* (3rd ed.). Baltimore: Williams and Wilkins.

Klare, George. 1974–1975. Assessing readability. *Reading Research Quarterly* 10: 62–102.

Law, Gwillim. 2011. Error in the Fernandez Readability Formula. May 27, 2011. Http://linguistlist.org.

Liberman, Kenneth. 1981. Understanding Aborigines in Australian courts of law. *Human Organization* 40: 247–255.

Liberman, Kenneth. 1985. *Understanding Interaction in Central Australia: An Ethnomethodological Study of Australian Aboriginal People.* Boston: Routledge Kegan & Paul.

Leo, Richard. 2008. *Police Interrogation and American Justice.* Cambridge, Massachusetts: Harvard University Press.

Mildren, Dean. 1999. Redressing the imbalance: Aboriginal people in the criminal justice system. *Forensic Linguistics* 6(1): 137–160.

Organization for Economic Co-operation and Development. 2012. Program for International Student Assessment (PISA). Retrieved May 24, 2014, from http://en.wikipedia.org/wiki/Programme_for_International_Student_Assessment#2012.

Ramirez, Linda Friedman. 2007. *Cultural Issues in Criminal Defense* (2nd ed.). Huntington, New York: Juris Publishing, Inc.

Ramirez, Linda Friedman, Leslie Nori Kay and Katherine Weber. 1994–1995. When language is a barrier to justice: The non-English speaking suspect's waiver rights. *Criminal Justice* 50: 2–6.

Renteln, Alison. 2004. *The Cultural Defense*. Oxford and New York: Oxford University Press.

Rock, Frances. 2007. *Communicating Rights: The Language of Arrest and Detention.* Basingstoke, U.K. and New York: Palgrave Macmillan.

Rogers, Richard, Amor Correa, Lisa Hazelwood, Daniel Shuman, Raquel Hoersting, and Hayley Blackwood. 2009. Spanish translations of Miranda warnings and the totality of the circumstances. *Law and Human Behavior* 33: 61–69.

Rogers, Richard, Kimberly Harrison, Daniel Shuman, Kenneth Sewell and Lisa Hazelwood. 2007. An analysis of Miranda warnings and waivers: Comprehension and coverage. *Law and Human Behavior* 31: 177–192.

Shepherd, Eric, Anna Mortimer and Reza Mobasheri. 1995. The police caution: Comprehension and perceptions in the general population. *Expert Evidence* 4(2): 60–67.

Shuy, Roger. 1998. *The Language of Confession, Interrogation, and Deception.* London and New Delhi: Sage.

Solan, Lawrence and Peter Tiersma. 2005. *Speaking of Crime.* Chicago and London: University of Chicago Press.

Stygall, Gail. 2002. Textual barriers to United States immigration. In Janet Cotterill (ed.) *Language in the Legal Process*. Basingstoke, U.K.: Palgrave Macmillan. 35–53.

Tello, Nelia. 2012. Police reforms: The voice of police and residents in Mexico City. *Journal of Policing and Society* 22(1): 14–27.

Tiersma, Peter. 1999. *Legal Language.* Chicago: University of Chicago Press.

Walsh, Michael. 1994. Interactional styles in the courtroom: An example from northern Australia. In John Gibbons (ed.) *Language and the Law*. London: Longman. 217–233.

Weiner, Tim. 2002, June 17. Mexico begins to wade through morass of police corruption. *New York Times*.

12

Negotiating the Right to Remain Silent in Inquisitorial Trials

Fleur van der Houwen and Guusje Jol

Introduction

Cautions are formulas that inform suspects and witnesses of their rights during interviews with legal officials. Various studies of police cautions (e.g., Solan and Tiersma 2005; Ainsworth 2008; Carter 2010) have highlighted their importance, given that the police statements that result from a suspect's interrogation are at the very basis of subsequent criminal procedures. The statements serve as pieces of evidence as they "travel the legal trajectory" (see Blommaert 2005: 76; Heffer, Rock and Conley 2013; D'hondt and van der Houwen 2014, for the notion of text trajectories). What suspects say at this stage indeed can, and often will, be used against them, overriding later statements a suspect might give in court when examined by the judge, as we will see. While police cautions have received a lot of scholarly attention, similar cautions given in court have received little attention. Cautions are usually not used in court proceedings in common law jurisdictions, but they are a part of the court proceedings in the Dutch inquisitorial legal system.

The Dutch criminal court is inquisitorial in nature, in the sense that the judge has an active role and examines the suspect in court. But before a judge can examine the suspect, the latter must be given a caution. The duty to give the caution in the Netherlands is legislated in section 29:2 of the code of criminal procedure (Wetboek van Strafvordering, hereafter referred to as WvSv), which stipulates that suspects are advised prior to questioning that they are not required to answer questions: *Voor het verhoor wordt de verdachte medegedeeld dat hij niet verplicht is tot antwoorden* ("Before the interrogation, the defendant is informed that he is not obliged to answer").[1,2]

This brings us to two further clarifying remarks. First, an important difference between the justice system in the Netherlands and many common law systems is that the right to a lawyer is not an integral part of the Dutch caution. Although suspects who have been arrested must be advised that they have the right to consult a lawyer (HR June 30, 2009, NbSr 2009, 249; interpreting ECHR November 27, 2008, no. 36391/02, *Salduz v. Turkey* and ECHR December 11, 2008, no. 4268/04, *Panovits v. Cyprus*), this is not a standard procedure in court or with suspects who are not officially arrested.[3] In this chapter, when we refer to the caution, we mean the advice of government officials (police or prosecution or judge) to suspects that they have the right to remain silent. Another terminological issue that we would like to clarify here is the use of the word "suspect." In the Netherlands the term *verdachte* ("suspect") is used throughout the criminal procedure, including the court proceedings. Although a person is not referred to as "suspect" in Anglo-American systems once they are in court (where they are "the defendant" or "the accused"), we use "suspect" to reflect the Dutch inquisitorial system we are describing here.

The suspect's right not to answer questions is an interactionally difficult task to negotiate for both judges and suspects. Suspects obviously do not want to incriminate themselves but also will want to be perceived as cooperative because judges may take into account their *proceshouding*, or "procedural attitude," which relates to the position a suspect takes within the trial, for example, demonstrating regret, being (un)cooperative, being open (e.g., about motives for the crime), remaining silent, and so on. This can be important for judges when deciding on a suspect's sentence (HR March 3, 1964, NJ 1964, 400; HR November 12, 1974, NJ 1975, 41). For example, a procedural attitude in which the suspect claims her or his right to silence can be viewed negatively by a judge (Spronken 2009: 88). Moreover, claiming one's right not to answer is a dispreferred response, interactionally, because it (a) does not provide an answer that has content, and (b) does not "count" as an answer and therefore does not fit the (technical) question-answer format. That is, invoking "one's right" does not fulfill the preference for moving the interaction along (or progressivity, see Stivers and Robinson 2006). Another complexity is that the examination in court is not the first questioning of suspects. Preceding the court hearing suspects have been interrogated by the police when they presumably were also given a caution. This means that their statements to the police, which should be as much as possible in "their own words" (section 29:3 WvSv), but which are written down by the police,[4] are part of the evidence, and may be quoted from by the judge as well as the prosecutor or lawyer (see van der Houwen 2013; van der Houwen and Sneijder 2014).

In this study we investigate the discursive mechanisms surrounding cautions in a setting where, as explained above, this has been given relatively little attention, namely courtroom hearings. We illustrate how the tensions surrounding cautions play out interactionally for both suspects and judges. For suspects, there is a tension between not being required to answer questions and being cooperative, and for judges, between giving the caution and needing to examine the evidence in order to make a judgment. (See also Komter 1998: 6–10, for a brief discussion of the dilemmas involved for both judges and suspects.) Furthermore we show how statements prepared at earlier stages in the legal process, and for which the suspect was also cautioned, can play a central role in court, especially in those interactional contexts where suspects use their right not to answer questions (or not to answer them fully or as projected by the question).

Data and Method

The data for this study come from two different corpora of Dutch criminal trials. The larger corpus of audio files of 31 cases was collected in the 1990s (see Komter 1998 for a more elaborate description) and a smaller corpus consisting of both audio and video recordings of five criminal trials was collected in 2008. Dutch criminal trials are inquisitorial in nature and the judge(s) take an active part in examining the evidence. Trials are also adversarial in nature in the sense that the prosecutor and defense lawyer each present a particular point of view, namely, that of the state and the suspect(s), respectively.

Dutch criminal trials are organized as follows. The court consists of one judge in lesser cases, and three judges in more serious cases. The court is assisted by a clerk. The system does not include a jury, nor are there lay judges. Once all court participants have entered the courtroom, the (chairing) judge verifies the name, place and date of birth, and current address of the suspect. The (chairing) judge gives the caution "You have to pay close attention but you are not required to answer questions" (or a variant thereof) and then gives the floor to the prosecutor to read out the indictment, stating the offenses of which the suspect is accused. Then follows the longest part of the trial, in which the court examines the evidence by questioning the suspect and referring to and reading from the case file. Both the prosecutor and the lawyer have a chance to question the suspect and any witnesses who have come to the court. The questioning tends to be inquisitorial in nature and does not generally resemble the direct and cross-examinations that are typical of adversarial systems. After the examination, the prosecutor and then the defense lawyer can read their statements. Both parties also have the opportunity to react to each other's statements. The suspect then has the last word before the trial is closed, after which the judge gives a judgment (either immediately in cases chaired by only one judge or after two weeks when there is a panel of three judges).

In this chapter, we draw our examples from both the beginning of the trial, when the judges give the caution, as well as from the part of the trial when the judge examines the evidence. It is in the latter part of the trial that we see how the caution is interactionally negotiated during the questioning phase.

Transcripts have been anonymized and English translations are given in italics below the Dutch original; transcription conventions are added in the appendix. The method we used for analyzing the data is Conversation Analysis (e.g., Heritage and Clayman 2010).

Findings

In the following analyses of extracts from our corpus, we first show (in the section that follows) the different forms that cautions can take and how they relate to the suspects' right not to incriminate themselves (this caution usually occurs at the beginning of a hearing). In other words, we are interested in how legislation as written down in the WvSv is invoked in the courtroom. In the section titled "The Right to Remain Silent during the Examination of the Evidence" we demonstrate how the various tensions surrounding the suspect's right not to answer questions are negotiated during the examination of the evidence by the judge. Finally, under the section "The Right to Silence and the Role of the Case File," we show how, when suspects claim their right to silence, the judge can invoke the case file as a way of answering a question that the suspect does not answer.

CAUTIONS IN COURT: THE INITIAL FORMULATION OF THE RIGHT TO REMAIN SILENT

Before they start their examination, criminal trial judges are required to follow certain steps (section 273 WvSv). As mentioned in the section "Data and Method," the chairing judge must first ask suspects their full name, place of birth, date of birth, address where the suspect is registered, and address where the suspect currently resides (which might be a prison, for instance). This verification is followed by a caution, informing suspects that they have to pay attention and that they are not required to answer questions. An example is given in Extract 1; J = Judge, S = Suspect.

Extract 1. Case 13: You are not required to answer questions (see appendix for transcription conventions)

1 J: (u bent) Piet van Doorn?
(you are) Piet van Doorn

2 S: jawel meneer.=
yes indeed sir=

3 J: =30 december 1953 in Geldermalsen geboren,
=born December 30 1953 in Geldermalsen

4 (weet) u zich thans in het huis van van bewaring in Utrecht?
you (find) yourself currently at the detention center in Utrecht
5 meneer Van Doorn u moet goed opletten wat hier voorvalt,
Mr. Van Doorn you have to pay careful attention to what goes on here,
6 → u bent niet verplicht om vragen te beantwoorden.
you are not required to answer questions
7 gaat u maar zitten, (2)
you can sit down (2)
8 luistert u naar de heer officier.
please listen to sir prosecutor

The caution itself can be short and formulated as in section 29:2 of the WvSv, shown in Extract 1, line 6. It does not have a fixed formulation and is not read from a prepared script; thus, there can be variation in the way it is expressed. A common formulation in our corpus is shown in Extract 2.

Extract 2. Case 12: . . . if you do not want to
1 J: meneer Rutten u moet goed opletten wat hier voorvalt,
Mr. Rutten you have to pay careful attention to what goes on here
2 → maar u bent niet verplicht om vragen te beantwoorden als u dat niet wil.
but you are not required not answer questions if you do not want to.

Here, the judge gives the standard caution but adds “if you do not want to.” It is an addition that appears to make the caution more comprehensible because it emphasizes that the suspect has a choice whether or not to answer questions; that is, the option that the suspect would not want to answer is made explicit. Interactionally, the addition of “if you do not want to” may make it easier for the suspect indeed not to answer questions. At the same time, however, the choice that the suspect has is made dependent on what the suspect “wants” and the fact that it is a *right* of the suspect is de-emphasized. So, this addition reframes the suspect’s right to silence as a choice; however, what is not said is that the choice to remain silent can imply that the suspect is an “unwilling,” and hence uncooperative, suspect, the kind of identity that may not be favorably viewed in court.

Other formulations (not analyzed in this chapter) emphasize the fact that the suspect is present in a criminal trial and that as a suspect has the right to not answer questions as well as formulations that highlight that suspects, while not required, are allowed to answer questions (Extracts 3 and 4).

Extract 3. Case 1A (new): You may but you do not need to

1 J: → uh meneer Roenier u bent hier als verdachte
uh Mr. Roenier you are here as a suspect
2 → en dat betekent dat u niet hoeft te antwoorden op vragen
and that means that you do not need to answer questions
3 S: (dat heb ik begrepen)=
(I have understood that) =
4 J: → =het mag wel maar het hoeft dus niet
you may but you do not need to

Extract 4. Case 3A: You may of course answer if you want to

1 J: heren voor jullie beiden geldt dat je op vragen geen antwoord hoeft te geven
gentlemen for both of you it holds that you do not need to answer questions
2 → we zijn tenslotte voor een strafzaak hier
after all we are here for a criminal trial
3 → je mag natuurlijk wel antwoord geven als je wil
you may of course answer if you want to

One last example comes from a case in which the suspect, who made a confession, is also interrogated as a witness, in relation to another suspect (Aurelia). The judge explains the difference between being a suspect and a witness for the court.

Extract 5. Case 1A: . . .but about Aurelia the truth

1 J: over u <u>zelf</u>,
about yourself,
2 u hebt over u zelf een bekennende verklaring afgelegd dus zo moeilijk is dat niet,
you made a confession statement about yourself so it isn't that hard,
3 maar als het over u g- <u>u</u> gaat,
but if it is about you,
4 u bent verdachte,
you are a suspect,
5 → 'n verdachte mag zwijgen,
a suspect is allowed to remain silent,
6 → 'n verdachte mag <u>zelfs</u> liegen,
a suspect may even lie,

7 → hoewel dat soms niet verstandig is,
even though that is not wise sometimes,
8 → maar u mag dus over u zelf zeggen wat u wil,
but you may thus say about yourself what you want,
9 → daar hoeft u ook niks te zeggen,
there you do not need to say anything,
10 → maar over Aurelia de waarheid.
but about Aurelia the truth.
11 is dat allemaal duidelijk?
is that all clear?
12 ja? want dat kan best lastig zijn.
yes? because that can be quite tricky.

In contrast to common law jurisdictions, suspects are allowed to lie (Melai 1980: 537), whereas witnesses who lie could be accused of perjury. This is, however, the only example in our corpus in which a judge advises a suspect that he or she is allowed to lie. And, as we can see, the judge immediately mitigates this utterance (line 7) by adding that it is not wise to do so sometimes. Presumably the judge makes the legality of lying by suspects explicit in this context because the suspect is also a witness in the trial of another suspect, a role in which lying *would* have legal consequences.

In these first examples, we have seen that cautions in court can take different forms. The WvSv does not prescribe a particular form for cautions so that judges can express them in different ways during the court procedures (thus emphasizing different aspects), possibly depending on the suspect (see for instance van der Houwen and Jol, under review, for the cautioning of juvenile suspects that takes a more elaborate form). Similarly, suspects who claim their right to silence (at the police station or in court) also do not need to do so according to a specific linguistic formulation, in contrast to what Ainsworth (2008) has shown for suspects in police interrogations in the United States. Another difference is that government officials do not have to stop the questioning once a suspect invokes her or his right to silence. Consequently, suspects who do not want to answer questions will have to say so for every question. As a result, they might answer some questions but then claim their right to silence for other questions. In the next paragraph we explore in more detail how judges and suspects handle this turn-by-turn negotiation.

THE RIGHT TO REMAIN SILENT DURING THE EXAMINATION OF THE EVIDENCE

Section 271:1 of the WvSv states that the chairing judge must ensure that no questions are asked which could result in statements that could be argued to have been given involuntarily. Furthermore, section 271:2 states that neither the chair nor any of the other judges should show any belief regarding the guilt or innocence of the accused. However, judges need to go over the evidence and verify the indictment because they have to base their judgment only on that which has been put to the court. In addition to the case file, the suspect is the most important source of information, and people interviewed by police as witnesses to the crime are generally not interviewed in court. When examining the evidence judges will verify if what is in the indictment is correct and complete (Kronenberg and de Wilde 2005). Judges, hence, face a dilemma (Komter 1998: 6–11) in that they must question suspects to hear their version of events, but need to do so while also acknowledging suspects' right to not answer questions and to not incriminate themselves.

Komter also discusses how suspects face a dilemma (1998: 10), namely, the right not to incriminate themselves and the fact that not answering questions can be seen as incriminating themselves nonetheless. We would want to add to this dilemma that there is also something else at stake: namely, that suspects presumably also want to show a cooperative attitude. As mentioned earlier, a suspect's noncooperative procedural attitude may influence the eventual sentence; that is, judges are allowed to consider suspects' procedural attitude and whether they take responsibility for the acts that, according to other evidence, they have committed (Schuyt 2009: 76–77). Although this is in accordance with the Dutch legal doctrine, from an interactional point of view, the negative inferences drawn from a noncooperative procedural attitude are at odds with suspects' right to silence as stated in section 29:1 of the WvSv. In the examples that follow we show how some of these tensions are negotiated during the examination phase.

Extract 6 comes from a case in which the suspect is accused of rape and extortion. The judge's turns in lines 13 to 21 are also discussed in Komter (1998: 6–7), where the suspect's intervening turns have been removed. We discuss these turns in their larger and more detailed interactional context. The suspect has claimed his right to silence up to this point. The extract starts right after the prosecutor has read the indictment, before which the judge had read the suspect his right to silence.

Extract 6. Case 10-2: The court would like it (Mr. Leeds = S/suspect; Ms. Mathijs = victim)

1 J: meneer Leeds,
Mr. Leeds,

2 → u <u>weet</u> dat u niet op vragen hoeft te antwoorden want dat heeft u voor die tijd ook niet gedaan,
you know that you do not need to answer questions because you have also not done that before that time,

((explanation: the judge infers from several occasions on which the suspect has used his right not to answer questions, that he is familiar with this right; 'before that time' is also unclear in Dutch, presumably it means 'up till now'))

3 → maar bent u van plan om vandaag wel een verklaring af te leggen of niet.

but are you planning today to actually give a statement or not,

4 S: wel, om het eerlijk te zeggen is het (wel de) zaak is gewoon het is nul komma nul.

well, to be honest it is a case it is just zero point zero.

((explanation: the utterance is ungrammatical because the suspect re-starts this utterance several times. He basically asserts that the prosecution has no case))

5 (zeer) komma nul komma nul.

(very) comma nil comma nil.

6 want kijk kijk naar Mathijs.

because look look at Mathijs. ((victim))

7 zij ziet er prima uit hè [( )

she looks great, right [(. . .)

8 J: → [(als u praat) tegen ons dan zullen wij wel met mevrouw Mathijs spreken.

(if you talk) to us then we will talk with Ms. Mathijs.

9 [ja.

yes.

10 S: [ja ik bedoel het is gewoon een antwoord toch?

yes I mean it is just an answer right?

11 ja dus ik zie gewoon al dat soort dinges,

yes so I just see all those sort of things,

12 zijn alleen maar (.) onzin.

are only just (.) nonsense.

13 J: → jawel [maar om nou te kijken wat er gebeurd is,

yes [but in order to look at what happened,

14 S: [allemaal onzin

[all nonsense

15 J: → vindt de rechtbank het wel prettig,

the court would like it,

16 → maar nogmaals u hoeft niet te antwoorden,
but again you do not need to answer,
17 als u ook vertelt wat uw lezing van het verhaal is,
if you also tell what your version of the story is,
18 (.) tot dan toe heeft u eigenlijk eh nog niks gezegd,
till then you haven't really eh said anything yet,
19 dus eh (.) [de vraag is gaat u wat
so eh (.) [the question is are you going to
20 S: [(ja maar)
[(yes but)
21 J: verklaren of gaat u niks verklaren.
going to give a statement or are you not going to give a statement.

The judge makes various attempts to get answers from the suspect while simultaneously reading the suspect his rights. The first attempt (line 2) is couched in a reiteration of the suspect's rights, stating it as knowledge the suspect has because he has claimed his right before. The judge's first attempt to get an answer is prefaced by *maar* ("but," line 3), which appears to be a "segmentation signal" (Redeker 1994), segmenting the previous interrogations and conclusion (that the suspect must know his rights) from what the suspect will do now. The but-prefaced utterance is followed by an emphatic Dutch *wel* (the opposite of *niet*, English "not"). The contrastive *wel*, which we translated with English "actually," creates an opportunity for the suspect to change course and to give a statement in court.

The next part of the extract starting with line 13 is also discussed in Komter (1998: 6–7), who points out the judge's "double message," that is, that the court would like to hear the suspect's answers at the same time that it emphasizes the suspect's right to silence. We discuss this "double message" in more detail and in the context of the preceding interaction, showing how this is a dilemma that the judge struggles with at a turn-by-turn level. Furthermore, we show exactly how the judge makes it difficult for the suspect not to answer the court's questions.

After the judge's first attempt, the suspect starts talking about things not relevant to the question (in a fairly confusing way) and furthermore breaks the conversational rules of the court, as is apparent from the correction that the suspect should address the court and not Ms. Mathijs (the victim) directly (line 8). The suspect continues his view that it is all nonsense, a view the judge acknowledges with *jawel* (line 13) (which we translated as "yes" but might be closer to "well yes"), followed by the contrastive conjunction "but" to reintroduce the previously unanswered question about whether the suspect will give a statement. In reintroducing this unanswered question, the judge ignores the suspect's claim that it is all nonsense (line 14). The judge's use of contrastive *maar* ("but") in line 13 is consistent with the use of *maar* by police officers interviewing children in Jol and van der Houwen's (2014) analysis, which finds that *maar*-prefaced questions in that context can disqualify a previously given answer, and pursue a renewed response. This time the question is couched in terms of what "the court would like" (lines 15 and 17), highlighting the court's function (i.e., to judge; even if formulated casually; line 13). The judge thus gives a motivation for wanting a statement from the suspect and refers to the institution in which the examination of evidence takes place. The judge self-interrupts, however, giving another reference to the suspect's right to silence (line 16), demonstrating that he does not want to pressure the suspect and that the institutional orientation in the previous utterance (what the court would like, line 15) might be interpreted as such. However, the judge's following talk emphasizes the benefit of giving a statement, as a chance to give "your version," while ignoring the fact that such a statement can also be used against the suspect. The judge, furthermore, constructs the suspect's claim to silence as a shortcoming; the court "would like it" if the suspect gives his version (presented as if the suspect would do no more than please the court), but so far he "really" did not say anything (line 18), followed again by the question as to whether or not the suspect will give a statement (lines 19, 21).

To summarize, in Extract 6, the court's invitation to the suspect to tell his story (lines 15 to 17) and the reference to the caution (both in line 2 and in line 16) not only show a double message (Komter 1998) but also show the various ways in which the judge tries to convince the suspect to talk. The reference to the right not to answer cancels out any pressure that the suspect might feel to answer questions. Yet referring to this right also underlines the pressure that is put on the suspect given that the judge frames "talking" as a desirable and "innocent" activity. Thus, referring to the caution *enables* the judge to ask a question that may be considered coercive (in line 3), while also making clear that the suspect's rights have been observed.

The next extract comes from a case in which the suspect was involved in a hotel robbery. The suspect admits he took part in the robbery but has been refusing to answer questions regarding his agency or motive (see also the last example in this chapter) and says he was doing as he was told. The suspect's answers are generally brief: he answers mostly "correct" when the judge reads out his earlier statements, and "incorrect" when the judge asks verifying questions when reading statements of others involved in the robbery. Preceding Extract 7 the chairing judge has examined the suspect and now asks if the other judges have questions.

Extract 7. Case 16: A bit contradictory (J3 = third judge)

1 J3: ja ik heb eigenlijk twee vragen.
yes I actually have two questions.
2 vindt u uzelf iemand die eh (2) zich la- makkelijk dingen laat zeggen door een ander. (5)
do you think of yourself as someone who eh (2) easily does as he is told by others. (5)
3 u komt hier over als iemand die precies weet wanneer die (mee wil doen).
you come across here as someone who knows exactly when he (wants to join in)
4 → u zegt nee daar zeg ik niets over,
you say no I am not saying anything about that,
5 → andere dingen geeft u wel een antwoord,
other things you do answer,
6 → (3) ik vind dat een beetje beetje (.) tegenstrijdig eigenlijk. (6)
(3) I find that a bit bit (.) contradictory actually. (6)
7 vindt u dat ook? (7)
do you think so too? (7)
8 S: ((zacht:)) nou kan wel.
((soft)) well could be.
9 J3: wat zegt u?
what do you say?
10 S: dat kan wel. (3)
that could be (3)

The third judge on the panel of three introduces his agenda, stating he has two questions. The first question (line 2) poses a dilemma for the suspect: if he answers affirmatively he denies his own autonomy; if he answers negatively, he rules out the possibility of blaming his accomplices for his own misbehavior and thus limits the possibilities for defending himself against the charge. The suspect withholds an answer, remaining silent for five seconds. By not answering the question the suspect avoids commitment to either of the two harmful implications.

The judge then confronts the suspect with the assertion that he comes across in court as someone who knows "exactly when he wants to join in" (referring to the robbery) but who then also claims his right to silence when asked about this (line 4), while at the same time answering other questions (line 5). The judge concludes that this (nonanswering versus answering) is contradictory (line 6), a conclusion that (although not necessarily logical) challenges the suspect's choices in answering and not answering questions and which implies that if the suspect might be trying to defer responsibility to his accomplice, the judge does not believe him. Again, the suspect does not fill in the slot that is created by the judge's question, still avoiding the dilemma and a pause of six seconds follows. The judge does not stop, however, and follows up with a question that hence requires an answer now (line 7). The question is formulated with a preference for agreement, namely, an agreement with the judge's assessment that it is contradictory that the suspect does not answer some questions and does answer other questions. If the suspect does not agree, he goes against the preference organization. If he agrees with the judge, he confirms that his answers to some questions and his silence after other questions are indeed contradictory. Because "being consistent" conveys reliability in legal context (cf. Shuy 1993), appearing inconsistent would complicate his own position. The suspect indeed treats the question as a dilemma he tries to avoid by delaying his answer by seven seconds, the longest pause so far. And the pause is not broken by the judge. The suspect then formulates a soft and evasive "well could be." The judge initiates a repair (line 9). Although this could be interpreted as an attempt to get a different (less evasive) answer, the suspect treats it as a hearing problem by repeating his answer, now louder and also formulated a bit more firmly, "that could be" (see Svennevig 2008). The example shows, then, that when the suspect claims his right not to answer a question (at the police station as well as in court) this is not necessarily accepted and it is something the suspect can be made to account for (see also the judge's question in line 7).

In Extract 8, the judge makes explicit that the suspect is being uncooperative. The extract comes from a case where the suspect, a minor, is accused of stealing an iPod, together with two other minors. Earlier in the trial the suspect gave an answer to the chairing judge's question but then later gave a slightly different answer when the same question was further pursued by one of the other judges. In the exchange just before this extract, the judge and suspect negotiate the likely truthfulness of the suspect's claim that he did not hear his co-suspect utter a threat to the victim of the robbery.

Extract 8 (1). I do not want to force you into something, but...

1 J: of moeten mijn collega's dan ook weer aan <u>jou</u> vragen stellen;
or do my colleagues then also have to ask <u>you</u> questions again;

2 en dan –
and then -

3 (.)

4 dat er dan toch weer een iets ander antwoord komt dan (.) bij mij;
so that again a slightly different answer comes out than {the one} you gave me

5 (. .)
6 S: hoezo,
how so,
7 J: nou ja;
well;
8 hoezo,
how so,
9 (. .)
10 nou ja ik bedoel;
well I mean;
11 → i-ik wil je niet ergens toe dwingen,
I-I do not want to force you into something,
12 maar (ik zie/misschien) dat je advocaat even met jou moet uh
but (I see/maybe) that your attorney should for a moment uh
13 even overleggen
for a moment discuss with you
14 over de proceshouding van jou.
your procedural attitude

This extract begins with the judge referring to an earlier part of the examination in which further questioning led to an answer that was adjusted. In referring back to this, the judge treats the answer the suspect gives as possibly not the "final" or "real" answer. The judge, hence, makes explicit that he questions the suspect's truthfulness. The suspect postpones his answer (line 5) and then asks for an explanation ("how so," line 8), sidestepping the damaging nature of the question.

The judge constructs his answer as a dispreferred turn using "well" (lines 7 and 10), hedging and delay (lines 8, 9, and 11), and reformulation ("I mean," line 10). He states he does not want to *force* the suspect (line 11), which makes relevant the rule that statements must be given voluntarily (section 271:1 WvSv). Subsequently the judge suggests that maybe the lawyer should talk to her client about his procedural attitude. This suggestion runs counter to the rule that aims at avoiding undue pressure, not only because of "but" (line 12), but also because of the cautious way in which he formulates the suggestion. Whereas the reference to section 271 is formulated as a (negative) extreme case (force), the judge hedges his directions with "maybe" and assigns the task of "discussing" to the lawyer as agent, taking responsibility away from the suspect. By referring to the suspect's "procedural attitude" (which is less personal than, say, "how you answer questions"), the judge implies that the suspect's answers are unexpected and suggests that the lawyer's discussion with her client about procedural attitude will result in a different approach to her client's way of answering.

Extracts 6, 7, and 8 highlighted different aspects of how judges and suspects, during the examination in court, negotiate their respective dilemmas associated with the caution. In Extract 6, we saw how the judge orients to the suspect's right and the legal rule that a suspect does not have to reply, while also pressing the suspect to satisfy the court and tell his story. In Extract 7, we saw how the judge does not accept the suspect's silence, constructs it as contradictory with other questions that the suspect does answer, and pursues an answer. The right to silence is thus transformed interactionally into an activity that should be done consistently, and that can be scrutinized critically. In Extract 8, we saw how the judge carefully addresses the suspect's procedural attitude. In both Extracts 6 and 8, the judge includes a reference to the suspect's right to not answer questions. This works in at least three ways: (a) it takes some of the pressure off the suspect, but (b) it also treats the question at hand as possibly pressing and (c) it allows the judge nevertheless to pose that question while ensuring that the suspect's rights have been observed officially. Probably this is important not only for the suspect, but also for the court; if the court has not followed all the rules, a conviction may not "hold" in appeal courts. Reminding the suspect of his rights thus can provide an opportunity for the judge to pursue answers to questions while at the same time avoiding objections, either directly or in appeal procedures. All three extracts show how a judge treats the suspect's contributions as noncooperative in relation to the examination of evidence and how, despite the right to silence, judges try to elicit answers or a particular kind of answer.

THE RIGHT TO SILENCE AND THE ROLE OF THE CASE FILE

Although judges make an effort to elicit answers from suspects, the suspect's oral statement in court is not the only source of information that judges have about the case. The case file contains—among other documents—the suspect's statements given to the police at an earlier occasion as well as statements by witnesses, victims, and professionals (e.g., medical experts or psychologists), that is, statements containing voices that might also be able to provide answers to the questions a judge has. It is important to note that it is the indictment composed by the prosecutor (and not, say, the suspect's or victim's story) that judges verify when examining the evidence. Thus, judges must manage a vast number of sources, written or spoken, that need to be reviewed. According to the immediacy principle, judges can base their judgment only on evidence that is read or summarized aloud for the court. In the next examples the case file is not just read out, but also used as an authoritative source that can provide answers to questions in the ongoing interaction.

Extract 9 comes from a case in which the suspect allegedly shot and seriously injured two men. The suspect is Turkish, and there is an interpreter (I) present.

Extract 9. Case 18: But I do ask why he did not want to say anything anymore (I = Interpreter)

1 I: hij zweert op zijn vader en moeder dat hij het niet gedaan heeft.
he swears on his father and mother that he did not do it.
2 J: ja hij heeft verklaringen afgelegd bij de politie, %tolk%
yes he made statements at the police station, %interpreter%
3 weet ie nog wat ie daar gezegd heeft, %tolk, verdachte%
does he still know what he said there, %interpreter, suspect%
4 J: nee even ja of nee hè?
no, just yes or no right?
5 eh weet ie nog wat ie gezegd heeft bij de politie,
eh does he still know what he said at the police station,
%verdachte%
%suspect%
6 I: ik weet het.
I know it.
7 J: ja en was dat de waarheid,
yes and was that the truth,
%verdachte%
%suspect%
%tolk, verdachte%
%interpreter, suspect%
8 I: ik heb de waarheid verteld.
I told the truth
9 J: → waarom heeft hij op het laatst eh niks meer (.)
why did he not {say} anything anymore in the end (.)
10 → ja dat is wel zijn zijn recht
yes that is indeed his his right
11 → maar ik vraag toch waarom ie op het laatst niks meer z- heeft willen zeggen,
but I do ask why in the end he did not want to say anything anymore,
12 bij de politie,
at the police station,

%tolk, verdachte%
%interpreter, suspect%

13 I: want ik had het eh eerlijk gezegd bij de politie. (2)
because I told it eh truthfully at the police station. (2)

14 J: ja, maar de politie had toch allerlei vragen kunnen we in de stukken lezen,
yes, but the police did have all sorts of questions we can read in the case file,

15 → en daar heeft ie op het laatst geen antwoord meer op willen geven.
and in the end he did not want to answer them anymore
%tolk, verdachte%
%interpreter, suspect%

16 I: wat ik wist heb ik antwoord op gegeven
what I knew I answered

17 en die dingen die ik niet weet (.) ik heb geen antwoord erop. (2)
and those things that I do not know I have no answer for them. (2) ((in slightly ungrammatical Dutch))

18 J: ja, nou zo staat het er niet maar goed.
yes, well that's not what it says but okay.

19 e::hm (.) ik zal eh (.) meneer een eh aantal dingen voorhouden die er in de stukken staan,
e::hm (.) I will eh put a number of things to the gentleman that are in the case file,

In lines 1 to 6 the judge and suspect jointly create common ground, intermediated by the interpreter.[5] They determine that the suspect's statements to the police are accessible to both, and in lines 7 and 8 they jointly confirm that the suspect is still committed to these statements and thus can still be held responsible for them.

Having established the status of the police statement, the judge then problematizes the statement, or rather how it came about. The judge asks the suspect for an account of why in the end he did not say any more to the police officer but then interrupts herself with "yes that is indeed his [. . .] right" (line 10), referring to the caution that is also given at the start of police interrogations. She then continues her request for an account that she embeds in a "but" and an emphatic do-support construction (translated from the Dutch *toch*) in which she mentions the suspect's right to not answer questions but also counters it. The suspect responds, via the interpreter, to the possibly damaging inference that the suspect was uncooperative (as the procedural attitude may be taken into account by the judge when deciding on a sentence) and formulates his answer (in line 13) to avert the inference "because I told it [. . .] truthfully at the police station." The judge shows dissatisfaction with this answer and counters with "yes but" (Pomerantz 1984) and invokes the case file as an authoritative source, saying that the police had more questions that the suspect did not want to answer. In doing so, the judge recasts the suspect's "I told it [. . .] truthfully at the police station" (formulated as a voluntary act of giving a statement) as a series of questions and (partly lacking) answers and as such (re)constructs the suspect's attitude as noncooperative based on the case file.

After talking to the interpreter the suspect responds again (via the interpreter) to the damaging implication that he did not want to cooperate. The suspect answers that he gave answers to the questions to which he knew the answers (and as such conveys a cooperative attitude), but to the things he did not know, he did not answer. With this last move the suspect gives a less damaging alternative to not wanting to answer: he did not have the knowledge to answer. And, in so doing, he attempts to neutralize the damaging inferences of the judge's questions, thus negotiating his dilemma.

The suspect's account is met by the judge with "well," indicating objection, followed by another referral to the case file "that's not what it says" and "but okay," which closes down the topic for the time (line 18). The reference to the case file as an authoritative source of information highlights the judge's agenda when questioning the suspect; it shows how the judge checks the suspect's account in court against what she read in the case file (and specifically those parts that the prosecutor has drawn upon in writing up the indictment) (see also van der Houwen 2013). The judge then follows with the procedural announcement that she will now put to the suspect what is in the case file.

We have seen in this extract how the reference to the caution is embedded in a series of argumentative actions by the judge and how the suspect's selective use of his right is questioned and made problematic. Our last example comes again from the case in which the suspect was involved in a hotel robbery (see Extract 7).[6]

Extract 10. Case 16: You have said at the police station . . .

1 J2: wat is er dan eh volgens u precies gebeurd,
what then exactly happened according to you,
2 voordat eh (2) voordat u daar bij het Iris hotel binnenkwam? (.)
before eh (2) before you entered the Iris hotel there
3 S: ik wist niet dat er eh een overval plaats zou vinden. (4)
I did not know that there eh would be a robbery. (4)
4 J2: waarom bent u dan naar het Iris hotel toegegaan,
why then did you go to the Iris hotel,

5 en daar naar binnen gegaan?
and enter?
(12) ((*some background noise and leafing through pages*))
6 S: → wil ik niet op antwoorden.
I don't want to answer.
7 J2: wat zegt u?
what do you say?
8 S: daar wil ik niet op antwoorden. (.)
I don't want to answer that. (.)
9 J2: → <u heeft eh bij de politie gezegd dat eh >
<you have eh said at the police station that eh>
((*5 seconds leafing through pages*))
10 ((zacht:)) even kijken waar het staat, (4)
((soft)) let me have a look where it is,

((lines 11–21 omitted in which the judge quotes directly and indirectly from the suspect's statement))

22 (.) u heeft bij de politie gezegd toen ik de auto geparkeerd had,
(.) you said at the police station when I had parked my car,
23 kreeg ik van mijn mededader te horen wat er ging gebeuren.
I heard from my accomplice what was going to happen.
24 hij vertelde mij wat hij van plan was.
he told me what he was planning to do.
25 hij vertelde mij vrij weinig.
he told me very little.
26 wat weet ik niet meer.
what I do not recall.
27 → wel kon ik aannemen,
but I could assume,
28 → dat er iets ging gebeuren,
that something was going to happen,
29 → wat niet door de beugel kon. (.)
that was not acceptable.
30 ik wist toen eigenlijk nog niet,
I did not actually know then,
31 dat er door ons een overval gepleegd ging worden. (2)
that a robbery was going to be committed by us.(2)

32 blijft u bij wat u daar bij de politie heeft gezegd? (2)
do you stick to what you told the police?(2)
33 → dus dat betekent dat (.) u wel wist,
so that means that (1) you indeed knew,
34 → dat er iets ging gebeuren wat niet door de beugel kon. (.)
that something was going to happen that was not acceptable.
35 S: klopt. (.)
correct. (.)

The judge's question in line 4, which inquires about the motive the suspect had in entering the hotel, is met with the suspect claiming his right to silence (line 6). The judge asks the suspect to repeat his answer and postpones a more substantial reaction. Although the judge's request for a repeat could be interpreted as offering the suspect an opportunity to rethink his answer (e.g., Mazeland 2008: 167–169), the suspect treats the judge's utterance as a hearing problem by repeating his answer a bit more emphatically, adding the deictic pronoun "that" (daar) and emphasizing the first part of the answer (Svennevig 2008; see also our discussion of Extract 7). The judge does not in any way acknowledge the suspect's response, but instead introduces the suspect's statement (line 9) and leafs through the documents searching for the evidence to put to the suspect (line 10). The judge quotes from the suspect's statement at some length, partly quoting directly, partly indirectly, and partly summarizing. The judge moves to direct quotation in line 22 when he arrives at the passage that will answer the question from line 4—why the suspect went into the hotel (see also van der Houwen 2012 on different ways of referring to the case file and how this is related to the foregrounding and backgrounding of information).

The suspect in court (line 3) and in the police interview (lines 30 to 31) holds the same position, namely, that he did not know that there would be a robbery. In lines 22 to 31, however, we appear to see some remnants of questions and report writing by the police (e.g., Komter 2013; see also endnote 3). The statement the suspect made and which is written down by the police should be as much as possible in the "suspect's own words" (section 29:3 WvSv; see also endnote 3). We cannot know for sure, obviously, but it would be hard to imagine that the suspect voluntarily formulated "but I could assume, that something was going to happen, that was not acceptable" (lines 27 to 29). It is a statement that clearly assigns some agency to the suspect, something that the police would want to establish. (We see an even stronger example of police wording entering the suspect's statement in line 23 where the suspect is quoted as using the word "accomplice," implying that he has committed a crime.) The importance of the suspect's agency in the event is also emphasized in court, first by the judge's question (line 32) and then by the judge's formulation (line 33 to 34; Heritage and Watson 1979) of this particular part of what he read from the suspect's statement. This formulation draws out the legal implication that the suspect went into the hotel knowing "that something was going to happen that was not acceptable" and that the suspect has a guilty conscience (cf. "legal formulations" in van der Houwen 2005, 2009; see also Edwards 2008). It also is a formulation that the suspect confirms (just as he likely did in the police interrogation). In Extract 10, then, we see again how the judge draws upon the case file as an authoritative source of information that can provide answers to questions the judge has and that are not readily provided by the suspect in court.

Extracts 9 and 10 illustrate how the judge negotiates the various sources of information, not only from the suspect in court who is being examined but also from the case file, containing the suspect's voice as mediated by the police, as well as the (also mediated) voices of various other parties, such as witnesses. With Extract 9 we emphasized how the suspect's right to silence, when claimed, is not necessarily accepted by the judge without problems; the suspect is pressured to account for his selective use of his right not to answer questions. And when this pressure does not provide a "sufficient answer" (see van der Houwen 2013; van der Houwen and Sneijder 2014), the judge resorts to the case file. With Extract 10 we illustrated specifically how a suspect's earlier statement may be used as a "surrogate answer," that is, how the suspect's prior voice (as recorded by the police) is animated to answer the question that the suspect in court is not required to answer and indeed has refused to answer.

Conclusion

In this chapter we have analyzed how cautions play a role in the Dutch courtroom, a context where cautions are not given in the common law system, and where their use in the inquisitorial system has received little scholarly attention. We have demonstrated how discursive mechanisms surrounding the caution in court work at different levels. At a more surface level, under "Cautions in Court: The Initial Formulation of the Right to Remain Silent," we have shown the different forms that cautions take in the Netherlands and how the formulation of the caution itself can emphasize different aspects of the caution. In the section "The Right to Remain Silent during the Examination of the Evidence," we examined the judges' reference to the caution later in the proceedings, when they try to elicit the suspects' story during the examination of the evidence. Referring to the caution not only reminds the suspect of her or his rights but also highlights and legitimates the nature of the judges' questions for those at the trial as well for a court of appeals. Our turn-by-turn analysis highlights the dilemma for the suspects: despite their right to silence during the courtroom hearing, not providing answers can disadvantage them in terms of judicial assessment of their procedural attitude. In the last section ("The Right to Silence and the Role of the Case File"), we demonstrated how statements drawn up earlier in the legal trajectory are invoked in court. Judges can request clarification of earlier statements, even if a suspect has claimed her or his right to silence, and the statements can be used to question and counter the suspect's clarifications. The case file can also serve to answer questions for the suspect in situations in which her or his answer is not in line with the story constructed by the prosecution when composing the indictment, a document that is the point of departure for the in-court examination of suspects by judges. We saw, hence, how the statements drawn up by the police can interactionally overrule the caution given in court.

This chapter shows how difficult it can be for suspects to exercise their right to silence in court, even in a legal system that mandates that judges must explicitly advise them that they are not required to answer the questions they are about to be asked. While advising them of this right, judges have various ways of making it difficult for suspects to exercise it. Thus a question arises about the extent to which suspects who answer questions in court, despite being advised of their right to not answer them, are indeed consenting to provide these answers.

Acknowledgments

We would like to thank the editors for their helpful comments and feedback. This study has been funded by NWO Programmatic Research in the Humanities, Grant No. 360-70-240.

Appendix: Transcription Conventions

(2)	pause of 2 seconds
(.)	pause shorter than 0.1 second
(. .)	pause longer than 0.1 second, not measured exactly
=	no noticeable silence between two sequentially following speaker's turns or between intonation units by the same speaker
Over[lap] [over lap]	stretches of speech between square brackets overlap with stretches of speech in the next line
(xxx)	the transcriber is not sure what is said
((comments))	comments by the transcriber
{translate}	words between {brackets} are added in English to improve the translation

%other language%	comments between %% indicates which participants communicate in another language
→	key utterance(s) for the analysis
strong fall.	intonation unit-final strong falling intonation
fall;	intonation unit-final slightly falling intonation
rise,	intonation unit-final slightly rising intonation
strong rise?	intonation unit-final strong rising intonation
emphasis	underscored words or syllables are emphasized
int-	(self) interrupted speech
lo:::nger	the speaker has lengthened the preceding sound; the more : symbols, the longer
<slower>	words or syllables between < > signs are produced slower
>faster<	words or syllables between > < signs are produced faster

Notes

1. In 2002, there was a brief political discussion when a right-wing party wanted to abolish the suspect's right to silence after their leader Pim Fortuyn was shot and killed. The suspect, Volkert van der Graaf, was shortly after arrested and claimed his right to silence, causing public outrage as people wanted to know why he had murdered Pim Fortuyn.

2. This duty applies to police officers as well as public prosecutors and judges.

3. This may change in the future. EU Guideline 2013/48/EU, issued on October 22, 2013, prescribes that suspects must be advised about their right to a lawyer (section 14).

4. It is beyond the scope of this chapter to discuss the construction of police records, but see for instance Coulthard (2002), Van Charldorp (2011), Rock (2001), or Jönsson and Linell (1991) for different kinds of analyses.

5. In this analysis we assume that the relation between the original turns and the translations is unproblematic because (a) we cannot know how well the translation covers the meaning of the original utterance and (b) the participants in the interaction do not (observably) treat the translations in an problematic way. Of course, we are aware that more thorough study of the translations by speakers of both languages may reveal difficulties in translations because one-to-one translations are (nearly) always problematic.

6. See also van der Houwen (2013) for a related analysis of this extract.

Cases Cited

DUTCH JURISPRUDENCE

HR March 3, 1964, NJ 1964, 400.
HR November 12, 1974, NJ 1975, 41.
HR June 30, 2009, NbSr 2009, 249.

International Jurisprudence

Panovits v. Cyprus, ECHR December 11, 2008, no. 4268/04.
Salduz v. Turkey, ECHR November 27, 2008, no. 36391/02.

References

Ainsworth, Janet. 2008. "You have the right to remain silent ..." but only if you ask for it just so: The role of linguistic ideology in American police interrogation law. *International Journal of Speech, Language and the Law* 15(1): 1–22.

Blommaert, Jan. 2005. *Discourse: A Critical Introduction*. Cambridge: Cambridge University Press.

Carter, Elisabeth. 2010. *Analysing Police Interviews: Laughter, Confessions and the Tape*. London: Bloomsbury.

Coulthard, Malcolm. 2002. Whose voice is it? Invented and concealed dialogue in written records of verbal evidence produced by the police. In Janet Cotterill (ed.) *Language in the Legal Process*. New York: Palgrave Macmillan. 19–34.

D'hondt, Sigurd and Fleur van der Houwen (eds.). 2014. Quoting from the case file: Intertextuality in judicial settings [Special Issue]. *Language & Communication* 36.

Edwards, Derek. 2008. Intentionality and *mens rea* in police interrogations: The production of actions as crimes. *Intercultural Pragmatics* 5(2): 177–199.

Heffer, Chris, Frances Rock and John Conley (eds.). 2013. *Legal-Lay Communication: Textual Travels in the Law*. Oxford: Oxford University Press.

Heritage, John and Steven Clayman. 2010. *Talk in Action: Interaction, Identities, and Institutions*. Oxford: Wiley-Blackwell.

Heritage, John and Rodney Watson. 1979. Formulations as conversational objects. In George Psathas (ed.) *Everyday Language*. New York: Irvington Press. 123–162.

Jol, Guusje and Fleur van der Houwen. 2014. Police interviews with child witnesses: Pursuing a response with *maar* (= Dutch but) prefaced questions. *International Journal of Speech, Language and the Law* 21(1): 113–138.

Jönsson, Linda and Per Linell. 1991. Story generations: From dialogical interviews to written reports in police interrogations. *Text* 11(3). 419–440.

Komter, Martha. 1998. *Dilemmas in the Courtroom: A Study of Violent Crimes in the Netherlands*. Mahwah, New Jersey: Lawrence Erlbaum.

Komter, Martha. 2013. Travels of a suspect's statement. In Chris Heffer, Frances Rock and John Conley (eds.) *Legal-Lay Communication: Textual Travels in the Law*. Oxford: Oxford University Press. 126–146.

Kronenberg, Mathieu and Bas de Wilde. 2005. *Grondtrekken van het Nederlandse Strafrecht* [The Fundamental features of Dutch Criminal Law] (3rd ed.). Deventer, the Netherlands: Kluwer.

Mazeland, Harrie. 2008. *Inleiding in de conversatieanalyse*. Bussum, the Netherlands: Coutinho.

Melai, Alfred. 1980. De positie van de verdachte in het strafgeding. *Delikt & Delinkwent* 10: 533–537.

Pomerantz, Anita 1984. Agreeing and disagreeing with assessments: Some features of preferred/dispreferred turn shapes. In J. Maxwell Atkinson and John Heritage (eds.). *Structures of Social Action*. Cambridge: Cambridge University Press. 57–101.

Redeker, Gisela. 1994. Maar nu even iets heel anders—*maar* als segmentatiesignaal. In Ronny Boogaart and Jan Noordegraaf (eds.) *Nauwe Betrekkingen*. Amsterdam: Stichting Neerlandistiek VU. 213–221.

Rock, Frances. 2001. The genesis of a witness statement. *Forensic Linguistics* 8(2): 44–72.

Schuyt, Pauline. 2009. *Verantwoorde Straftoemeting*. Oegstgeest, the Netherlands: Kluwer.

Shuy, Roger. 1993. *Language Crimes: The Use and Abuse of Language Evidence in the Courtroom*. Oxford: Blackwell.

Solan, Lawrence and Peter Tiersma. 2005. *Speaking of Crime: The Language of Criminal Justice.* Chicago: University of Chicago Press.

Spronken, Taru. 2009. Titel II De verdachte. In Tineke Cleiren and Hans Nijboer (eds.) *Tekst & Commentaar Strafvordering* (8th ed.). Deventer, the Netherlands: Kluwer. 69–154.

Stivers, Tanja and Jeffrey Robinson. 2006. A preference for progressivity in interaction. *Language in Society* 35(3): 367–392.

Svennevig, Jan. 2008. Trying the easiest solution first in other-initiation of repair. *Journal of Pragmatics* 40: 333–348.

Van Charldorp, Tessa. 2011. *From Police Interrogation to Police Record.* PhD dissertation. Oisterwijk, the Netherlands: BOXPress.

van der Houwen, Fleur. 2005. Negotiating disputes and achieving judgments on *Judge Judy*. Unpublished PhD dissertation. Los Angeles: University of Southern California.

van der Houwen, Fleur. 2009. Formulating disputes. *Journal of Pragmatics* 41(10): 2072–2085.

van der Houwen, Fleur. 2012. The foregrounding and backgrounding of information: Reporting practices by judges in criminal court. Paper presented to the 3rd European Conference of the International Association of Forensic Linguistics: Bridging the Gap(s) Between Language and the Law. Universidade do Porto, Portugal.

van der Houwen, Fleur. 2013. Reported writing in court: Putting evidence "on record." *Text & Talk* 33(6): 747–769.

van der Houwen, Fleur and Guusje Jol. Under review. Juvenile court: Creating (an atmosphere of) understanding.

van der Houwen, Fleur and Petra Sneijder. 2014. From text to talk in criminal court: Prosecuting, defending, and examining the evidence. In Sigurd D'hondt and Fleur van der Houwen (eds.) Quoting from the case file: Intertextuality in legal settings [Special Issue]. *Language & Communication* 36: 37–52.

13

"No Comment" Responses to Questions in Police Investigative Interviews

Elizabeth Stokoe, Derek Edwards, and Helen Edwards

Introduction

What are suspects' rights in an investigative interview with police officers, and how do suspects exercise them? This chapter investigates the way a particular right within the British system, that suspects "do not have to say anything," is explained to them by officers, and then realized in suspects' "No comment" responses to questions. This right is explained as part of the "caution," which is a key element of a standard opening of police interviews that follow the requirements of the Police and Criminal Evidence Act for England and Wales (PACE 1984; see Stokoe 2013), as amended by the Criminal Justice and Public Order Act 1994, Part III, sections 34–37 (CJPO 1994). The "caution" stipulates a right to remain silent under questioning, along with a caveat on the possibility of negative inferences being drawn from the exercise of that right; the "caution" is broadly similar to the "Miranda warning" given by police officers in the United States prior to questioning a person in custody. Although the codes in England and Wales and in the United States grant the suspect's right to silence, there is a key difference that is relevant to the analysis we provide in this chapter. Miranda essentially warns about the potentially negative consequences of saying anything, which "can and will be used against you in a court of law." In contrast, the caution in England and Wales essentially warns against silence, in that any answer provided later in court, but withheld initially under police questioning, is liable to being treated skeptically, as fabrication: "it may harm your defence if, when questioned, you fail to mention something you later rely on in court." The extent to which the "caution" establishes or, in its post-1994 version, undermines, a right to silence has been a matter of some controversy since its inception (e.g., O'Reilly 1994). This chapter focuses on instances in which suspects under police questioning in England exercise their right not to answer questions, by use of the standard response formula "No comment." We examine the design, uses, and consequences of that response, in and for its specific environments in recorded police questioning. Some suspects are advised by co-present lawyers to "not answer" in response to particular sorts of police questions (Edwards and Stokoe 2011). However, lawyers do not always persist with this advice once given, and suspects do not always adhere to it.

The chapter is located in a wider context of conversation analytic (CA) work on social interaction in legal settings (e.g., courtrooms, police stations, emergency services, prisons, legal documents, lawyers' offices). Indeed, in his groundbreaking collection of papers on ethnomethodology, Garfinkel (1967: 105) examined jurors' decision-making practices in the allocation of blame and in "recommending remedies" (see also Manzo 1996 on jury interaction, and see Bittner 1967; Cicourel 1968; Sacks 1972; Sudnow 1965; Wieder 1974, for other classic ethnomethodological studies of legal institutions). Another key conversation analytic study was Atkinson and Drew's (1979) investigation of the organization of cross-examination in courtrooms, focusing on the design of lawyers' questions, particularly those that were designed to allocate blame, and of witnesses' responses to such questions (see also Pollner 1974; Maynard 1984; Beach 1985; Pomerantz 1987; Bogen and Lynch 1989; Komter 1998; Burns 2001; Galatolo 2007; and Lynch 2007, on courtroom interaction of various kinds). Other sites of investigation include the everyday workings of law firms (e.g., Travers 1997); the production of legal texts and records (e.g., Meehan 1986; Summerfield and McHoul 2005; Komter 2006; Van Charldorp 2013), and encounters between citizens and the police (e.g., Meehan 1989; Sharrock and Watson 1989; Whalen and Zimmerman 1990). Interaction in places such as courtrooms can constitute some of the most highly consequential moments in people's lives.

Rigorous analysis of "live" (i.e., recorded) police interviews comprises a minority of work on interaction across legal settings. In contrast to numerous studies of suspects' and police officers' post hoc reflections about their interviewing technique, style, and experience (e.g., Holmberg and Christianson 2002; De Fruyt, Bockstaele, Taris and Van Hiel 2006; Kassin, Leo, Meissner, Richman, Colwell, Leach and La Fon 2007; Dando, Wilcock and Milne 2008), there are far fewer studies of actual interactions between officers and arrested suspects. Within the smaller body of work that analyzes real-life police interviews of suspects, grounded in linguistics and discourse analysis as well as CA, much attention has been paid to officers' questioning strategies, issues of power and coercion, and the elicitation and design of suspects' accounts (e.g., Watson 1983; Wowk 1984; Linell and Jönsson 1991; Shuy 1998; Komter 2003; Heydon 2005; Benneworth 2006; Edwards 2006; Haworth

2006; Edwards 2008; Johnson 2008; Stokoe and Edwards 2007, 2008; Stokoe 2009, 2010). Some have analyzed the physical and embodied aspects of police interviewing, such as how the interview room itself becomes a resource for interaction (LeBaron and Streeck 1997), or how gaze direction between participants can play an important part in the emotionality of an interview (e.g., Kidwell 2006).

With regard to the "caution" itself, Rock (2007) has conducted detailed linguistic analyses of both its written text and the spoken event, though her analysis falls short in focusing on the kinds of phonetic and other details that are crucial to a conversation analytic approach to interaction analysis. Nevertheless, Rock shows how police officers' explanations of suspects' rights, while based on written text, are diverse and personalized. This chapter extends Rock's work by focusing on a specific feature of investigative interviews in which suspects exercise their right of silence—that is, to not answer questions put to them by police officers. Although "No comment" responses (which are overwhelmingly used in preference to mere silence) are sometimes commented on in other work on police interviews, they are referred to casually rather than selected as the analytic focus of research. We examine the way suspects' rights to not answer questions are explained to them, and then how such (non) responses are occasioned, and how they work interactionally in the live unfolding of investigative interviews.

Data and Method

We draw on a corpus of 125 British police interviews with suspects, recorded by officers as part of standard police procedure and subsequently digitized, anonymized, and transcribed by the authors. The data were collected as part of a funded study of community disputes.[1] We identified all cases in which "No comment" turns were present, as well as other turns that delivered a similar function of not supplying the required answers to questions. We identified the location of these turns within the overall landscape of police-suspect interviews, and the sorts of responses that interviewing officers gave to "No comment" turns. Therefore, we focused closely on the sequential placement, action orientation, design and uptake of these turns. In the data extracts that follow, the title (e.g., "PN-4") specifies the source of the extract within a larger corpus (e.g., police interview number 4). Abbreviations for participants include "P" (or P1, P2, etc.) for the interviewing police officer(s); "S" for the suspect being interviewed; "L" for the lawyer, who is a solicitor or other legal representative advising S (in all cases, these were appointed by the police; none of the suspects in our sample already had their own solicitors on hand); and "A" for an "appropriate adult," where present, who was usually accompanying a child. Names that could identify persons and places, including police officers, have been anonymized. Data transcripts use punctuation and other symbols to mark prosody rather than grammar, according to the conventions for CA (Jefferson 2004).

Analysis

The analysis is organized into two broad sections, each presenting findings about the sequential and action-oriented environments for "No comment" responses. The first section focuses on spontaneous (in terms of the local interactional sequence) suspect-initiated "No comment" responses. The second section examines lawyer-initiated "No comment" responses, including cases in which suspects do or do not follow the lawyer's advice.

SUSPECT-INITIATED "NO COMMENT" RESPONSES

In this first analytical section, the extracts show how suspects invoke their right to "not say anything." We see how suspects do this when solicitors are and are not present, as well as variations in whether or not suspects maintain "No comment" responses throughout their interviews or in parts.

In the first extract, the suspect is an 18-year-old male who has been arrested for assault. No lawyer is present and, following the opening part of the interview (establishing the interview's time and date, identification of those present, and delivery of the standard "caution"; see Stokoe 2013), S responds with "No comment" to every question asked by P. We join the interview after P has explained the caution to S, which he does verbatim (it is generally available written on a card): "You do not have to say anything, but it may harm your defence if you do not mention when questioned something which you later rely on in court. Anything you do say may be given in evidence, okay?"

Extract 1: PN-14

P: D'you understand what the caution mea:ns,
S: Yeh.
(0.2)
P: Wha– (0.2) what do you think the caution means.
(0.5)
S: U- (0.4) dunno. Heh heh [heh
P: [Right I'll- I'll explain

then.= before we go any further n' you start actually
telling me anything it's important that you fully
understand that. .hh Caution is there that you do not
have to say anything. .h So you don' have to answer
questions, you don't have to speak on this interview.=
S: =Yeh
P: .h But if you don't it may harm your defence. Okay, so
if you go to cou:rt, .h yeh? u:h and they say why did
this person not answer these questions on interview,
.h the court may draw their own conclusions from that.=
The court might think well (0.2) has this person got
something to hide, .h why didn' he explai:n on the day
of the arrest or on the interview to say that .hh so
anything you do say may be given in evidence, may be
used in court, .h but if you don't say anything which
is your ri:ght then (.) the court mi:– might ask why
you hadn't done that. O[kay?
S: [Yeh.
P: .h So y– you are okay with what the caution [means
S: [Yeh.
P: and you're (okay) to continue. .h[hh
S: [Yeh
P: Still don't want a solicitor?
S: No.
P: Okay mate. .hhh Tell me about last night then Tom.
(2.0)
S: No comment
(0.4)
P: [No comment.]
S: [( )] No.
P: Ri:ght that's a gre:at start okay.

In the opening of the interview, prior to the start of Extract 1, S has given his name and date of birth in response to P's request for him to do so. In none of the persistent "No comment" interviews did suspects use the response in that preliminary environment. S also answered a question about why he did not want a solicitor to be present. In the extract, he also responds to questions about his understanding of the caution (lines 25, 27). Note that P's explanation of the caution offers an elaboration (lines 18 to 19) of why it may be *in S's interests* to answer questions. So, although P informs S that it is his "right" to not "say anything," this is inserted into a statement about the negative inferences it makes available.

At line 34, in response to P's request for S to "Tell me about last night then Tom" (line 32, the use of "then" implies that this is an expectable way to proceed, to move from preliminaries into direct investigative questioning), S answers, "No comment." P responds by repeating "No comment" (line 36), emphasizing the "No," which S confirms (line 37), which in turn P acknowledges with "Ri:ght" (line 38), and adds a probably ironic assessment: "that's a gre:at start." The description of S's first and only (thus far) "No comment" as a "start" anticipates that it is, indeed, heard by P as how S may continue. Indeed S goes on to reply "No comment" to all further questions through to the end of the interview, shown here:

Extract 2: PN-14 (*continued*)

P: Is there anything further in relation to what we've
(0.2) £talked at length about today:,£ .h that you
wanna tell me.
S: No comment.
P: Oka:y, (2.4) wi:th eight minutes twenty five on the
clock, (0.2) I'll cease that interview there.

Having responded "No comment" throughout the interview, S says it again in his final turn (Extract 2, line 4), rather than "No," maintaining the stance. Note P's further ironic formulation of the interview content as "What we've £talked *at length* about today:,£" (emphasis added) where the pound signs show the start and end of a "smiley" voice quality (Jefferson 2004). There is a sense, conveyed by these ironic remarks from P, that S's "No comment" responses are, in this setting, a recognized and understandable stance toward being questioned, while also being somewhat perverse in the sense that a question normatively expects an answer (Schegloff 2007). S has every right to adopt this stance, as P's "caution" made plain. However, P also has the right to continue putting questions to S well beyond the point at which "No comment" is the likely response, thus getting it on record for every individual question that S chose not to answer.

An *ironic* uptake by the police interviewer, to a suspect's "No comment" responses to questions, occurs in some other interviews in our collection. Extract 3 follows P's delivery of the caution, and P's account of what S is accused of, and the reason for his arrest.

Extract 3: PN-15

1 P: Okay so (0.6) >over to you< wha- what happened on that
2 night,
3 (0.7)
4 S: No comment.
5 P: Right. (.) °Excellent.°
6 (0.5)
7 P: >Okay< I'm gonna read from the statement u:m ((. . .))

In this case, P's acknowledgment, "Right" (line 5), is enhanced by the possibly ironic "Excellent" (see Antaki, Houtcoop-Steenstra and Rapley 2000, on the uses of "high-grade assessments"; and Edwards 2000, on the ironic uses of extreme case formulations), before proceeding with his set of interview questions. Again, S's first "No comment" response to P's first substantial (investigatory) question informs P that the interview will be constrained by S's recognizable strategy and it is common that, when done in this position, at the beginning of the interview's main investigative phase of questioning, suspects generally maintain such a strategy throughout, although officers continue to ask further questions. Again, P's expression "Excellent" may be an ironic orientation to the interactionally peculiar, almost absurd, practice of continuing with a series of questions to which is it understood that no substantial answer will be forthcoming. In fact, it is the design and function of the formulaic response "No comment" to occupy that interactional slot, providing a succinct response in its correct location, while avoiding answering any and all specific questions.

Extract 4 provides another example of an ironic receipt of a "No comment" response. We join the interview after S has already issued several "No comment" responses to questions about the alleged offenses, which are threats to murder and also criminal damage regarding the property of neighbors with whom there appears to have been a long-running feud. The extract opens as P asks S for his account of the history of events leading up to the alleged offenses.

Extract 4: PN-45

1 P: .hhh u:h this is your opportunity no:w John, whi:le
2 we're on tape, while you're represented, .h to (0.2)
3 uh maybe give any explanation no::w .h as to: .h
4 what has happen:ed involving the Penrose family: .hh
5 uh that may have led (0.2) to (0.2) what is alleged
6 to have happened last night.
7 S: No comment.

(0.5)
P: Okay £that was a ↓mouthful to get over for a [no=
S: [Yeh
P: =comment reply ↑wasn't it.£
(0.2)
P: There you go. .hhh U:h the allegation is that ((. . .))

In lines 1 to 6, P not only asks S a question, but builds a case for answering it, given that S has displayed a "No comment" stance to previous questions. P has remarked, prior to the extract, that S has said things to P off record on other occasions in the past about a continuing feud between S and his neighbors. In what appears to be an effort to obviate a further, immediate "No comment" response from S, P builds the importance of this "opportunity," on record and with a lawyer present, to provide that historic account of "what has happen:ed involving the Penrose family:" that may explain S's side of what he is now accused of doing. S nevertheless responds immediately with "No comment" (line 7). P's formulation "a mouthful to get over" (he is referring to his extended question and its buildup in lines 1 to 6), and the expression "There you go" (line 13), combine with a marked shift in tone of voice at line 9 from deliberate and emphatic toward jocular, to treat S's response ironically. Again, we have an oriented-to sense of the absurd, in the continuing elaboration of questions and explanations by P, in the face of a stubborn series of "No comment" responses from S.

In Extract 5, a teenage suspect is present with his father (A) but no solicitor. The suspect has been arrested for harassment of his neighbors. Again, we join the interview as P explains the caution to S.

Extract 5: PN-31

P: Okay an' that is you do not have to say anything but
.hh it may harm your defence:, if you do not mention
when questioned, .h something which you later rely on
in court. .h Anything you do say may be given in
evidence. Okay, you happy with that?
(0.3)
S: Ye[h.
A: ['kay=
P: =Right. .hhh Um (1.0) I've had cause to go and speak
to a chap by the name of Davi:d (0.3) Jenkinson.
(0.7)

P: And he lives at forty fi:ve (0.2) Stonycroft Road.
(0.5)
P: Which i:s virtually opposite your house.= Is that
all right
(0.5)
S: (°°spose so°°)
P: An' you live at two Honeywell Terrace
(0.6)
S: Yeh
(0.6
P: Y'have to speak (0.5) so the microphone c'n hear you.
(0.7)
S: No comment.
(0.3)
P: Are y'GOIN' NA- oh is he going no comment. °Okay.°
Right.

Having given his name and address, S's response to P's first substantive (crime-relevant) question is an almost inaudible "spose so" (line 17), and then a "Yeh" to once again (having already done so as part of the interview's preliminaries) confirm his own home address (line 20). However, following P's exhortation to speak clearly for the sake of the tape recording, S then replies, "No comment" (line 24). In fact, P's questioning does more than merely affirm the preliminary business of where S lives. P is now entering the main investigatory part of the interview, formulating S's house as "virtually opposite" that of the complainant, establishing that S knows that to be the case and that he knows who lives there. So P is starting to build connections between S and his accuser. Once S makes his first "No comment" response, P pointedly remarks on it (line 26). Note how P stops to repair and restart his "Are y'GOIN'" (addressed to S) by inserting an "oh" (a change-of-state token: Heritage 1984) and readdressing it to S's father. The repaired remark at line 26 nicely displays the action that P is doing, in marking S's "No comment" as significant beyond its specific moment. There is the formulation "is he *going* No comment," (emphasis added) which packages the "No comment" response as scripted (Edwards 1994), which is to say, likely to be repeated throughout the interview. P is showing, right from S's first "No comment" response, that "No comment" is recognizable not merely as a particular answer to a particular question, but as a *stance*, displayed by a *formulaic* expression, which enables P to project how S may proceed from then on. Recall also Extract 1, with "that's a gre:at *start*." (Emphasis added) In ways similar to other interviews in which parents are co-present, P's redirection of his question to S's father implies that this may be a strategy that the boy and his father may have planned in advance. S does indeed maintain his "No comment" responses until the end of the interview.

In Extract 6 the suspect has been arrested for criminal damage to his neighbor's fence. S has a solicitor, "Mr. Evans," present.

Extract 6: PN-32

P: Anything you do say may be given in evidence. .h
Are y'happy- (0.2) you understand what the caution
mea:ns,
(2.1)
L: It's what I've just explai:ned t'you,
P: Yeh.
(0.2)
P: Yu- y'ok↓ay with that yeh,
(0.2)
P: A'right no problem at all. .hhh Right. .h I've given
(0.2) mister Evans a form what we call (0.2) form
eff one two one which explains your rights to the
tapes (.) on conclusion o'the interview. *A'right*
that's somethin' c'n discuss but the form's there
now. .h Okay y'r happy to proceed with the interview
(0.2)
S: Ye:h
P: °Okay no problem at all.°
(0.6)
P: .pt.hhh Right.
(0.6)
P: Approximately:: (0.5) ten to four this afternoo:n,
(0.5) u:::h my colleague an' I: (.) attended (.)
your address back garden of your address and spoke
to you there.
(0.2)
P: Can you: (0.3) tell me exactly what happened,
(0.3)

29 P: during the time that we were there.
30 (0.3)
31 S: No comment.
32 (0.2)
33 P: °Okay. No problem at all.°
34 (2.2)
35 P: I believe that you live at thirty four Staveley
36 Road (0.3) on the: (name) estate in ((city)). .hh
37 Can you:: (.) tell me how long you've lived there.
38 (0.7)
39 S: No: comment.
40 (0.3)
41 P: °Okay.°

In Extract 6 his lawyer has apparently already explained the caution to S (line 5), so there has been some communication on that between L and S prior to the interview. As P moves into the interview's main investigatory phase, with an open-ended invitation for S to provide his version of the events at issue (lines 27 to 29), S responds with a simple, unelaborated "No comment" (line 31). Note P's "Okay" acknowledgment of this and the additional "No problem at all" (line 33). In proposing it as "No problem at all," P orients to the normative expectation, whether in a police interview or elsewhere, that a question deserves an answer. The "at all" upgrades it to an extreme case formulation (Pomerantz 1986), emphasizing the remark. It also implies that P is not going to *pursue* answers to specific questions: that "No comment" is an acceptable and consequential response.

In summary, then, across the first six extracts, we have seen "No comment" operate as a recognized, formulaic stance taken by suspects toward police questioning, that police officers acknowledge as such, generally on its first occurrence (it does not require many repetitions to be recognized as a stance rather than a one-off response), and that they may, but not always, treat ironically. In Extract 6 we saw indirect evidence of S's lawyer orienting S to the possibility of issuing "No comment" responses to questions. Extract 7 shows another lawyer directly recommending the device, with which (a different) S appears to be not thoroughly familiar, despite this being his second formal interview. Indeed, as we show later in this article, this particular suspect is inconsistent in his use of the device. Here, S is a teenage boy accompanied by his mother (acting as "appropriate adult") and a solicitor, and there are two police officers present.

Extract 7: PN-110b

P1: Again I'll ask you do you understand the caution?
S: Yeh.
P1: Okay great. .hh Right then. Um (0.5) u-u- just to-
(0.4) summarize from what we were on about from the
last interview- .h[hh
S: [Can I say one thing.
(0.8)
S: On my solicitor's advice here
P1: Yeh,
L: Uh huh
S: I don't wanna answer no more questions.
L: [Right.]
P1: [Right.] Tha- tha- that's your prerogative. However,
(.) um unfortunately I still have to ask you the
questions.
S: So what do I say.
L: No [comment.]
P1: [y-] y'can say whatever you wish.

As in previous examples, in the interview's preliminary phase S has given his name, age, and address, and has answered questions about his understanding of the caution. However, as P begins to move into investigative questioning (lines 3 to 5), S inserts a sequence preface (line 6) to an announcement (line 11) that, on his solicitor's advice, "I don't wanna answer no more questions." A possible consequence of this announcement would be that of forestalling the continuation of the interview. However, as P asserts (lines 13 to 15), that is not going to happen. It is at this point that S asks how he is supposed to go about invoking his right ("your prerogative," line 13) to say nothing. It is interesting that S does not assume that he can simply remain silent; his inquiry to L, "So what do I say" (line 16) implies that he needs *something* to respond with. L provides at line 17 the standardized wording, the "No comment" *device for doing* not-answering. In overlap, P asserts that S can nevertheless "say whatever you wish" (line 18). When P asserts that he does nevertheless "still have to ask" questions, the "have to" alludes to the part of the caution that advises it will be a matter of record if S refuses to answer any question that may be put to him again later in court. So we see here, played out in sequential detail, a motivation for the creation and use of the "No comment" response itself, as a way of officially, and recognizably, and not merely actually, not answering.

In Extract 8, although S responds to P's investigative questions with "No comment," he does in the first instance offer a statement of his own, "for the um benefit of the court" (lines 9 to 12). At the start of the extract, P has just completed the caution. The extract is given here in enough length to show how P produces, and how S deals with, a series of substantive (investigative) questions following S's "No comment" responses.

Extract 8: PN-5

P: [..] D'you understand that.
    (0.2)
S: Yeh.
    (0.2)
P: O:kay mister Johnson. .hh Um <u>wh</u>en you were arr<u>e</u>sted,
(0.2) you <u>a</u>ctually said that you didn't do it. Have
you got anything <u>e</u>lse (0.3) you'd like to add to
that?=
S: =Y<u>e</u>:h. for the um benefit of the court (0.2) u:h
mister <u>Re</u>ynolds is a (0.2) heroin and crack addict,
with an alcohol problem, (0.2) and was trying to get
money off of me, (0.3) and that's all I have to say.
    (1.2)
P: Okay thank you mister Johnson,
    (2.6)
P: °Ri:ght. Okay.°
    (2.6)
P: R<u>i</u>::ght.= <u>I</u>f I can just um <u>a</u>sk you then mis- um
mister Johnson, (0.3) um (0.5) when- when the
officers arr<u>i</u>:ved we actually (0.2) u:m (0.3) <u>f</u>ou:nd
the stereo that was <u>d</u>amaged (0.2) outside (0.3) on
the p<u>a</u>vement from uh (0.3) twenty nine Oxford Road.
.hhh Can you just tell me (0.2) in your own words
<u>h</u>ow that came to be there- down on the pavement.
    (0.6)
P: If [you (would)
S: [No comment.
    (1.3)
P: °Okay,°
    (6.5)

P: You know who the stereo belonged to?
(1.7)
S: No comment ( ).
(12.0)
P: °O::kay,°
(2.5)
P: Did you eh, (0.7) £did you throw the stereo out of
the window.£
S: No comment.
(15.0)
P: °O:kay.° =.h u:m
(5.7)
P: When- when it came to the um- (0.3) when you were
arrested, (0.6) u:m (0.5) the officer came in and
arrested you mister Johnson, (0.3) u:m did you: (1.2)
did you do anything when the arrest took place?
(1.5)
S: No[:
P: [Remember anything happening,
S: comment.
(0.7)
P: (°*No comment*°)
(7.0)

Having made his initial statement concerning his alleged victim's character and motives (lines 9 to 12), a topic neither invited nor pursued by P, S concludes the turn with the words "that's all I have to say." He then proceeds to respond "No comment" to questions that P puts to him. The "No:" at line 48 is not a stand-alone "no," which would be a substantive answer to the question that precedes it, but part of the turn completed in line 50, a "No comment," which is then quietly echoed by P at line 52. Following each of S's "No comment" responses (lines 27, 33, 39, and 48 to 50) there is a substantial gap of silence, punctuated by P's quiet, almost inaudible acknowledgment "Okay" or, at line 52, a quiet, confirmatory echoing of the response. When P eventually begins another question, it is not the same question again, neither precisely repeated nor paraphrased, but another aspect of the event: whether S knew who owned the damaged stereo (line 31); whether he threw it out of the window (lines 37 to 38), a question delivered with an audibly "smiley" voice quality (P is presumably orienting to the unlikelihood of S confessing this action);

and whether S recalls anything else happening or having done something at the time of the arrest (lines 46, 49). We later discover that this latter incident concerns a separate accusation (see Extract 9) involving the police officer who arrested him. This is a pervasive pattern in our data: that P generally acknowledges S's "No comment" responses with an "Okay," and moves on to a *different aspect* of the event in question, rather than pursuing an answer to the same specific point.

Later in the same interview, S is asked about the second charge of resisting arrest, and we join the interview as P further alleges that S scratched the arresting officer, "PC Kent." Here, S deviates somewhat from the routine production of "No comment" responses.

Extract 9: PN-5 (*continued*)

P: He's also saying that when you: when you did pull
awa:y, (0.5) u::m (1.6) the actual handcuffs u:m
(1.9) (kind of) scratched (the hand of) my colleague
PC Kent.
(0.4)
P: U:m (1.3) how- how did that scratch: come about with
PC Kent's hand d'you know that?
(1.5)
S: Um: (0.3) no: (0.6) comment, (.) either, (0.3) but no.
(1.2)
P: °O:kay.°
(0.4)
P: U:m well he's got here that- (0.5) you've actually:
you've scratched him as you've pulled awa:y, .h um so
did y- did you intend to scratch PC Kent when you uh
S: No comment.
P: pulled away from him?
(3.0)
P: °Okay.°
(0.5)
P: ↑Have you anything to uh (0.4) tell us about the whole-
whole ni:ght and the arrest in question,
(3.2)
S: Fact that you've u:m (1.5) took a:: (0.3) heroin
addict's (0.3) statement (0.8) um no sorry I haven't.

No I haven't got anything else to say.
(1.2)
P: You hav↓en't got anything [to say] about the whole=
S: [No:.]
P: =matter at all
(0.9)
P: D'you deny: u:m (1.0) the actual stereo bein- (0.5) did
you damage the stereo at all.
S: No comment.

Again, in Extract 9, S repeatedly produces a "No comment" response to evidential questioning, and P produces a delayed and quietly delivered "Okay" acknowledgment (lines 10 to 11, and 18 to 19) before proceeding to another, though related, question. There is a variation at line 10, where S adds "either, but no" to his initial "No comment," which P initially treats (line 11) in the same manner as a straightforward "No comment." However, S's same-turn repair of the answer to "but no" converts the turn into a denial rather than a simple "No comment," and this elicits from P a pursuit of what S is denying (lines 13 to 14) and, in refuting that denial, whether he did it on purpose (line 15; see Edwards 2008 on the pursuit of intentionality for actions and their consequences, in police questioning). A clearer deviation starts at line 24, where in place of his usual "No comment" response, S again invokes his opening statement about the status of his accuser as a heroin addict. Rather than a straightforward exception to saying "No comment," however, this is also not an answer to the question but, rather, an account for not commenting. Its status as an account is specifically marked by the "so" at line 25. S's formulation at line 26, "No I haven't got anything else to say" adds the notion of nothing *else*, which P then formulates in extreme terms at lines 28 to 30, "*anything* . . . about the *whole* matter *at all*." (Emphasis added) P then goes on (beyond the end of the extract) to elicit from S a series of "No comment" responses, for the record, to a succession of question formulations concerning the alleged event. The earlier insertion of an opening statement by S, following the caution (see Extract 8), is a recurrent, though not universal, feature of interviews that then proceed with "No comment" responses to questions.

As Extract 9 starts to show, a sense of the functional import of "No comment" responses can be gained from examples in which the suspect does not always make use of them. Rather than being randomly distributed, however, these variations in response may display S's own analysis of the different status of specific questions, as sometimes being legally consequential or evidential, or else merely preliminary or contextual. We return to interview PN-15, which we visited briefly in Extract 3. The suspect has been arrested on suspicion of the criminal offense, one recent Friday night, of "causing actual bodily harm" to his accuser, another man, who has provided a witness statement. Having received a couple of "No comment" responses from S, P is using the accuser's witness statement as a basis for pursuing an account from S of his actions and locations on the night in question.

Extract 10: PN-15

1 P: ↑What d'y'normally do on Friday night when y're (0.9)
2 when y're out 'n about.
3 (2.2)
4 S: With my girlfriend mainly.
5 P: Right. W- were you with your girlfriend on this night.
6 (0.4)
7 S: U:::::h no comment.
8 (1.9)
9 *((P continues to read from the witness statement,*
10 *which contains the location Cranston Bridge Road))*
11 P: D'you know where Cranston Bridge Road is?
12 (1.3)
13 S: Yep.
14 (0.2)
15 P: Yeh. Okay is that- (.) close to where you live?
16 (0.2)
17 S: Yep.
18 P: Right.
19 (0.5)
20 P: Is it possible that you was around the area (0.4) of
21 Cranston Bridge Road at about half past ten on that
22 night?
23 S: No comment.
24 (2.4)
25 P: °Okay.°
26 (1.0)
27 ((*P reads more from the witness statement*))

In Extract 10, the questions to which S answers "No comment" are at lines 5 and 20. Both questions directly concern S's actions and location on the specific night in question, with regard to when and where the alleged assault took place. In contrast, the questions to which S provides substantive answers are those at lines 1, 11, and 15. These are general or background questions, not specific to the alleged incident. In this interview, then, S displays, through selective uses of "No comment" or else of informative answers, an understanding of the particular applicability of "No comment" answers to questions directly pertinent to the alleged offense. As we have seen elsewhere, P's response to "No comment" is to move on, following a delay (lines 8 to 10, and 24 to 27). This contrasts with P's pursuit of the topic following S's informative answers (lines 4 to 5, 13 to 15, 18 to 20). Clearly, "No comment" has a special status for both S and P, both in terms of the interactional contingencies it responds to, and the consequences that it generates.

LAWYER-INITIATED "NO COMMENT" RESPONSES

We have seen that the status of "No comment" is generally recognized by participants in police questioning as *the* recognized, formulaic device for not answering specific questions in accordance with the right to silence stipulated in the caution. This normative recognition applies even in the breach, which is to say, even where it is *not* what S says at the appropriate juncture, as we saw particularly with regard to Extract 7. We move now to examples where "No comment" responses are directly instigated by the lawyer present, and to further examples of how the device is oriented-to in the breach: that is, when suspects are inconsistent in spite of their lawyers' advice. Lawyers sometimes spontaneously advise clients not to answer a question, this advice being occasioned by some feature of P's questioning or of S's answering. In such cases, lawyers display suspects' "rights-in-action"; that is, they invoke suspects' rights to "not say anything" that police officers have stated at the outset as part of the formal caution.

We return to the case seen in Extract 7, involving interview PN-110b. That was the second of two interviews with the same suspect. Extract 11 is from the first of those interviews, PN-110a. This is one of a number of cases in which the suspect does not consistently follow his lawyer's advice to restrict answers to "No comment," sometimes to the exasperation of the lawyer, the appropriate adult (in this case, a parent), and even the police officer who is asking questions. Again we are able to see how "No comment" is not simply an uncooperative response, but part of a recognized, orderly way to engage in a police interview. In Extract 11, the suspect, "John," fails to produce "No comment" responses despite his lawyer's attempts to stop him from talking. In each case, what we see is that S does not maintain that "No comment" stance. John is a juvenile suspect, whose parent is also present as an "appropriate adult."

Extract 11: PN-110a

L: Actually John I–*u– my advice to you no:w is that
you've explained your (side of the) story= 'f you don't
want t'say any more about it don't. Let's wait and see
what the– the CCTV– it won't stop them asking the
questions possibly, .hh but I'm saying that (.) >youknow<
you've- (0.4) you've explained your side of the story=
S: =Mm
L: and let's see what the CCTV throws up.
(2.5)
P: Okay.
(1.3)
P: ↑Well (0.5) goin' on from there then, (.) what you're
sayin'is that u- this security guy's approached you:
he's grabbed hold of you. .h and y– you've u- uh (0.4)
made two comments to him. .h One is you're lucky you
don't bomb 'im ou:t (0.2) and your other is to [get the=
S: [Yeh
P: =fuck off her.
S: Ye:h.
P: U- so in that (0.2) [duration of–]
S: [We was– we was] havin' little
ar:gu↓ments like (0.3) you prick an' tha:t,
P: Right.
S: And he was like laughing at me 'n that.
P: Right so you've just expanded slightly more on what
you've just sai[d
L: [If you don't js take my advice and not
say any more about it.
(0.6)
P: Is there anything el:se that you: said to that security
guard?
S: No comment.
(0.2)
S: Not really.
P: °Okay.°

36 (0.7)
37 P: Well s-security guard says other- other[wise.
38 S: [Heh
39 P: As you would probably appreciate he would.
40 ((*P now reads from the guard's statement concerning what S allegedly said to him*))

L's initial advice (lines 1 to 8) is that S has said enough about the incident in question, and does not have to say any more. Following a minimal receipt of that advice by S (lines 7 and 9), P continues the questioning at line 12. Rather than making no reply, nor indeed using the standard "No comment" formula, S then proceeds (lines 17, 19, 21, 24) to answer P's questions, even adding further details of his own (lines 21 to 22), which P remarks on (lines 25 to 26). At this point, L remarks (lines 27 to 28) that her advice not to answer is not being followed by S. Then, in response to a further question from P, S finally issues a "No comment" response (line 32) but adds the modifying turn increment "Not really." Following his acknowledgment "Okay," P follows up S's "Not really" with a return to the same precise topic: that is, what S allegedly said to the security guard. Recall the same consequence in Extract 9, in which the same suspect's shift from "No comment" to "but no" elicited further pursuit by P of the same precise topic, based on the witness's statement that contradicts S's denial. Having something more substantial than "No comment" to work with, even something as minimal as S's "but no" or "not really," P is entitled to stay on topic and not move on.

In Extract 12, from the same interview, L again attempts to get S not to answer.

Extract 12: PN-110a

1 P: Okay. What d'y'do durin- (0.4) y'kno:w (.) while sh-
2 you're with– (0.7)
3 L: If you don't want to answer any questions [about Sally]=
4 S: [°I know I]=
5 L: =[you do not have to]
6 S: =[know I know I know I] know°
7 (0.5)
8 S: Heh °heh°
9 (0.4)
10 S: °Pass.°
11 (0.2)

12 P: But yeh what– what d'y'do with- um S- Sally I mean
13 during the da:y pass time away or
14 (2.5)
15 S: Don't ask.
16 (o.2)
17 P: Sor[ry?
18 S: [Nothing really,
19 L: No comment will do fine thank [you,
20 S: [No comment.
21 (0.8)
22 P: O:kay.
23 (1.3)
24 P: Ri:ght. Okay.
25 ((*P shifts topic to items found at S's home*))

At line 3, L cuts into P's question concerning what S gets up to with his girlfriend Sally, advising S that he need not answer this line of questioning if he does not want to. The formulation of L's advice not to answer is somewhat hedged and conditional (lines 3 to 5, "If you don't want to . . . you do not have to"), rather than simply advising or instructing S not to answer. S laughs briefly at this repetition of L's advice (which has already been given several times), and says "Pass." This response, "Pass," is a conventional term used on British television quiz shows, telling the questioner to proceed to the next question. But it is not "No comment." Accordingly, P restarts the question begun but broken off at lines 1 to 2 ("What d'y'do . . . while you're with . . .") and completes it in lines 12 to 13. The "but" at the start of line 12 is P's acknowledgment that he is asking a question in spite of what has just been said by L and S. Again, S responds to P's questions (lines 15 and 18) until L intervenes with the more direct instruction, "No comment will do fine thank you" (line 19). This intervention stipulates the formula "No comment," which S immediately repeats, precisely and in overlap (line 20), and which P now acknowledges as closing the sequence (lines 22 to 25).

Following some further abortive attempts to get S to stop answering P's questions and to stop providing additional, uncalled-for versions of events, L focuses directly on S's repeated failure to consistently follow her advice. Extract 13, from S's second interview PN-110b, follows an unrecorded "off-tape" break called for by L, for a private conversation with S.

Extract 13: PN-110b

1	P2:	Were y'on y'r own or with: Sally.
2		(0.4)
3	S:	With Sally.
4		(1.4)
5	S:	°No comment°
6	P2:	°Ri:ght.°=
7	L:	=John it's either no comment or you're going to
8		answer questions.
9	S:	I've go- I've go- I keep forgettin' to say it.
10	L:	You do:n't you just think you're doing the [right thing.
11	P1:	[C'm on John
12		y- y- y- gone t- (.) you've ↑admitted going to this
13		guy's hou:se [right?
14	S:	[No com[ment.
15	P1:	[Just stop messin' abou:t.
16	S:	No comment.
17		(0.3)
18	P1:	Right.
19		((*P1, sounding exasperated from line 12, now persists with questioning S on the same topic*))

In answer to P2's question at line 1, S provides a substantial answer (line 3) and then, after a delay, a quietly delivered "No comment" (line 5), which P2 acknowledges (line 6). It is at this point that L, with an exasperated tone, pointedly addresses John by name at the start of his turn (line 7) and exhorts him to select a consistent stance in the interview, to either answer questions or, as advised by L, to say "No comment." Addressing someone by name at the start of a turn has been noted to mark discontinuity and disaffiliation with the action or stance of the prior turn (Stivers 2008; Butler, Danby and Emmison 2011). Note again that this is the specifically formulated advice for what to say: "it's either *no comment* or . . ." (line 7), rather than, say, "either don't comment or. . . ." The use of "it's," and of "going to" (line 7) mark this as "scripted" advice about how to proceed generally, rather than just on this one occasion. S accounts for his inconsistency in following that advice, as memory failure (line 9), to which L's response is to revise the account in S's favor, as admirably motivated, to do "the right thing" (line 10). At line 11, P1 cuts into that formulation by L and attempts to restart S's narrative of events (lines 11 to 13), to which S now provides the formulaic response suggested by L, "No comment" (line 14). Note how, like L did previously, P1 exhorts John by name "C'm on John . . ." at the start of his turn, to take a different stance. S's inconsistency appears also to have exasperated P1, whose objection formulates it as "messin' abou:t" (line 15), which S should "Just stop." However, S has now learned his lines, and repeats "No comment" (line 16). P1 acknowledges that (line 18) but, instead of moving to another question topic, S's pervasive inconsistency apparently gives P1 license to continue along the same line (following the end of Extract 13). S's failure to consistently follow his lawyer's advice not to answer occasions the appeals that L makes, and S's accountability (line 9) for that consistency, and also P1's intervention (lines 11 to 15). These interactional moments further display the special value in this setting of the normative, formulaic response "No comment."

Discussion

In police questioning, the response "No comment" provides suspects with a means of exercising their right, as stipulated in law and in the preliminary "caution" (cf. the "Miranda warning" required of police officers in the United States), to not answer police questions. It is a response with specific design features, being brief and succinct, indeed minimal, referencing merely the absence of comment with no additional, potentially troublesome notions that might provide for further inferences or uptakes, such as "No comment *at the moment*" or "*I don't wish to* comment on that" or "I *have nothing to say* about that." A simple "No comment" adds nothing about the speaker's intentions, state of knowledge, preferences or desires to speak or not speak, all of which might risk pursuit within the interview or later in court. Suspects using this device are not merely saying nothing, nor even refusing to say anything, but simply, economically and efficiently asserting their right to say nothing and, in doing so in this precise manner, obviating as much as possible whatever inferences might be drawn from doing so, as are warned against in the caution.

"No comment" also has the virtue of being standard and formulaic. This makes it immediately *recognizable as the action of* not commenting, which is different from merely saying nothing. It provides an appropriate and minimal response token in the position in which an answer is due, thus promoting the interview's progressivity (cf. Stivers and Robinson 2006) in a manner that an indefinitely extended silence would not. In other words, "No comment" is not merely a nonanswer, but an action in its own right, a *device for doing* not-answering, in observable accordance with the law. Further, its formulaic design permits it (though of course, this is not cause-and-effect) to regularly forestall the police officer's pursuit of an answer to each *specific* question. This is in contrast to what tends to occur if S says anything other than "No comment," including even a paraphrase of it, as we saw in Extract 12. Therefore, far from being an uncooperative stance, a consistent "No comment" response is treated by all participants as a recognized, legitimate, and effective way of conducting a police interview, in a way that orients to legal requirements. We saw particularly in Extract 10 that selective use of "No comment" can display a suspect's analysis of which questions are especially pertinent to the crime for which he or she has been arrested, and which questions are less troublesome to answer. However, as Extracts 11, 12, and 13 showed, a suspect's inconsistency in the use of the device may cause difficulties, disruption, and some exasperation for all participants.

One of the issues within and beyond police interviewing, concerning the caution and the right to silence, is the extent to which the revised version of the caution, now including the caveat about inferences that may be drawn from a suspect's refusal to answer questions, amounts to a weakening or even removal of the suspect's right to silence. There are instances in the extracts examined here, in which a police officer provides, and may repeat during the interview, a colloquially enhanced version of the caution's caveat, as in Extract 1: "The court might think well (0.2) h̲as this person got something to hide." The issue is: what use is a right to silence, if silence is potentially to be treated as evidence of guilt? It can be argued that a right to silence must be a right to have silence *respected* as not some kind of quiet confession. After all, in the absence of torture or a law *against* silence, nobody needs a law to enable them to say nothing, although they may need a law to give them the confidence to say nothing with impunity. Nevertheless, it is not a straightforward matter to assign to police questioners some kind of coercive basis for persuading a suspect to forgo their right to say nothing. Given the 1994 change in the law, the revised caution, and the practice in courtrooms of drawing negative inferences from a suspect's silence when previously interviewed, a police officer's advice to answer questions may sometimes be in the suspect's best interests. In that case, it is the change in the law itself that risks being considered coercive.

Appendix: Transcription Conventions

The following transcription conventions are based on and slightly adapted from Jefferson's (2004) glossary of transcript symbols.

Temporal and Sequential Relationships

[	A left bracket indicates the onset of overlapping speech
]	A right bracket indicates the point at which overlapping utterances end
=	An equals sign indicates latched speech (no break or gap between talk)
(0.5)	Silences are indicated as pauses in tenths of a second
(.)	A period in parentheses indicates a hearable micropause (less than two tenths of a second)

Aspects of Speech Delivery

.	A period indicates a falling intonation contour
,	A comma indicates continuing intonation
?	A question mark indicates rising intonation contour
_	An underscore indicates a level intonation contour
:	Colons indicate lengthening of preceding sound (the more colons, the longer the lengthening)
ye-	A hyphen indicates an abrupt cutoff sound (phonetically, a glottal stop)
yes	Underlining indicates stress or emphasis, by increased amplitude or pitch
YES	Uppercase letters indicates noticeably louder speech
°yes°	The degree sign indicates noticeably quiet or soft speech
°°yes°°	The double degree sign indicates whisper
^	A caret indicates a sharp rise in pitch
↓	Down arrow indicates shift into especially low pitch
↑	Up arrow indicates shift into especially high pitch
>yes<	Indicates talk that is noticeably faster than surrounding talk
<yes>	Indicates talk that is noticeably slower than surrounding talk
yes	Asterisk indicates a "croaky" or "creaky" voice quality
hh	The letter "h" indicates audible aspirations (the more hs the longer the breath)
.hh	A period preceding the letter "h" indicates audible inhalations (the more hs the longer the breath)
y(h)es	"h" within parentheses within a word indicates "laugh-like" sound
£yes£	A pound sign indicates smile voice

Other Notational Devices

(guess)	Words within single parentheses indicate likely hearing of that word
((coughs))	Information in double parentheses indicate the transcriber's descriptions of events rather than representations of them
( )	Empty parentheses indicate hearable yet indecipherable talk

Notes

1. Economic and Social Research Council (ESRC) Grant No. RES-148-25-0010, "Identities in Neighbour Discourse: Community, Conflict and Exclusion," held by Elizabeth Stokoe and Derek Edwards.

References

Antaki, Charles, Hanneke Houtkoop-Steenstra and Mark Rapley. 2000. "Brilliant. Next question ...": High-grade assessment sequences in the completion of interactional units. *Research on Language and Social Interaction* 33(3): 235–262.

Atkinson, J. Maxwell and Paul Drew. 1979. *Order in Court: The Organisation of Verbal Interaction in Judicial Settings*. London: Macmillan.

Beach, Wayne. 1985. Temporal density in courtroom interaction: Constraints of the recovery of past events in legal discourse. *Communication Monographs* 52: 1–18.

Benneworth, Kelly. 2006. Repertoires of paedophilia: Conflicting descriptions of adult-child sexual relationships in the investigative interview. *International Journal of Speech, Language and the Law* 13(2): 190–211.

Bittner, Egon. 1967. The police on skid-row: A study of peace keeping. *American Sociological Review* 32(5): 699–715.

Bogen, David and Michael Lynch. 1989. Taking account of the hostile native: Plausible deniability and the production of conventional history in the Iran-Contra hearings. *Social Problems* 36(3): 197–224.

Burns, Stacy. 2001. "Think your blackest thoughts and darken them": Judicial mediation of large money damage disputes. *Human Studies* 24(3): 227–49.

Butler, Carly, Susan Danby and Michael Emmison. 2011. Address terms in turn beginnings: Managing disalignment and disaffiliation in telephone counseling. *Research on Language and Social Interaction* 44(4): 338–358.

Cicourel, Aaron. 1968. *The Social Organization of Juvenile Justice*. New York: Wiley.

CJPO (1994). *Criminal Justice and Public Order Act 1994, Part III, Sections 34–37.* London: HMSO.

Dando, Coral, Rachel Wilcock and Rebecca Milne. 2008. The cognitive interview: Inexperienced police officers' perceptions of their witness/victim interviewing practices. *Legal and Criminological Psychology* 13: 59–70.

De Fruyt, Filip, Marc Bockstaele, Ruben Taris and Alain Van Hiel. 2006. Police interview competencies: Assessment and associated traits. *European Journal of Personality* 20(7): 567–584.

Edwards, Derek. 1994. Script formulations: A study of event descriptions in conversation. *Journal of Language and Social Psychology* 13(3): 211–247.

Edwards, Derek. 2000. Extreme case formulations: Softeners, investment, and doing nonliteral. *Research on Language and Social Interaction* 33(4): 347–373.

Edwards, Derek. 2006. Facts, norms and dispositions: Practical uses of the modal *would* in police interrogations. *Discourse Studies* 8(4): 475–501.

Edwards, Derek. 2008. Intentionality and *mens rea* in police interrogations: The production of actions as crimes. *Intercultural Pragmatics* 5(2): 177–199.

Edwards, Derek and Elizabeth Stokoe. 2011. "You don't have to answer": Lawyers' contributions in police interrogations of suspects. *Research on Language and Social Interaction* 44(1): 21–43.

Galatolo, Renata. 2007. Active voicing in court. In Elizabeth Holt and Rebecca Clift (eds.) *Reporting Talk: Reported Speech in Interaction*. Cambridge: Cambridge University Press. 195–220.

Garfinkel, Harold. 1967. *Studies in Ethnomethodology*. Englewood Cliffs: Prentice-Hall.

Haworth, Kate. 2006. The dynamics of power and resistance in police interview discourse. *Discourse & Society* 17(6): 739–759.

Heritage, John. 1984. A change-of-state token and aspects of its sequential placement. In J. Maxwell Atkinson and John Heritage (eds.) *Structures of Social Action: Studies in Conversation Analysis*. Cambridge: Cambridge University Press. 299–346.

Heydon, Georgina. 2005. *The Language of Police Interviewing: A Critical Analysis*. Basingstoke: Palgrave Macmillan.

Holmberg, Ulf and Sven-Åke Christianson. 2002. Murderers' and sexual offenders' experiences of police interviews and their inclination to admit or deny crimes. *Behavioral Sciences & the Law* 20(1–2): 31–45.

Jefferson, Gail. 2004. Glossary of transcript symbols with an introduction. In Gene Lerner (ed.) *Conversation Analysis: Studies from the First Generation*. Amsterdam: John Benjamins. 13–31.

Johnson, Alison. 2008. "From where we're sat . . .": Negotiating narrative transformation through interaction in police interviews with suspects. *Text & Talk* 28(3): 327–349.

Kassin, Saul, Richard Leo, Christian Meissner, Kimberly Richman, Lori Colwell, Amy-May Leach and Dana La Fon. 2007. Police interviewing and interrogation: A self-report survey of police practices and beliefs. *Law and Human Behavior* 31(4): 381–400.

Kidwell, Mardi. 2006. "Calm down!": The role of gaze in the interactional management of hysteria by the police. *Discourse Studies* 8(6): 745–770.

Komter, Martha. 1998. *Dilemmas in the Courtroom: A Study of Trials of Violent Crime in the Netherlands*. Mahwah, New Jersey: Lawrence Erlbaum.

Komter, Martha. 2003. The interactional dynamics of eliciting a confession in a Dutch police interrogation. *Research on Language and Social Interaction* 36(4): 433–470.

Komter, Martha. 2006. From talk to text: The interactional construction of a police record. *Research on Language and Social Interaction* 39(3): 201–228.

LeBaron, Curtis and Jürgen Streeck. 1997. Built space and the interactional framing of experience during a murder interrogation. *Human Studies* 20: 1–25.

Linell, Per and Linda Jönsson. 1991. Suspect stories: Perspective-setting in an asymmetrical situation. In Ivana Marková and Klaus Foppa (eds.) *Asymmetries in Dialogue*. Hemel Hempstead, U.K.: Harvester-Wheatsheaf. 75–100.

Lynch, Michael. 2007. Law courts as perspicuous sites for ethnomethodological investigations. In Stephen Hester and David Francis (eds.) *Orders of Ordinary Action: Respecifying Sociological Knowledge*. Aldershot, U.K.: Ashgate. 107–19.

Manzo, John. 1996. Taking turns and taking sides: Opening scenes from two jury deliberations. *Social Psychology Quarterly* 59(2): 107–125.

Maynard, Douglas. 1984. *Inside Plea Bargaining: The Language of Negotiation*. New York: Plenum.

Meehan, Albert. 1986. Record-keeping practices in the policing of juveniles. *Urban Life* 15(1): 70–102.

Meehan, Albert. 1989. Assessing the "police-worthiness" of citizen's complaints to the police: Accountability and the negotiation of "facts." In David Helm, W. Timothy Anderson, Albert Meehan and Anne Warfield Rawls (eds.) *The Interactional Order: New Directions in the Study of Social Order*. New York: Irvington. 116–140.

O'Reilly, Gregory. 1994. England limits the right to silence and moves towards an inquisitorial system of justice. *Journal of Criminal Law & Criminology* 85(2): 402–452.

PACE. 1984. *Police and Criminal Evidence Act 1984*. London: HMSO.

Pollner, Mel. 1974. Mundane reasoning. *Philosophy of the Social Sciences* 4: 35–54.

Pomerantz, Anita. 1986. Extreme case formulations: A way of legitimizing claims. *Human Studies* 9: 219–229.

Pomerantz, Anita. 1987. Descriptions in legal settings. In Graham Button and John Lee (eds.) *Talk and Social Organization*. Clevedon, U.K.: Multilingual Matters. 226–243.

Rock, Frances. 2007. *Communicating Rights: The Language of Arrest and Detention*. Basingstoke, U.K.: Palgrave Macmillan.

Sacks, Harvey. 1972. Notes on police assessment of moral character. In David Sudnow (ed.) *Studies in Social Interaction*. Glencoe, Illinois: Free Press. 280–293.

Schegloff, Emanuel. 2007. *Sequence Organization: A Primer in Conversation Analysis* (vol. 1). Cambridge: Cambridge University Press.

Sharrock, Wes and Rod Watson. 1989. Talk and police work: Notes on the traffic in information. In Hywel Coleman (ed.) *Working with language: A Multidisciplinary Consideration of Language Use in Work contexts*. Berlin: Mouton de Gruyter. 431–449.

Shuy, Roger. 1998. *The Language of Confession, Interrogation, and Deception*. London: Sage.

Stivers, Tanya. 2008. Stance, alignment and affiliation during story telling: When nodding is a token of preliminary affiliation. *Research on Language and Social Interaction* 41(1): 31–57.

Stivers, Tanya and Jeffrey Robinson. 2006. A preference for progressivity in interaction. *Language in Society* 35: 367–392.

Stokoe, Elizabeth. 2009. "For the benefit of the tape": Formulating embodied conduct in designedly uni-modal recorded police-suspect interrogations. *Journal of Pragmatics* 41(10): 1887–1904.

Stokoe, Elizabeth. 2010. "I'm not gonna hit a lady": Conversation analysis, membership categorization and men's denials of violence towards women. *Discourse & Society* 21(1): 59–82.

Stokoe, Elizabeth. 2013. The (in)authenticity of simulated talk: Comparing role-played and actual conversation and the implications for communication training. *Research on Language and Social Interaction* 46(2): 1–21.

Stokoe, Elizabeth and Derek Edwards. 2007. "Black this, black that": Racial insults and reported speech in neighbour complaints and police interrogations. *Discourse & Society* 18(3): 337–372.

Stokoe, Elizabeth and Derek Edwards. 2008. "Did you have permission to smash your neighbour's door?" Silly questions and their answers in police-suspect interrogations. *Discourse Studies* 10(1): 89–111.

Sudnow, David. 1965. Normal crimes: Sociological features of the penal code in a public defender office. *Social Problems* 12(3): 255–276.

Summerfield, Tracey and Alec McHoul. 2005. Family as a commonsensical device and its place in law. *International Journal for the Semiotics of Law* 18(3–4): 243–261.

Travers, Max. 1997. *The Reality of Law: Work and Talk in a Firm of Criminal Lawyers*. Aldershot, U.K.: Ashgate.

Van Charldorp, Tessa. 2013. The intertwining of talk and technology: How talk and typing are combined in the various phases of the police interrogation. *Discourse & Communication* 7(2): 221–240.

Watson, D. Rodney. 1983. The presentation of victim and motive discourse: The case of police interrogations and interviews. *Victimology* 8: 31–52.

Whalen, Marilyn and Don Zimmerman. 1990. Describing trouble: Practical epistemology in citizen calls to the police. *Language in Society* 19: 465–492.

Wieder, D. Lawrence. 1974. Telling the code. In Roy Turner (ed.), *Ethnomethodology: Selected Readings*. Harmondsworth, U.K.: Penguin. 144–172.

Wowk, Maria. 1984. Blame allocation, sex and gender in a murder interrogation. *Women's Studies International Forum* 7(1): 75–82.

NAME INDEX

SUBJECT INDEX

www.ingramcontent.com/pod-product-compliance
Ingram Content Group UK Ltd.
Pitfield, Milton Keynes, MK11 3LW, UK
UKHW020849150926
475595UK00003B/88

9 780199 945351